CITIZEN PEROT

CITIZEN PEROT

HIS LIFE AND TIMES

Gerald Posner

RANDOM HOUSE   NEW YORK

ISBN: 0-679-44731-8

Random House website address: http://www.randomhouse.com/

Printed in the United States of America on acid-free paper
24689753
First Edition

Book design by Bernard Klein

To Trisha, my wife,
who, by her complete honesty and simple belief in the truth,
is my constant inspiration and guidance

Preface

This book has changed in scope since I first proposed it to Random House in late 1994. I had envisioned a brief biography of Ross Perot as part of a detailed study of his 1992 presidential campaign and a discussion of third-party politics. After speaking to some of Perot's friends and associates, I changed my direction. Perot's 1992 campaign did not, as I had expected, provide a blueprint for future independent races. Rather, the character of Perot's run for the White House was invariably tied to his personality. Understanding him became the focus.

I did not, at first, call Perot, or try to interview him, although he was aware of my project. My hope was that I could finish most of my research prior to seeing him. However, before I was ready to ask for an interview, he called in August 1995, upset over some questions I had raised with his son-in-law Clay Mulford. He had become uncomfortable because he realized I was now writing about his life. Although dozens of journalists had done so before and an unauthorized biography was published in 1990, this was different, and Perot knew it. Not only had I spoken to some of his closest confidants, but I had conducted hundreds of interviews independent of him and reviewed thousands of pages of documents about his life. And he had no control over the content of the book.

After several contentious telephone conversations, he accepted the new direction I had taken. I made it clear to him that the book was centered more on the public aspects of his life than the personal. As a result, he allowed my wife, Trisha, and me to interview him for two days last November in Dallas. After that, Perot and I continued our talks by telephone for the next six months. From the beginning, no question was off limits, and he encouraged me to ask the most difficult and challenging ones. If not sure of an answer, he would often research it himself. He would occasionally provide names of others who might be of assistance.

Perot also supplied documents. They included everything from an internal company booklet about its business practices to cables and notes from FBI agents; copies of personal letters written on Perot's behalf by government officials; interviews about Perot conducted by a friend; and even some of his private papers, ranging from a poem he wrote as a teenager in which he worried about the plight of a youngster poorer than himself to a long essay he wrote as a midshipman about "The History of Honor at the United States Naval Academy."

Also among the documents was a fifteen-page report he had prepared for me entitled "Ross Perot: Outline of His Life." It begins with a brief biography. There are then three pages listing fifty-nine awards Perot has been given, from the Winston Churchill medal to one from the National Business Hall of Fame. (Perot prefaces the awards section by writing, "Neither Ross Perot nor anyone representing him has ever sought awards or recognition.") Another two pages are devoted to the nearly $120 million in philanthropic gifts Perot has donated to a variety of organizations, ranging from hospitals to schools to the Salvation Army to the Boy Scouts. The final two pages expound on his pride in his five children, especially his only son, Ross Jr. After listing some of Ross Jr.'s achievements in school, sports, and the military, Perot writes that his proudest moment came when Ross Jr. called him to say he had been chosen as one of America's Most Outstanding Young Men, and that he wanted his father to sit next to him at the awards ceremony. "He is 'big Ross,'" writes Perot. "I am 'old Ross.' I live in my son's shadow, and there is no better place for a father to live."

He also sent along a twenty-eight-page paper entitled "All I Know About Business," which was his gift to Ross Jr. upon his graduation from college. In it Perot summarizes his precepts for business success in a series of exhortations ("It should be pursued with the same positive spirit one brings to an athletic contest"), sprinkled with caveats about overemphasizing money ("Never let money become your goal"). Perot also advises his son to avoid hiring graduates from the top business schools ("Their loyalty is to themselves, not to the company") as well as "people who drink every day," "people with marriage problems," and "social climbers." He even warns about lawyers ("Washington lawyers . . . have no sense of ethics regarding their clients," "New York lawyers charge too much [and] are not very effective," and "California lawyers are really fast . . . be careful").

Perot follows much of the advice he gave to his son. Although he is worth several billion dollars, he is largely without pretense, still personally retrieving his car from the company garage, making his own calls, and often eating lunch at a nearby barbecue joint, Dickey's, chatting with local laborers.

Perot believes his motives are always pure. For every episode I raised with him in which I thought he had a questionable role, he had an explanation that made him sound blameless. To Perot, that explanation should be the final word. However, there were sometimes interviews and documents that challenged his recollections. In those cases, I have presented the conflicting views. There are many such incidents in Perot's life.

The Perot I came to know is complex and contradictory. He engenders fealty and esteem (a few proclaimed they would give up their lives for him), but also fear and contempt (several were so frightened that they demanded anonymity and in one case insisted on frisking my wife and me for electronic surveillance equipment, suspicious that Perot had sent us). This is a troubling paradox that any examination of Perot must confront.

Could the man described by some as a superior judge of character be the same person capable of relying on apparent charlatans? Could the business executive bent on saving the life of a child he never met spend his time on an effort that would destroy the career of somebody else, whom he had also never met? Could the former Boy Scout who spoke of America as a Norman Rockwell painting be the secretive billionaire who directed private investigators to pursue those whose activities he questioned?

The extent of his cooperation, especially for an unauthorized biography, is rare for someone like Perot. While he will not agree with all my interpretations of the often conflicting evidence over major events in his life, I have done my best to evaluate the facts fairly. This book presents his unique life and the quest for power that I believe has driven it, stripped of the mythology that has built up around him.

Contents

CITIZEN PEROT

ONE

___□___

The Boy from Texarkana

Near the end of Ross Perot's hour-long interview on *Larry King Live* on February 20, 1992, King asked the Dallas business tycoon for the third time if there was any scenario in which he would run for president. Perot stared into the camera and finally said he would be willing if "you, the people, are that serious—you register me in fifty states." It seemed spontaneous. Perot later insisted it was "impulsive" and bristled at the idea he had long considered such a move.[1]* The reaction of his family and friends also seemed to indicate the decision was abrupt. Margot, his wife, was "surprised."[2] Mort Meyerson, his chief business colleague, refused to believe his wife when she told him.[3] Tom Luce, Perot's longtime attorney, nearly fell off his treadmill as he watched the show.[4] When Luce called his law partner, Clay Mulford, who also happened to be Perot's son-in-law, Mulford thought Luce was joking. "I watched the tape of the King show," says Mulford, "and Bette [Perot's sister] watched it, and we both thought it was spontaneous."[5]

For several months, though, Perot had had daily discussions about whether he should run for president. He had kept those conversations a secret, even from his family and closest advisers. The two men he was talking to had been virtual strangers to him. One was Jack Gargan, a retired Florida businessman who ran the

---

* In this book, when a person is quoted in the present tense, it indicates an interview by the author. The past tense is used for quotations from other sources.

anti-incumbency organization THRO (Throw the Hypocritical Rascals Out). The other was John Jay Hooker, a courtly Nashville lawyer who had made and lost several fortunes while unsuccessfully dabbling in politics with three failed runs for governor and the Senate. Gargan was a political activist on the fringes of American politics; the melodious-toned Hooker, on the other hand, counted prominent friends in places from publishing to politics. Neither had ever spoken to the other. Early in 1991, they independently decided that the country was heading for ruin, accelerated by weak leaders and a lack of vision. In searching for a persuasive leader, each had settled on Perot.

Gargan's approach was to invite Perot to address THRO at a November 1991 gathering in Florida. That invitation also initiated a series of telephone conversations between them. At a late May 1991 meeting in Perot's Dallas office, Gargan told him he "had to run for president because our country was headed on a sure path of fiscal and moral disaster." Perot seemed intrigued by the idea. "There was no hesitation," recalls Gargan. "I am familiar with the term *buying signal*—you say to someone, 'Do you want the blue one or the white one?' and if they say, 'The white one,' then you at least know they want to buy. So I threw out the buying signal by talking about possible vice-presidential mates if Perot ran for president—you don't consider vice-presidential candidates unless in your own mind you are a presidential candidate. But after a while, Perot said, 'Jack, I am a businessman, not a politician. I really don't think you should pursue this idea. I would make a poor politician because I am a man of action. If I see a poisonous snake, I don't call a committee, I kill it.' I told him, 'Ross, I am a man of action too, and when I see a man who should be president, I don't just ask him, but I'll draft him if I have to.' "[6]

Five days later, Gargan proposed drafting Perot to an enthusiastic group of political activists attending a mini-convention in Kansas. He said that Perot was "too modest to seek the office, but I think he's too patriotic to refuse it." Later that day, an excited Gargan pulled his car into the rear parking lot of a Kentucky Fried Chicken and called Perot on his car phone. "Ross, I just want you to know that the draft movement to make you president was started earlier today here in Kansas City."[7] The following day,

June 2, the local paper, *Kansas City Star,* declared, "You heard it here first: A campaign to draft H. Ross Perot for president of the United States was launched at 4:16 P.M. Saturday in Kansas City. Credit Jack Gargan . . ."[8] It received no other attention.

During the next few months, Gargan and Perot had dozens of telephone conversations, with Gargan "pushing him very hard to run for president . . . I really was twisting his arm, and kept appealing to his sense of duty."[9] Perot never closed the door and, by this time, had accepted Gargan's invitation to address THRO's annual gathering. On August 30, 1991, Gargan, at his own expense, sent out nine thousand copies of a press release announcing the formal draft-Perot campaign. Again, the media did not pick up on it.

In November, almost four months before the *Larry King* appearance, Perot spoke at Gargan's anti-incumbency conference. "Perot gave a 'clear out the barn' speech," remembers Gargan. "It was a campaign speech—a speech of somebody running for president." Gargan had paid for signs and placards proclaiming ROSS FOR BOSS and PEROT FOR PRESIDENT. "I told a whole bunch of people that if his speech went over well," Gargan recalls, "to start yelling, 'Run, Ross, run! Run, Ross, run!' His speech was great. At the end of it, the place exploded, people stomping their feet, and they really went crazy. They loved this guy. I got up and said, 'Well, I don't know about you folks, but I think this is the guy who ought to be the next president of the United States.' " The crowd started chanting "Run, Ross, run!" The posters bobbed up and down. A woman near the front seemed faint with excitement. Ross Perot waved his hands as if to quiet the crowd, but he was beaming.

Unknown to Gargan, John Jay Hooker had also started a campaign to persuade Perot to run. The six-foot-two Hooker, fond of white suits, Panama hats, and gold pocket watches, placed his first call to Perot's office in October 1991. Perot returned it the same day, and Hooker informed him that he was calling for one reason—"because I want you to run for president."[10] That was the start of more than two hundred telephone conversations during the following four months, leading up to the *Larry King* appearance. Hooker, a forceful and persuasive speaker, worked incessantly on bringing Perot into the race. He stressed the country's decline, and challenged Perot with examples of personal courage from Andrew Jackson to Muhammad Ali. "I was merciless," Hooker recalls. "I told him it was his duty, I appealed to his patriotism, said that his mother would want him to do it, pleaded with him that he was the only one who had the drive and spirit for it. And he was listening. You don't spend the dozens of hours on the phone we spent talking about this unless you are interested."[11]

By Christmas 1991, Hooker had enlisted the country's leading expert on ballot access, Richard Winger. At Hooker's request, Winger sent a memo that showed the qualifying date and the number of signatures required for getting on the ballot in each of the fifty states. "I sent that memo to Ross," Hooker says, "and wrote across it, 'Ross, here's the answer—let's go!' " After receiving it, Perot called Hooker, still protesting he was not interested. "Look, Ross, you have to do this," Hooker urged. "I had a very strong feeling on Christmas Eve," says Hooker, "that Ross was seriously considering it. I could see him moving along. He began asking the next questions. And he talked more about the possibilities for America. He had softened his no. It was like a girl—he was starting to show some leg."[12]

On February 5, just two weeks before the King show, Perot visited Nashville to address a group of businessmen. The night before his speech, Perot and Hooker spent four hours in an intense discussion at Perot's hotel suite. "We sat down and got at it," Hooker says. "That was the night. We stayed in our suits and ties, no alcohol, no food, just water. I used every argument I knew. It was an Eisenhower-type opportunity—the American people are thirsting, a third of the people are independents, we can carry two or three states, and if it is close enough we can get to the House of Representatives, and if we get it there, who knows what will happen? He listened very intently. Very intently. He was the judge, and I had my case before him. Then he finally said, 'Maybe if they qualify me in all fifty states.' And I said immediately, 'That can be done. That's what that piece of paper says!' Then he said, 'Well, that's not going to happen, it's not possible, and I'm not going to start a campaign.' There was no doubt that he was not going to lift his finger, but he was looking for a draft. At the end of that four hours, I knew I had him. I had him."[13]

The following day, after a local radio appearance, Perot spoke to the business leaders. When asked repeatedly by a local reporter if he would consider a presidential bid, Perot finally relented. "If you feel so strongly about this, register me in fifty states. If it's forty-nine, forget it. If you want to do fifty states, you care that much, fine, then I don't belong to anybody but you." The next day, *The Tennessean* ran a small story about Perot's willingness to run if his name was placed on the ballot in all states.

Hooker now went to Bert Lance, the ex–Carter administration budget chief, to discuss the best way for Perot to make a national announcement. John Seigenthaler, former editor of *The Tennessean,* was another Hooker friend. "Because I knew King well," recalls Seigenthaler, "I called King and told him that Hooker was very much interested in Perot running and thought he would run. I told King that if the right question were put to Perot, he would answer it the right way."[14] King then started to talk to Hooker. "He told me that Perot was not going to say yes after one question," says King, "but that I could get him to say it if I was persistent. That is why I kept coming back to it in the interview."[15]

In the frenzied aftermath of Perot's appearance on King's show, Hooker and Gargan were surprisingly forgotten. To their chagrin, Perot never mentioned them. He was adamant that he had not thought previously about running for president—he had only responded, off the cuff, to growing public discontent over the two-party system, not to personal ambition. During the campaign, when reporters asked Perot press spokesman Jim Squires about Hooker and Gargan, he discounted their roles. "He [Perot] does not ascribe his decision to the particular advice of either of them," Squires said. "Both of these people were calling him, but gee, he gets zillions of calls."[16] Perot himself dismisses the influence of either man. "Good Lord, why in the world would you think they have an effect on decisions I am making? This is all tedious, little gossip."[17] He no longer even speaks to them.

But Gargan and Hooker are upset that Perot refuses to acknowledge that they had any effect on his decision. "He has been intellectually dishonest with me," says Hooker. "He knows that I am the architect of this thing, and he has not only failed to acknowledge my role, but he has denied it, and it has filled me with contempt for him. It does not have a damn thing to do with me, it has to do with him. I am sure he has treated people like that all his life. You would have to go way back in Ross Perot's life to find out why he is like this."[18]

Henry Ray Perot,* the last of three children, was born on June 27, 1930, into a middle-class Texarkana family. His father, Gabriel Elias Perot, known as "Big Ross" even though he was just over five feet tall, was a successful cotton broker in a town where the largest crop was dubbed King Cotton ("The heart of my business success, my Harvard Business School, was [learned] in my father's cotton office," says Perot).[19] Perot's mother, Lulu May Ray, was a secretary at a local lumber company before marrying and becoming a housewife. The little boy and his sister, Bette, grew up in a strictly disciplined, devoutly Methodist house. "Being sick was not an excuse for missing Sunday School and church," Perot remembered. "Only dead kept you away."[20]

Although the backdrop for Perot's early years was the Great Depression, he has only the fondest memories of his family ("I had the finest parents any could have, just too good to be true") and of Texarkana ("a magic place where there was a wonderful spirit in the community"). Perot describes his childhood as idyllic and simple, similar to moments depicted in the Norman Rockwell paintings that now adorn his office walls. "That's my life," Perot has said about Rockwell's *Breaking Home Ties*, which depicts a tired father and son sitting on the running board of a car, a collie beside them. Saturday evenings were spent at his grandmother's listening to radio shows, or sometimes the family drove downtown and parked near the bus station to see who was coming through town. For entertainment, Perot's father would often tell them stories on the rear porch. "That's where I heard all the great stories about Texas cowboys," recalls Perot.[21] Once a month,

---

* Perot (pronounced PEE-row in Texarkana) was initially named after his maternal grandfather, but when he was twelve, his parents legally changed his name to Henry Ross, in memory of their first child, Gabriel Ross, Jr., who had died of a stomach disorder at the age of three, in 1927. However, Perot was called by neither name in the household, as his parents and sister, Bette, called him "Brother."

they went to the movies (after his parents' deaths, Perot spent $800,000 to refurbish the Saenger Theater, the city's most opulent, and have it renamed the Perot Theater). The big event in town each year was the arrival of the Ringling Bros. Circus. At home, according to his sister, Perot immersed himself reading Grimms' fairy tales, Hardy Boys stories, Horatio Alger, and *Boy's Life;* the radio shows his father allowed him to listen to included *Amos 'n' Andy,* Red Skelton, and *Fibber McGee and Molly.*

Texarkana, as the largest city in the isolated East Texas prairie, had its share of problems. With large military bases nearby, it boasted the region's largest red-light district. The town was racially segregated, and virtually the only contact whites had with blacks was as domestic help. The blacks that worked for his father carried Big Ross's business card to flash in case other whites gave them trouble.[22] Once, during World War II, a black man was charged with raping a white woman. A furious mob dragged him from the jail, and burned and hanged him on the outskirts of town. Word spread quickly overnight, and some of Perot's friends went to look at the body the next day before it was taken down from the tree.[23]

But Perot's family life insulated him from any unpleasantries. He idolized his father, whom he considered his best friend. Since his father's cotton business was seasonal, it meant that nine months of the year he was home early, and in a pasture across from their house, he taught Ross to ride horses. "I loved to break horses," recalled Perot, who also broke his nose that way. "I can't even remember how many times he broke his nose," says Bette. "When he would get thrown and knocked out, my father would put his head under some water and he would come right to."[24] Perot says, "I was small and was good at it. It was okay as long as my mother did not hear about it."[25] And once a year, in what Ross says is a "cherished memory," his father took him to Fort Worth's Fat Stock show, a premier rodeo-and-livestock event.

His mother, quiet and religious, fed so many hoboes from the trains that passed through town that the family's curbstone had a mark painted on it to direct other drifters her way.[26] She was a soft-spoken woman (Perot calls her "magic"), and while she would not raise her voice or hit her children, her stare was enough to silence them.[27] "She could *also* lecture us for hours if we misbehaved," Bette remembers, but she notes that Lulu did so privately, so Bette and Ross were not humiliated in front of each other.[28] "There were no Miranda rights at our home," Perot recalled. "Life was miserable if word got back home that you misbehaved. . . . If I threw chewing gum down in the street, somebody would call my parents. They knew that my parents wanted to be called. Since everybody in town knew you, there was never a place where you could just kind of go crazy, and you were one hundred percent accountable."[29] Ross felt it was important to please his mother, and he heeded her advice that he always set high goals for himself.

One thread that runs through the memory of his childhood is that his family struggled through the Depression. "We didn't have much," he says. "They sacrificed for us."[30] He remembers that one year his father had to sell a favorite horse to buy Christmas gifts. The Perots, however, did own a good home in a respectable area of town.* They were active in the church, and Lulu May was one of the founders of the Ladies Garden Club.[31] "They were wellbred and genteel," said Ellen Crow, a childhood friend. "They had a car and a brick home. They were in the country club. In fact, some of us were kind of envious."[32] The Perots paid seven dollars a month in tuition to send Ross and Bette to Patty Hill, a private grammar school that mixed a classical curriculum with artistic creativity and Bible recitations. "Those of us at public school actually thought of kids at Patty Hill as snobs," says Herbert Wren, a Texarkana native who used to ride horses with Ross at shows and competitions.[33]

Perot likes to recount how enterprising he was as a youngster. "All of my work experiences," he says, "were good work experiences—and none of them paid me unless I performed."[34] Starting

---

* The family home was sold years later, but when Perot made his fortune, he repurchased it. The bricks had been painted over. Perot wanted to return the house to its original condition but was told the bricks were too old to sandblast. He had the walls dismantled, the bricks turned around so their unpainted sides showed, and then rebuilt piece by piece so it looked exactly like it was when he grew up in it.

at the age of seven, he sold Christmas cards, bridles and saddles, flower seeds in the spring, and then the *Saturday Evening Post*.[35] He began earning money from a favorite pastime—breaking horses, for a dollar each. But his fondest memories are of his newspaper routes in some of the poorest white and black areas of town. Perot says that as a thirteen-year-old he confronted the publisher to force a special arrangement that paid him more than double the going rate, since no one else wanted to deliver to those areas. He sometimes threw his papers from his horse, Miss Bee, and other times rode a bicycle as other carriers did.[36] "Dad's paper route—we were raised on that story," said Perot's daughter Nancy. "It was like a childhood myth, a fairy tale."[37]*

Perot's small stature kept him from succeeding in sports, but his highly competitive streak was evident in other pursuits. He joined the Cub Scouts just after his twelfth birthday, and as Perot has stated, it was his "first opportunity to set goals and achieve them."[38] He reached all ranks: Bobcat, Wolf, Bear, and Lion. He raced through the program with such enthusiasm that in 1942 he became an Eagle Scout after only thirteen months (two to four

---

* However, in 1990, a controversy arose over Perot's story. Two of his childhood friends, J. B. Rochelle, and B. W. "Sonny" Atchley, told author Todd Mason that they remembered things differently. Rochelle claimed he, not Perot, was the first to deliver to the black ghetto. Atchley said that Perot had delivered the papers on his bike. The tales of delivery by horseback were "bullshit. It's harmless. It makes good copy," said Atchley. Upon hearing this, Perot was furious. He called Atchley and Rochelle several times. "They were totally disoriented," says Perot, "and then I explained it to them." He also told Atchley he might sue Mason and his publisher, and demanded that Atchley write a retraction. Atchley finally sent Perot a four-page handwritten letter, saying, "My recall of some 48 years ago was not correct," and "I regret that this matter has caused you some grief." "I did not write an apology," Atchley told me. "He's just so damn sensitive about everything." J. B. Rochelle also received several calls from an agitated Perot. For six months, Perot bombarded Mason and his editor, Jeffrey Krames, with letters and more than a dozen phone calls, warning them that "all my lawyers read it [the book], and they're salivating." He sent Krames a large map of Texarkana with his bicycle route outlined block by block, together with a prepared letter of retraction, which Krames never signed. Perot claims he decided not to sue only because "I figured out what lawyers cost, [and then] I said to hell with them." The author spoke to several Texarkanans who clearly recall Perot breaking horses as well as delivering his papers by horseback in a poor black neighborhood.

years is average).* "Something happened to Ross in that scout troop, something clicked," recalled Ed Overholser, a classmate. "It was extraordinary. It was the competition for that Eagle badge that really set Ross apart. He went after it like nothing I had ever seen, competing with another boy in the troop to get the Eagle badge first. . . . Even at twelve, you could see that part of him that wanted to succeed."[39]

"He seemed to try a little harder at most things,"[40] recalls Herbert Wren. Perot practiced tennis at a neighbor's court and, when he was proficient, challenged a classmate who also happened to be the starting tailback for the high school football team. He was ecstatic when he won. During another summer, he decided to become the best diver among his friends, and practiced back flips hours daily, wearing a T-shirt to lessen the water's sting. Losing was not something he tolerated well; he was incensed at being a runner-up in his high school's "best all-around" student competition.

Although only an average student, he starred on the debate team, and teachers appreciated his confidence and politeness. His classmates also generally liked him, and while he made friends easily, he seemed to bond more with his family than his peers. A number of acquaintances say that the "take-charge" attitude that came over him after the Boy Scouts was occasionally overbearing, although mostly they seemed amused when he barked orders at camp or regaled them with dreams of how he could become a board member of General Motors by gathering proxies from minority stockholders.[41] "Ross thought a lot of himself, even then," a classmate says. "He's always had a very healthy ego."

"When he set out to do something, he did it," recalls a classmate, Hayes McClerkin, the former speaker of the Arkansas House of Representatives. "That type of discipline was unusual at that age. For instance, we all learned to drink and smoke. Ross never got involved in drinking and smoking. Never. He was never tempted

---

* Perot's scouting possessions are ensconced in a glass case at the Ross Perot Scout Service Center, which Perot built for the Boy Scouts shortly after he made his fortune. When I visited, the clerk at the desk was eager to show the well-worn copy of Perot's scout handbook, evidence, she said, of "how much he studied the scout philosophy."

because his peers were doing it.* But he was still part of the group. He was prudish, but we overlooked that because that was his way."[42] The boys in Perot's circle of friends got in little trouble, but in any case, he pulled away from their more boisterous outings.

When Perot was sixteen, his hometown received national attention when a serial killer, dubbed by the press as the "Phantom Murderer," brutally killed four teenagers, including a girlfriend of one of Ross's schoolmates. The phantom was never caught. Life in the small town was noticeably affected, including a curtailment of dating by teenagers Perot's age.[43] "You had parlor dates," recalls Sonny Atchley. "You would go over to a girl's house and listen to records and talk. But no one went out. There was a lot of fear back then." The phantom may have affected Perot less than his friends. Shy with girls, and with his face dominated by his broken nose and jug ears, he did little dating.[44†]

By seventeen, Perot felt constricted in Texarkana. He had already traveled beyond the East Texas plains, frequently visiting Shreveport, Louisiana, and one summer he hitchhiked to Mexico.[45] He particularly admired a neighbor, Josh Morris, who left Texarkana for the naval academy at Annapolis. "I had never seen the ocean or a ship, but when Josh went, I knew where I wanted to go," Perot recalled.[46] He applied but, without political influence, did not receive an appointment. Instead, in 1947, he enrolled at Texarkana Junior College, where his discipline and competitiveness soon set him apart. In his first year he revived the school's yearbook, and in his second was elected the class president. At the time, the college was deciding whether to expand by investing in new property. Perot was an adamant proponent of

---

* "Now, I don't drink, and I don't smoke," Perot told me, "and people always ask why, and my answer is that my dad asked me not to. That's it, and thank God he did. Because for all I know, I would be an alcoholic. Or I would smoke four packs a day. I don't know. When you get hooked, you get hooked." His father was sensitive about liquor, says Perot, because "he had a younger brother that he helped get through college—my dad had not finished high school—and he had a drinking problem, and it just broke my father's heart."

† Strangely, the only fear that Perot ever expressed about living in Texarkana was his concern that the Nazis were going to attack. "We were absolutely convinced that the Germans would bomb us any night. We were focused on the fear that we were a target."

acquiring the additional land, and he successfully made his case directly to the dean and the college board (the school, now called the Texarkana Community College, is still on the land Perot encouraged it to buy).

"At first, I thought he was an ordinary student," says Claude Pinkerton, Perot's second-year speech teacher. "But I soon realized he was a leader, very mature, and had a fine personality."[47] Pinkerton also says that "he was likely involved in too many projects outside school."

Jimmy Crowson, a few years older than Perot, had already served in the navy by the time he was on the student council, when Perot was president. "People voted for Ross because they knew that he wasn't afraid to tackle a job and be a spokesman for them," says Crowson. "But most important, he absolutely believed in himself."[48] Perot says that by electing him class president his peers let him know he was a born leader. He has maintained ever since then that his forays into public life have been motivated not by ambition but by the prodding of others. "All the way back to my childhood in Texarkana, for some reason people kept electing me to lead whatever group I was in," he says. Those leadership skills are, to Perot, "kind of like finding out you can play the piano by ear or something."[49]

As in high school, a few classmates found him too domineering. The same feelings prevailed among the teachers. "He never changed his ideas about certain things," says Pinkerton. "He was very outspoken. One or two instructors in the college at the time thought he was just a little too cocky. One of them went as far as to say he was rather obstinate, and a little belligerent with her."[50] The only girl he dated for several months, Jane Maxwell, remembers him as "always in the middle of everything, driven, very intense."[51]

In 1949, after two years at junior college, Perot received the good news that his appointment to the naval academy had finally been approved. Arkansas senator W. Lee (Pappy) O'Daniel was retiring, and one of his last official acts was to recommend the persistent youngster from Texarkana. On his nineteenth birthday, Perot entered the naval academy.

TWO

The Godless Navy

"Everybody said, 'You will hate the naval academy because the environment is so disciplined,'" recalled Perot. "Well, I got there and I loved it."[1] The academy's regimentation suited him. He liked the fact that once the new recruits received their uniforms and became midshipmen, family background, political connections, and wealth were unimportant. During the first summer, "plebe summer," recruits were put through the naval equivalent of boot camp. "Because he was so short," recalls Bob Lowell, one of Perot's roommates, "he was always at the far end, since everything you do at the academy is according to size—the tall ones are up front, and the little ones are in back. Ross was always in back— but that didn't make any difference to him. Somehow, he seemed to surface to the top because of the type of person he was."[2] Again, Perot did not excel at sports, although he was chosen as a coxswain for a rowing team where his light weight and strong voice were ideal. In academics he remained an average student, finishing in the middle of his class (453 out of 925 students). But it was during that first summer that Perot impressed his classmates in a debate competition. "He did a superb job," according to Arlis Simmons, a classmate. "The whole class knew who he was. That's really how he got started."[3] James Chelsey, who was often paired with Perot in physical-education classes, began calling him "Senator Perot."

The navy was looking for more than bright students and good football players—it had a regimen to identify leaders. Perot excelled. "Every year, people in the academy were ranked by their peers," says another classmate, Mark Royston. "If I was in a bunk sleeping, how happy would I be to have this guy on the bridge on watch? Leadership quality is the number one factor, and decision-making ability is number two. Ross certainly wasn't the biggest guy there, and he didn't look like a military guy, but he was always, from day one, a standout—someone you would accept as a leader."[4] Three times a year, all midshipmen were evaluated by classmates, students in the class above, and their commanding officers. Based on the evaluations, combined with grades and athletic achievements, stripes (up to six) were awarded. Perot earned four stripes, which was remarkable considering his grades were average and he had no athletic accomplishments. He ranked in the top 1 percent of his class in leadership. In his second year he was elected class vice-president, and then president in each of his last two years. The academy's officers selected Perot for a listing in "Who's Who Among Students in American Colleges and Universities" in both his junior and senior years. He also headed the honor committee and rewrote the honor code. According to Perot, when one midshipman had violated the code, "but because of who his parents were, everybody wanted to sweep it under the rug," Perot threatened to resign as class president. The offending classmate was then punished. "He was perfect for the honor committee," says classmate Lowell. "Ross was very ethical. Black was black and white was white. There was simply no shade of gray for him."[5]

As in Texarkana, he was popular with his classmates but his personal life was subdued. He avoided partying and drinking, remained timid with women, and attended dances but did not date. However, in his senior year—when he was twenty-two years old—Perot met Margot Birmingham, a pretty, blond, eighteen-year-old junior from nearby Goucher College. She came from a genteel Pennsylvania family that traced its roots to William Penn. One of Margot's friends, who was seeing another midshipman, finally talked her into a blind date with Perot. On October 18, 1952, the two met. Although Perot says that "it was love at first sight," Margot was more ambivalent. When she returned to Goucher, her friends asked her what he was like. One remembers that Margot simply said, "Well, he was clean."[6] (She doesn't remember her exact words, but thinks she described him as "clean-cut.")

They soon started dating, and Margot, like others, was attracted to his energy and sense of humor. "I remember thinking during one of those first weekends," she recalled, " 'I wonder what it would be like to live on a ranch in Texas?' He was the first Texan I ever met. But at the same time, I was afraid of being swallowed up by another strong man, like my father. He was smart enough to recognize that."[7] In June 1953, Perot graduated from Annapolis. His parents and sister, Bette, drove from Texarkana and met Margot. "We were worried that she wouldn't like us," Bette said. "Maybe we weren't fine enough. But the minute we met her, we saw that she fit right in."[8]

But Perot did not rush Margot into making a commitment. While she remained in school, he left Annapolis for active duty aboard a destroyer, the U.S.S. *Sigourney*. He reported on his birthday—he was twenty-three—just as he had when he entered the naval academy. The *Sigourney*'s cruise lasted nine months, with stops in twenty-two countries. "I got all the dirty jobs as junior officer," recalls Perot.[9] The Korean War was still raging, and Perot and his shipmates took their responsibilities, and the possibility of combat, seriously. "From Norfolk, Virginia, to Midway Island, I could teach the dumbest guy in the navy how to do heart surgery," Perot said. "They'd learn how to perform first aid, how to keep the hatches closed. 'Cause we were going into combat. And I preached to standing-room-only audiences on the fantail of that destroyer. . . ."[10] During the first few Sundays, Perot says, "I thought I was Billy Graham."[11]

By the time the ship reached Midway Island a truce had been declared and Perot suddenly found himself without a congregation. "You couldn't teach a guy to put a Band-Aid on," he complained. "And you sure couldn't get him to go to church. All these reborn guys disappeared on me right there at Midway." Perot now became the permanent shore-patrol officer because, as one shipmate recalled, he was the only sailor who "didn't drink, didn't swear, and didn't mess around with women."[12] Perot remembers that it "wasn't pretty, because they were in bad shape . . . tattooed and drunk." He retrieved his shipmates in drunken stupors from Asian whorehouses, extricated them from street brawls, kept them from being arrested for public lewdness, and brought them back to the *Sigourney,* often enduring a profane outburst at his interference.[13] He laid them out on the ship's deck, where they often became sick. By the time the destroyer reached the Mediterranean, Perot had new problems, like chasing men running naked on the beaches. Many were detained by the local police. "I hauled more guys out of jail," he recalled, "in the first two or three days than I ever will in my life."[14]

The transformation of the crew disgusted Perot. The profanity, drunkenness, and womanizing offended him, as did the lack of officer discipline. Perot had little difficulty restraining his own desires and did not understand why his fellow Annapolis graduates could not—or why the ship's officers did not—exert more control.

But Perot suppressed his disdain, and to his shipmates and commanding officers he was the epitome of a young and promising officer. The *Sigourney*'s captain, Bernhard Lienhard, soon appointed Perot chief engineer, a position usually reserved for more experienced junior officers. Perot was also chosen to attend "legal justice school" and became the ship's prosecutor for court-martials. He obtained convictions in all nineteen cases he tried.

In December, Perot was promoted to lieutenant junior grade. However, that satisfaction was short-lived. Lienhard had been replaced late in 1954 by Commander Gerald J. Scott, an officer with a loose and relaxed style. Scott did things that were not technically against the rules—such as letting the crew gamble or amusing the sailors by firing a gun from the bridge at empty cans tossed over the side—activities the stricter Lienhard would have prohibited. Perot shared Lienhard's absolutist view of morality and regulations, and soon clashed with his new captain when he insisted that fish be served on Fridays for the ship's Roman Catholics and refused to appropriate structural parts belonging to another ship. Also, according to Perot, he opposed Scott's demand for liquor while at sea and his desire to redecorate his cabin with money from the crew's recreation fund. "And I wouldn't give it to him," says Perot, who ran both the recreation fund and the ship's liquor and narcotics stocks. "He just couldn't believe that some kid was saying, 'You can't have a drink; you can't have the money.' "[15]

Scott has called Perot's charges "hogwash," and said he was "happy just if someone gave me a bunk," but he also admits that he does not remember many of the events Perot discusses. "I have no specific recollection of him or any other specific junior officer."[16] Shipmates who served with Perot support his version, and were not surprised that he said no to Scott. "He [Perot] was strictly by-the-book," recalled Ed Ditzel. "There was no deviating."[17]

For several months, Perot fretted over his intensifying dislike for Scott. He wrote to his family and to Margot expressing his frustration. He sometimes interrupted his daily on-deck jogs to complain to other shipmates.[18] Perot now felt trapped in the navy. In return for an appointment at the naval academy and the government providing an education free of charge, Perot and the other cadets had to complete a period of active service. Although not clear, it appears the navy expected Perot to serve four years.* In early March 1955, Ross's father, Gabriel, wrote his congressman, Wright Patman, asking for his advice on how to "have him [Ross] get out at the end of his two years of duty. . . . Ross does not want to make this a career."[19] Patman wrote back the next day with the straightforward advice that Perot "talk with his Commanding Officer about it and get his Commanding Officer's advice first."[20] Three weeks later, on April 1, Perot submitted a letter of resignation to Captain Scott, requesting that he be released immediately from active duty and placed in the naval reserve.[21] Since he had been a naval academy class president, his request, and the reasons behind it, were carefully considered. Perot's letter vividly presents the twenty-four-year-old's beliefs, and is a precursor of the philosophy he eventually used to tremendous success in private business. His tone is that of an indignant prude.

---

* The minimum had been two years, but during the Korean War that was increased to four. The four-year period evidently applied when Perot graduated from the naval academy and began serving aboard the *Sigourney*. The navy has searched its records and claims it cannot find precisely what the active-duty obligation was for 1953 graduates.

His first complaint was with a system that rewarded on "seniority rather than on ability," and he was incensed there was little "incentive for competition." "Having been reared in an atmosphere of competition," he wrote, "I find myself unable to alter my philosophy to one that permits a person to serve his time in grade, maintaining a good record, and awaiting promotion. I would prefer a career where extra effort brings results, and where seniority is insignificant compared to ability and willingness to produce." He confessed that he had "felt little sense of pride on being promoted to lieutenant junior grade," since all of his acquaintances had also been promoted and the "deciding factor seems to me to be the time in grade instead of capability."

Then Perot expressed his dismay over the loose morality the navy tolerated. "I have found the Navy to be a fairly Godless organization (with the exception of the Naval Academy), according to my personal beliefs. I do not enjoy the prospect of continuing to stand on the quarterdeck as Officer of the Deck in foreign ports, being subjected to drunken tales of moral emptiness, passing out penicillin pills and seeing promiscuity on the part of married men. I have observed little in the way of a direct effort to improve a man morally while he is in the Navy or even hold him at his present moral level. I constantly hear the Lord's name taken in vain at all levels." He condemned such language as "blasphemy," and found it "unsatisfying to live, work and be directed in an atmosphere where taking God's name in vain is part of the everyday vocabulary."

His third point concerned the prevalence of ulterior motives. He observed that the "average career officer . . . avoids making decisions or taking action that might have a negative effect on his career." Perot condemned the idea that officers routinely decided what was best for their careers rather "than deciding on the sole basis of right and wrong. . . . I would prefer to make my life's career in a field where men are more self-reliant and the threat of disapproval is not the paramount consideration when making decisions."

Finally, he did "not feel that the Navy is an ideal environment in which to rear a family" because of the frequent relocations. He summed it all up by concluding that "continuing to serve as a Naval officer will only result in the continued training of an officer who desires to be released."[22]

When his father received a copy of Perot's letter, he again appealed to Congressman Patman, as well as to Senators Lyndon Johnson and Price Daniels, to use their influence to help his son cut his commitment to the navy by half. Lulu, Ross's mother, called Patman directly. At the same time, at the suggestion of his commanding officers, Perot submitted to the secretary of the navy a less indignant request for his release. In an April 27 letter, just three weeks after his original letter, his tone was softer. The new appeal still chastised the navy for occasional "complete deviation" from the high standards taught at the naval academy, but said his main reason for wanting out was that he had a "change of mind" about making the navy "my career," and wanted to "establish myself permanently in one community . . . to enter the occupation of my choice as soon as possible." Moreover, he complained that his naval training in subjects such as fire and damage control and ship handling would have "little carry over value" for his business career, which he was "already quite late in preparing for . . ."[23]

Perot and his family also debated using a "hardship" excuse to facilitate his exit. Gabriel Perot had been ill during the late spring, and Ross had taken leave to visit his father. They discussed whether that illness should supersede his other reasons for leaving. While Gabriel wrote Congressman Patman, "It would be best not to use the hardship case,"[24] Perot had already initiated that plea in discussions with senior officers. The navy did not buy it, and on May 18 officially concluded that "no hardship exists."*

---

* Over the intervening years, Perot has changed his reasons for wanting an early discharge. In 1971, he told *The New York Times Magazine* that "the promotion system and the seniority system and the waiting-in-line concept were just sort of incompatible with my desire to be measured and judged by what I could produce." Yet during the 1992 presidential campaign, Perot again spoke to a reporter for the *Times Magazine* and this time said his reason for asking out was that "my father was very ill. That's what was driving this. He wanted me to be with him if I could." At another point, he blamed Captain Scott's alleged requests for special breaks for souring him on the service. Subsequently, a prepared statement issued during the 1992 presidential campaign attributed the reason to Perot's confusion over the extent of his active-duty obligation: "Perot raised the question in 1955 about whether or not his original obligation of two years was back in effect, because the war was over." On another occasion, he told an authorized biographer that it was all a misunderstanding.

In the late spring of 1955, Perot met with the commander of the destroyer division that included the *Sigourney*, Captain G. H. Miller. There, the naval academy class president who was a debating champion and ranked number one in leadership used his most persuasive arguments to win an early release. Perot even told Miller that he wanted to be a social worker upon his release and would work with young people. Miller was not impressed. He decided that Perot's resignation should not be accepted, and also found that he was "emotionally maladjusted for a regular Navy career."[25] Destroyer force commander Rear Admiral J. C. Daniel then reviewed the case and also urged that Perot's request be denied, though he concluded that Perot was "too immature to be entrusted with the leadership responsibilities inherent in sea duty."[26] Daniel recommended that Perot be transferred to an administrative position for the remaining two years of his service. Perot's complaints inevitably affected the evaluation reports filed by his superiors. They had been outstanding in his early service aboard the *Sigourney*. Now, Scott chastised Perot for placing the ship in "embarrassing position[s]" and for having personal views that "conflicted with the loyalty to the service demanded of commissioned officers." In a separate letter sent to the chief of naval personnel, Scott wrote that "I have had many private discussions with him [Perot] in a sincere effort to broaden his views in this regard, but the results were not successful."[27]

Perot was devastated and, again through his father, appealed to politicians for help. Typical of the entreaties was Gabriel's letter to Wright Patman that said Ross had "never been given a copy of the specific charges," and that his son demanded an investigation of his abilities, immediate detachment from his ship, and "a personal interview be granted with the Secretary [of the navy]."[28]

"I was not going to compromise my principles and what I had been taught," says Perot.[29] Perot, a junior grade officer, finally got a hearing with Vice-Admiral James L. Holloway, the chief of naval personnel. "Holloway had been superintendent of the naval academy while I was there," Perot remembers. "He had some sense of who this kid was. He went all the way through this and inserted into my file that all this negative stuff was to be removed from [my] file in two years. . . . Holloway was determined that a junior officer should not be penalized for standing on the principles that had been drilled into his head at the naval academy."[30]* However, while Holloway may have been sympathetic to Perot, he nevertheless denied his request for an early discharge and ordered him to report to the antisubmarine aircraft carrier *Leyte*.

Perot had barely arrived on his new ship as a gunnery control officer when his father had a massive heart attack in Texarkana in early November. Granted leave, he immediately returned home. "Either my mother or me lived in that hospital," Perot later recalled. "The night before he died, I had a long talk with him. I left to get some sleep, and when I woke the next day, he had died." It was the first close family death he experienced, and Perot was depressed and worried about leaving his mother. Margot flew to Texarkana for the funeral. To Perot, that simple act seemed to cement their relationship. "It meant a lot," recalled Bette.[31]

Within days of his father's burial, Perot returned to the *Leyte*. His new shipmates did not know him, so no one is able to comment on whether he somehow seemed different. What is evident at least from his naval record is that after his father's death, Perot again exerted his tremendous discipline, determined to serve his remaining time aboard the *Leyte* without incident. He began receiving high marks in his evaluations, and his commanding officer gave him additional responsibilities as a gunfire control officer and as an assistant navigator.

The pace of his letters to Margot picked up. She had graduated from Goucher College and now taught at a nearby boys' military school. From Perot's letters, she had come to view him as "strong and honest." "I knew that much," she recalled. "And I knew life would never be dull if he was around. It may not sound romantic, but it was. He was an overwhelming presence."[32]

Perot now kept a picture of Margot on his desk, and even spoke of her to some of his shipmates. During September 1956, he took

* The navy apparently never expunged Perot's file of the information. In 1992, when he was running for president, journalist Art Pine of the *Los Angeles Times* obtained a copy of the file. It became the basis for an article about Perot's fights with his ship's captain and his desire for an early discharge. Routinely, military records are not available to the public. Perot believes the Bush administration leaked a copy of his file in order to embarrass him.

leave to travel to Greensburg, Pennsylvania. There, on September 13, they married.[33] Margot, by her own account, "was very happy as a navy wife," and she and Ross rented a furnished one-bedroom apartment near his duty station at the Quonset Naval Air Station. The Perots were frugal ("It is a trait he got from our father," said Bette) and saved most of Ross's salary.

It was only a matter of months before Perot's naval service would end, and he began thinking of what he should do as a civilian. The answer was right in front of him on the *Leyte:* The computer age had arrived in the military. The machines were simple and they allowed Perot to gain some rudimentary knowledge of computers at a time when few people knew anything about them. But he did not so much foresee the opportunity for a career in that new field as fall into it.

Perot was on the bridge of the *Leyte* executing naval maneuvers. An IBM executive was on board at the invitation of the secretary of the navy. He was impressed watching Perot control the small flotilla. When the *Leyte*'s captain told the executive that Perot was soon leaving the navy, he approached the bridge.

"Young man, would you like an interview with IBM?"

"Mister, I am twenty-seven years old," Perot remembers saying. "I have worked since I was seven, and you are the first person who has ever offered me a job. I always had to look for work. You bet I would like to have an interview with your company, and I don't even know what you do."[34]

In June 1957, Perot was finally discharged from active duty (he served an additional five years in the naval reserve). IBM offered him a job in Connecticut, but Perot was adamant that he would work only in Texas. IBM relented and arranged for another interview. The Perots packed everything they owned into the back of their 1952 Plymouth and set off for Dallas.

THREE

"Bring Me the Guys Who Love to Win"

Perot's transition from the navy to IBM was easier than it would have been to any other American corporation in the early 1960s. IBM, dominant in the burgeoning but little appreciated field of computers, prided itself on an almost cultlike loyalty among employees. Its system rewarded hard work and demanded high moral standards, all-important to Perot after his run-in with military bureaucracy. Perot's naval uniform was merely replaced by a corporate one (dark suits, white shirts, conservative ties).

The early brilliance he exhibited at the naval academy returned when he was a trainee at IBM's Dallas office in 1957. In class he was vocal, "a step above the rest of the recruits," according to one of his instructors, Jane Onofrey, and in the field he was aggressive and innovative.[1] In one particularly difficult computer installation, Perot moved a cot into a customer's office and stayed there until the job was finished. With that level of commitment, he finished at the top of his sales class.[2] Office manager Henry Wendler remembered him for another reason. "I want your toughest accounts," Perot told Wendler in their first meeting, "because I want to make some money."[3]

IBM's commissions for salesmen were lucrative, paying for both sales and the installation of equipment. However, to ensure employees had a stake in keeping customers satisfied, returned equipment was deducted directly from the salesman's paycheck. Wendler gave Perot and Dean Campbell, another salesman, twenty accounts. Perot took the two most difficult ones, South-western Life Insurance Company and Texas Blue Cross. Initially, his style was too aggressive, but after a lecture from Wendler, he refined his approach, practicing his technique on co-workers. He was a quick learner, and soon established himself as one of the best in the Dallas sales office. At Southwestern Life, his assignment was to figure out how to salvage a $1.3 million computer sale made by his predecessor. The machine at issue, the IBM 7070, was the largest of its time, and after agreeing to take it, South-western Life realized its capacity was far greater than required. Perot's solution was to find another company that needed computer time but did not have the money to buy a machine. He convinced Southwestern Life to lease the 7070 to other companies during its unused hours. Perot even found a local government agricultural agency willing to become the first client. Although he was not the first person to think of computer leasing, he was one of the few who applied it to save his sales.

Dean Campbell and Perot had agreed to split their commissions, but Perot wanted to keep the entire commission on South-western Life. He argued that he had done all the work and its fee was larger than anything Campbell could earn on his eighteen accounts. Campbell refused, and they submitted the dispute to their managers, who, to Campbell's shock, sided with Perot. "I nearly dropped dead there," said Campbell. "I said, 'I'm splitting this team right now. I know what it is costing me this time. God knows what it will cost me next time.' "[4]

Perot's good fortune was not limited to work. On November 7, 1958, about a year into his IBM stint, the Perots had their first child, and only son, Ross Jr.* On that same day, Perot's mother moved from Texarkana to Fort Worth, adjoining Dallas. Lulu became a regular visitor at the Perots' two-bedroom duplex, much to her son's delight.

At IBM, he continued to carve out a reputation as a super-salesman, popular with management but not always well liked by his co-workers. Some of them considered him a loner, skipping the

---

* After Ross Jr., the Perots had four daughters: Nancy was born in 1960; Suzanne, in 1964; Carolyn, in 1968; and Katherine, in 1971.

morning coffee chats, avoiding lunches or evening drinks, all in favor of extra time with his customers.[5] Perot further alienated his colleagues by boasting that he worked harder than anyone else. "Look, the only thing I'm doing different from the other salesmen is that I work all day and they don't."[6] "He wouldn't have won any popularity contests in the office," admitted office manager Wendler.[7] Commanding the top of the sales charts, Perot was so successful that there were complaints Wendler had given him plum assignments.

While Perot's commissions and reputation grew through 1960, the following year brought some unsettling changes. Wendler was transferred to Washington, and Perot did not have as good a relationship with his replacement, Paul Williams. Perot was further disappointed by a change in the commission rules, with strict new quotas—once a salesman met a quota, extra sales resulted in a series of regulated bonuses, meaning less compensation for the star performers.

But unknown to IBM, Perot had taken some steps in case the new changes proved unbearable. He began spending more time at Texas Blue Cross. There he learned the basics of handling data processing from a client's perspective, and picked up details that eventually helped him tailor the business proposals for his soon-to-be computer service. Moreover, he encountered Blue Cross executives who would be key to the early expansion of his business, including a young claims adjuster, Merv Stauffer, who eventually became Perot's most trusted aide for personal and extracorporate affairs.

A showdown was inevitable when IBM set Perot's quota for 1962. The company knew he had been working on a sale of its most expensive computer, the 7090, to the Graduate Research Center of the Southwest. IBM established his quota so that single sale of the 7090—which he made in January 1962—would satisfy it. Perot has since claimed that the sale meant he could not earn any more money that year. Actually, the more he sold, the larger his bonus would be. Even his booster, office manager Wendler, acknowledged that Ross exaggerated the rule: "If you sold 100% of your quota, you didn't stop there. You could go to 200%, 300%, 500% and get more commissions."[8] But Perot goes further, saying that by remaining at IBM he took an 80 percent reduction in his commission rate and that he tried unsuccessfully to interest management in his idea of a data processing service business.[9] "Everyone heard me out at IBM," he recalls. "They said, 'eighty percent is hardware and 20 percent is software, and we have the hardware locked up.' The 20 percent looked small to IBM, and looked big to me."[10] IBM tried to keep Perot by offering him a transfer, which he declined.

After meeting his quota in January, he decided he could do better on his own.* "It was the same old story," said Perot. "If I had stayed in the Navy, I probably would have retired as a captain because I would have been too controversial. I would have been too direct. If I'd stayed at IBM, I'd be somewhere in middle management getting in trouble and being asked to take early retirement."[11] Perot realized that the same data processing services he intended to offer—such as automated billing, payroll, inventory, accounting—would put him in competition with several established companies, including IBM. But from his experience with customers, he felt that while IBM put much effort into selling computers, it was not adept at helping the clients use the machinery. A large market existed for leasing idle time on those machines. He was convinced that if his new company could operate on low overhead, it could effectively compete against much larger and established firms. "There weren't many people who understood computers," he says. "There was a tremendous demand . . . [but] I realized that people did not want computers, they wanted the results that came from computers. And that was the idea for EDS [Electronic Data Systems]."[12]

Sitting at the small Formica kitchen table in his apartment, armed with a stack of yellow pads, Perot nightly scribbled his concepts for a new company. When he went on vacation with

---

* Perot says he decided to leave and form his own company, spontaneously, after seeing a quotation from Henry David Thoreau in a *Reader's Digest* at a barber shop. The quote, "The mass of men lead lives of quiet desperation," seems quite introspective for a man who begs off analytical issues by protesting, "That's more philosophical than I like to get," or, "That's too cosmic." Yet he has a copy of the December 1961 *Reader's Digest* encased in the mini-museum of artifacts built around his life that fills the anterooms of his Dallas office.

Margot, he took along his pads, filling thirteen of them with his left-handed scrawl.[13] He planned a meritocracy where résumés and graduate degrees mattered less than performance and achievement. What he wanted were employees much like himself, self-motivated and resentful of bureaucracies. "I wanted people who are tough, smart, self-reliant, absolutely honest," Perot recalls, "people who have a history of success since childhood and people who love to win. After that, bring me people who hate to lose."[14]

Many concepts came from IBM, with Perot fine-tuning them to fit his philosophy—a dress code of dark suits, long-sleeved white shirts, and conservative ties; no slacks for female employees, except on snow days; no facial hair for men.* Alcohol was banned from lunches and business meetings. "If we have a married employee who has a girlfriend," he commented, "we terminate him. He's got a lifetime contract with his wife, and if she can't trust him, how can I?"[15] Perot planned an austere and strict environment. "We made it very clear what our culture was, what our standards were, including our ethical standards," he says, "and if that didn't excite you, then you were not going to come. 'I don't want to be part of an organization that is that rigorous.' Great—better you know it beforehand. It can't be good for us if it is not good for you."[16]

As his birthday had previously marked significant events in his life (reporting to Annapolis and the *Sigourney*), Perot waited until June 27, 1962, when he turned thirty-two, to incorporate Electronic Data Systems. His only employee was Betty Taylor, a secretary. The board of directors consisted of his wife, mother, and sister. He had no computer. "Starting EDS was months of terror," recalled Perot, "because we didn't have any money. And we didn't know what we were doing."[17] He boasts that he started his company with only $1,000 (the original check is framed in his office),

---

* Those rules were not relaxed until 1980, when men could sport mustaches and colored shirts, and women could wear trousers year-round. Yet, even then, EDS preferred conformity. In 1983, a computer programmer who converted from Roman Catholicism to Orthodox Judaism was fired when he then grew a beard. The employee filed a complaint with the Equal Employment Opportunity Commission, and a federal judge eventually reinstated him, holding that EDS had discriminated, based on religion.

but neglects to mention that this was the minimum requirement for incorporating any Texas company. The Perots, however, had a financial cushion in case the venture did not prosper. Ross had collected his full 1962 wages from IBM because of his January computer sale, and had started work as a part-time data processing consultant for Texas Blue Cross; Margot earned a second salary as a schoolteacher. The consulting work paid him $20,000 a year (the equivalent of $84,000 in 1996), and to make matters even cozier, Perot established EDS's offices on the fifth floor of Dallas's Blue Cross headquarters, for $100 a month in rent. "He was both an employee and a tenant," recalls Tom Beauchamps, general counsel and later president of Texas Blue Cross. "Ross was Blue Cross in the morning and EDS in the afternoon."[18] Typically, Perot later claimed he did not take the Blue Cross job because he wanted it or needed the money, but only because they asked him "to help out."[19]

During his EDS stint, Perot made telephone calls trying to land his first client. He called over a hundred companies that owned IBM 7070 computers to find out whether any of them needed extra computer capacity. He had made a deal with one of his former IBM clients, Southwestern Life Insurance Company, to lease the off-hour shifts on its computer. His seventy-ninth call, to Collins Radio in Iowa, brought his first deal. In need of more computer time, Collins took over Southwestern Life's machine every weekend for four months. Perot pocketed the difference between what he paid Southwestern for its computer and what he charged Collins—nearly $100,000 by the project's end.[20] That profit allowed Perot to hire his second employee, Tom Marquez, a salesman at the Dallas IBM office. Marquez was an ideal Perot recruit—short on experience, but a natural and talented salesman. In February 1963, Marquez made EDS's first sale for computer services to potato-chip maker Frito-Lay.[21]

The deal was consummated with a bit of smoke and mirrors because Frito-Lay had little idea of how small EDS was. "I used odd numbers [to bill them] like $5,128 in those days," admitted Perot, "to make it look like I knew exactly what I was doing and had figured everything down to the last penny. And I would say, 'We want you to pay us in advance.' And they would say, 'Why?'

And I would say, 'Well, that's customary in the computer business.' In fact, if they hadn't paid me in advance, I couldn't have paid my people."[22]

"Things were pretty simple then," Marquez said. "All we had to do was go out and sell. With no product and no prior customers, the thing we were selling was each other. I told 'em what a great guy Perot was, and he told 'em what a great guy I was."[23]

Perot hired more employees for the Frito-Lay project. Most of the early recruits came from raids on IBM. He knew that IBM invested almost $10,000 in training costs for each recruit, and with the IBM culture ingrained, they could easily adapt to EDS. In 1962 and 1963, IBM's Dallas office lost some of its most aggressive young workers. EDS's third employee was salesman Milledge "Mitch" Hart, who had also attended the naval academy. Quickly behind him came salesman Charlie Miller, systems engineering manager Jim Cole, engineers Cecil "Rusty" Gunn and Tom Downtain, and software developer Bob Potter. Later, more programmers came from IBM in Houston.

Obviously, Perot could not offer new employees what IBM did. While he did guarantee a year of their salary, he was frugal, often paying new employees less than they had previously earned.[24] Discussing salaries was grounds for immediate dismissal. There was minimal health insurance, no disability coverage, and no pension plan. But what Perot did offer was a chance to get in on the ground floor of a promising new company. "If you are successful and help me build EDS," he told Tom Marquez, "you'll be taken care of. If not, there's nothing to it."[25] After a while, Perot rewarded good work with EDS stock, at the time worthless but, again, holding the possibility of wealth if the company succeeded (also, by making the employees part-owners, he increased their incentive to make it prosper).*

The advice given to new workers was simple: "Do what makes sense." As for travel and business expenses, Perot reminded them

---

* Even small gifts of stock eventually proved very profitable. For instance, in 1963, Perot visited every employee's wife and thanked each for her patience by giving her 100 shares of EDS stock. Twenty-five years later those shares were worth more than $200,000.

of their stock ownership: "Spend the money like it was your own." While staff meetings were held at the Blue Cross offices, the account teams worked at the client's site (as Marquez noted, "We told the client that was the way it was done, but actually we didn't have any money") and used rented computers to do processing (EDS did not even own its own computer until 1965).[26]

Every new recruit was interviewed by, and had to be approved by, every employee. The hiring questionnaire kept expanding, including such pre–Equal Employment Opportunity Commission questions as religion and race, but also such innocuous ones as "What do you consider the greatest accomplishment of your life?" Perot insisted on meeting the recruits' wives (the early employees were almost all men) to make them feel as though they were joining part of a large family.*

After Perot had taken the best from IBM's Dallas office, he started raiding other area companies, bringing in key people, including EDS's future chief financial officer, Tom Walter (he had served with Perot on the *Sigourney*), and Bill Starnes, a former naval academy classmate. Systems engineers Bob Watkins and Joe Wright came from Texas Instruments. Those early EDS workers had an esprit de corps. There were few executive titles, and Perot made it a point to be accessible, having lunch with his workers and calling them into the office for a visit if he had not seen them in a while.[27] Employees felt as though they were pioneers in a burgeoning new field, confronting—and often beating—the less nimble IBM. Perot acted as though each campaign to win a new customer were a military battle. "If we blinked we knew we would lose, and we beat them [IBM] five times out of five," he says. "That gave everybody the confidence that this company could really be something."[28]

Not only did new employees work long hours, but many did not take a vacation the first two years.[29] During the days, they concentrated on selling new accounts and servicing existing ones. At night, they packed the files of their customers into cars, drove

---

* Rob Brooks, an EDS recruiter in the late 1960s, told me that the "real agenda" for visiting the wives "was that we wanted to see who wore the pants in the family. If the wife was too strong, we could veto the hiring at that point."

to downtown Dallas, and used rented computers to write software programs and to produce printouts of payrolls, profit-and-loss statements, and ledger sheets.[30] That kept EDS overhead to a minimum. The personal cost to employees, however, was sometimes greater. "EDS was your life," says Marquez. "It was survival."[31] "When I went there, I had no idea how many hours I would work," recalls former engineer Tom Downtain. "We worked night and day on those projects. After two years, and the third project, I was burned out for the first time at the company. It took a toll on our families."[32]

But Perot remained a great motivator, and often when employees thought they could not continue, he personally urged them on. While he kept his small workforce working at a fever pitch, he concentrated on bringing in new accounts. "And I would get long-term, ten-year contracts, as opposed to ninety days, which is what your computer hardware would get," recalls Perot. "I knew this could be a really solid, stable business. You sign them up for ten years, and as they grew, you grew, just on that account."[33]

Mitch Hart, who became the company's president directly under Perot, was also a sales specialist, as was Tom Marquez, who quickly became one of Perot's closest friends. "The company was strong on the sales end," says Downtain. "What it actually needed were more technical people. Ross was not involved in the details of the systems. He had the big ideas. He loved to have ideas, and we couldn't grow without them. But it took those of us in the technical departments to go out and make it happen."[34] "You can't run a technical company with technicians," countered Perot. "You've got to run it with businessmen."[35]

But the marriage between the two, salesmen and technicians, worked fairly well. By the end of 1964, EDS had over a dozen employees, $400,000 in gross revenues, and a $4,100 profit.[36] Even after two and a half years, it was only a mildly successful start-up, still struggling to carve out a solid niche in the computer-services business. But unknown to Perot and his fellow workers, the following year, 1965, would revolutionize EDS and bring tremendous profits. The federal government, on the verge of establishing Medicare and Medicaid, was about to become Perot's biggest customer. EDS would never be the same.

FOUR

---□---

Welfare Billionaire

Early on, Perot had targeted the government as a major EDS client, forming a subsidiary, EDS Federal Corporation, only for that business. In the spring of 1963, Perot had pitched an ambitious idea to the Department of Defense to provide the military a backup to its computer system in case of war or disaster.[1] Then vice-president and fellow Texan Lyndon Johnson liked the idea, but officials concluded that EDS did not have "any experience with the government in such a role."[2] Though the proposal was a long shot, Perot was upset that he was not allowed to present it to higher-ranking officials.

Sensing he did not have the right political contacts prompted Perot to hire Jack Hight, a former IBM lobbyist with excellent Washington connections, to start EDS's first satellite office in the capital. Through Hight, EDS bombarded the Johnson administration with ideas, including a broad plan to assist federal agencies in "improving their letter writing and handling of mail, and to conduct research in automatic data processing as it applies to Federal records."[3] Perot flew to Washington in April 1965 to lobby Paul Popple, Johnson's assistant.[4] Popple was impressed. He even considered granting the contract unilaterally, but backed away after being warned by the Bureau of the Budget of the possibility of "criticism of a 'sole source' contract for such services."[5]

But while Perot made little headway in selling the government one of his grandiose schemes, the passage of Medicare and Medicaid legislation on July 30, 1965, established an unprecedented opportunity for computer service companies like Perot's. Medicare created a new class of recipients, granting federal health benefits to people over the age of sixty-five, while Medicaid supplemented or replaced an amalgam of existing programs for indigent citizens. Part of Lyndon Johnson's Great Society, Medicare and Medicaid fundamentally changed health care, entitling nearly 30 million people to benefits. However, Congress did a better job of analyzing the costs than establishing the mechanics for the new system. Filling in lists for eligibility, forms for benefits, reimbursement procedures by doctors and hospitals, statements for treatment, and claims for additional coverage all meant that tens of millions of pieces of paper had to be processed without jamming the system.

Under the federal legislation, existing state medical organizations—primarily Blue Cross (for the hospitalization portion) or Blue Shield (for the physicians' portion)—had responsibility for implementing the legislation and were allowed to subcontract the claims work and the data processing. That subcontracting work—developing and servicing computer systems and processing the claims—was EDS's chance to move into an enormous market. And if he could develop a computer system in Texas for processing health claims, he could use that model, with only slight modifications, in other states. Moreover, EDS already did data processing for Texas Blue Cross and rented an office in its building, and Perot was a $20,000-a-year employee. That gave him the inside track on one of the largest state contracts. "We tried to carve out industries like financial services, banks, and insurance," says Tom Downtain. "But the biggest things that turned EDS around were the Medicare projects."[6] "The volume of paperwork was unbelievable," recalls former EDS executive Ken Riedlinger. "Nobody knew what to do, so it created a great opportunity."[7]

Although the legislation passed in 1965, Medicare did not become effective for a year while people were enrolled into the program. Because the federal government reimbursed the state carriers for the costs of their subcontracts, the regulations were explicit that if any "subcontract was primarily for Medicare purposes," the contract had to be approved by the secretary of health, education, and welfare. On June 28, 1966, EDS signed an agreement to supply computer time for Medicare work for Texas Blue Cross/Blue Shield.[8]* The Texas agreement had not been submitted for approval.[9] The Social Security Administration (SSA) did not even know about the Texas Blue Cross–EDS deal until a year later, when a disgruntled Blue Cross employee informed them, claiming a conflict of interest.[10] The SSA was disturbed by what it discovered. Texas Blue Cross had given EDS the business without any competitive bidding, and there was no written record of the contract negotiations.[11] Also, as part of its Medicare work, EDS had restructured Blue Cross's existing computer contract with IBM into three separate agreements, potentially increasing the cost to Blue Cross for the same data processing.[12]

Equally troubling, the EDS–Blue Cross agreement omitted a standard clause granting the government the right to inspect EDS's books to ensure it was not overcharging and making an unreasonable profit. Finally, when the SSA learned that Perot was employed by Blue Cross, it was troubled that in his job there, as chief of the data processing department, he was responsible for supervising EDS performance on its Medicare contracts.

Because of these concerns, the Social Security Administration gave Texas Blue Cross explicit instructions to avoid the appearance of any conflict of interest. In mid-November 1967, the SSA sent assistant director William McQuay to Dallas to discuss the issues with Blue Cross president Tom Beauchamps. McQuay warned that the next contract had to be competitively bid so that "the Government could determine that it was getting the most favorable deal for the work that was being performed under the Medicare program."[13] He expressed concern about Perot remaining a Blue Cross employee. Later that month, Thomas Tierney, the SSA director of health insurance, wrote to Beauchamps, demanding to review a draft of any new contract before it was signed and reminding him to solicit several competing bids. He, too, questioned Perot's employment.[14]

---

* Medicaid was implemented in Texas in September 1967, increasing the number of recipients by another 25 percent. EDS also handled that computer work.

The SSA also sent a delegation to review EDS's books. Perot initially said the auditors could see the records, but when they arrived, he changed his mind and refused.[15] The government representatives were furious, and put Perot on notice that he would have to open his books under any new contract.[16]

Texas Blue Cross ignored the warnings and exhortations from the Social Security Administration and signed a new contract with EDS on January 5, 1968. Although Blue Cross's contract to act as the Medicare carrier for the federal government was only for one year, it had signed a broad three-year deal with EDS, worth more than $5 million.[17] Again, there was no competitive bidding, no access to EDS's books, no record of the negotiations, and no draft sent to the Social Security Administration for preview. Perot, however, did quit Blue Cross on December 15, 1967, only two weeks before the new contract was signed.[18] "How close is close," an SSA official told congressional investigators.[19] Even Beauchamps admitted that Perot's employment was "not a good permanent relationship."[20] EDS's rental of office space from Texas Blue Cross also ended in 1967, when Perot finally moved to a new Dallas headquarters.

Incredibly, nobody in Texas even told the Social Security Administration that a new contract had been signed, and it did not get a copy for six months. Officials were "shocked" when they learned the details.[21] Social Security analysts estimated that the total cost of processing each claim in Texas was $0.36 and that a fair profit for EDS was to charge $0.55, a 50 percent gross profit margin. EDS actually charged $1.06, nearly a 200 percent gross profit.[22] Of additional concern was whether EDS double-counted some claims.[23]* Thomas Tierney reviewed the new contract and wrote to Beauchamps that he found some EDS charges to be "exorbitant" ("atrocious," concluded other SSA officials).[24] The

---

* In Kansas, for example, audits showed that from 1968 through 1972, EDS overcounted the number of claims it processed each year—by no less than 8 percent inflation, to as much as 35 percent. Moreover, four years after EDS and Texas Blue Cross had signed their new contract, SSA officials were startled to discover that in the first month of the agreement, January 1968, 73,280 claims were processed, but EDS charged, and was paid for, a total of 168,063 (an inflation of 129 percent). The SSA never determined what created that discrepancy.

SSA demanded access to EDS's books to determine whether its charges were reasonable. Perot argued that EDS performed the work more efficiently, and cheaper, than the government could, and the SSA should not worry about how much profit he made from processing each claim. "IBM is the world's largest natural monopoly," complained Perot. "And it doesn't have to tell the state what its costs are."[25] (Actually, IBM allowed the government to examine its books on Medicare computer contracts.)[26]

SSA officials again traveled to Dallas to ask Perot to open EDS's books to auditors. "Practically, what we did the entire day," recalled Walker Evans, the chief of the SSA's contract division, "was listen to sales pitches by Ross and his staff as to what a wonderful job he could do if he could take over the whole Medicare computer program. We left about—well, it was shortly before five o'clock, and we achieved nothing. . . . Ross was of the attitude that he did not want to share his knowledge, his know-how with the Government. He wanted to be competitive . . . but when it came down to actually contracting, he did not want any competition."[27] "Under our contract, they had no right to audit," insists Perot. "No right to audit! That was the whole key. They thought they could run over us. In the words of one of these guys, he said, 'Ross, I'll grant that you are doing for a dollar what we used to do for five dollars, but I think you figured out how to do it for a dime.' I said, 'I wish I had.' "[28] EDS was the first subcontractor to refuse to open its books.*

To the SSA, one of the most controversial clauses in the 1968 Blue Cross contract was a quarter-million-dollar payment to EDS for the development of a computer program to process Medicare claims. The government argued that since it paid for the program, it owned it (common practice at the time was that if the govern-

---

* Actually, EDS later made available the books of its government-related subsidiary, EDS Federal (EDSF), for examination by government auditors. "Mort [Meyerson] had the solution," Perot told me. "Just let them audit. There was nothing there. They went away after that." However, those records did not reveal actual profits, since EDSF made large, indistinguishable lump-sum payments to EDS for computer time, the services of systems engineers, and overhead. "I can assure you," says Meyerson, who ran health care for EDS, "and I was right in the middle of this—that we did not make obscene profits. We made fair profits, considering the level of service we provided."

ment paid for the development of such a program, it either got title or the right to use it).[29] EDS refused to relinquish title. "They had no right to it," says Perot. "[With] all our customers, not just Medicare, we own the program."[30] Eventually, Tierney backed down over the vehement objections of his staff ("We paid for this system and Perot has exclusive use of it," complained one).[31]

The EDS program, developed with the help of Texas Blue Cross and paid for by federal funds, was the same one that Perot kept reselling at a significant profit to other states. "The computer program we were making became quite standardized from one to the other," says Tom Downtain.[32] The issue was of no small consequence, because between 1966 and 1971, the year of a congressional hearing on the subject, the federal government paid EDS $36 million (the company had only $400,000 in revenues in 1964). Its closest competitor during the same time, Applied Systems Development Corporation, received just $275,000.[33] Moreover, EDS's pretax profits, which were 1 percent in 1964, had zoomed to 40 percent (government analysts estimated that in its Texas Medicare work, profit margins were over 100 percent).*

Unknown to the SSA, not only had Texas Blue Cross obligated the government to pay for that program, but it also worked with Perot and his employees to create it, and then helped them win other Medicare contracts. "We didn't know anything about computers," recalls Eugene Aune, then claims manager for Texas Blue Cross, "and they didn't know a damn thing about health care benefits. So they would bring a program back to us, and we would adjust it, tinker with it, show them how it had to work to administer health care provisions. EDS would then put that into computer language. Meanwhile, we trained the new EDS people so they could go out and win the bids at other states. Other state managers might call on us, and we didn't mind trying to assist his sales efforts."[34]

The Social Security Administration was also unaware that another Perot relationship with Blue Cross/Blue Shield raised a

---

* Although EDS was built almost entirely around Medicare work during this time, Perot downplayed the dependency, even telling *The Dallas Morning News* in 1970, "We don't like government business. We don't do any business direct with the government."

potential conflict of interest. James Aston was president of Dallas's largest bank, the Republic National. He was also an influential director of Blue Cross who mobilized the effort to grant EDS its lucrative three-year contract. Perot signed that deal in January 1968. EDS received an $8 million loan from Aston's bank the following month, with the Medicare contract serving as collateral.[35] When Perot's company went public later that year, Aston and some other Republic officers apparently ended up with EDS stock, although federal investigators were never able to determine whether it was a gift, sold to them at a preferential price, or bought at the market.[36] (Perot, who eventually became a director of the Republic National Bank and years later—in 1988—underwrote a multimillion-dollar bailout of the then failed bank, insists the loan was "fully collateralized," and dismisses the issue of any conflict of interest as "just total hot air.")[37]

While the fight over Texas Blue Cross was the first for Perot, controversies continued in other states in which he initially won data processing contracts. In California, in 1969, a contract that guaranteed EDS its largest profit margin was approved, without any inquiry, by the director of the state's Department of Health Care Services. The following year, the director of the agency went to work for EDS.[38] (Eventually, the California auditor investigated the EDS/state relationship and issued a critical report that highlighted a half-million dollars in unverifiable EDS charges such as "general and administrative services" and "technical personnel services.")[39] In New York, the Bureau of Health Insurance raised allegations of overcharges and duplication of cost.[40] Yet the criticisms did not slow Perot's drive to dominate the Medicare field. EDS was able to cite statistics that showed performance generally improved and costs were lowered once it took over a contract. Those figures impressed most state health care officials. Also, since the industry and technology were new, many states excused the problems as growing pains.*

---

* Perot provided the author with a 1973 internal EDS booklet titled "Make It Happen—EDS Health Care Performance," in which he sets out to justify EDS's domination of the health care field. EDS's performance was better than any other subcontractor, argues Perot, and even better than the Social Security Administration's Model Medicare System. He also insists that the criticism about

By the time of the congressional investigation into its practices, of the $23.2 million paid to all Medicare subcontractors in 1971, EDS received $20.7 million, or 90 percent of the market share, prompting some state regulators to call, in vain, for an antitrust investigation.*

Within a few years, the giant revenue stream and bloated profit margins fundamentally altered the nature of EDS. Hiring grew at such a fast pace, starting in 1966 and 1967, that recruits were no longer interviewed by everyone in the company. Some of the best talent, which later led the company in the seventies and eighties, arrived during this time, most notably Mort Meyerson, a Fort Worth native, the son of Russian and German Jewish immigrants. The twenty-seven-year-old Meyerson, who came from Bell Helicopter in January 1966, quickly became Perot's point man on health care, and one of his most trusted advisers. Top engineers, such as Les Alberthal, Gary Fernandes, and Ken Riedlinger—all employees who, years later, would vie with Meyerson for the company's presidency—also arrived during this burst of expansion.

As EDS lost its small-shop atmosphere, it developed more of the corporate structure that Perot disliked. When the company finally left its Blue Cross offices in 1967, it settled into a modern thirteen-story tower at Exchange Park, off Harry Hines Expressway in Dallas. For the first time there were executive suites as Perot and several officers took the thirteenth floor, while the second floor became the computer center. The building was renamed for EDS. But the office atmosphere was not always as good as the

---

sloppy work "grossly misrepresents" EDS, and that the federal inquiry into EDS business practices may have been inspired by a group inside the Social Security Administration who wanted to take away EDS's state contracts so they could do the work themselves.

* One SSA official later testified that when news of the congressional inquiry leaked in Washington, the assistant deputy director of program operations, James Calhoon, who was a constant booster of EDS, had become "quite excited and nervous" and ordered that all papers concerning the EDS subcontracts be destroyed. Under oath, Calhoon said, "To the best of my recollection, that is not what transpired." Another Medicare employee said Calhoon ordered him to destroy a staff memorandum recommending against awarding EDS a contract to process Arkansas claims. Calhoon said he ordered that memo destroyed because "it was poorly drawn."

cosmetic changes, as some employees now had mixed feelings about the company's founder.

While Perot kept his well-liked policy of ignoring résumés and concentrating on achievement, several early workers say that as the company grew, he developed a confrontational management style that was, as one put it, "good cop/bad cop, all rolled into one." "When Ross pulled you aside for a project," recalls a co-worker, "he gave you every opportunity to sink or swim based on your own talents. He made all of us reach inside and achieve things that, as kids in our twenties, we didn't think was possible. He could literally come down and visit you, give you an assignment, and make you feel like you had been touched by God. That was his gift as a motivator. But at other times, almost always one-on-one in his office, he could be vicious. He sat there and asked questions rapid-fire. And when he found one you couldn't answer, he'd scream, 'Are you stupid? What the hell is the matter with you? How stupid can you be?' But then a few days later he'd stop by and talk to you and make you feel that he was only interested in you and your life, and then everything would be fine until the next outburst. It was like two different people."

A female employee remembered the first time Perot yelled at her. "He ripped my heart out," she recalls. "It was so humiliating. 'You're so stupid,' he kept saying. My father had a bad temper, but no one had ever spoken to me like that. It was almost like it amused Ross to tear people down." But she stayed, as did most employees. Some remained only for the money. "He treated me like a dog, but I made a fortune because of him," admits one. But more often, Perot's better qualities created fierce loyalty in his employees. "Most of the time," says the woman who was so harshly yelled at, "he exhibited some of the most unique characteristics of leadership. He could make you want to work for him, to follow him. A lot of us got caught up in that web and just tried to ignore the abuse."

"In business you've got to know your own strength and weaknesses," Perot later said, "and then concentrate on what you do best. My strength is being able to motivate others."[41]

"Ross was a great motivator," agrees one of his closest executives, "but he was also unpredictable. Sometimes I could love the

guy and hate him in the same day. I think a lot of us felt like that."
After a while, new employees learned to watch for the telltale
signs that Perot's volatile temper was about to blow. One eyebrow
arched. His ears flushed red. One eye slightly crossed. "Then you
just knew it was coming," recalls a former executive, "and you
grabbed your chair and waited for it to end." "We all got it at
some point," says another executive who worked closely with
him. "You would just walk out of his office feeling like dirt."
("How many people said that?" Perot demanded to know when
told of the numerous complaints about his explosive management
style. He swore that he never "penalize[d] anyone for an honest
mistake" and believes that only a small minority of the thousands
who worked for him have such complaints.)[42]

Some of those who worked closely with Perot say that a more
callous side of him may have shown at this time because he was
worried that the rapid influx of new employees might dilute the
carefully crafted EDS cult. Perot's problem was the requirement,
in those states where EDS won a contract, that it had to offer jobs
to all the state employees in the data processing operations it took
over. "There were times when the company would double overnight because we took someone on or over," recalls Bill Gayden,
one of EDS's star performers, who arrived in 1967. "It was harder
to control the quality of the employees we took en masse."[43]

In California, EDS gained not only its largest group of employees but also its biggest number of complaints. While Perot fretted
over the quality of his new employees, they in turn worried about
EDS's practices and reputation. The clean-cut EDS workers
swarmed into the data processing centers like paramilitary teams
and intimidated some with their dedication and straight-arrow
approach. They were sometimes called "storm troopers" behind
their backs.

When a group of keypunch operators, fearing the long hours
and tight salaries on which EDS had earned its fame, voted to
unionize at an EDS site, Perot closed the shop rather than accept
the union (EDS defeated union organizers in over 150 subsequent
elections). "I'm all for unions," he said, "but we don't need
them."[44] While Perot could shut out organized labor, he had more
difficulty in getting his dress code accepted in the age-of-Aquarius

California. San Francisco's leading newspaper columnist, Herb Caen, wrote a scathing article titled "Space Age Company Has Stone Age Dress Code." EDS exacerbated the problem by toughening its code for California, banning miniskirts, flat shoes, long hair, colored eye shadow, gaudy jewelry, or "mod looks." Questionnaires given to state employees included such diverse questions as what church they attended, what indebtedness they had, and how often they paid their bills.[45]

"We were told," recalled a former female employee, "that EDS had taken over and that we were all working for them. The dress code was explained. . . . If you didn't go along there was no place for you. Either you signed the new contract by the next day or you had to leave the premises. Immediately. There wasn't even an arrangement for personal property. You couldn't go back to your desk and get your personal articles. And all the time they had a security guard thrown around the computers. . . . Anyone who even discussed salaries got fired."[46]

Black employees encountered the greatest difficulties. Bushy Afros, popular in the late sixties, had to be cut, and there were complaints that EDS managers sometimes referred to them as "boys." "We were considered undesirable," recalled Hardy Green, a black employee of the California Physicians Service in 1969, "because we didn't fit the EDS image. The EDS image was a white image, as white as the shirts we had to wear."[47] Of twenty black employees who worked in the operations department, more than half were fired within two years. Others were demoted. Although some of those fired charged racism, and EDS did lose several Unemployment Insurance Appeals Board hearings, Perot is adamant that he and EDS were not biased. "I don't care what your color is, I don't care what your race is, I don't care whether you are a man or woman," he insists. "I am interested in what you can do, and I am interested in what you have done lately, once you are here."[48] He points to an early black employee, DeSoto Jordan, one of his chief lobbyists, as well as executives Tom Marquez, a Mexican, and Mort Meyerson, a Jew, as signs of his open-mindedness.

There is little doubt that EDS was a virtual bastion of white males—as were most Southern companies in the late 1960s.

Several executives who worked with Perot for over twenty years say that his view of blacks was similar to that of many of his generation who were raised in a segregated atmosphere: condescending but not racist. "He was not a sheet-wearing racist, no way," one told me. "When he got wealthy, he actually liked to think of himself as the 'great benefactor of Dallas's Negroes.' "*

Beyond secretaries, women were also scarce in the company. Anne Ellis, a systems engineer, and Diane Folzenlogen, a financial expert, were two of the few. Folzenlogen ended up on EDS's board of directors, and Perot remembers, "*Forbes* magazine, sometime in the mid-sixties, ran a story that I had a woman on the board of directors of EDS, and the kind of mood was, 'Has this guy lost it? How could anybody have a woman on their board?' "[49] "That's just an after-the-fact, using a quirk to point out that from the earliest time EDS always had a woman in a strong place," says former EDS executive Ken Riedlinger. "She was basically a secretary, and she didn't have any decision-making authority."[50] But even those women who arrived years after Folzenlogen felt that while Perot gave them responsibilities, there was a "definite limit as to what you could do and where you could go in EDS." "We didn't have any female role models," remembers one. An associate who worked with Perot says, "Ross thought women were great secretaries and public relations people. That was about it." One woman, who started as a secretary in the late 1960s, was grilled over the fact that she had been divorced for nearly ten years. "They thought I might be emotionally unstable because of my divorce," she recalls. "And I had a child, and they thought maybe that meant I couldn't do the job. Both Ross and Mitch [Hart] warned me, 'Don't bring your personal problems to work.' "

A former executive recalls numerous discussions he had with Perot. " 'Why have all these women?' Ross would ask. 'You're just throwing away company money as all they will do is get married and have babies and follow their husbands around. All we are doing is wasting money on them.' We would say, 'Ross, it's not

---

* Others recount jokes about blacks that Perot sometimes told. "Ross did tell those jokes," says Ken Riedlinger, "but he certainly was not a racist. It was more a matter of his background than any real bias."

legal.' He'd become exasperated and say, 'Oh, hell, you just don't understand.' " Perot says, "I can't compete with these little guys [babies]. I couldn't, because the mother instincts just took them away from me."[51]*

"Ross finally realized the realities of federal law, because EDS was in serious trouble for a long time because we had no blacks or women in any real position," says Ken Riedlinger. "Blacks worked in data centers or as janitors, and women were secretaries. Ross just wanted to build an army of young marines."[52] It was not until 1983, following race discrimination complaints by four black EDS employees, that the Labor Department ordered EDS to produce an affirmative-action plan.

But a single event in 1968 overshadowed all of Perot's problems over the propriety of his Medicare contracts, the rapidly changing nature of his workforce, and the occasional charges of bias or insensitivity. Perot had decided to take EDS public, and Ken Langone, a smooth-talking executive with a small New York investment-banking firm, R. W. Pressprich and Company, had won the right to be the underwriter. He promised Perot an initial stock price ($16.50) that was an extraordinary 118 times EDS's earnings. (A normal stock offering is set between ten and twenty times earnings; based on the EDS formula, IBM's stock, trading at $92 as of this writing, would be worth more than $1,000 per share.)

There were several factors that allowed EDS to command such an inflated price. The company was just showing the effects of its new multiyear Medicare contract with Texas Blue Cross. The same company that in 1965 had revenues of $865,000, with pretax profits of $26,487 (3 percent of revenues), finished its 1968 fiscal year with more than $7.5 million in income and a 31 percent pretax profit of $2.4 million.[53] Those numbers greatly impressed investors at a time when high-tech stocks were already

---

* Although over 40 percent of the eventual EDS workforce was female, only 5 percent of the women ever got to management or supervisory levels. "Ross was concerned about that image," recalls a colleague, "and that is why in the late sixties he put Folzenlogen on the board. She was his token." Since Perot left EDS in 1986, 31 percent of management or supervisory positions at EDS have been held by women.

the darlings of Wall Street. Moreover, EDS's prospectus was careful to emphasize that the company was a strong supplier of computer services in several industries, including insurance, finance, and health care (the lawyers for the underwriting had to scuttle Perot's own draft of the prospectus, written in Horatio Alger terms: "All alone, against overwhelming odds, with little money . . .").[54]

"There was no way you could tell from that prospectus that almost all their money was from Medicare," says James Naughton, who served as the general counsel of the 1971 congressional investigation into EDS. "There was virtually no way to find out that this was a one-industry firm, since they passed themselves off as well rounded."[55] The prospectus also omitted any information about the government investigation into EDS's Medicare work (morality aside, Perot was not legally bound to disclose the government probes, since they were not official criminal or civil investigations).

With spectacular growth in revenues and profits, a generalized business description, and no reported problems, EDS was set to go public. Langone and Perot limited the number of shares offered for sale (of 11.5 million outstanding shares, only 650,000 were offered), further raising a possible bidding frenzy for the new shares. On September 12, 1968, EDS went public. It was one of the most successful offerings of the year. Investors snapped up the shares at the opening bell and drove the price up during the trading day to finish at almost $23. Ross Perot, who owned 10 million shares, was worth $230 million overnight. (At their peak, a year and a half later, the shares traded at $162.50, or 500 times earnings, with Perot worth more than $1.5 billion.)

"Now keep in mind," said Perot, "once you have money, life changes." The media were suddenly interested in discovering his secrets for success. There was no press spokesman at EDS. Initially, Tom Marquez answered the calls, put the reporters on hold, and then ran down the hall to get a quote from Perot. Nobody spoke for EDS but Perot, and he started doing his own interviews. Instead of selling a product, the super-salesman was now selling his image. He regaled the press with tales, from growing up in the Depression in Texarkana and delivering papers by horseback to understanding the value of work and earning a dollar. *Fortune* proclaimed him "The Fastest Richest Texan Ever," and missed EDS's Medicare dependency when it reported, "Today, much of E.D.S.'s revenues come from insurance companies in the Dallas area."[56] *The New York Times* declared him "surprisingly modest" and concluded that not only did he have no political ambitions, but he even kept politics out of his own company. It was the start of the Perot mythology. "He was good theater and good copy from the start," says a former EDS executive.

With his wealth, Perot suddenly had a newfound respect. Soon after his spectacular stock market debut, Donald Kendall, the chairman of PepsiCo, invited Perot to meet presidential candidate Richard Nixon to give a talk about the ways computers could be used in a campaign. Perot saw the Nixon meeting as a doorway into Washington power—the boy from Texarkana was about to step onto the national scene as the ultimate insider.

FIVE

The Ultimate Insider

The spectacular stock success of Electronic Data Systems, and its booming run on Medicare contracts, further threatened the company's carefully crafted personality. That problem was resolved in 1968 by focusing on a new pool of employees—returning Vietnam veterans. Since his new employees knew little, if anything, about computers, Perot established a trainee program emphasizing system engineering, which EDS sorely needed. "Ross figured that while these people may not have gone to graduate school," says Tom Meurer, who arrived from the air force and was in the first trainee class, "they were married, and they were hungry to get a career going. These were people who knew how to work twenty hours a day."[1] "Pay was equivalent to service pay," recalls Rob Brooks, who arrived from the military in 1968. "We had no reference point to other industries, as to whether our work hours and routine were 'normal.' EDS became the norm for us. It was a great move for Ross—he got a group of kids willing to work hard who were used to taking orders without questioning authority."[2]

"We had thousands of Vietnam veterans," recalls Perot. "We [EDS] put a very high priority to hiring people coming right off the battlefield, because they were very mature. They were twenty-seven years old, and forty in terms of maturity. And no matter how much of a load we placed on them in the training program— and we tried to make it very rigorous—this was a huge cakewalk for them; nobody was shooting at them. And they knew what stress was—not getting shot at was not being under stress."[3]

An aggressive EDS recruiting program searched for the Vietnam vets. Of the 323 employees when the company went public, nearly 30 were recruiters. Dubbed the "Wild Bunch" by Perot, they had the company's most grueling schedule, traveling in ten-day stretches, with only three days of rest in between. He gave them their slogan: "Eagles don't flock. You have to find them one at a time." Recruiters lasted an average of two years before burning out. Using a twelve-page form, they would interview recruits fourteen hours a day in their hotel rooms, and then send only a select few to Dallas for even more extensive interviews. The recruits had to be approved by all they met, and even write an essay answering "What did you accomplish in your life from age six?" Only one in thirty had the fire for which EDS was searching.

The recruiters were selling both Perot and EDS, telling veterans that if they accepted the challenge, they too might find wealth. Keeping in mind the things he was searching for when he left the navy, Perot offered the veterans an opportunity to succeed based almost solely on hard work and achievement. (Perot, still careful with a dollar, had the new employees sign an agreement that if they left within a year, they had to repay the cost of their training, which ran to several thousand dollars.) "If we, the recruiters, did our job," recalls Rob Brooks, "the people were willing to pay us to work for EDS."[4]

As the number of returning veterans increased, EDS recruited directly on military bases, advertising in *Stars and Stripes* and holding seminars that hundreds attended. After the recruiters had worked the crowd, Perot walked in and gave a talk that was a folksy discourse on the American dream tempered by the challenge of the special EDS culture. "It's like a cold shower," Perot later remarked. "You're either attracted by it or repelled by it. If you don't like it, there are a lot of other opportunities."[5] The company pulled between 80 and 90 percent of its recruits from veterans, giving it a military flavor unique among American corporations.[6] "EDS attracts people who would love to be on a SWAT team," said Portia Isaacson, a former employee.[7] "They are like the Marine Corps," commented business author Tom Peters. "Heck, they *are* the Marine Corps."[8]

By 1969, the year that Perot dropped a ban against hiring single men, the company had over 1,000 employees, and two years later the workforce had tripled. Although it was impossible for Perot to meet everyone arriving in Dallas and the satellite offices, he walked the floors, and if he saw something he didn't like, he told a manager. Perot also stopped by the trainee classes several times a week and gave pep talks about the EDS philosophy. "We had uncluttered minds," says Tom Meurer, "and Ross molded us, very effectively, into his view of industry and competition. He made us feel we were part of a special enterprise."[9]*

While the new recruits trained in computers, Perot used some for his personal projects. He had not sat still after the stock market conferred great wealth, but instead had formed the Perot Foundation for philanthropic bequests, and had also begun to indulge an interest in public affairs. New employees worked on such non-EDS projects as studying requests for which schools and hospitals were worthy of receiving money, considering real estate for EDS expansion, and investigating unsolicited requests for assistance that came across Perot's desk. "Ross almost created two different sections within EDS," recalls a colleague. "One was the straight business end—that was Meyerson, Alberthal, Fernandes, and the rest pursuing new accounts, operating the Medicare contracts, and expanding the client base. Then there was Ross, getting a letter from someone about a missing daughter, and he would pull four or five employees and form a team to follow up. If you performed well for him, then he kept going back to you for extracurricular events. And he loves to compartmentalize things. No one who works on a project knows all the pieces but him. He certainly did that in splitting assignments that were for him versus those that were just for EDS. There were people he liked who did a lot of work for him personally, but they did very little work for EDS."

* Perot was so effective in instilling his philosophy into the recruits that the company was later criticized for a lack of diversity. Perot bristled at the idea: "That is hardly a Nazi youth camp. What gets under my skin? Anybody who says anyone who works here is a clone."

One of those whom Ross took an instant liking to was twenty-eight-year-old Tom Meurer, the only liberal arts major in his EDS training course in 1968. Perot called Meurer into his office and asked whether he could develop a plan to utilize computers in the upcoming fall presidential campaign. Although Meurer had been at EDS for only six months and knew little about computers, he had taught United States foreign policy at the air force officer training school, making him the only EDS recruit with a political/history background. "So I spent a couple of weeks in the library, and came back to him with a game plan," recalls Meurer. "Perot took that and went to New York and made the presentation, which Nixon liked."[10] But Nixon wanted more than just a Perot employee—he also wanted Perot's money. "I can give you money," Perot told him, "but I can do better than that—I can give you people."[11]

When he returned from New York, Perot again called Meurer into his office.

"Tom, would you like to work for Nixon?"

"Well, I never really thought about it."

"There's a guy called John Erlichman coming through here, and if you'd like to talk to him, I'd be glad to set it up."

Erlichman met Meurer a week later and invited him to be an advance man for Nixon (advance work involves setting up campaign rallies and appearances before the candidate's arrival). Perot told Meurer, "If you want to work for the campaign, you can, and I will pay for it. When it is over, you come back to the same place you were at in the company. You won't lose any time."[12]

Perot loaned seven EDS workers to the Nixon campaign.* Two other 1968 military recruits, Stuart Reeves and Vern Olsen (both now EDS senior executives), joined Meurer in advance work.

---

* Perot later got into trouble with the IRS when it was discovered he had deducted the salaries of the EDS employees who worked on the campaign. Nixon officials intervened for Perot and were "modestly helpful" in resolving the dispute, according to the administration's internal files. A lawyer who worked with Perot told me that in later years, when Perot pulled EDS employees to work on special projects, he agreed to reimburse the company for their salaries because there was a question under securities law whether they were legitimate corporate projects or whether they amounted to personal service for Ross. "There was never a clear line in Ross's mind between EDS's public business and his personal business," says former EDS executive Ken Riedlinger. "He just did it all. Mort

Meurer and Olsen reported to Erlichman, while other EDS workers reported directly to Nixon aides Pete Flanigan and John Mitchell. Perot stayed informed of everything that transpired. He instructed Meurer to call him every evening with a status report. Meurer did so, and those daily conversations helped form a special bond between the two. Perot also stayed in touch with his other workers, summoning them occasionally to Dallas for updates on the campaign. "That's why he wanted to use our people," says a former executive. "Ross basically likes to inject himself into a situation, not to watch it from the sidelines. Those 'volunteers' were his way of knowing what was going on from the inside."

When Nixon won, Perot and the EDS "volunteers" attended the inaugural. For Perot, Nixon's victory was the beginning of a special relationship with the White House. Both Haldeman and Erlichman liked the work done by the EDS staff. Haldeman was impressed enough by Meurer to offer him a permanent position as a deputy assistant on the president's staff. Meurer decided to stay with Perot ("I was the only one of the Watergate crew that turned it down— those who stayed ended up in jail," recalls Meurer). Perot, impressed by Meurer's loyalty, made him part of his personal staff.

While Perot liked having Meurer around the EDS offices, he would sometimes "loan" him back to Nixon for special projects. Six months after the election, in response to an Erlichman request, Perot sent Meurer to spend several months on a computer project in California, with then Nixon domestic adviser Daniel Patrick Moynihan. In the fall of 1969, Erlichman called Perot and asked to use Meurer as an advance man when Nixon went on the road for early preparatory work for the 1970 congressional elections. Meurer covered everything from preparing campaign stops to setting Pat Nixon's trip to Peru after a major earthquake to taking the Nixons to the Texas-Arkansas football game in 1969.

But loaning Meurer and other EDS workers was only one way Perot built special leverage with Nixon. Starting immediately after the election, through Nixon's chief of staff, H. R. Haldeman, and

---

[Meyerson] was always worried after we became a public corporation because Ross really used EDS like his own wallet. He thought, 'Well, hell, I own the company, it is mine.' "

presidential assistants John Erlichman and Alexander Butterfield, Perot began making proposals to boost Nixon's domestic popularity, particularly over the war in Vietnam.[13] The administration's internal files are replete with scores of references to Perot's calls, submission of ideas, and requests for conferences, as well as meetings with Nixon.[14]*

Perot initially intrigued Nixon's aides—"The man bears watching," said special counsel Charles Colson.[15] Perot's ideas ran a broad spectrum—from a telethon to a panel discussion. At one point he telephoned Haldeman, pushing a variety show, and wanted the White House to help get Bob Hope to appear (the show never happened).[16] The memos reveal that Perot, in grander moments, even discussed buying the ABC television network to recast the news coverage.[17] Later, he inquired through Erlichman if it was possible to buy *The Washington Post,* but Tod Hullin, Erlichman's assistant, informed him that "it is our understanding it is not for sale."[18] (Perot is emphatic that most of the proposals mentioned in the administration's papers were actually proposed by White House officials and usually rejected by him.)[19]

In May, special assistant to the president James Atwater met Perot at EDS's office to discuss Perot's belief "that the turmoil on campus could be quieted if the moderate, responsible student leaders were encouraged to play more of a role in the life of their schools," thereby countering "the minority of revolutionaries." Perot offered to subsidize the costs of a program to "build the qualities of leadership in student moderates."[20] To do this, he promised to transport 2,500 students to an Honor America Day, built around a celebration of the administration, though in the end he paid for only 300.[21]

But Perot's ambitious programs were meant to gain him more than entry to the White House or to enable him to boast to his Texas friends about his Washington connections. He often used his access for favors. Some were simple personal accommodations such as obtaining passes for friends to tour the White House;

---

* Most of this chapter is based upon documents reviewed in the Nixon Presidential Papers Collection, maintained at the National Archives at College Park, Maryland.

requesting that Erlichman allow Ross Jr. (then age ten) to attend the moon launch at Cape Kennedy (attendance was restricted to people over the age of sixteen, but Perot complained, "Senator Ted Kennedy was able to clear his young son for one of the recent launches, so apparently clearance is possible [at least for Democrats]");[22] arranging for his mother to attend a presidential "prayer breakfast";[23] or getting autographed pictures of Nixon (he received two, personally inscribed, after complaining that he had received one signed by a machine—"They will be treasured by the Perot family for many years to come," Perot wrote Nixon).[24]

Not all the favors, however, were innocuous. One arose when EDS lost a part of its Medicare contract in Southern California, worth $1 million a year in revenue, to California Blue Shield. HEW secretary Bob Finch noted that "Perot [was] mad as hell . . . as a result, and bitched to WH [White House]."[25] Although Finch thought that EDS had simply lost the contract because its charges to process the claims were too high, the White House ordered him to intervene and try to overturn the deal and return it to Perot.[26] Finch and Frederick Malek, a Nixon aide, intervened on Perot's behalf "but became involved too late to turn it around without inordinate flak," concluded Haldeman assistant Gordon Strachan.[27] Although the contract was not renewed, the Social Security Administration released $400,000 to EDS that it had previously refused to pay because of a question of overcharges on processing Texas Blue Cross claims. Malek concluded that Perot "won one and lost one" with the administration at HEW.[28]

Another problem Perot wanted addressed by the White House involved 36.3 acres that he had rented from the Army Corps of Engineers. Adjacent to public land at the Grapevine Reservoir in Denton County, Texas, Perot's $110-a-year lease expired at the end of 1968. The Army Corps of Engineers decided not to renew it, claiming that the land was needed for increased tourism and that Perot had repeatedly violated the terms—blocking public access to the shoreline with a fence; landscaping the land for his private use; and using the property to corral his horses. An investigation by the Department of the Army concluded, "What is involved here is an effort by Mr. Perot, under the guise of a grazing lease, to create a private area bordering the reservoir for his personal use. That violates important policies concerning public use of government lands."[29]

At this point, the White House got involved. Erlichman wrote to Lieutenant General William Cassidy, chief of engineers for the Department of the Army, "It has been called to our attention that the lease of Mr. H. R. Perot of Dallas . . . has not been renewed." Erlichman said he had "carefully reviewed the facts" and it was "most difficult for me to understand" why the land should not be re-leased to Perot.[30] Tom Cole, an assistant to presidential adviser Arthur Burns, left no doubt about the importance in a memo to Erlichman aide Ed Morgan: "H. R. Perot of Dallas, Texas, was the most substantial Nixon backer in 1968. Besides outright financial contributions, a number of Perot's employees' time was donated to the campaign. . . . Perot is *extremely* interested in having this lease approved. I leave the matter in your good hands."[31] The White House carried the day, and a few months later the matter was solved completely to Perot's satisfaction.[32]

As the land dispute was pending, Perot met with Nixon to discuss his most ambitious plan. He offered to spend $50 million on buying television time to boost Nixon's image—Perot thought television was "the most powerful social instrument ever developed."[33] On May 16, 1969, Perot met with Nixon and Haldeman about the best use of his $50 million and proposed airing a national town meeting, the same idea he would raise in his 1992 presidential campaign. Haldeman wrote in his diaries, "P[resident] anxious to do something, not sure what. Perot the same."[34]* Roger Ailes, then a Nixon aide, worked up some of the prime-time costs.

During this time, Nixon appointed Perot as one of eight directors of the newly formed Richard Nixon Foundation, whose goal was the construction of the Nixon Library.[35] Two months later,

---

* Although Nixon accepted the $50 million offer, Perot never delivered. In 1992, Perot denied even making the offer, although the administration's internal documents are replete with references to it (an aide's handwritten notes of one meeting quote Perot asking Nixon, "How could I spend $50 million for you?"). Rather, Perot claimed that Nixon aides solicited him with "fantasyland numbers . . . and beautiful and strange ideas." When confronted with the contemporaneous memos, Perot curtly said, "I can't control what people scribble on pads."

presidential adviser Pete Flanigan urged interior secretary Rogers Morton to have Perot fill a vacancy on the Naval Academy Board of Visitors, since he "has been a generous and imaginative supporter of the Administration and President Nixon's campaign."[36] Perot was made chairman, although the White House, trying to keep a low profile on its relationship with Perot, was insistent that no press release be made on the appointment.[37]*

By now, White House officials were so comfortable with Perot that they now approached him with their own ideas. Erlichman solicited his views on what "specific national goals [should] be achieved by our bicentennial" as well as the possibility of holding "town meetings all over the country [to] discuss our national goals . . ."[38] When Nixon aide Alexander Butterfield asked Perot if he would be interested in uniting different private groups into a single organization to push the idea that "the silent majority speaks out in support of national unity, peace with honor, etc.," he reported to Nixon that "Ross is more than amenable."[39]

Near the end of Nixon's first year in office, Perot was approached about establishing a "pro-Vietnam Committee," but agreed only to become a member.[40] Perot's service on that panel coincided with his own burgeoning interest in the war. Murphy Martin, a popular Dallas news anchor for the CBS affiliate, WFAA, was partly responsible for Perot's enthusiasm.[41] In 1969, Martin took four women whose husbands were missing in action to Paris, where they tried to meet the North Vietnamese negotiating team. When he returned to Dallas, he put together a documentary, and he asked Perot to preview it in the hope that he might agree to sponsor the show. "In it was a young man, Ricky Singleton," recalls Martin, "whose mother was one of the four ladies that went to Paris. And that young man had never seen his father. And Perot

---

* As part of that appointment, Perot had to submit his résumé. There are some minor factual errors—he says he "attended public schools" when growing up in Texarkana, when he actually went to the private Patty Hill school. He also boasted that his current wealth is "in excess of $400,000,000, and [it] will be used extensively to improve the quality of life in the United States." Among his principal interests, Perot listed "creating greater respect for the federal government . . . improving relationships between law enforcement agencies and the people . . . relieving college unrest . . . national defense." He also cited the Perot Foundation as being "active in Negro business opportunities and ghetto problems."

leaned forward and said, 'Do you mean that boy has never seen his dad?' Well, you know how Ross feels about his own father. As a result of that, he sponsored our show. About a week later, Perot said to me, 'Why don't we form an organization, United We Stand, in support of the POWs and MIAs.' And we did it."[42]

Perot had already been discussing the formation of United We Stand. "Ross was thinking in broad terms," says Tom Meurer. "He had this feeling—'We have this war over there, and we've elected a president, and whether you agree with the guy or not, we've got to get behind him.' And that became United We Stand."[43] At the White House, Perot spoke to Alexander Butterfield "to make sure before he moves that his actions will not conflict with ours."[44] According to Butterfield, Perot first suggested "a dues-paying organization which hopefully would grow and grow and grow . . . the money to be used for producing year-round educational television programs which give equal time to pro and con views on 'great national issues.' "[45] Perot wanted to start United We Stand with a separate advertising campaign that would include coupons at the bottom of the ads, where people would fill in their names, addresses, zip codes, and Social Security numbers. He intended to computerize the membership rolls by congressional districts, hold programs on such issues as tax reform, and put government "back in the hands of the people"— themes that would recur in his 1992 organization, United We Stand America. Beyond United We Stand, Perot also suggested a massive advertising campaign (full-page ads in a hundred of the largest papers and magazines, plus Boy Scouts delivering handouts door to door) to encourage Americans to write letters in support of the POWs. Perot offered to take the letters personally to the Paris peace talks.

Butterfield consulted with Haldeman, Erlichman, Secretary of State Kissinger, and Bryce Harlow, Nixon's political counselor, before recommending that the White House approve both plans. Even though they were "massive in terms of size and cost," Butterfield concluded they were "highly commendable in principle."[46] Forming his own public pressure group, however, did not mean that Perot would implement every White House idea for polishing Nixon's image. In one instance, Perot initially refused to cooperate with a Nixon request to pay for the manufacturing and distribution of a SILENT MAJORITY pin. Disappointed, Haldeman noted that Perot thought the phrase *silent majority* was passé and Perot had determined that "any of his resources which are expended for pins, buttons, bumper stickers, decals, etc. should emphasize a theme which will best serve the long-term objectives . . . and *that* theme (for Ross) is 'United We Stand.' He has already had something like 1 million bumper stickers made and the same approximate number of decals."[47] Perot finally did agree to distribute the SILENT MAJORITY pins with his own UNITED WE STAND mailings, but only reluctantly and after persistent requests from the White House. Butterfield told Haldeman, "This morning I swallowed my pride and made one final call to the Perot headquarters. . . ."[48]

In general, however, Perot was cooperative (although he sometimes insisted, to the consternation of some aides, that "the president has to ask me" before he undertook a project).[49] Yet Haldeman was able to coax Perot to set his massive ad campaign to coincide with Nixon's November 3, 1969, speech on Vietnamization and a new United States policy. "What Haldeman wanted," recalls Meurer, "was a White House announcement, and then a rising groundswell from below. It was very much orchestrated."[50] Perot approached several New York advertising firms in order to launch his blitz of full-page newspaper ads as well as television spots but was told two weeks was too little time. He returned to Dallas, called Merv Stauffer and Tom Meurer into his office, and instructed them to create the campaign. "We pulled recruits from all over EDS," remembers Meurer, "and around the clock for one week, we wrote, printed, and delivered maps to newspapers so those ads could be run."[51] They also filmed astronaut Frank Borman for a special about Vietnam, which aired about a week later. The White House worked with Perot to ensure the campaign was helpful. William Safire, then a Nixon speechwriter, approved the ad copy for the newspapers, while Alexander Butterfield reviewed the television script.[52] Nixon's staff quickly discovered that Perot had a short attention span and was ready for another challenge the minute one was completed. "Having wrapped up final plans for this Sunday's program at noon today, he's already bored!" one aide wrote to Haldeman.[53]

Those November ads included coupons that encouraged people to show their support for the president by sending donations directly to United We Stand. At the end of the television special, Frank Borman made another appeal for money, saying, "Your personal check or IOU . . . stands for a positive expression of confidence in America. . . . Send your checks or IOUs immediately to United We Stand."[54] No accounting was ever made public, even though within two weeks of the advertising blitz, Perot told Alexander Butterfield that he had received "a minimum of three million coupons to date."[55]

Administration officials were not concerned if Perot profited from the projects. They were convinced that Perot and United We Stand would continue to be a unique ally. Haldeman thought that his November work had been "almost unbelievable" and that Perot was "an amazing resource," though his "problem is his *total* lack of sophistication" [emphasis in original].[56] Nixon thanked Perot personally in early December.[57]

It was shortly after that meeting with Nixon that Perot became involved in his first venture that captured the public imagination— an audacious idea to deliver medicine and food, at Christmas, to American POWs in North Vietnam. According to Perot, the idea originated with Henry Kissinger and his deputy Alexander Haig— "The government asked me to do it," he said.[58]* Actually, Perot came up with the ambitious plan on his own, in a conversation with Murphy Martin. "We were sitting in his office on Exchange Park, about ten days before Christmas," recalls Martin. "We were frustrated, having been stonewalled at almost every turn for what we were trying to do for the POWs. And just as conversation, I

---

* Haig, who was one of Perot's biggest boosters in the administration, told *The New York Times* in 1992: "I would not say we formally asked him to do it as such, but we endorsed the concept. There were a number of things that Ross conceived of, including ransoming the prisoners with his own capital." Perot adamantly denies ever offering to pay ransom for the POWs, although he admitted in 1970 that he was willing to "build facilities, supply food, clothing and other non-military items needed by the North Vietnamese people in exchange for the prisoners of war. . . . As a practical matter, we are willing to spend huge sums. . . ." Perot said he would "certainly" consider spending $100 million on the "supplies."

said, 'It's a shame we can't just pack up a Christmas dinner and send it to each one of them' [there were 1,420 known POWs at the time]. And he leaned forward over the desk and said, 'Let's do it!' That's how it started."[59] Perot had already sent Tom Meurer, with two POW wives and a couple of reporters, to Vientiane, Laos, on December 10 to generate some press coverage over the issue of captured Americans.

The 1969 Christmas delivery to Vietnam was the type of project Perot relished. The odds seemed greatly against him, and he almost single-handedly mobilized dozens of workers at EDS and chartered two Braniff jets. One jet was loaded, in nine days, with thirty tons of gifts, food, and medicine.* Some of the items included in the cargo were Bibles, thermal blankets, inflatable rubber mattresses, underwear, vitamins, and more than fourteen hundred Christmas dinners (according to an internal administration document, those dinners were "canned . . . and neatly packed by the Boy Scouts"). Perot also brought fifty Honda motorcycles and five hundred Sears, Roebuck catalogs in the hope he might be able to barter with village chiefs for information about MIAs.

That same plane—carrying two dozen journalists and an eight-person team from the Red Cross, as well as Perot, Murphy Martin, Tom Marquez, and several other EDS employees—flew to Vientiane (the closest U.S. embassy to Vietnam) to wait while North Vietnam decided whether it would accept the gifts. The second plane flew to Paris with the wives and children of POWs, who were to make a direct appeal to the Vietnamese embassy. Unknown to the press and public, the administration was secretly helping. "We were able to give Ross a good bit of behind-the-scenes assistance during the past week," Alexander Butterfield wrote to the president. Assistance had been given to a "most appreciative" Perot from diverse government branches, including Defense, Customs, the Surgeon General's Office, and even the Postal Service.[60] "It had to be closely coordinated with the federal

---

* Perot refused to pay the $30,000 insurance premium from Lloyds of London to cover the Braniff planes flying into a war zone. Instead, he told Braniff that he would buy it new planes, worth over $7 million each, if he lost the ones he chartered.

government," Perot later admitted. "But nothing could occur that would make it look like a government effort or it would have no credibility with the Vietnamese."[61]

While the White House was initially pleased with Perot's gambit, officials soon fretted about his independence and there were indications that he might not adhere to the strategy that had been mapped out. "The assumption all along was the North Vietnamese would not allow Ross and his 2 gift-laden planes into North Vietnam," Butterfield wrote to Nixon in a confidential memorandum on the afternoon of Saturday, December 27, 1969. "After widely publicizing their repeated refusals, Ross was to leave the goods with orphaned children in South Vietnam and herd his entourage home by way of India and Europe . . . holding numerous enroute press conferences to continue high-lighting Hanoi's 'thoroughly unreasonable' rejection of food, clothes, medicine, etc. and its 'inhumane treatment of captured persons.' We hate to see him divert from his plan, but have little hope now that he won't."

The reason for Butterfield's concern was that in Vientiane, Perot spontaneously told the press he intended to turn the cargo over to *North Vietnamese* orphans if he could not deliver it to the POWs. The White House was stunned, sending a cable to Perot urging him to change his mind, since it would cause "considerable undue embarrassment . . . for it would be only a matter of days before the Communist propaganda machine would turn the gesture into an admission of war crimes guilt on our part . . ."[62] Perot preferred his own alternative and ignored the White House entreaty. He persisted until the North Vietnamese rejected his offer, claiming they would only accept "American goods through the normal delivery channel,"—i.e., Moscow.

But Perot was not dissuaded. Again the White House was worried. Butterfield sent another confidential memo to Nixon, saying that "Ross is [now] seriously considering releasing the goods to the Soviets—something which we have asked him not to do. Henry [Kissinger] is quite concerned for if Ross does as Hanoi suggests, the generous 'private citizen' act of giving food, gifts, and medicines to the U.S. POWs will be lost to a heavy dramatization of Soviet benevolence. There is just no reason why we should make the Soviets look good on this one."[63] On the day

Perot's plane was to leave Vientiane for Moscow, Haig and Kissinger again sent urgent cables to Perot, virtually pleading with him not to go. "And Perot said, 'Wrong! We are going to Moscow,' " Tom Meurer remembers. "We just kind of disappeared to do our own thing."[64] "The White House just didn't understand Ross," says a former EDS executive. "They just thought he was some wealthy guy who would write checks for them and do their bidding. But Ross doesn't spend his money unless he has some control over how it is used, and once you put him in the game, Ross sets his own rules. He's not very good at any position but coach, and that is difficult to be when you are supposed to be doing it for the president."

The White House was so irritated with Perot's unpredictability that it even tried, unsuccessfully, to cancel the plane's clearance for takeoff. Once airborne, Perot discovered the direct route to Russia was blocked, since India and Pakistan had denied him the right to fly through their airspace. The North Vietnamese also added another restriction: They would not accept packages weighing more than 3 kilos (6.6 pounds) and larger than nine-by-twelve inches. This meant that most of the cargo would have to be repackaged. The North Vietnamese thought that would stop the flying caravan, which, to their dismay, had started to receive international press attention. But Perot had the plane fly to Anchorage, Alaska, where Meurer had radioed ahead for assistance. At the airfield, they were met by military units, local volunteers, and even some Boy Scouts. The gifts and medicine were weighed and repacked into small parcels. Despite the Alaskan winter, the volunteers finished the task in under ten hours. "Perot never had any doubt that we could get it done," recalls Murphy Martin.[65]

Moscow, however, remained out of reach, as the Soviets now refused to allow the plane to land. So Perot flew over the North Pole to Copenhagen instead. The North Vietnamese had set a deadline of December 31. Perot tried everything, including meetings with the Soviet ambassador and a late-night telephone call to Soviet premier Aleksei Kosygin, but the deadline finally expired. "The American ambassador was of no help," says Tom Meurer. "We just thought that the American government had decided to close everything down before it got out of control."[66]

Although Perot did not deliver the cargo, the entire event was a public relations coup, casting the North Vietnamese as callous and focusing international attention on the POWs. Much to Perot's delight, conditions for American prisoners improved inside the North Vietnamese camps. The episode also made Ross an instant celebrity. "It focused world attention on Perot," says Martin. "And he continued to ride the crest."[67] He did his first tour of the talk-show circuit. "Some of us started to think that the trip had been more about Perot than about the POWs," says one former White House official. "And that trip made us realize that he actually thought he knew what to do, better than anyone else. He never considered the possibility that anyone else could be right. When it comes to foreign policy and people's lives, that cowboy approach could be dangerous."

The Perot who returned home now seemed more aggressive with the White House. He told Nixon aides that he had several issues he would discuss only with the president—including that the "federal government can do so much more than it is now doing," and that the man he had met in Southeast Asia who directed the Red Cross "is bordering on insanity." He also wanted to complain about the "flak" he claimed he was receiving from Kissinger.[68] White House aides were not anxious for him to see Nixon, but Perot insisted. After several weeks, Butterfield told Haldeman, "I went through some stalling motions which I fear are getting a little old-hat to Ross. He cut me short by saying, 'Either the President would like to get a firsthand report on this matter or he wouldn't. It's as simple as that. We're both busy men, so there is no sense in wasting either person's time.' "[69] Just before midnight on Thursday, January 29, Perot called Butterfield at his home. He again demanded a meeting with Nixon. Butterfield was concerned by "Ross's statements to me to the effect that he has been deluged with queries by the press as to his precise connection with the White House—and more importantly, the White House's influence on his 'POW relief activities' . . ."[70]

Despite the advice of his advisers that he only send Perot a thank-you letter for the Christmas trip, Nixon decided to meet with him. The day before, Butterfield briefed Nixon, warning him that "upon several occasions he [Perot] has expressed to me his utter amazement over the fact that since his return from the round-the-world trip (in which he spent more than $600,000) 'no one seems to be particularly concerned, grateful, or even curious.' "[71] Butterfield suggested Nixon emphasize "our continuing interest in his support," and the "need to keep his activities totally independent of the White House."[72]

On Sunday, February 1, Perot went to the White House (to mollify White House aides, he agreed to keep his Washington trip a secret).[73] Nixon congratulated him on his Christmas trip, but Perot had other things on his mind. He proposed small "action teams" that would tackle problems in the State Department and HEW and, most important to Perot, on the POW issue.[74] The president told Perot the ideas were good ones, but within a week the administration had put them on the back burner. Sensing he had been given the brush-off, Perot declined to help Chuck Colson with a public relations project. In a formal letter to Haldeman, he said that his first priority was to United We Stand. "I want my reasons in writing so that there could be no confusion about my thinking," he wrote.[75] According to a former cabinet officer, "We realized that unless it had his name on it, he wasn't going to do as much for us anymore. He was starting to like the limelight."*

Encouraged by the success of his Christmas trip, in the spring of 1970 Perot returned to Laos. Besides some EDS employees (Meurer and Marquez) and a press contingent (Martin) he also took some wives of missing American servicemen. In Laos, Perot claimed to have met with U.S. embassy and Pathet Lao officials, and said he learned that large numbers of American POWs were held in Laos (see Chapter 13, "Missing in Action," for a fuller discussion). Perot continued to Saigon, where he visited North Vietnamese and Viet Cong prisoners of war. Later that autumn, back in the States, he mobilized United We Stand to hold rallies across the country to generate support for the POWs. In one of his

---

* Perot seemed to enjoy publicity, even when he was ostensibly avoiding it. For instance, in the summer of 1969, he gave an "anonymous" contribution of $2.5 million to the Dallas public school system. However, a Dallas publicist had spread the word about Perot being the donor even before the donation was announced by the city. Two days after the gift, both Dallas newspapers featured front-page stories quoting Perot extensively.

more dramatic moves, he built replica bamboo cages simulating the conditions in which U.S. prisoners were sometimes kept by the North Vietnamese, and displayed them on the steps of the Capitol before sending them on a nationwide tour.[76]*

At the White House, there was growing unease about Perot, but Charles Colson, special counsel to the president, was one of the few who had taken an outright dislike to him. "Ross Perot came in and dazzled Alex [Butterfield] and the President, that he could get the POWs back; he came in with a big POW kick. The guy was an amazing operator. I didn't know anybody in the whole four years that I was in the White House who was able to muscle themself in quicker into the President's own confidence. . . . The President was absolutely taken with this guy, totally."[77]

Colson had direct reason to be upset, as he had been the one charged by Haldeman with coordinating yet another Perot pledge,

* In 1992, Perot claimed that after his second trip to Southeast Asia, the FBI informed him that the North Vietnamese had targeted him for assassination and that they had hired the Black Panthers to carry it out. FBI officials found no evidence of such an assassination order or warning. But Perot went further, alleging there was an actual attempt: "The most significant effort they had one night is five people coming across my front lawn with rifles," he said. But Paul McCaghren, who headed Dallas police intelligence operations in 1970, believes that "it did not happen. There were only about eight people here that belonged to the Black Panther party. Two of those people worked for us, and they told us every day what was happening." Perot said he had not told the police or the FBI about the attack, even though Dallas police records show that on at least fourteen occasions during 1970 and 1971 Perot and his security team had asked for police help investigating incidents as minor as vandals throwing bricks at his mailbox. Perot claimed the five armed men were chased away by a guard dog, who had bitten a "big piece out of the seat of one of the guys as he went over the fence. We thought we would be able to find that person, because if you take a tremendous hit to your seat, you bleed profusely." Perot told another reporter that "when the dog came back, he had a piece of a guy's fanny in his mouth." Harold Birkhead, an ex–marine sergeant who was responsible for the dogs and security at the Perot house, said, "I neither saw it on my watch or even heard about it on somebody else's watch." No hospital in the Dallas area reports treating anyone for such a wound near that time, and indeed Perot now says that the day after the incident, he and two friends called local hospitals trying to find the wounded assailant, to no avail. When reporters at a 1992 press conference challenged Perot over his inability to provide any confirmation, he snapped, "I'm not going to get into that with you because it's none of your business. I'm not going to—hey, look, I don't have to prove anything to you people to start with."

$10 million, to form a conservative, pro-Nixon think tank. Colson had lawyers establish a general framework to be funded by Perot. Perot went to Colson's office, and after they exchanged pleasantries, Colson asked him if he was going to put up the money. "Yes," Perot told him.[78] "So, we got everything set up," recalled Colson, "and I called him up and said, 'We're ready to start funding it.' He came up with one stall after another. It was absolutely amazing. But all the while he was stalling, he was still getting in to see the President. He'd call up Alex Butterfield or he'd show up at seven o'clock in the morning . . . and say, 'I'd like to meet the President at seven-thirty.' They'd walk him in through the French doors from the Rose Garden, and he'd visit the President and go out."[79] After six months of trying to get the money, Colson said, "my patience was running out," and one night, before a White House white-tie dinner, Colson confronted Perot. Perot sat on a sofa in Colson's office, as Colson, still in his shorts while getting dressed, challenged him. " 'If we don't see some money within a week, I'm going to decide that you're nothing but a phony.' He left my office. . . . He never put up a nickel. He parlayed that offer . . . into access, which ended up costing him nothing. It is one of the most effective con jobs I ever saw in the White House."[80]

"That type of confrontation wouldn't bother Ross in the least," says one of his former colleagues. "Whatever you say to him one-on-one, he will just deny your version if he doesn't like it. Not only will he say what he wants, but Ross could look you in the face and say he never met Colson or doesn't even know who Colson is, and he could almost convince you he's right." Perot, in 1992, countered that the think tank was Colson's idea and that he rejected it since it did not have anything to do with the POWs.[81] He further says that Colson was constantly approaching him with "unusual" proposals, and was upset because Perot always said no. At least one administration official, communications director Herb Klein, corroborated Perot's version. "I was afraid that Colson, in his fashion, would try to exploit him [Perot] in a way which was not good for the effort and not good for Ross Perot himself, and I think that occurred on a couple of occasions."[82]

Although Colson was at the heart of some growing dissension in the administration regarding Perot, the pro-Perot faction still held sway. His failure to deliver on his $50 million media promise and the $10 million think tank was simply an aberration, his boosters thought. The administration kept inviting Perot to White House dinners; it sent officials to Dallas to solicit his advice on national issues, kept him abreast of public opinion polls, and even allowed him to brief the Joint Chiefs of Staff on his Vietnam trip.[83] In February, the same month that Perot refused to help Colson, Nixon named him one of eight recipients of the Distinguished American in Voluntary Action award.[84] Three months later, Nixon appointed him to the Advisory Committee on the Arts for the John F. Kennedy Center for the Performing Arts (Margot Perot was also later given an appointment to that same committee).[85] Later, when a limited, bound edition of Nixon's inaugural address was sent to a select list, Rose Mary Woods, Nixon's personal secretary, wrote to Perot that "no list of friends who should receive them would be complete without your name" and that Nixon wanted Ross to have it "as a reminder of his deep appreciation for your friendship and support over the years."[86]

Behind the scenes with the administration, Perot continued pushing for preferential treatment on a variety of personal and business matters, and delayed helping unless he saw progress on pending requests. For instance, the White House formed the Townhouse Operation in 1970 to raise large donations from wealthy contributors for funding Republican congressional candidates in the fall elections. Perot initially told Nixon's personal attorney, Herbert Kalmbach, that he would give $250,000.[87] But White House officials were soon grumbling as Perot attached conditions to his gift—that he "personally meet individually with every candidate we propose . . . to assure himself (1) that they have a 'plan to win' and (2) that they are philosophically and personally acceptable." He also demanded that Haldeman call him to confirm that his contribution was a priority, and that he "in no way be identified as a contributor to these candidates." He further insisted that "the HEW situation vis-a-vis his company must first be resolved" (Perot was trying to get HEW to drop its investigation into EDS's Medicare contracts).[88] Holding out the promise of contributing $25,000 to Ronald Reagan's gubernatorial race, he met with Reagan to complain about the loss of EDS's Medicare contract in Southern California. Perot did not make a contribution.[89] Nor did he give any of the $250,000 to the Townhouse Operation, prompting Jack Gleason, a Nixon staffer responsible for fund-raising on that project, to comment, "At least the oilmen keep their word."[90]

Despite its aggravation with Perot, the administration continued to help him. In the spring of 1971, John Erlichman awarded EDS a $62,000 contract to conduct a "state of the art" study on controlling costs in future national health care programs. The contract, signed by Nixon's deputy assistant Kenneth Cole and EDS president Mitch Hart, was not advertised for bids, nor was it announced in the Department of Commerce's *Business Daily,* despite government regulations requiring such published announcements (all civilian contracts valued at over $10,000 had to be published).[91] When that news became public the following year, the administration acknowledged that it had placed EDS into a "preferred" position for substantially more federal health care business, and that it was unusual for the White House to issue such a unilateral contract.[92]

Although concerned about press criticism, the White House did not back away from Perot. For instance, when Perot tried to persuade Congress to scrap the Social Security Administration's model computer system in favor of using EDS as its sole processor of claims, the White House applied pressure. "There was never anyone raising doubts about our [model system] until the Nixon administration came in, and then there was some interest in our dropping our own model system and letting him [Perot] have a really free hand," recalled Robert Ball, then commissioner of Social Security.[93]

By the time of the congressional investigations into EDS's state Medicare contracts in 1971, White House officials were finally concerned about overt interference, stalling Perot on his continuing demands for a meeting with HEW secretary Elliot Richardson. Kenneth Cole wrote to Haldeman aide Gordon Strachan, "It would not be wise to arrange a meeting. . . . Perot has been pushing anxiously requesting this meeting since Mar of '71."[94] Cole had visited Perot in Texas, and later reported that Perot was "consistently bitching about HEW" and felt that "HEW [was] trying to screw him."[95] In private notes made later by Strachan, Cole indicated that Perot wanted to meet with Richardson because of his concern over the "investigation on the Hill indicating hanky panky that started EDS—4 months of hearings—EDS did illegal things at start; exercising undue influ[ence] (monopoly) on market."[96] At another point in the notes, Cole noted that "Perot believes [he is] home free on [the] hearings." Events showed Perot's confidence in the administration was not misplaced. Even without allowing Perot to meet Richardson, the White House made its feelings clear to Richardson and other HEW officials. The Social Security Administration dropped its complaints against EDS regarding its charges on state Medicare contracts, and the congressional investigation eventually fizzled without that help. While the SSA said that EDS's failure to open its books to auditors made it difficult to determine whether its costs were reasonable or not, it nevertheless concluded that EDS's costs seemed reasonable when compared to those of other plans. "We're not interested in profits, just costs," said an SSA spokesman.[97] The following year, it was as though the fight with the Social Security Administration had never taken place. EDS was back in business, with HEW awarding it another large contract, and the only concern for Nixon aides being whether the award would seem connected to Perot contributions to Nixon's campaign (Perot had not given any money, although EDS officials had secretly given more than $200,000 to Nixon's reelection).[98]

But despite the favors, the tension between the administration and Perot worsened in early 1971. The White House was annoyed with what it viewed as Perot's cycle of promising more than he could deliver, getting a favor in return, and then not following through. It was also bothered by his abrasiveness when it did not take his advice on issues. Perot, on the other hand, felt the White House had taken his help for granted and started ignoring him. "The one thing the guys in the White House want is a puppet they completely control," he says. "And I have never been willing to be their puppet."[99] When he bumped into then United Nations ambassador George Bush, he complained "that he hasn't been getting very much White House attention of late," and also griped that during a recent *Life* magazine interview, when Nixon was asked to name people he frequently spoke to, he did not mention Perot.[100] When Perot later met political strategist Murray Chotiner, he was "miffed" no one had asked him to participate in the upcoming 1972 reelection campaign.[101] "It is difficult to please Perot," wrote one Nixon aide.[102] In an attempt to mollify Perot, Nixon's deputy assistant Dwight Chapin wrote a seven-point memo in February 1971, urging that Perot be consulted more on issues such as the Family Assistance and Welfare Program, the long-range economy, and the notion of the "volunteer army." Chapin also noted that somebody should talk to Perot about his recent complaint that he was not on Nixon's Christmas card list. "If all of the above is taken care of," Chapin wrote, "I am sure that Perot's problems with us will diminish rapidly."[103]

But the suggestions in the Chapin memo were ignored. "We were getting tired of Perot telling us how to run the government," recalls one White House official. "And nobody had been keeping count on what he had done for us recently, so it was very possible that it had turned into a one-way street, only benefiting his desire to be a player." Eventually, Haldeman asked his top aide, Gordon Strachan, to make an "assessment of H. Ross Perot in terms of commitments and delivery of money or material and Perot complaints and administration responses.[104]* Strachan consulted with thirteen Nixon aides and administration officials who had dealt with Perot. Even when Perot had delivered on his promises, there were caveats. His donation of seven men to the 1968 campaign had led to the IRS fight over his subsequent tax deductions for their services, and the administration had to "intervene to obtain a settlement." After he "became obsessed with the humanitarian POW issue in December 1969, [h]e played off Hughes, Haig, Colson, and Butterfield to the point where Alex

---

* The assessment done by Strachan is represented in the Nixon presidential papers both in its final January 12, 1972, memo to Haldeman and in a January 8, 1972, draft, with Strachan's handwritten notes. Also, there are twenty-seven handwritten pages of notes of discussions with other administration officials in preparation for the memo. All of these documents were used in reconstructing this section.

told Perot that he didn't understand the issues and should 'goddam stop calling.' "

Strachan also highlighted instances in which Perot had made promises and then failed to perform. He had pledged $250,000 for the 1970 congressional elections "but delivered nothing"; he promised $50 million "for the benefit of the President" and $10 million for a pro-Nixon think tank but did not give anything; he committed $500,000 to the National Center for Voluntary Action (Margot was on the board of directors) but "withdrew this pledge," since he "would not give a dime to the Administration until the POW's are free"; he did not contribute any money to the Nixon Foundation, though he was on the board of trustees; and in a private campaign to enhance Nixon's popularity, he failed to "produce a [nationwide] motorcade or delivery of letters," and though he agreed to "put 500,000 names on computer, Perot [again] did not deliver (in 1992, Perot claimed he did not give the addresses because the administration wanted them "for political purposes").[105] According to Nixon aide Richard Moore, Perot was a "lot of big talk, [and] turned out to be B.S."[106] When Perot called Haldeman in early 1972, Haldeman wrote in his notes that Perot complained he had "never had a personal relationship with the P[resident] . . . [and] he really supports the P[resident] and he would like to feel he had a relationship with him. . . . This is actually a little farfetched because Perot, of course, has reneged on almost everything he's promised to do for us, but I told him I'd see what we could work out."[107]

But there was one area of the Strachan memo where Perot's interests had melded ideally with those of the administration. It was an investment by Perot of $5 million in November 1971 in the giant Wall Street brokerage firm of du Pont–Glore, Forgan. Nixon administration officials, concerned about the weak condition of Wall Street brokerage firms and the effects on the market if one failed, encouraged Perot to make the investment. Perot, on the other hand, motivated by his desire to expand his business far beyond Medicare and Medicaid, and intrigued by the allure of conquering Wall Street, made the worst business decision of his young career.

SIX

Wall Street Fiasco

EDS's stock had been a star performer on Wall Street since it went public in 1968. Even a stock market crash in 1969 seemed to leave it unfazed, although the shares of most companies plummeted. EDS did not reach its peak ($162.50) until the spring of 1970. Then, on April 22, the decline that other companies had suffered over a year hit EDS in a single day. The sell-off started in the morning, and since there were so few publicly traded shares, the selling pressure exaggerated the slide. The stock dropped from 150 to 90, knocking $450 million off Perot's net worth. For most Wall Street traders, the one-day EDS crash, along with Perot's personal loss, became the permanent image of the 1969–70 panic.

Yet Perot had emerged from the bear market better off than most—he still had $1 billion, and had not made the mistake of placing EDS in debt by borrowing when its stock had soared. Instead of being disappointed in Wall Street, Perot thought he could take advantage of the frenzied market activity. Through the bull market of the late 1960s, trading volume had consistently set records, often reaching 15 million shares a day (in June 1968, it passed 20 million shares for the first time). Those trading levels would not be matched again for ten years.[1] For six months during 1968, the volume was so great that the New York Stock Exchange closed on Wednesdays to allow traders to catch up on the backlog of orders.

The stock exchange's problems were mirrored in brokerage firms, whose back offices (the Wall Street term for data processing, marketing, and cashiering) were drowning in paper, causing significant delays. Reconciling trades became a major problem, and there was even difficulty in locating stock held for clients. Perot saw the glut of paper as a ground-floor business opportunity, similar to the one he had envisioned in the Medicare field. No private electronic data processing firm had yet created a software system that could be sold to other brokerage firms, the way EDS had sold its Medicare system, developed in Texas, at substantial profits to other state Medicare programs.

Wall Street's readiness for the development of a single system coincided with Perot's need to find a new growth industry for EDS. In 1970, there were rumors of congressional inquiries into EDS's Medicare contracts (they actually began the following year), sending a warning that the days of keeping EDS's books and records closed might be nearing an end. Disclosure threatened the fat profit margins that had fueled the company's success. EDS stock had traded at such high prices before its April slide because the company had annually increased profits by more than 100 percent—a spectacular growth rate, but one virtually impossible to sustain.[2] However, to keep the stock propped up, it was important to find new business in virgin industries, where the same type of profitable long-term contracts as those originally fashioned in Medicare could be made.

Rudy Smotney, a partner at R. W. Pressprich and Company, the New York underwriter that had taken EDS public, thought he had found the ideal Wall Street firm—Francis I. du Pont and Company—in which to get EDS its first data processing contract. Founded in 1931 by Francis I. du Pont, the great-grandson of the founder of one of America's largest family empires, E. I. du Pont, it was the third largest brokerage house in the country in 1970. Managed by Francis's son Edmund and firmly controlled by the du Pont family, it had 95 branch offices and 1,500 brokers. The du Pont back office had expanded from 20 employees to almost 150 in two years, and there was excessive waste and duplication of effort, making it look like the ideal cleanup for EDS.

"We took a trip to Dallas," recalls Peter du Pont, a nephew of the senior du Ponts and a former manager of the back office. "Ross gave us a big show—we talked to some people he brought in, how customer relations worked—and we were reasonably impressed. He was entertaining, telling us stories about how he had telephoned Khrushchev, or someone like that, from a phone booth. Our only negative was when one person we spoke to, from a Dallas insurance company, who should have really been beating Perot's drum, was negative—not on EDS, but on Perot, because Perot was flying around the world doing all these things, and this guy was having some difficulties. He said, 'I want the son of a bitch here so I can get some help on my problems.' But even with that, we liked Perot—he was a real dynamo."[3]

In July 1970, only three months after EDS's stock slide, Perot traded 100,000 shares of the company (worth $3.8 million) to buy Wall Street Leasing, a computer services subsidiary of du Pont. This move allowed EDS to take over du Pont's back office. Although there had been some disagreement among the du Pont family about whether to sell the subsidiary to Perot, the company was in a cash crunch and needed the fresh capital.[4]

Du Pont had been paying Wall Street Leasing $3 million a year for its back-office work. EDS made a new eight-year contract that averaged $8 million annually. That deal appeared to provide Perot a major inroad into Wall Street, giving EDS the chance to develop software that could become the industry standard. But Perot and EDS had entered a sick industry. Indeed, though large brokerage firms were inefficiently run and needed computerization help, after the 1969–70 panic many were in financial difficulty. The freefall in share prices, combined with the sinking trading volume as small investors withdrew from the market, had eroded profits. The market's reversal was so quick and ferocious that by early 1970, several firms were forced to merge to survive. In May 1970, the stock exchange, worried that some brokerage firms were inflating their capital figures (brokerage houses were supposed to keep a minimum of their assets in cash), moved to establish the Crisis Committee, a self-regulating body of leading Wall Street executives. It was chaired by Lazard Frères partner Felix Rohatyn. By the time the committee was formed, five small brokerage firms were in liquidation, creating a shortage in the stock exchange's special trust fund, established to protect investors in case companies collapsed. Almost immediately, the Crisis Committee was confronted with yet another near collapse, that of Hayden, Stone and Co., an eighty-four-year-old Wall Street institution with nearly 100,000 customers.[5] "We all feared that if one of the large firms went under," recalls Rohatyn, "the whole exchange could come down, and we could have a major financial crisis. So there was a very high priority on maintaining stability for the three or four large firms that were trouble."[6] After five months of intensive efforts and backroom negotiations, Hayden, Stone was saved by September. But immediately after came Goodbody and Company, a preeminent Wall Street house and the fifth largest in the country, with almost a quarter-million customers (one of its co-founders was Charles Dow, after whom the Dow Jones Industrial Average was named). By late October, after another frantic effort, the Crisis Committee arranged for Merrill Lynch to rescue the ailing firm.

Losing almost $8 million in fiscal 1969, the du Pont firm emerged as the next possible casualty of the stock market slide. The company had expanded too quickly during the bull market, and when the market turned, it was overextended. It tried to strengthen itself by merging with two other brokerage houses— Glore, Forgan and Staats and Hirsch—in July 1970, the same month that Perot took over the back-office operations. But both Glore, Forgan and Staats and Hirsch were also in trouble, and neither could help du Pont.[7] By early November, du Pont needed an infusion of fresh capital, but the du Pont family refused to contribute. In an unprecedented move, the stock exchange's board of governors censured du Pont and fined members of its management for allowing such a rapid depletion of capital.[8]

As the Crisis Committee looked for a savior, Perot emerged as the natural choice. Besides his wealth, he had the motivation that if du Pont failed, EDS would lose one of its largest data processing contracts, the $8 million a year to run the du Pont back office. That could cause EDS stock to take another significant hit. As added insurance that Perot would be receptive to a request for money, members of the Crisis Committee enlisted Nixon administration officials to encourage him, warning that if du Pont failed, the consequences could be devastating. John Mitchell, Pete Flanigan, and even fellow Texan John Connally told Perot that his investment was an important one for the country.

At the personal request of Nixon, Pete Flanigan, formerly a top executive at Wall Street's Dillon Reed, made the most persuasive pitch to Perot.[9] On December 4, 1970, Flanigan wrote to Nixon: "I talked to Ross Perot. He is planning to go ahead with his investment in DuPont Glore Forgan. The reasons for this investment are to a large extent his recognition of the national importance in not having DuPont fail at this time. I told him you were appreciative of this move and agree with him that this is important in the national interest. We also agreed that his investment had substantial profit potential if he was able to develop the appropriate applications on his computer technology."[10]

Perot later insisted that he invested in du Pont because Nixon aides "got down on their hands and knees," pleading with him to invest.[11] He even complained that he was singled out as the man who could save Wall Street because "they were looking for a sucker," and "they assured me the maximum exposure I could have was 5 million."[12] Yet White House officials like Flanigan and Nixon's attorney, Herbert Kalmbach, were convinced that Perot's primary motivation was profit and that he had "overstated" his reliance on the administration.[13]

In addition to blaming the government, Perot also claimed that he was induced to invest because "a who's who of Wall Street and a who's who of the banking community came to me and pleaded with me to bail it out."[14] But Felix Rohatyn, who remains one of Perot's few boosters on Wall Street, says that Perot's investment in du Pont benefited all parties. "It was in our interests to get him involved in this thing as heavily as possible, and it was in his interest as well. . . . Perot had a big interest because he had a company with such a high multiple [price of EDS stock as figured as a multiple of stock price to company earnings] that the earnings generated by the du Pont contract helped the multiple and was actually worth hundreds of millions of dollars to him. Also, it was an opportunity for him to get other work on the Street. Perot has put a little bit too much emphasis on the public service aspect."[15]

Even Bill Gayden, a Perot confidant who was involved with du Pont, admits, "We not only thought we would develop a system that would work for other Wall Street companies and for the stock exchange, but there was also this other side, where we thought we were going to make ourselves richer. And we were under a lot of pressure. I wasn't even thirty years old. And I was going with John Connally, secretary of the treasury, to David Rockefeller's apartment for breakfast to talk about borrowing millions of dollars. We were young kids from Texas and were so mesmerized by it, enamored by the du Ponts and all the social power of the East—it was all a great draw."[16]

But Perot was not as impressed. Instead, he considered the du Ponts pompous and barely competent. This attitude was evident in negotiations to establish the amount he should invest in du Pont and what he should receive in return for that investment. Perot was tough (as he described it, "plain old beady-eyed business"), and was irritated that "I'm being treated like a raider when I'm trying to help."[17] He lectured them about how poorly they managed their company, and how he would revolutionize the way Wall Street did business. The du Ponts, on the other hand, disliked being rescued by someone as nouveau riche as the upstart Texan.[18]

"To Edmund, it just seemed as if the firm was being taken over by Perot," recalls Peter du Pont, "and he resented it—'Here was this little fellow who ran data processing and now he is taking away my firm that I took years building.' That is where Edmund and Perot had a parting of the ways. My feeling was that we had been led astray and that Perot was taking advantage of a bad situation."[19]

Perot had agreed to a $5 million loan. However, before the terms were finalized, du Pont's annual audit revealed the firm had lost more than realized—a record $17.7 million—the previous year. An additional $5 million was needed. Although Perot was initially angry, he soon realized that a $10 million loan would give him more leverage, and he set about to wrest even greater concessions. The du Ponts resisted, but the Crisis Committee made it clear they had few alternatives. On December 16, a deal was completed. Two EDS executives delivered a $10 million certified check to du Pont. The firms' partners agreed to raise an additional $15 million, but if they failed (which they did) Perot would receive a 51 percent controlling stake in the company.

"Ross Perot just closed his deal to make a major investment in DuPont, Glore Forgan," Pete Flanigan wrote to Nixon in mid-December. "Bunny Lasker [chairman of the New York Stock

Exchange and a close Nixon friend] feels this is the last of the 'bad apples in his basket' and that the securities industry has no further major firms in imminent danger."[20]*

One of the first things Perot did after his investment was to meet with Crisis Committee chairman Rohatyn. "They said, 'Look, if we are going to save the Street, we want to get something out of this,' " recalls Rohatyn, who agreed that indeed they did deserve something. "But they actually overreached—they wanted the data processing business of the entire stock exchange. They wanted to be treated like major players on Wall Street. They wanted people to recognize that they were doing something for the community, even though they were also serving their own self-interests, and they did not want to be looked upon like rubes from the sticks."[21] With the help of Nixon aide Flanigan, EDS did get a $250,000 consulting contract to study computer options for the stock exchange. Eventually, many of the recommendations in EDS's final report were adopted, with the notable exception that EDS itself was not hired.[22]

Quickly, however, Perot was less concerned with winning new business than with solving the problems at du Pont. Within two months, it was evident that $10 million was not enough to save the firm and that a rescue might require over $50 million. When Perot heard the news, he seemed surprised and threatened to pull out and let du Pont collapse.[23] "They said it was a $5 million problem," he said, "so we waded in like Boy Scouts and then found out the vault was out of control. . . . All the capital was gone."[24] "When we got inside the company it was much worse than we expected," concurs Mort Meyerson. But other observers, such as Felix Rohatyn, are skeptical that the Perot group did not realize the full extent of du Pont's problems. "It was a high-risk investment, not a safe one," concludes Rohatyn, "and there was no question about that to anyone."[25] EDS had been doing the data processing of the back office since July 1970, where it encountered all the firm's internal figures. "They ran the figures for

---

* Within the next few months, the Social Security Administration approved payment of five government data processing contracts that had been delayed because of questions concerning possible EDS overcharges.

six months," says Peter du Pont, "so to say they didn't get control of the vault is a bit of bullshit."[26]

But by late April Perot had negotiated a new deal. In return for a $55 million loan, he would own 81 percent of du Pont (he eventually ended up owning 100 percent). Perot also asked Pete Flanigan to help persuade the stock exchange to indemnify him for losses, which it did to the extent of $15 million.[27] Also, Perot was successful in getting the Federal Reserve Bank to make an unprecedented exception concerning how much stock he had to use as collateral in securing the $55 million loan. Normally, $157 million in stock would have been set aside as collateral, but the Federal Reserve cut the requirement in half for Perot.[28] Perot's final requirement for the deal was Edmund du Pont's resignation as general manager. On May 14, 1970, Perot took control.* "It's okay to take the du Ponts' money," Perot later said. "They haven't worked for it in two generations."[29]

Mort Meyerson, the head of EDS's health care division, was thirty-three years old when Perot asked him to go to New York to run du Pont. That Perot completely trusted Meyerson and felt confident he would institute the changes Ross sought was more important than the fact he knew nothing about Wall Street and managing a brokerage house. Still, Perot kept abreast of Meyerson's progress through securities attorney G. Michael Boswell, who observed the New York operation during the week and then flew every Saturday to Dallas for a briefing with him.

Almost immediately after Meyerson settled into du Pont, he tried to infuse the EDS culture into Wall Street. It did not work. "They were very military," recalls Rohatyn, "very by-the-book, certainly different than people up here." EDS, with its dress code and ban on facial hair, rubbed Wall Street the wrong way from the start. "There was a culture clash you wouldn't believe," said Perot lawyer Boswell.[30] Perot viewed the beards, fashionable clothes, and three-martini lunches as emblematic of a poor attitude that would lead to failure in business. "One of our philosophies is that

---

* Edmund du Pont later sued Perot, charging that Perot breached his fiduciary relationship by using inside information, gained from EDS computer programmers working on the company's books, to induce the du Ponts to give him control of the company. The suit was unsuccessful.

we fire people," Perot said. "We fired those who thought our objectives were too Boy-Scoutish and would not support them."[31] Although some EDS executives wanted to modify the strict rules for du Pont, Perot would not. When Perot visited New York and ran into one of his employees, Gary Griggs, wearing a blue shirt, he told Meyerson, "I'm here with Griggs and I don't know whether to kiss him or shake his hand."[32]*

But the tension between Perot and Wall Street was deeper than a clash over clothing styles. "Ross is not overly endowed with humility," said Walter Auch, who was later a chairman under Perot. "He did not have a high regard for management on the Street, and was not reluctant to say so."[33] Perot did not help matters by publicly criticizing his new industry. He said that "nobody ever talks about making money for the customer," and charged that most stockbrokers "wanted to shoot dice" and risk the average person's "fruit-jar money."[34] He even raised the possibility of paying brokers based on what they earned for clients, as opposed to a commission for each transaction. In full-page national newspaper advertisements, Perot proclaimed that the new du Pont would cater to the small investor—"For 38 years of my life, I was a 'little guy.' There are so many of us. We are America."[35] At special luncheons, Perot scolded investment analysts about their business practices. "He tried to impose his provincial attitudes on some pretty sophisticated people here, who consider themselves to be every bit as energetic and entrepreneurial as him," said Alan Abelson, a prominent *Barron's* columnist. "And his style left something to be desired. He came across as a super–Boy Scout."[36]

Du Pont did not respond to Perot's shock therapy. One of his early decisions was that the recruiting philosophy that had worked for EDS in 1968—hiring Vietnam veterans—would work for du Pont. In the first two months after the takeover, more than six hundred veterans were hired and sent to the du Pont Educa-

---

* Perot once referred to men who wore blue shirts as "sissies." "Ross doesn't have a very high impression of men he thinks are homosexual," says a former EDS executive. In 1992, Perot told a *New York Times* reporter that "as far as he knew," he had never met a gay person. Earlier, he had told ABC News that his gay employees were "brilliant people, doing outstanding work" who "worked directly for me."

tional Center in Los Angeles. There they received a crash course as stockbrokers, plus a motivational program that incorporated much of the EDS philosophy (the recruits had to sign contracts that if they quit after the training course, they owed du Pont $25,000). "We are hiring men at the rate of 50 a month," boasted Perot. "I don't want anybody that has any brokerage experience. We want to vaccinate these fellows in a different way."[37] While veterans fit comfortably into EDS since most of the employees were like-minded, du Pont was different, and military training did not always lend itself to becoming a successful broker. Moreover, the resentment among du Pont's existing workers grew, and several hundred left within the first eight months. In one instance, the entire sales office in Decatur, Illinois, quit and walked across the street to join a rival.[38]

Although Meyerson made some progress in turning around du Pont's operations, the rest of the company remained troubled. "One of his problems was that he put some real sleaze types in key positions," recalls Peter du Pont, who stayed at the firm after Perot's takeover. "Meyerson was extremely bright, but a bad guy for the job. He didn't have much humility, and he really didn't know how to act on Wall Street. He could have had the best people on the Street, but through arrogance, and not being willing to listen to other people, he hired a lot of second-rate people."[39]

There were also bad business decisions. "I don't think they ever realized what type of business this is," comments Felix Rohatyn. "They were never able to hire the people they needed to as the business was changing from an individual broker one to an institutional one. Du Pont had no merger-and-acquisition activity, no investment banking capability. Even in the retail end there were dramatic changes as fixed commissions were going out the window. It happened too fast for them."[40] A key blunder was maintaining 110 of du Pont's 120 branch offices, at a time when most brokerage houses, due to reduced volume and customer demand, were consolidating. By keeping the offices open, Meyerson kept costs inflated at a time du Pont could ill afford it. During the first two years of the Perot-Meyerson tenure, the firm lost $32 million.[41]

An extended market rally that brought renewed volume to the stock exchange and encouraged the return of small investors—the heart of the retail brokerage business—might have pulled them through. There was a brief market run-up in 1972, and Perot tried to capitalize with a massive advertising campaign, but the market peaked in early 1973 before plunging again. Yet many analysts thought stocks were due for a fall rally. Perot and Meyerson counted on that rally, and further expanded their business by proposing to merge with another respected brokerage house, Walston and Company, in July (earlier in 1973, Perot had invested $4 million in Walston, winning the rights for EDS to do the back-office work and to put Mort Meyerson and Bill Gayden on the Walston board).

As du Pont–Glore, Forgan's fortunes worsened through early 1973, the stock exchange demanded that the firm put more money into capital reserves by July 1. Perot had a creative solution that avoided putting in more cash. By merging the sales and back offices of du Pont and Walston, Perot hoped to save costs while boosting revenues. But there was a final hurdle. The Walston board had to approve the merger.

It met on Sunday, June 30, only one day before the stock exchange's deadline for bringing du Pont into capital compliance. The Walston family controlled half of the twenty board votes and rallied against the merger. They knew their firm was weak from several years of a languid market, and since it was much smaller than du Pont, they feared the problems of the larger firm might sink them as well. The heated meeting lasted from the early morning until past midnight. Since Perot was not there, Meyerson shuttled between telephone calls with him and the meeting. According to Meyerson, the meeting was "the tensest, roughest I've ever seen."[42] When one of the Walston loyalists, George Robson, became ill and returned to his hotel room, Meyerson's bloc refused to let Robson vote by phone, although the Walston policy had long permitted that.[43] With Robson gone, the Perot faction approved the merger by one vote. "It was the most awful experience of my life," recalled Jack Walston.[44] Jack and his brother, Carl Walston, were fired the following month.[45]*

---

* Mrs. Nella Walston, widow of the founder of Walston and Company, later unsuccessfully petitioned a court to void the merger. The only silver lining for

Du Pont Walston seemed promising on paper. With 143 branch offices, 2,800 salesmen, and 300,000 customers, it had overnight become the country's second largest retail broker, behind only Merrill Lynch. In fiscal 1973, du Pont Walston supplied almost 20 percent of EDS's $111 million in income. "Conceptually it was good," says Peter du Pont, who was fired during the merger, "since if you put them together, the plant you need to service it is smaller, and you have the same sales force. But it didn't work that way. It was too late. Both Walston and du Pont were too sick by then."[46]

Problems quickly surfaced. The Walston employees were as unhappy being under the EDS culture as the du Pont workers once were, and that made them ripe for raids from other brokerage firms. More than five hundred of its best salesmen left for competitors. Perot was so concerned that he filed suit against E. F. Hutton in September to stop the raiding. The autumn stock market rally never materialized, and du Pont was further buffeted by the Yom Kippur War and the Arab oil embargo. Although Meyerson managed to cut costs by $4 million a month, the company lost $10 million in its first five months. "When we grossed over $12 million in October and still lost money," said one du Pont Walston official, "I knew our goose was cooked."[47]

In September, Perot insisted he would "stick it out until we can turn this thing around."[48] But when he studied the six-month forecasts, he was shaken by the predictions for continuing poor performance. In January 1974, Perot flew to New York and had a stormy meeting with the du Pont Walston board. The decision was made to dissolve the firm and sell the retail business and the company's nineteen-floor Manhattan headquarters. Although Wall Street had been filled with rumors that du Pont Walston was in deep trouble, the news of its demise still was a surprise. In many Wall Street offices there was glee that Perot, perceived as a smug interloper, had failed. "When they finally went under," admits

---

Perot during the ten-year legal morass that resulted from his Wall Street venture was that he engaged the services of a young Dallas lawyer, Tom Luce, from a four-member firm. Luce would eventually become one of Perot's closest confidants, and his firm would grow fat on Perot business. Today, it is one of Dallas's largest law firms with more than 150 attorneys.

Felix Rohatyn, "I thought they were poorly treated."[49] Perot spent another $16 million in closing and selling the du Pont Walston's retail operation. Du Pont's back-office operation was left intact, but it had lost its only data processing client in Walston. While Meyerson wanted to stay in New York and find new customers, Perot overrode him (in 1974 the remainder of the du Pont firm filed for Chapter 11 bankruptcy protection).*

Ross Perot was publicly silent after the announcement from New York of du Pont's failure. But privately, his anger was evident. One employee who was with Perot on the day he told Meyerson to close the operation said, "It was the lowest I ever saw him. He was exhausted, but he was also tyrannical about it, screaming at people all day. If you had anything to do with him, he took it out on you. He had people in tears that day because of the way he treated them." It was his first public failure, costing him between $60 and $70 million. But in no way did it humble him. Rather, he blamed the loss on his unquestioning patriotism—the notion that if he had not been asked by the government to save Wall Street, he would never have answered the call to go to New York. Years later Perot said, "This is a great business to work in but a terrible one to be an owner in. Where else are there so many mediocre people with absolutely unbelievable incomes?"[50]

Perot tried to salvage what he could from the du Pont debacle, but his misfortune continued. Since the money he lost on Wall Street was as an individual investor, not as a corporation, he was not entitled to write off his loss. He decided instead to lobby the House Ways and Means Committee, chaired by the powerful Arkansas representative Wilbur Mills. In Washington, Mills had been a steady booster of Perot and EDS. He sometimes called the

---

* In 1978, the court-appointed trustee for the bankrupt du Pont Walston filed a $90 million suit against Perot and many EDS associates, charging fraud, misrepresentations, and deception, including Perot's purported failure to disclose the extent of du Pont's financial troubles and to reveal a stock exchange study that predicted the combined firm would last only eight months before failing. Perot settled the suit the following year for $6.7 million. That settlement was the only time he was disappointed with his new attorney, Tom Luce. When presented with the settlement papers, Perot grumbled, "Jimmy Hoffa's attorneys don't settle. They win and he's a crook. I'm not, and my attorneys want to throw in the towel. Maybe I need Jimmy Hoffa's attorneys."

commissioner of Social Security, Robert Ball, and urged the government's computer system for Medicare be dropped in favor of "letting him [Perot] have a really free hand."[51] Unknown at the time, EDS executives had secretly donated $100,000 to Mills just three years earlier (March 30, 1972), by passing checks through seventeen "dummy" committees (the donations were discovered in Senate Watergate files).* After the Mills contribution, Perot also gave more than $27,000 to twelve other members of the Ways and Means Committee.[52] On November 4, 1975, at 10:30 P.M., on the last day of a prolonged tax writing session, Democratic congressman Phil Landrum of Georgia introduced an amendment to a major tax bill. It entitled investors who had capital losses of more than $30,000 to a refund for any taxes paid on capital gains in previous years. Perot stood to recoup $15 million. Privately, committee members dubbed the bill the "Perot amendment," as it was drafted by one of Perot's lawyers, former IRS commissioner Sheldon Cohen.[53] After a few minutes of perfunctory debate, it passed 20–14 (ten recipients of Perot contributions voted for the amendment).[54] However, when word leaked that Perot would be a beneficiary of one the biggest tax breaks in congressional history, he suddenly flip-flopped, criticized the amendment, and even said he would not take advantage of it if it passed. His about-face ensured that it was killed in conference.

Perot was at a low point. National magazines and newspapers that had praised his brilliance when EDS went public in 1968 suddenly questioned his judgment.[55] With the loss of the du Pont Walston income, EDS stock tumbled, and after the announcement of the company's shutdown, it traded as low as $11 a share. Perot's net worth had dropped from the heady days of 1970, when it topped $1.5 billion, to $100 million. But that was not all. The same month Perot closed du Pont Walston, EDS lost a $584,000-a-year Medicare contract with Kansas Blue Cross/Blue Shield. Soon, ten other state health insurance officers announced that they intended to competitively bid EDS's contracts upon their expiration.[56] EDS would soon record the first of several consecu-

---

* The gifts were legal when made, but a week later, a new law banning such secret gifts went into effect.

tive years of declining revenues. "The only area of the company making money was health care," says Ken Riedlinger, who had successfully led EDS teams to capture health care contracts in eight states during his seven years at the company. "Everything else was losing money, and a lot of people had gotten taken in the Wall Street thing."[57] Perot knew Riedlinger was right. Worried about having lost his opportunity to move into a new industry in Wall Street, Perot now decided to return to the company's core field—the government and Medicare. When he visited the new secretary of health, education, and welfare, Caspar Weinberger, his reception was anything but friendly. Perot vaguely recalls the meeting, and says he asked Weinberger to stop picking on EDS in seeking audits. But Weinberger recalls the meeting quite differently, and in considerable detail. Perot produced a letter from the White House urging that Weinberger try to help him.

"I want the data processing contracts for Medicare," Perot told Weinberger.

"Well, these are very big contracts, and they are already awarded," Weinberger said.

"I can do them for half."

"That would be interesting. Very interesting. I don't award the contracts myself, but if you have a proposal to make, why, we have a board downstairs that does that. If you have the lowest responsible bid . . ."

"No, no, no, you don't understand." Perot was agitated. "I gave five million bucks to Nixon, and I want that contract now!"

"You are absolutely correct, Mr. Perot, I don't understand. We don't do business that way. If you are going to do anything at all, it would have to be by competitive bid."

"But this letter is from the White House." Perot's voice rose as he waved the paper at Weinberger.

"Well, the White House doesn't write many letters like that, that I know of, but I can't believe that if you have something worthwhile, the White House wouldn't want you to get it by competitive bid."[58]

"He stormed out of my office," says Weinberger, "and that was the last I saw of him. Now, I've heard that he used those tactics elsewhere, that same sort of technique and that same sort of intimidation. This is a very unpleasant man." (Asked years later by a reporter whether his government contacts helped him compete for federal jobs, Perot said, "Gosh, no. If I go around making calls at a senior level, that becomes a news story.")[59]

Perot's reception by Weinberger was another reminder of how the Nixon administration had soured on him and his string of broken promises. Near this time, a reporter for *Newsweek* asked Perot about the political influence he wielded with the administration. Perot actually downplayed his influence, and complained about the public's perception that he had "some kind of close relationship [with Nixon]. It was never there."

Rebuffed by an administration increasingly consumed with Watergate, Perot left Washington power politics, licked his wounds from Wall Street, and returned to Dallas to regroup EDS and his troops.

SEVEN

"*I'm Not an Investigative Personality*"

The relationship between Perot and the Nixon administration further deteriorated in 1973, when the POWs started coming home as part of the peace treaty between North Vietnam and the United States. The government wanted an official celebration in Washington. Perot decided to give his own party in San Francisco. "They were all buried in Watergate, but they lusted in their hearts to have the ultimate media event," Perot later said.[1] When Haldeman asked Perot to postpone his event until after the White House celebration, Ross refused. "That guy [Haldeman] was your classic instance of someone who got to be where he was because he was good at blowing up balloons in campaigns," recalled Perot.[2] For his POW party, Perot enlisted his employee Tom Meurer, who had done advance work for Nixon. "Perot said, 'Throw them a party,' " Meurer recalls. "I knew where the right points were. I had thrown ticker-tape parades for Nixon, and suggested one of those, and Perot said, 'Great.' "[3] Meurer arranged for appearances by John Wayne, Clint Eastwood, Red Skelton, and other entertainers. The San Francisco event was further enhanced by a group of Green Berets who had infiltrated North Vietnam to free POWs at a camp at Son Tay (the prisoners had been moved days before their arrival). Perot flew most of them in from Thailand, where they were still based. "It cost Ross over $250,000 for that weekend," says Meurer.[4]*

---

* The deputy secretary of defense, Bill Clements, was Perot's contact in the government who helped bring the Son Tay raiders to the party. Clements, a fel-

It was further evidence to the POWs, many of whom had heard snippets about Perot while imprisoned, that he cared more about them than the government did. Meanwhile, White House aides fumed over Perot stealing the limelight. Although Nixon later toasted the POWs at a black-tie reception on the White House lawn, Perot knew that the administration had not forgiven him. "Whatever relationships I had with the White House were destroyed," he later said.[5]

But as important as the POW issue was to Perot, he still had a business to attend to. After he finished closing du Pont in 1973, his attention returned exclusively to EDS the following year. His top priority was finding a new location for the company, since it had outgrown its Exchange Park headquarters. Perot decided that if he had to move EDS, it presented an opportunity for the company to recapture its original ethic. He searched for a site where he could create an insulated atmosphere, and found it in an affluent north Dallas neighborhood, the site of a former country club, Preston Hollow. The land was zoned for one-acre residential lots, but that did not dissuade Perot from purchasing it and beginning a battle with the neighborhood association over the proposed commercial development. He sent three female employees to call on the neighbors and tell them that, as one executive said, "they were in for the fight of their life if they opposed our development plan." The eventual compromise with the neighborhood suited Perot, giving him a twenty-five-year deed. He agreed to leave nine holes of the golf course bordering the south, west, and north sides of his proposed development. With a creek running along the eastern boundary, the neighborhood residents felt as though there were a buffer between them and the new headquarters (the main building could not be seen from the public street). It also provided Perot the shield from the outside world that he sought for his new site.

Perot built a twelve-foot-high fence around the compound's 180 acres, and security guards patrolled the perimeters. The grounds

---

low Texan, later served two terms as the state's governor, and also became an EDS board member.

were impeccably maintained, with the grass even spray-painted green during Dallas's dry periods. Once past a guard's gate, visitors proceeded a quarter mile along a curved driveway (which was flanked by dozens of flags representing states and countries with EDS offices) to the modern seven-story headquarters and adjacent computer center. There, clean-shaven men with army haircuts, in the EDS uniform of dark suits, white shirts, and spit-shined shoes, enthusiastically greeted visitors and took them around the grounds in a double-time gait. The climate-controlled buildings were kept cool enough so that workers never had to remove their jackets, even in the summer. Employees were encouraged to stay on the "campus" for their recreation—it had a small fishing pond, lighted tennis courts, jogging tracks, a swimming pool, a softball field, and even a family picnic area. "This place was designed to keep our people healthy and happy," boasted Perot.[6] "It was like another world," recalled one competitor who visited the site. "Everything was extremely clean, very efficient, almost eerie in that everything seemed a little too perfect. The following year I saw the film *Stepford Wives*, and I realized what it was that had bothered me."

Although the sheltered and homogeneous atmosphere was important to Perot, it was not enough, by itself, to reverse EDS's fortunes. The firm had lost some of its earliest clients, including Frito-Lay, PepsiCo, and Continental Emsco, and had failed to win some major new contracts, making mistakes that would have been unthinkable five years earlier. The biggest blow was the failure to close an enormous data deal with United Airlines, after having gotten a letter of intent that it was imminent. The mystique of being able to tackle and master every project, no matter how difficult, had been lost. Competitors, including IBM, at first slow to respond to the EDS challenge, had by the early 1970s mobilized efficient divisions to pursue the same data processing contracts, beating EDS on accounts that had previously been Perot's exclusive domain.

During the first two years after its corporate move (1975–76), EDS had its first declining earnings (it took EDS three years to return to the net income it had when it was flying high with du Pont). Perot tried investing in new start-up companies like a catalog for videocassettes and electronics, but that venture quietly folded after three years of no profits.[7] There was even heresy among Perot's chosen employees, some of whom were leaving. Tom Meurer, one of his closest aides, went to Hunt Oil.[8] Rob Brooks, one of the company's star recruiters, left with eight others, who felt "we were tired of working our tail off for nothing."[9] Perot could not imagine why anyone would want to leave EDS. The company had an award, Recruiter of the Year, and the names of the winners were engraved on a prominent plaque. When any of the winners left the company, Perot wanted to remove their names.[10] "If you left the company," recalls Tom Downtain, "usually you never heard anything more about that person, no matter how good Ross thought they had been when they were there."[11] Downtain, who was employee number seven, lasted a few more years (until 1977) before leaving.

"There was a definite burnout ratio with Ross," recalls one executive who was close to Perot. "He works at an incredible level of intensity, and a lot of people just lost the fire to put up with all the headaches that could mean when you were on a project and he was all over your back. We used to say, only half joking, that a lot of the time it was as though Ross asked you to go climb a sheer ice glacier and report back to him. Then you would go ahead, climb the glacier, almost kill yourself in the process, and report back. And he would say, 'Okay, now do it without gloves.' After a while, a lot of people who thrived on that in the beginning just figured there was an easier and less pressure-filled way to make money. Plus, some of us thought Ross was acting a little squirrely on some things."

What that executive thought was "squirrelly" was Perot's tendency to periodically obsess about personal security for him or his family. Those who worked with him noticed that this trait seemed more pronounced once Perot became a public figure, following EDS's wildly successful stock offering and his trips to Southeast Asia. Yet there was little predictability to what would concern Perot.

"The thing that has always puzzled me about Ross is the paranoia that I see manifested there," says Rob Brooks. "Even when one of his children was born at Presbyterian Hospital—and this is only when he had publicity associated with the POW issue, and some publicity regarding his success as a businessman—he had the floor at the hospital where his wife, Margot, was having a child cordoned off, with security guards at each end. I mean, the paranoia was just unbelievable. Let's say Ross was going to fly to New York. He would have his secretary make reservations on five or six different flights, and no one knew for sure which one he was going to be on—that sort of thing. I never understood the basis for that.

"But the contradictory thing about that is that once or twice a week he will go over to Dickey's Barbecue, by himself—you can see him in line—and he sits there and eats a sandwich in the corner all by himself. I have seen him drive down Forest Lane honking away. He goes alone to get his haircut. He's hard to figure."[12]

Although the mid-1970s was the same period when Perot claimed a squad of Black Panthers, acting on a Viet Cong hit contract, had scaled the wall around his house before being chased off by guard dogs, he bragged to Washington politicians and reporters that he traveled without an entourage or bodyguards. But unknown beyond a small circle at the company was that Perot's apparently conventional car (a black four-door Chevrolet Caprice) was a special bombproof vehicle, protected by bullet-resistant Kevlar. "It had everything," recalls Tom Marquez, who had helped arrange the order together with Perot's aide Merv Stauffer. "It had places for guns, pits where you could shoot, and a double battery. It looked just like a normal car, except when you got to a tollbooth, you had to open the door to give the money because the windows were so thick you couldn't roll them down. Ross was like a kid in a candy store when we gave him that car."[13] Perot liked the Caprice so much that he later bought a Chevrolet Suburban rebuilt by the same San Antonio company. "Then they had a little machine gun they were coming up with," says Marquez. "It was going to be the competitor for the Uzi [a renowned Israeli automatic weapon]. Ross liked it so much that he wanted to buy the whole damn company."[14]*

* One executive recounted an evening when he left a hotel with Perot and the Caprice had been moved by the parking lot attendant. "We had a bellman start

In the late seventies, when Perot was doing work for Texas governor Bill Clements on the war on drugs, he became convinced that another assassination order had been put out on him and that the man who was going to carry it out was Charles Harrelson (actor Woody Harrelson's father, currently in jail for murdering a federal judge). A local FBI official did not take Perot's fears seriously. Furious that the FBI did not react, Perot assembled his own security team to follow Harrelson.[15] The Harrelson matter was one of many incidents in which Perot began relying on private security. Permanent guards patrolled the grounds of his house and the EDS complex. Dallas police officials believe that Perot has hired more policemen (scores of them) in their off-duty hours than any other Dallas resident. Day and night, a Dallas police car sat in the driveway of his home (the house itself is surrounded by a ten-foot-high wall and is under constant video surveillance). Retired FBI agents frequently work for him.*

In addition to hiring private security guards for his protection, Perot also used them, and their techniques, at EDS. Polygraphs were occasionally used to resolve issues of employee misconduct (people who refused to submit to one were fired if other evidence pointed to guilt), and background investigations were done on many new applicants.[16] Perot kept track of license plate numbers in the EDS parking lot in an attempt to track some workers who were arriving late and leaving early, and during particularly heated fights for contracts, employees on the "bid team" would be physically searched to ensure they did not remove any paperwork that could assist the opposition. Perot also used investigators to check on the backgrounds of competitors, and even several key executives at EDS. He personally interviewed the investigators he hired. One told me that in his initial meeting with Perot and Merv Stauffer at EDS's headquarters, Perot "presented a hypo-

---

the car while we waited over by the hotel's entrance," the EDS employee recalled. "Just in case someone had put something in it, we figured he was the most expendable of the three of us."

* When Perot later helped Governor Clements on a task force on drug abuse, he asked the state to build a heliport on his estate apparently so he could make a fast escape from drug lords or assassins. His neighbors successfully fought the idea.

thetical situation about somebody in the company doing something wrong. He then asked me if I would put a tap on the phone. 'No,' I told him. 'What if I ordered you to do it,' he asked. 'Well then, I would just say you've got the wrong guy.' Perot dropped it and we talked about other things. When I left, Stauffer walked me over to the door, put his arm around me, and said, 'By the way, when Ross asked you about the phone taps, you gave the right answer.' " However, according to Ken Riedlinger, one of the company's star salesmen and a protégé to Mort Meyerson, "Most people at my level assumed their phones were tapped at EDS. All the officers I ever talked to about it assumed their phones were tapped, and I felt that way about mine. We would have been surprised if we weren't investigated."[17]

"This was almost a Ross Perot genetic disposition. . . . Find the dirt," recalled his former general counsel Richard Shlakman.[18] For instance, Perot later used the same investigator with whom he'd discussed phone taps for a variety of assignments, including internal fraud and embezzlement cases. He also compiled personal information on business competitors and the private lives of at least two leading EDS executives, and did background checks on some of the young men who dated Perot's daughters. ("There was no tailing or surveillance on their dates, just simple stuff like background crime checks," says the investigator.) When Perot heard that a senior vice-president was seen at a party with a woman other than his wife, he assigned the same investigator to the case. "I want to know everything they do together," Perot told him. The investigator followed the vice-president throughout Europe and the United States. "Perot loved to collect information, those personal facts of a perverse nature," recalls the investigator. "Perot was titillated by it. And he is unique among businessmen I worked for, because most of them, when they asked me to check someone out, were relieved when I returned with nothing. Perot, however, expected that I should always find dirt, and thought I had not done my work right if I returned with nothing."

Perot kept to a minimum the number of employees in his company who knew about his private and security affairs. None were closer than Merv Stauffer, who oversaw each case as directed by Perot. Yet while senior executives were familiar with Stauffer's responsibilities and Perot's predilection for security, there was little reason for most employees to ever suspect such things. Indeed, the image most workers had of Perot was of a gifted motivational leader who cared about their welfare. The firm is replete with stories of Perot arranging for doctors, flying medical teams in for a crisis, or arranging special education or scholarships for the disadvantaged. "For many years, there was no disability program at the firm, so the policy was 'Trust me,' " recalls a former Perot colleague. "Most of the time it worked, because Ross saw to it that people who were loyal to him were paid in turn by loyalty from him. That meant that if you or your family needed Ross, he would be there, and be just as single-minded as he is when he is trying to win a contract or get something he wants, he will be just as determined in making sure that he helps solve your problem, whatever the cost." Many employees felt as though Perot honestly cared for them, that he had forged special relationships with them, and his instances of great generosity reinforced that attitude. Mort Meyerson, for instance, in recalling an incident in which his wife spilled Drāno in her eye, recounted how Perot rented a Learjet the following day and flew her to Johns Hopkins. Although some employees felt that Perot only helped because it was a means of guaranteeing loyalty and indebtedness, Meyerson's reaction was typical of many who were recipients of Perot's largesse. "[At the time] I wasn't an executive, just a beginner, and here he was, going to the limit for me and my wife. Imagine what I felt for that man. Imagine the loyalty. I would have walked through a wall for him."[19]

The high achievers at EDS thrived on Perot's intense focus and ever-constant challenges. Since EDS encouraged performance and honored it with extra compensation and more responsibility, many overlooked Perot's quirks and instead developed a loyalty to the organization that is rare in most companies. Bill Gayden and Tom Walter gained Perot's complete trust and were two of the few people who could get Perot to reconsider a decision.[20] Merv Stauffer and Tom Marquez were also close. Others, like Les Alberthal, Gary Fernandes, and Ken Riedlinger, had become the company's best performers, especially on health care, yet they lacked the influence of Perot's inner circle. But the person who continued to have a unique relationship with Perot was Mort

Meyerson. "When I came back to Texas after du Pont, I arrived in a 1967 Volkswagen, all very low-key," says Meyerson. "The culture of EDS is that if you produced, that was all that mattered. It didn't matter I had failed at du Pont. Ross had said to me, 'It is like you are trying to grow cotton on a rock without rain. So it couldn't be done.' "[21] Although only a vice-president, Meyerson wielded more influence with Perot than president Mitch Hart and chief financial officer Tom Walter. "We always got along, even though we are very different people," says Meyerson. "I was trying to reorganize the company, trying to change everything. I was in his face about everything they were doing. And the fact that he didn't slay me is a miracle, an absolute miracle. He must have smelled something so that he would put up with that grief."[22]

Perot began bypassing EDS president Mitch Hart, and turned increasingly to Meyerson. Although some thought Meyerson's enhanced status had made him demanding, few doubted his strong contribution to the company. Meyerson would eventually be voted, three years running, the most outstanding executive in the computer services industry by business publications and financial analysts. Perot later said, "Morton Meyerson was the central personality in EDS for the last ten years [1976–86]. . . . He ran the company. I did not deal with security analysts. I did not go to the managers' meetings except typically to make a speech and go to dinner."[23]

The first thing Meyerson did when given his new responsibilities was to drive across the country visiting all the EDS accounts. He promoted the aggressive Ken Riedlinger to regional manager in charge of selling health care contracts. As competition increased for the state Medicare contracts, Riedlinger used a dual approach: Some employees looked for the dirt on competitors, while others moved into "war rooms" in state capitals, pressured the politicians and health commissioners, and produced thick and persuasive proposals faster than other competitors.[24] The results were mixed. Riedlinger's teams won new contracts, starting in 1975, in North Carolina and Alabama and one in a particularly nasty fight in Tennessee, where a competitor seemed to have better connections with the governor's office.[25] Yet in 1977, EDS lost two large contracts in Massachusetts. Governor Michael Dukakis canceled one because the selection committee awarded it to EDS after ignoring a lower-priced bid. Dukakis nullified the other because the selection committee included executives from a company that was an EDS business partner in another state.[26] That same year EDS dropped out of competition for a $24 million-a-year New York City Medicaid contract, which promptly went to a rival, Bradford National Corporation. The following year, EDS lost a $12 million-a-year California contract to another competitor.[27]*

Audits of EDS's government work, under way by the General Accounting Office (GAO), eventually highlighted a host of problems and substandard work on some Medicare contracts, including a "very high error rate in its claims processing" and "a lack of responsiveness" to beneficiaries.[28] In Illinois, EDS had nearly half a million backlogged claims, including many black-lung compensation cases. There its work was so bad that the government imposed a $2.9 million penalty, leading the government's Health Care Financing Administration to establish a special unit to monitor the firm.[29] In other cases, the audits discovered that EDS had destroyed thousands of claims and letters in an attempt to reduce the enormous backlog of unfinished work or that improper accounting procedures led to flawed financial reports. The GAO also charged that EDS had an unfair advantage on some major contracts by obtaining advance information on competitors' bids.†

The company's president, Mitch Hart, resigned in 1977, although most employees thought Perot had fired him.[30] Perot continued grooming Meyerson for the job. Meyerson, meanwhile, helped the company find partial salvation from its dependence on the health

---

* While EDS had its difficulties during this time, Perot was doing very well in his private investments. He had accumulated a sizable real estate portfolio that was booming along with Dallas during the mid-1970s, and was also the owner of Petrus Oil and Gas Company, which eventually held oil and gas revenues worth hundreds of millions of dollars. Perot's lifestyle, which had been subdued immediately after the success of his public stock offering, had become more luxurious; he acquired several homes, private planes, a helicopter, a cabin cruiser, and one of his favorite recreational toys, speedboats.

† By 1978, EDS felt so adrift that Perot hired outside consultants to study employee attitudes and suggest changes. The results of that survey eventually prompted Perot to allow mustaches and colored shirts for men, and slacks for women.

care field when he moved EDS into another government area—the military. Led by Meyerson, the firm had won a $100 million contract from the army (taking it away from IBM made it even sweeter).[31] With that foundation, it also started expanding its overseas operations, an area where Perot and other executives saw great potential, since governments and private industries were some ten years behind the United States in the use of computers. The company's first major overseas contract was for a university in Saudi Arabia, followed quickly, in late 1976, by a $41 million pact with the Iranian social security system. EDS's 1978 annual report praised its Middle Eastern growth, proclaiming that it was "a choice assignment for the 200 EDS people from the U.S. and Europe who are working there."[32]

By the time that annual report reached shareholders, however, Perot was only a few weeks away from facing one of his greatest personal challenges—in Iran—and the outcome would forever alter the public's image of him.

EIGHT

Escape from Iran

On December 28, 1978, Perot was having breakfast with his family at his mountain retreat in Vail, Colorado, when he was interrupted by a call from Bill Gayden, president of EDS's international division. At first, Perot thought it might be bad news about his eighty-two-year-old mother, who had bone cancer and had been hospitalized with a broken hip on Christmas Eve (Perot had joined his family in Vail only the day before, leaving his sister, Bette, to watch Lulu). Gayden did have unsettling news, but it was about EDS: Two top executives had been arrested in Iran. No charges had been filed, but it appeared to be a corruption investigation, and their bail was set at a staggering $12.75 million. "Get Tom Luce [EDS's outside counsel] into the office," Perot told Gayden. "Call the State Department in Washington. This takes priority over everything else. I don't want them to stay in that jail another damn minute!"[1]*

Perot was furious with himself because he had not followed his own instincts three weeks earlier to pull all his employees from

---

* Much of this chapter is based upon the account presented by mystery writer Ken Follett in his international best-seller *On Wings of Eagles*. However, while Follett's rendition presents the most detailed account of the crisis in Iran and Perot's subsequent rescue mission of his employees, it is the authorized version, over which Perot had full editorial control. The book suffers from that, and this chapter attempts to counterbalance it with some contrasting witnesses and viewpoints.

Iran. The signs of a collapse of order had been evident for almost six months, with accelerating social unrest as revolutionary mobs took to the streets with increasing frequency and vigor. There had been particular warning signs for EDS. In June, the Iranian Ministry of Health and Social Welfare missed its monthly $1.4 million payment to the firm. EDS had one of its largest data processing contracts in Iran (potentially worth $90 million), which called for everything from issuing social security cards to 32 million Iranians to organizing national payroll deductions and processing claims while trying to minimize some of the endemic fraud.

Paul Chiapparone, the EDS manager for Iran, tried to get the Iranians to renew their monthly payments, but was unsuccessful in a climate of increasing anti-American sentiment. In September, martial law was declared, and the day after, army troops killed over a hundred demonstrators in downtown Tehran. The following month, the minister of health and social welfare, Dr. Shoja Sheikholeslamzadeh, and his deputy, Reza Neghabat, were arrested as part of the shah's program to ferret out corruption in government and thereby boost the popularity of his weakening regime. Both had been closely allied with EDS. A third ministry official who was arrested, a Dr. Towliati, was actually on the EDS payroll (at $5,000 per month). Their replacements did not return Chiapparone's calls.

By year's end, rifle shots were frequently heard in the streets, electricity was repeatedly cut off, and essential services, from hospitals to banks, were often interrupted by the unrest. On December 2, the first day of a national strike called in protest against the shah's regime, seven hundred people were killed in street fighting. Jay Coburn, the EDS director of personnel in Iran, had a card pushed under the door of his apartment that said: "If you value your life and possessions, get out of Iran."[2] In December, a smaller EDS project, to computerize the bookkeeping of the shah's bank, the Omran, was halted when mobs threatened the employees.

Finally, Chiapparone sent a letter placing the Ministry of Health and Social Welfare on notice that if it did not pay promptly, EDS might stop all its work. It was a calculated threat, since if EDS followed through, the social security system would grind to a halt, further exacerbating the shah's problems. On December 4, EDS repeated the threat to stop work unless it was paid.[3] That same day, Perot ordered his staff in Dallas to "evacuate everyone."[4] EDS flew almost all of its 131 American employees and 220 dependents out of Iran on December 8. But Gayden had persuaded Perot to leave a skeleton staff of about ten senior men. Evidently, Perot did not know that Bunny Fleischaker, an American living in Tehran, had already warned EDS executive Jay Coburn that her friends at the Ministry of Justice were planning to arrest Chiapparone and the manager of the social security contract, Bill Gaylord. Coburn did not believe her.[5]

Perot returned to Dallas the same day he received the news of the arrests of Chiapparone and Gaylord, and began urgently seeking help to obtain their release. Among those called were Henry Kissinger, Alexander Haig, former ambassador to Iran (and CIA director) Richard Helms, and aides to Secretary of State Cyrus Vance. Perot sent Tom Luce and Admiral Tom Moorer, former chairman of the Joint Chiefs of Staff, to Washington to meet with State Department officials.

After forty-eight hours, Perot became convinced that the officials were not doing anything to bring about his employees' release. He was doubly incensed, because the officials did not seem to show enough concern, nor did they move fast enough to satisfy him. Perot thought EDS "should be a top priority" and that the embassy staff in Tehran was "simply incompetent."[6]

"That's pure bullshit," says John Stempel, then acting political counselor at the U.S. embassy. "The ambassador and all the top consular officers were doing everything we could to resolve that case and ensure they received fair treatment. Perot deliberately obscures the case between what diplomats are supposed to do and what he would like them to do. The very fact that he had raised the profile by talking to so many prominent people made it very difficult for us to work out a quiet solution to the problem."[7]

"Perot's attitude was 'I want you to get my men out and forget about everything else,' " recalls Clyde Taylor, a deputy chief in the embassy's economic division. "What he forgot was that we had 25,000 Americans to worry about getting out of the country [more than 27,000 had left during the previous six months]. . . .

Perot jeopardized all of that by ratcheting the pressure on his case to the exclusion of the other Americans in the country."[8]

In Washington, the State Department also felt the heat from Perot's well-placed friends. "I got a constant barrage of calls about it, and couldn't get away from it if I wanted to," says Henry Precht, then the State Department's director of Iranian affairs. "Kissinger, the senators from Texas, even Senator Kennedy—because, I believe, Chiapparone had been from Massachusetts. Every day I began by calling Tehran, and the first question I asked the embassy was 'What have you done for EDS today?' That was because I knew that at some point later during that day the pressure to find out what we had done would start, and I had to have an answer. EDS was clearly on a higher plane than anyone else. Perot was certainly the most effective and persistent person I have ever encountered."[9]

Not only did Perot judge the official efforts in Washington and Iran as inadequate, but he became convinced that his employees had been criminally kidnapped, while the State Department and the embassy considered they may have been detained as part of an aggressive Iranian inquiry into possible corruption. "Our people on the ground worked on that," says David Newsom, then under-secretary of state for political affairs, "and in the end, couldn't confirm whether the Iranians or Perot were right."[10]*

The very idea that the State Department and embassy thought there could be any basis to a corruption charge against EDS infuriated Perot. However, American officials knew that almost every foreign company that worked successfully in Iran had to make payoffs, even if they were disguised as "legitimate" payments. "The Pahlavi Foundation [the private organization established by the shah and his family] got a cut," says former embassy official John Stempel, "or sometimes individuals close to the shah got money, or payments were made for travel and schooling for somebody's buddy, this kind of thing. I would be very surprised if EDS

---

* The general Iranian position, although never put into an indictment, seemed to be that since EDS had allegedly won the contract through bribery, it was invalid. Therefore, Iran wanted back the money it had already paid to EDS under the contract. The $12.75 million bail seemed a likely way to recoup some of the funds.

had not paid off. Now, whether they did it in traditional *baksheesh* [Middle Eastern term for a payoff] or not, I don't know, but nobody did business of that magnitude in Iran without arranging for some money to go to the Pahlavi Foundation."[11]

The American officials were even more suspicious of the EDS situation when they heard who EDS's Iranian agent was—Abolfath Mahvi. "This was a man who had been one of the most notorious 'five-percenters' [middlemen who took 5 percent of the gross value of a contract for greasing the government wheels]," says Henry Precht. "He had been very close to the shah, but his reputation had become so sullied that even the shah banned him from that kind of activity. . . . It was well known to everyone in Tehran that this was a guy who handled bribes."[12]

The issue of Mahvi and possible corruption and bribes is a very sensitive one to Perot. Although he has claimed that "we checked Mr. Mahvi every way to Sunday," neither Richard Helms, who was ambassador to Iran through late 1976, nor Roger Brewin, the embassy's economic counselor from 1974 to 1978, recalls Perot or EDS executives ever asking about Mahvi.[13] Whatever Perot found out about Mahvi, he felt comfortable enough to have dinner with him at Dallas's Petroleum Club in May 1975. Moreover, even when Mahvi was jailed for a month in Tehran in 1977 and questioned about allegations that he had supplied financial and sexual favors for the shah, EDS's Paul Bucha says Perot did not insist that he discover the reason for the investigation but that he nevertheless passed along information about it to Dallas.[14]

Years later, when Ken Follett wrote *On Wings of Eagles,* the authorized account of the Iranian affair, he acknowledged that in 1975, Mahvi helped EDS get its first Iranian contract, a document-control system for Iran's navy. "EDS, advised that by law they had to have a local partner, promised Mahvi a third of the profit," wrote Follett.[15] EDS had paid Mahvi $400,000 on that deal (EDS internal documents reveal that the sum was paid for "services rendered as agreed").[16*] In 1976, when the social security contract

* EDS, in 1977, gave a $400,000 loan to a Panamanian company, Cumana Investment Co., S.A., designated by Mahvi. Then later, EDS converted the loan to a payment for services. In 1977, another $200,000 was given by EDS, as a short-term loan, to an Iranian company in which Mahvi had an interest. Mr.

was being negotiated, Follett said, "Mahvi was on the blacklist" but that when it was about to be signed, he "was off the blacklist again [and] demanded that the contract be given to a joint company owned by him and EDS." Mahvi claimed to have helped EDS's contract pass through twenty-four different government bodies, and said he was responsible for a favorable tax clause built into it.

"Did we succumb to pressure?" said Paul Bucha. "We succumbed to the realities of life, and the realities of life were, he was off the blacklist, we wanted his help, we needed his help."[17]* EDS made payments to the Abolfath Mahvi Foundation, a charitable organization that supported educational objectives but that included a bylaw allowing the money to be used for Mahvi's poor or disabled relatives.[18] Iran's crown prince ran the Mahvi Foundation. "Mahvi eventually folded all of his businesses into the foundation," says former deputy minister Neghabat. "It had the added benefit that the money that went into it was tax-exempt."[19]

Also, EDS had to make other concessions to win the giant social security contract. At the final meeting, the health minister, Dr. Sheikholeslamzadeh, asked the EDS officers, "Where is my bribe?" The EDSers were taken aback. Then he told them what he wanted was that in return for the social security and bank of Omran data processing contracts, EDS should install computers in the office and residence of the Iranian queen, and that a hospital system should be developed for tracking an inventory of drugs in hospitals, via computers. "EDS agreed to both," recalls an Iranian official intimately involved in the negotiations. "The queen's work was worth $6 million, and the hospital work another $3 million. Nobody got personally richer from those deals, but in effect EDS had given Iran a $9 million discount off the value of the contract they had won on social security."

Mahvi did not repay it. EDS did not report those payments in its annual report to shareholders, and the Securities and Exchange Commission did not obligate them to, since they were considered too small to be "material transactions."

* When EDS was owed $10 million by the Iranian government on the social security contract, it again approached Mahvi and asked for his help. The deal struck was that if Mahvi could get the government to pay, he would receive $1.8 million. "It didn't help," says Paul Bucha. "We still didn't get paid."

"I guess the entire issue of bribery did not bother me," says Follett. "If Perot had been a different type of personality and the company had bribed everyone left, right, and center in Tehran, I would not have taken a moral attitude even toward that. However, this was a real issue. They had an Iranian partner [Mahvi], and Ross told me more than once that it was the law that if you wanted to work in Iran, you had to have an Iranian partner, and those partners were supposed to get a share of the profits. And, says Ross, 'I made them put their share of the profits into an educational trust and the trust was supposed to be building schools,' and, he says, 'I sent somebody to look at the buildings where they were building the schools.' Now, that tells you the extent to which he was interested in that question. Now, how far are you convinced by that? I think it wouldn't have been that difficult for someone, somewhere along the line, to pull a fast one here. They could have taken this American, in a jeep, out to somewhere in the backwoods, where they are building a casino, and said, 'Look at the schools we are building with EDS's profits,' and the guy would have said, 'That's great,' and would have gone back and told Ross. So I am not as convinced as Ross is of that story, but there is no question of his fierce concern that his company should not do anything disreputable. And there was then a question of how I was going to portray this in the book. And in the end, what I decided to do was to describe exactly what happened, just put in the facts. I didn't use the word *bribery* at all, but I thought, 'Let the reader draw his or her own conclusion.' Looking back on it, Ross shouldn't have done business in Iran. He's temperamentally unsuited for it."[20]*

By December 31, after three days of living at his office, sleeping on the floor, and eating cheese sandwiches, Perot decided to take things into his own hands. "Are you going to let two friends get killed in Iran just because our government sits around with its fin-

---

* Although Follett considers Perot's adamant stance regarding EDS and possible bribery in Iran to be solely a moral issue for Perot, it also carried legal consequences. Because of an earlier Senate investigation into bribes paid by Lockheed Aircraft Corporation, Congress had passed the Foreign Corrupt Practices Act. Under its terms, it was a felony for an American company to pay bribes in foreign countries.

ger in its ear," he later asked, "or are you going to get them out? I think you'd go get them out."[21] Within hours of the arrest of Chiapparone and Gaylord, Perot had briefly considered what might happen if negotiations failed. Now he started to gather a team that could rescue his executives. Ross directed two employees to "put together a list of EDS people who could help do it. We'll need men who know Tehran, have some military experience—preferably in Special Forces–type action—and are one hundred percent trustworthy and loyal."[22]

At midnight on New Year's Day, Perot received a telephone call from Henry Kissinger assuring him that Chiapparone and Gaylord would be released within half an hour in Tehran. Perot was initially ecstatic, but an hour later nothing had happened. The Iranians controlling the jail had not received word to release the EDS employees. "Perot closed his eyes," wrote Follett. "The worst had happened. Kissinger had failed."

At 2:00 A.M. on January 2, Perot had Tom Marquez call Colonel Bull Simons, the leader of the special forces team that had made a raid on a North Vietnamese prisoner camp in an unsuccessful effort to free American POWs. Perot, who had met Simons in 1973 at the celebration he hosted in San Francisco for the POWs, considered the colonel a hero. By the time of Marquez's call, Simons had retired from the military, and his wife had died the previous March. According to Follett, "He was sixty years old and he could not think of a single goddam reason for living another day. He stopped taking care of himself. He ate cold food from cans and let his hair—which had always been so short—grow long. . . . He started taking in stray dogs, and soon had thirteen of them, scratching the furniture and messing on the floor. He knew he was close to losing his mind. . . . Paradoxically, the only way to rescue Simons was to ask him to rescue somebody else."[23] Simons did not hesitate when asked if he wanted to help get Chiapparone and Gaylord out of their Tehran jail (he was so eager to help that he refused any money for his services).

Later that day, Perot met with seven of his employees, five of whom had flown in from EDS sites around the United States. All had served in the military and had spent time in Tehran for EDS, and most had combat experience. All were in their thirties, married, and had children. Two were black. Not a single one dissented when Perot asked them to be on the squad. The next day, January 3, the team met with Simons at Perot's weekend house near Lake Grapevine. There they discussed how to storm the Ministry of Justice in Tehran, the city-block-large structure that included the jail holding Chiapparone and Gaylord. During the following days, they did the planning for what was now Operation Hotfoot (Help Our Two Friends Out of Tehran)—including everything from smuggling guns into Iran in the false-bottomed portion of two large Louis Vuitton steamers to target practice at a nearby shooting range. In the Perot-approved language of Follett's book: "When they had started on January 3, they would have had trouble launching a rowboat as a team. Five days later they were a machine."[24]

As word spread around the seventh floor of EDS headquarters that a special mission was under way, a few of Perot's closest executives expressed misgivings. Tom Luce, his outside counsel, told him it was "idiotic."[25] When the State Department heard rumors of what Perot wanted to do, Undersecretary of State David Newsom called to "warn him about this idea of his."[26] "Whether he was successful or failed," says the embassy's Charles Naas, "there would be serious ramifications, and those of us left behind would pay the price."[27]

But Perot was insistent that Simons's team, dubbed the "Sunshine Boys," might be his only answer, as efforts to release the two men by paying the bail demanded by the Iranians had stalled.* One of the team's members left for Istanbul on January 8, and the remainder of the squad, including Simons, left for Paris on Wednesday, the tenth. From there they split, half the team getting to Tehran through Zurich, while the rest left from Paris. They established their Tehran headquarters at the Hyatt Crown Regency. Unknown to them, Perot, together with a lawyer from

---

* EDS tried to interest a bank in posting a letter of credit, and then once Chiapparone and Gaylord returned to the U.S., reneging on the payment, claiming that the bail had only been extortion. However, EDS chief executive officer Tom Walter had trouble locating a bank that did not have large outstanding loans to Iran, in which case the Iranians would merely apply the amount under the letter of credit against the existing loan.

Tom Luce's firm, John Howell, also left for Tehran, flying first to London and then to Iran. "Perot wanted to go to Tehran to kick ass in one last attempt at a legitimate solution," wrote Follett, "before Simons and the team risked their lives in an assault on the prison."[28] Perot arrived on a chartered Learjet, pretending to be an NBC staff worker, but passed through customs using his real name and passport. Chiapparone and Gaylord had been in jail for two weeks.

Within the first few days in Tehran, attorney John Howell met with Iranian prosecutor Hosain Dadgar, and was frustrated to discover that no compromise was possible over the issue of bail. Perot, meanwhile, visited the U.S. military headquarters, and then the embassy. " 'Mr. Naas, a Mr. Perot is waiting for you downstairs,' " Naas recalls his secretary told him during the early morning of January 13. "I nearly fell out of my chair."[29] He took Perot to the consul general, Lou Goelz, and the ambassador, William Sullivan. Perot did not like Sullivan's attitude. He had asked Sullivan if he could move from his hotel and stay at the ambassador's residence. However, U.S. Army general "Dutch" Huyser was staying there, and Sullivan had to turn Perot down.[30] "He [Sullivan] talked for a while, but did not sit down, and he left as soon as he could," wrote Follett. "Perot was not used to such treatment. He was, after all, an important American, and in normal circumstances a diplomat such as Sullivan would be at least courteous, if not deferential."[31]

Perot did not know that Ambassador Sullivan actually was his biggest supporter at the embassy, fond of Perot's high-profile involvement over Vietnam. "He liked Perot, and respected him," recalls John Stempel. "That was fortunate for Perot, because it was a terrible decision for him to come to Tehran. The ambassador had to intervene two or three times to avert an Iranian arrest of Perot." Perot, unaware of the background effort to keep him out of harm, ridiculed the ambassador and his staff as useless. "The State Department people never left the embassy," Perot complained. "They had no idea what was going on."[32]

On Tuesday, January 16, the shah, his family, and his personal entourage fled the country. Large crowds celebrated throughout Tehran. Two days later, Chiapparone and Gaylord were moved from the Ministry of Justice jail to the larger, and more secure, Gasr prison. Part of a military complex, Gasr was surrounded by two walls, one thirty feet high and another twelve feet high, plus inner sections cordoned off with barbed wire, and the entire complex was ringed with guard towers. When Simons's team learned the news, they were shattered, and Follett wrote that "their rescue team could not attack this place, not without the help of the entire U.S. Army. The rescue plan they had planned so carefully and rehearsed so many times was now completely irrelevant. There would be no modifications or improvements to the plan, no new scenarios; the whole idea was dead."[33] "Thank God that paramilitary operation never got off the ground," says Stempel. "It would have been a disaster. If the Iranian revolutionaries had found four or five yahoos with rifles, they would have thought they were CIA, and it could have been potentially terrible for the remaining Americans."[34]

Perot, deciding that a personal visit would be the best tonic for the flagging spirits of Chiapparone and Gaylord, went with two EDS employees and some of the embassy staff to Gasr prison. He signed the visitors' book with his real name, presented his passport as identification, and even stopped to chat with Ramsey Clark, the former attorney general, who was also visiting. The Iranians made no attempt to detain Perot, and he was even allowed to meet his imprisoned employees in a small ballroom in a building known as the "Officer's Club," instead of the dismal visitors' room in the prisoners' cell block. Chiapparone and Gaylord were overjoyed to see him (incredibly, Gaylord apologized to Perot for the mustache he had grown in jail, since it was against EDS rules). Perot brought books, groceries, and mail from their families, along with words of encouragement and some vague promises that if all else failed, "we will get you out of here by other methods."[35]

That night, Perot visited Simons, who was discouraged by Gasr's forbidding security. Simons thought of alternatives like trying to "bribe or blackmail this general who is in charge of the place." But he also told Perot, "There's a revolution going on here. Revolutions are predictable. The same things happen every damn time. You can't say when they'll occur, only that they will sooner or later. And one of the things that always happens is, the mob

storms the prisons and lets everyone out."[36] Since the bail negotiations were stalled with the Iranians and Simons's team was
stymied because of the security at the new prison, Perot decided to
leave Iran the following day, January 20. Again, he not only presented his real passport at the airport but was cleared on a VIP
basis before he caught a British Airways flight to London, where
he met Margot for a short holiday. "We were so happy he was
gone," says John Stempel. "He was too much of a loose cannon
while he was in Iran."[37]

Since an assault on Gasr was now impossible, Simons's team
was reduced by three members. It was still possible that a mob
might storm the prison. Simons instructed Jay Coburn that on his
next visit to Chiapparone and Gaylord, he should tell them that if
they were set free in such an episode, they should head immediately for the Hyatt, where the team was based. Coburn recommended using a twenty-three-year-old Iranian who had completed
the EDS training course and could be trusted to find Chiapparone
and Gaylord if they got out of prison and then lead them safely to
the Hyatt. (In Follett's book, the young Iranian is given the pseu-
donym Rashid.) Meanwhile, Simons and his team plotted the best
way to leave Iran once they were free. Kuwait was discounted
after an EDS employee flew there to check on the conditions and
discovered that the Kuwaiti authorities were forcing planeloads of
arriving Iranians to return to Iran. That left Turkey, and when
Simons decided an airport was too easy a place to be captured, he
chose the overland route. He bought two Range Rovers for
$20,000 each, and actually drove one, with Coburn and two
Iranians, to the Turkish border to ensure that there were no major
roadblocks or obstacles. The route to the border was clear.

Throughout January, the situation for the successor government
to the shah, run by Prime Minister Shapur Bakhitar, rapidly deteriorated. On January 24, against a backdrop of ever larger street
demonstrations, Bakhitar closed the airport at Tehran to prevent
Ayatollah Khomeini from arriving from Paris. During the following days, scores of pro-Khomeini demonstrators were killed by
government troops. By January 30, Ambassador Sullivan had
ordered the evacuation of all nonessential embassy personnel. On
Thursday, February 1, Khomeini arrived in Tehran, and 2 million

wildly enthusiastic Iranians overwhelmed the airport. In his first public statement, the Ayatollah told the throng, "I beg God to cut off the hands of all evil foreigners and their helpers." Simons, who watched it on television, turned to Coburn and said, "That's it. The people are going to do it for us. The mob will take that jail."[38]

Perot, impatient that his covert team now had no way to spring Chiapparone and Gaylord, made a final effort to arrange the bail. On February 5, a carefully crafted compromise by which the U.S. embassy agreed to guarantee the $12.75 million bail fell apart at the last minute when the Iranian prosecutor rejected it. But EDS did not give up. It turned to one of its clients, the bank of Omran, where the president was Dr. Sheikholeslamzadeh, the jailed minister of health and social services, with which EDS had its large contract.

In the week since the Ayatollah's return, his followers had established revolutionary committees that ran city services from the police to garbage collection. On February 8, more than a million people marched through Tehran, responding to Khomeini's call for the Parliament to resign and the military to mutiny. The following day, battles erupted at Tehran's two air bases between forces loyal to the shah and pro-Ayatollah contingents. Early on Sunday morning, February 11, some of the EDS employees went to the roof of their office building to watch the city's riots. Hundreds of men roamed the streets armed with automatic rifles. Molotov cocktails had started dozens of blazes. Two of the EDS workers, Bill Gayden and Keane Taylor, thought they saw smoke coming from Gasr prison.

Unknown to them, Gasr, as well as every other prison in Tehran, had been stormed that morning by large revolutionary crowds. Eleven thousand prisoners walked out of Gasr after the crowds moved in, and the guards offered no resistance. That did not surprise some, like John Stempel, who had contacts inside the revolutionary movement. "Several people had told me," recalls Stempel, "for a couple of days before the prisons were attacked, that they would be releasing political prisoners. The guards had started drifting away from places like Gasr, and the Revolutionary Council had decided it was time to move against them."[39] Yet in Ken Follett's book, the twenty-three-year-old ex-EDS trainee dubbed Rashid gave a rousing speech to the crowd milling in front of Gasr, started firing a rifle to further energize the mob, and then "wriggled through a window" to unlock the massive steel gates and let the mob inside.[40] Perot later said that ten minutes after Rashid's speech, "100,000 people were storming the prison."[41] "That's not the way it happened," recalls Reza Neghabat, the former deputy minister of health and social services who was imprisoned in the same cell block with Chiapparone and Gaylord. "I know that boy, and it happened without his help."[42]

The scene inside Gasr prison was chaotic, with thousands of prisoners, including an entire wing of mental patients, streaming into the courtyard and pressing to fit through the front gateway. Chiapparone and Gaylord thought they might die in the rioting about them. But within several minutes they had made it over a side wall and were ecstatic after six weeks of confinement. (Rashid actually waited outside the front of the jail for an hour and never saw Chiapparone or Gaylord when they came out.) Instead of dangerous mobs on the street, they found Tehran packed with people, but almost in a carnival atmosphere, shouting, "Allah akbar!" ("God is great!") People in neighboring offices and apartment buildings were at windows applauding the escaping prisoners. As Chiapparone and Gaylord walked and hitchhiked their way to the Hyatt, they were even passed by a former Gasr guard, now changed into civilian clothes and waving warmly from a passing car, shouting, "Mr. Paul! Mr. Bill!" The entire scene reminded Chiapparone of a New York parade. But until they reached the hotel, they were nervous something could go wrong. (Perot later told a crowded Dallas news conference that Chiapparone and Gaylord had to flee "through intense gunfire for about two miles on foot."[43])

When they finally arrived at the Hyatt, the lobby was nearly deserted. They began looking through the register for a name they recognized. The only familiar one was the lawyer, John Howell, but when they reached his room, no one answered. It was three hours before Barbara Schell, from the embassy's economic section, finally saw the two Americans dressed in prison uniforms and took them to Simons's room.[44]

Simons and his team took Chiapparone and Gaylord to a safe house on the edge of Tehran. Two days later, with Rashid as the driver and interpreter, the group left in two Range Rovers bound for the Turkish border. To safeguard their cover story that they were merely businessmen quietly driving home, they carried no weapons, but did carry over $250,000, hidden, in gold, Iranian rials, British pounds, and Deutschmarks, in case they needed to bribe anyone on the way out of the country.*

Perot wanted to ensure that the team had no problems leaving Iran. He flew to Washington, where his friend Governor Bill Clements, the former undersecretary of defense, put him in touch with a military command post that provided maps and satellite photos of the border crossing. Within two days, he was headed for Istanbul, in a chartered 707, to better oversee the operation's final phase.

"We made strenuous efforts to make sure they were received at the Turkish border," recalls former undersecretary of state David Newsom. "A rather frantic effort was mounted by the U.S. government to locate the people and find out what route they were leaving by. We intervened with the Turkish authorities as well."[45] Although Colonel Simons later called the trip to the border a "spring outing," it was a tough three days, with the team often stopped by local revolutionary cells and tribal leaders. Each proved harmless. At nearly midnight on Thursday, February 15, the team finally crossed the border into Turkey. That same day, the *Dallas Times Herald* ran a banner headline, PEROT MEN REPORTEDLY ON WAY OUT. OVERLAND EXIT ROUTE FROM IRAN INDICATED. Tom Luce, Merv Stauffer, and Tom Marquez in Dallas had tried to persuade the *Times Herald* to withhold publication until Chiapparone and Gaylord were safely in the U.S. The paper, which had known about the story while the men were still making their escape in Iran, decided to hold it only until the two were safely in Turkey. Perot was furious when he heard the news. "The Perot people had been telling us that we shouldn't release the story since it could put the

---

* The remaining EDS employees in Iran moved into the house of Lou Goelz, the embassy's consul general. They were flown out within a week on military transport. "They [EDS] did not bring the two men who were in prison to us for an exit," says the State Department's Henry Precht. "We got CIA agents out in a very sensitive operation. We could have easily gotten them out."

men in danger," recalls Ken Johnson, the former editor of the *Times Herald.* "We thought that was a crock. The real reason Perot was so pissed off was that a regional newspaper had foiled his plans for a big international press conference."[46]

Once everyone was back safely in the States, Perot and his rescue team were national heroes. Perot got the myth-building off to a strong start in his first Dallas press conference. "Our strategy became obvious—arrange for an Iranian to storm the prison," he told a room crammed with reporters. "We arranged it, yes . . . I'm not going to get into details."[47] In a subsequent speech, Perot elaborated a little more: "How did [Simons] know it would work? He was inside the mobs on the ground. He had the skin feel of being there."[48] Eventually, the story grew. "Simons and an Iranian employee of ours named Rashid spent time with the mobs outside the jail," Perot told a reporter. "Rashid formed a mob of his own and became a leader. When the right moment came, he paid off the local police to open up the [gun] magazine. Rashid threw weapons to everyone and yelled, 'It's up to us revolutionaries to free the political prisoners.' Rashid got the key and everyone started streaming out. The guards refused to shoot their own people."[49] (Rashid returned with Simons's team to Dallas, went to work for EDS, and in 1992 Perot took time out from his presidential campaign to attend Rashid's naturalization ceremony.)

"I heard one of the statements he made after he returned, a very dramatic one about the release," says David Newsom. "So I telephoned Perot and told him what he said was not exactly what we understood the facts to be. 'Well, the press never gets it right, you know,' he said, indicating to me that he knew there was some hyperbole in his story."[50]

Perot decided that the way to tell the Iran rescue story correctly was through a book. He formed a special EDS team to develop a list of possible writers.* "There were three criteria," says one of the executives who was involved in the search for a writer. "First,

---

* Whoever wrote the book would have to do so without the recollections of Bull Simons. He died on May 21, 1979, less than four months after returning from Iran. In April, Perot's mother had died after her long battle with cancer. Perot called two female EDS employees at almost midnight the night before his

the person had to put it into conversational English. Ross wanted to ensure the book could reach a lot of people. Second, the author had to be well known, but as Ross told me, 'not a drunk or druggie, like most of them are after they are successful.' " The book team developed a list of nearly seventy names, then started reading the books by those authors and gave Perot weekly updates. Follett had not made it on the list because his success was in fiction, and they initially did not think of him. The writer who was first chosen was Robin Moore, the author of *The Green Berets* (John Wayne starred in the movie version). Perot liked Moore, and gave him a contract. "He started really poking around and asked too many pointed questions," recalls one EDS official. "The next thing you knew, Ross voided the contract with him." A few other writers were contacted but declined. The staff working on the project began dreading the weekly meetings with Perot. At one meeting, Perot threw a book, *Eye of the Needle,* across the desk. "Margot is reading this," he said. "She said that's the guy we should have." There was a photo of Follett on the back cover. "He looks like a faggot to me," Perot said. "Forget it. Don't do anything about it." "We all knew what that meant," says one EDS executive. "When Ross says, 'Oh, don't do it,' he is really telling you to do it. We called Follett's agent in New York, who said that there was no way Follett would write such a book. But we really persisted because we were out of names."

Follett, after studying packets of information prepared by EDS about Perot and the Iran caper, decided it was worth a meeting. "The impression I had of Perot beforehand was this very superficial one that you get if you read his cuttings," says Follett, "that he was this gung-ho Texan businessman, with a rather militaristic approach, and so on. And I was, initially, very wary of him because he was, and is, in many ways the exact opposite of me—he's a conservative, I'm a socialist; he's a Texan, I'm Welsh; there's a differ-

---

mother's funeral. He ordered them to go to the funeral home and "pull out all the dead flowers from the bouquets sent by the EDS men. I don't want any dead flowers at Mother's funeral." At the office, Perot was strong and composed after his mother's death. However, after Simons died (he had been living in a guest cottage on Perot's property), several workers saw him cry at the office, the only time they ever saw him so emotional.

ence in age; I was brought up in the sixties, you know, free love and all of that, and Ross lives a quiet life, doesn't get drunk, doesn't do drugs, doesn't fool around with loose women*—so, I mean, there was a big distance between us, and I was very, very wary of him. And it was a real surprise to me that the two of us got along so well. We actually got along famously even from the start."[51]

When they first met, Follett recalls, "I did not want Perot to have an easy power of censorship, and he didn't want to tell me everything and have me go off and write a book that was either inaccurate or portrayed him as some sort of nutcase, or both. So we had this very delicate negotiation to do. And he wouldn't talk about that for one moment. He would not discuss it. All he would tell me was amusing anecdotes about what happened on this adventure. And I would occasionally say, 'That's terrific, but what are we going to do if . . .' and he would just tell me another funny story. So it was one of those cross-purposes things, and one of the things I discovered then is that if Ross doesn't want to discuss something, he will just tell you funny stories until you go away. And that's what he did at our first meeting. But actually, my agent worked it out, and we did it very simply. I made a deal with my publisher where they would give me a million-dollar advance on this book, and we just agreed that he could cancel the project at any time, but he would have to pay that million-dollar advance. He had a veto, but at least it would cost him. He didn't sign that deal until he was pretty sure it wasn't going to happen. I had no interest in doing any type of investigation over the book, which made Ross relax."[52]

After signing the contract, Follett moved to Dallas for six weeks, and his first working meeting with Perot made him wonder whether he had made a mistake. Perot met him in the private gym in his house and watched a televised Dallas Cowboys football game while paying only partial attention to Follett's questions. "He seemed bored," remembers Follett. But eventually, Perot liked Follett's work habits (he arrived at the office by 8:00 A.M. daily), and also that he was not too intrusive with his questions.

---

* Follett says, "The reason he doesn't drink, I am convinced, is that he wouldn't enjoy that slight feeling of loss of control that you get after a couple of belts."

Follett soon learned that Perot was sensitive about some matters. Once, with Perot in the room, Follett had a telephone conversation with an army colonel, getting some background for the book. "I made an error in judgment in assuming that this colonel was an old buddy of Ross's," recalls Follett, "when in fact he was just an acquaintance, but not a buddy. So I made this humorous remark about how I needed to check things out with him because Ross was always telling tall stories. Perot looked at me extremely coldly and, after I had hung up, told me he did not want me going around the country giving people the impression he said things that weren't true, because he had a reputation as an honest businessman, which he valued very highly. And I considered myself very firmly told off.

"We often disagreed in the following way. He would tell me a story about the adventure, and I would say, 'It is a great story, Ross, but it doesn't have any place in the book.' And the reason that happened so often is that this is a story with a cast, and because it is a true story, it rambles all over the place. And it wasn't long before I realized that my task was going to be to find some focus to drive the thing along in a straight line. So I was constantly eliminating stuff that he wanted to contribute. But he likes amusing anecdotes, so he would tell me the anecdote, and I would tell him it has no place in the book, and he would say, 'Come on, how can you turn down a great anecdote like that?' And I would say, 'Ross, I'm the writer. I know what has to go in and what doesn't. You don't.' "[53]

There were four drafts. The first one was only about 30,000 words long ("without dialogue," says Follett), more of an extended outline rather than a full manuscript. The rescue team reviewed drafts one and three. Perot reviewed every one and dictated his comments to his secretary, who then gave a copy to Follett. "I would incorporate what he had said into the book," says Follett, "or sometimes it turned out to be wrong, he may have remembered something a certain way . . . I would leave it out, or alter it some way. Obviously, he took a very close interest in it, and he read every word of every draft. He was probably the only person at EDS to have read every draft."[54] "I had an office near Ross's at the time they were working on the book," recalls EDS executive Ron

Sperberg. "There were people always going over those manuscripts, really managing it, making sure it was just right."[55]

Follett also showed the manuscript to embassy officials who had dealt with Perot over the rescue mission. "If it hadn't been for us," says John Stempel, "Perot would have been rotting in an Iranian prison. Instead, the book was written as though we were all cowering in the embassy and nothing would have happened if he hadn't come to Iran. That was just wrong."[56]

One of the most sensitive areas for Follett and Perot arose over how Chiapparone and Gaylord got out of jail. Follett, who admits that "there were times Perot might put in more drama than was absolutely necessary," says the issue of the jailbreak "would get up his nose. And I will tell you why. Because in that episode, he did show terrific courage, and he took risks. He handled it in a way in which no other American businessman would have handled it. And I think when you've stuck your neck out for something and somebody turns around and says, 'You were just lucky,' you are bound to be annoyed. So I understand his being upset at that. It is clear to me, and to anyone who reads my book carefully, that he didn't engineer the escape. It was a revolution, and the character, the Iranian boy Rashid, the account, the blow-by-blow account of how that jail was broken open, comes principally from Rashid. Nobody else knows the details of what went on. And although Rashid was there when all this was happening, and was egging people on, saying, 'Come on, let's do this, let's do that,' I hope I didn't give the impression that none of it would have happened if he hadn't been there. The jail would have been broken open anyway. It's like the storming of the Bastille. You always do that in a revolution—you let people out of jail. So that would have happened anyway."[57]

The published version of *On Wings of Eagles* (the original working title was *The Bull and the Peacock*) had a few detractors, primarily those familiar with the episode. "After reading the book, I lost all respect for Follett," says former embassy official William Lehfeldt. "It was just too self-serving for Perot," concurs State Department official Henry Precht.[58] "I told Follett that they were going to put his book on the fiction shelf if he wasn't careful," says John Stempel.[59] However, most commentators who were not familiar with the events in Iran were captivated by Follett's strong storytelling abilities (the book was a solid best-seller, selling over 300,000 hardcover copies). Seldom has a corporate tycoon ever had such a remarkable image-shaper. It was as though, overnight, Perot's recent stumbles with EDS and his failure on Wall Street became distant memories. The new image emblazoned into the public consciousness by saturation media coverage was that of the can-do Texas millionaire, someone who was willing to take great risks, and had the capability to pull it off.*

In the wake of the success of *On Wings of Eagles,* Perot filed suit in federal court in the northern district of Texas for the monies that Iran still owed EDS for the social security contract. The defense claimed that EDS had performed poorly on the contract (delays in paying medical bills increased under EDS from forty-seven days to sixty-one days, and there were specific charges of incompetence) and that bribery had played a key role in the contract's procurement.[60] The case went to trial in January 1980, during the height of the tensions over the fifty-two American hostages being held at the U.S. embassy in Tehran. "The bribery charges were hard to prove after the revolution," says Professor Bahman Fozouni, who worked in the health ministry and later taught political science at the University of California, "because suddenly all the deposed ministers and those close to the shah's court had the same goal as Perot and the EDS people, and that was to say there was no corruption—it was all done legitimately. Those who were still in Iran would be jailed for admitting to corruption under the shah's regime, and those who had made it out did not want to tarnish their new lives by talking about it. So that helped EDS."[61] Judge Robert Porter concluded that he had not seen any evidence of bribery, fraud, or public corruption "in the procurement of the contract" and granted EDS a judgment against the Iranian government, for over $19 million for money due under

---

* Perot bristled at criticism of his rescue mission. When the *National Review* was set to print a pointed article about the episode, Perot, who had learned in advance about it, called editor and publisher William Buckley and asked that it be dropped. Buckley told him the issue had already gone to press, but Perot, not dissuaded, told Buckley to kill the entire issue and send him the bill. Buckley declined.

the contract, interest, and legal fees. "It was a slam dunk, 100 percent win," boasted a jubilant Perot. "The courts found that our relationships with Mahvi were proper and legal and required by Iranian law—you just go step by step by step. Read the court case."[62] When President Carter eventually struck a deal with Iran in 1980 for the release of the American embassy hostages, he freed the country from all United States claims. However, since EDS's judicial judgment was exempt from Carter's compromise, Perot could still collect the money and was able to seize $16 million from an Iranian bank account in New York.

The capstone to Perot's final triumph in the Iranian affair was an NBC television miniseries made from Follett's book. Perot demanded, and got, script and casting approval (Richard Crenna played Perot). Edgar Sherick, the show's producer, said Perot was "never far away from the production" and that he had never had a project where "a living, vital person was so closely involved in the story we were going to tell."[63] In the miniseries, watched by an estimated 25 million Americans, Simons and his EDS team smashed into Gasr prison with their guns blazing, shooting Iranian soldiers posted in the guard towers. The Iranian prosecutor, Dadgar, was portrayed pursuing Simons's team, barely failing to capture them when Simons blew up an ammunition dump and crossed the Turkish border. Standing helplessly on Iranian territory, Dadgar shook his fist at Perot, who was jubilantly greeting his squad on the Turkish side (neither Dadgar or Perot was within hundreds of miles of the border).

Perot easily deflected any new criticism over the embellishments. "Now, in creating a miniseries, there is always a little dramatization," he said, "little things that are not exactly the way they happened. The biggest changes were: We didn't kill anybody—the guys were a little sensitive about seeing that . . . [but] not one has seen the ending without having tears come to their eyes, and these are not sissy guys."

Perot had several employees assemble a special commemorative book for each member of Simons's squad. (Perot went "crazy," according to one, over a photographer's airbrushing of a blood blister on Simons's face, and initially refused to pay for the photos.) Part of the commemorative book included some of the thousands of letters that had poured into EDS congratulating Perot and the team. Dozens of the letters were from people urging him to run for president. While looking through some of them, he turned to an employee.

"Do you think I should run for president?"

"President? No. King, yes."

The Perot myth had been cast.

NINE

Waging a Holy War

When Perot was in Iran in early January 1979, the governor-elect of Texas, his old friend from the Defense Department Bill Clements, appointed Perot chairman of the seventeen-member Texans' War on Drugs Committee. A successful war on drugs seemed straightforward to Perot. "We ought to quit putting teenagers in jail for stealing hubcaps if we can't put the big guys in jail for drug trafficking," he said.[1] An EDS employee he drafted onto his team says, "Dealing with drugs for Ross means tougher and longer sentences and more aggressive law enforcement, it's that simple."

As Perot began to turn his attention to the war on drugs, the daily operations of EDS were left to Mort Meyerson. In June, he was appointed president. The following month, Meyerson received his first profit-and-loss statement and was surprised that it was 75 percent below projections.[2] It prompted him to reorganize the company. As part of the retrenchment, several offices were closed and some employees let go. While Meyerson worked to revitalize EDS, Perot tackled the war-on-drugs campaign.

"Mort made that company work; he was the right person for the job at that time," says former senior executive Ken Riedlinger. "Ross was the leader, the motivator, but he didn't know that much about data processing. He never wrote a computer program. In 1979, when I had taken over commercial systems and I had to go in with him each month to go over the profit-and-loss statement, it was surprising because he was really fairly ignorant of basic management processes."[3]

"We read more about Ross in the newspapers during the next year than we saw him around the office," recalls one executive. "While he gave 110 percent to the drug effort, we actually flourished during that time. Ross had fathered the company, but once we were past the incubation point, he was not the best leader. He never built lasting relationships with customers, whereas Meyerson had vision and insight."

Perot spent more than $2 million of his own money to organize community action groups to spread antidrug messages among the state's youth, and brought nationally known substance abuse experts from around the country to symposiums and lectures in Texas.[4] "He basically spent the next year absolutely buried in drug issues—why we had a drug problem, the pharmacology of drugs . . . who was in jail," said Rick Salwen, then the third in-house lawyer hired by Perot.[5] Salwen, a bright young attorney from the Federal Aviation Administration, was chosen to be the chief researcher and legal adviser on the antidrug project. Perot turned his appointment into a personal crusade, talking to experts and visiting prisons, hospitals, police departments, and even addicts. Perot's committee promoted ways for parents to discover whether their children used drugs and then how to deal with it aggressively. He also encouraged corporate programs for selective drug testing of employees (it was not until 1984 that EDS instituted a urinalysis program for all recruits, security personnel, and senior managers and executives).

Although some civil libertarians criticized Perot for focusing almost exclusively on an antidrug message combined with stronger jail penalties, the commission's work received widespread public and legislative support. Opinion polls showed that most Texans thought the drug problem had worsened because penalties were too light, and Perot's suggestions of broader wiretap bills and central computer systems to organize information about suspected dealers complemented the militant attitude festering in the electorate.

At times, Perot's enthusiasm for his new role got him into trouble. In the fall of 1979, two undercover detectives in Tyler, Texas (not far from Texarkana), were attacked in their trailer by a man with a shotgun.* It looked like a professional hit, since the two detectives had spent the summer testifying against a hundred local drug dealers. Perot rushed to their aid, providing a safe house on one of his properties and private security guards who followed them everywhere, even into the judge's chambers for courtroom conferences. "They badly needed protection, and I gave it to them," boasted Perot.[6] However, it was later revealed the detectives were themselves addicts and had been dealing drugs and altering evidence in dozens of cases. All of the prosecutions based on their testimony crumbled. Perot was embarrassed for having jumped to an early conclusion before checking the facts.

Yet several months later he was at it again. "Go out to a rural airport, park your car, and watch what goes on in the middle of the night," he said. "[But] we've got judges in Texas who find no probable cause for a search when a plane flies in with no lights on, landing on a dirt strip."[7] Perot decided to develop a sting around an airstrip, luring traffickers with planes into his snare. He offered to buy a Caribbean island for U.S. Customs, build an airplane refueling station, and then recruit a team of commandos who would photograph the planes and plant tracking devices on the aircraft. In exchange, Perot wanted the government to grant him exclusive rights to supply necessary services, such as fuel. "If I'm going to buy a damn island down there," he told a Customs official, "I want my money back."[8] Perot hired a retired army lieutenant colonel, Richard Meadows, and sent him to the Caribbean to scout for an island. Meadows recruited six former U.S. military counterterrorist commandos, and one suggested to the Customs agent in charge of the Houston office, Frank Chadwick, that the team could also blow up freighters carrying drugs.[9] Customs rejected all of Perot's ideas as too risky.† According to a senior

---

* The detectives, Craig Matthews and Kim Ramsey, later married. Under the name Kim Wozencraft, she eventually wrote a best-selling novel, *Rush*, based on her experience.

† When the island proposal became public during the 1992 presidential campaign, Perot's press spokesman, James Squires, claimed that Perot had "no personal recollection" of such a plan. Perot went even further: "That's just another fictional story. There's no basis at all." Actually, the offer was detailed in a

EDS executive, when the Reagan White House later made overtures to Perot about possibly serving as the federal "drug czar," Perot said he would consider it only if "we can force every unidentified plane that crosses our border to land, and if they won't, then we will shoot them down." He did not get the offer.

Meanwhile, as chairman of the war-on-drugs committee, Perot directed attorney Rick Salwen to draft several bills, a sweeping package, to present to the Texas legislature. It included mandatory sentences, and tougher penalties for drugs sold near schools; made the sale of drug paraphernalia a crime; and required that pharmacists fill out forms in triplicate before they could dispense from a list of controlled drugs. A broad statute also allowed the seizure of drug dealers' assets. Perot sent several of EDS's female employees to help with the lobbying. ("Ross always thought women were great at public relations and lobbying," recalls one executive. "What old ornery Texas legislator could say no to a charming young woman pleading with him to make the state a safer place to raise families?") Perot was also helped by Rusty Kelley, then a staffer for the speaker of the legislature (Kelley went on to become a prominent Austin lobbyist and has since done work for Perot and his companies). "Ross likes to portray himself as the little businessman who just wins on issues because he is on the right side, but that's not the way things work in Texas," says one businessman who has competed against Perot on different projects. "He knows how to play the right cards in Austin all the time, with his army of lobbyists, and having a sixth sense for where the soft points are in the legislature or state agency. I have watched him do it time and time again. We could all take some pointers from Ross at knowing how to use power to get your way in the state capital."

As Perot's team arranged to present five draft bills to the Texas legislature, they increased the pressure on the politicians by bringing in Junior League members and PTA groups as well as busloads of concerned mothers and teachers from around the state, all to the capitol's doorstep in Austin. "It gave people all over the state

---

March 11, 1981, U.S. Customs Service memo, and both Customs agent Chadwick and an executive close to Perot confirm the offer.

confidence that they could pass laws to counter a bad situation in which their kids would grow up," says Salwen.[10] Perot appointed former POW and Vietnam war hero Robinson Risner as the point man on the parent and education issues (Perot and Risner later visited Nancy Reagan, and have been credited with giving her the idea for her "Just Say No" campaign). Two condominiums were rented in Austin, and an EDS team moved in. "We went to Cutter Bill's, a giant country-and-western store, and bought gear like cowboy hats and chaps and boots," recalls one of the EDS women. "That was because Tuesday night was 'speakers' night' at the Broken Spoke. It was a real popular bar, and on that night all the politicians were there, and we used to dance with them and talk about the bills and that they should vote yes when they came before them. Ross had really thought of everything." Perot accompanied Salwen to meet the most important politicians to ensure that the bills were on track.

In 1981, the legislature passed Perot's package. Governor Clements, in conjunction with Perot, sponsored a statute allowing easier wiretapping and surveillance ("We have to have a wiretap bill if we're going to get the people at the top," urged Perot).[11] Perot was satisfied with the result of his drug work. "Texas is the worst state to get caught in," he boasted after pushing passage of the legislation.[12]

Even as Perot was having success in leading the effort for tougher drug laws, EDS lost its most prestigious health care contract, the one with Texas Medicaid. The Texas Department of Human Resources had voted to give a $5 billion contract to a rival company from New York, Bradford National Corporation. The contract provided 14 percent of EDS's annual profits and, because of the way it was structured, allowed the winning company to earn interest on $100 million, held by the company on behalf of the state, for an "unpaid claims reserve." Moreover, Texas was the only state that paid on an insured basis, which meant that it paid each premium to the data processor, who then paid the claims. That meant EDS also earned interest, the "float," on several hundred million dollars a year. "There was no more lucrative state contract in the country," says a former auditor for Bradford. EDS had competed with Bradford in other states, earlier losing a New York City contract to them, and had even bought 5 percent of Bradford's stock at one time, considering a possible merger or buyout.

As disastrous as the loss was financially, it was also a personally intolerable blow to Perot. "It was happening in his own back-yard," recalls Ken Riedlinger, "and received massive publicity in Dallas."[13] Perot heard the news in London, and took the next flight back to Texas. Almost immediately after his arrival, he set about to figure out how to win back the contract. He was con-vinced that the only way EDS could lose was if Bradford had done something underhanded. According to one of the EDS executives who attended a hastily convened meeting, Perot stood up and shouted, "They are crooks! They bribed someone and we will find out who." Mort Meyerson stayed calm and replied, "I know one of their executive vice-presidents, and it's on the up and up." "That's the kind of soft-headed thinking that makes EDS lose business," Perot snapped. Meyerson fell quiet. When Perot later heard that Meyerson called Bradford vice-president Sol Seltzer, after hearing about the award, to offer his congratulations, Perot refused to believe it. "Mort's not a kamikaze," he said.[14] "It's one of the things that used to drive Ross crazy about Mort," says an executive who worked closely with both. "Mort made friends with EDS competitors. Ross thought it was heresy to ever talk nice to anybody who tried to take away business." The Bradford issue was simple to Perot: Convinced the rival company had done some-thing improper, he intended to expose it. "If he thinks he is right, that is all that matters," said his son, Ross Jr.[15]

"There's a [set] procedure you use when you think you have been wronged in a contract," recalled Les Alberthal, now the chairman of EDS. "That wasn't the means Perot used. He got into a holy war with Bradford, and basically out-muscled them."[16] "It was time for Ross's scorched-earth policy," says another executive who worked on beating back the Bradford challenge. "He was completely focused, and when he is like that, the rules just don't apply to him."

Perot brought in a different team to reverse the award of the contract to Bradford, by whatever means available. "What about

Mort?" one employee asked Perot. "Leave Mort out of this," he replied. "He doesn't have the stomach for this battle." Instead, Ross picked Riedlinger, the aggressive manager who had recently been appointed by Meyerson to oversee all the company's non-health-care projects. "Ken, you and Ron Sperberg are to find out whatever these guys have done wrong and get the smoking gun, do you understand? This is a gut issue and a gut contract. We are not going to lose this one, understood?"[17] "We formed a team for dirty work, which I ran," recalls Riedlinger, "another for clean work, to which I assigned someone and then watched over their work, and the third was the Texas political maneuvering, which was done by Ross personally."[18] EDS hired its first public relations firms, one in Dallas and the other in Austin, to control press coverage.

Perot complained to his friend Governor Clements, as well as to the state attorney general, Mark White. Perot flew around Texas to lobby state Human Resources Department board members: an attorney, Terry Bray; rancher Hilmar Moore; and businessman Raul Jiminez. At the same time, he filed a lawsuit seeking to void the board's award of the contract to Bradford. The board members quickly agreed to reconsider.

Perot argued that Bradford's victory was the result of either a flawed or a corrupt state bidding procedure. The process for the 1980 bid had actually started in December 1978, when Jerome Chapman, the commissioner for the state Department of Human Resources (DHR), directed the Health Services Division to start studying the best way to award the next state contract. During the following year, the Department of Human Resources settled on an exhaustive procurement program developed by its deputy commissioner, Wesley Hjornevik—the same one he had used when he ran procurement for NASA on the Apollo space program (Hjornevik had been the senior nontechnical employee at NASA).[19] It also happened to be the same procurement system under which EDS had won the 1976 Texas Medicaid contract.

The Department of Human Resources put out requests for five-year proposals, the longest term it had ever offered.[20] On August 1, 1979, more than a thousand letters were sent to potential bidders. Within a month, two dozen had expressed strong interest. One of those was Bradford, a rapidly expanding data processing services firm, with 3,500 employees and nearly twice the assets of EDS ($573 million). Bradford submitted its bid, although it was concerned that EDS and Perot might have an unassailable advantage. "I got a number of calls from national companies who didn't trust the honesty of our system, since EDS was not only the incumbent but also a Texas company," recalls Hjornevik. "Although I assured them it was an honest bid, some were doubtful. I would have liked more bidders."[21]

The final request for proposals was issued in February 1980. By that time, only six companies were still interested. Not only was Perot's entrenchment in Texas seen as a significant obstacle, but making a full proposal and presenting it to state authorities was expensive. The bid cost Bradford over a million dollars.

On April 1, 1980, the final bids were received. In the end, only Bradford challenged EDS. The two companies were required to submit references and a bid in two parts, one technical and the other pricing. The Bid Evaluation Committee consisted of twelve people, headed by Dr. Arnold Ashburn. "The leading lights on the evaluation committee were the same people who had monitored the performance of EDS on the existing contract," says Hjornevik.[22] The committee first studied the bid proposals and reviewed the references given by each. Then personnel from both companies were called to a series of meetings to clarify questions that arose from the initial review. Next, the evaluation committee conducted on-site inspections of each company. The committee spent three months reviewing the bids, and applied two hundred separate criteria to them. Eventually, eleven of the twelve committee members ranked Bradford first (the one who voted for EDS had it only one point ahead of Bradford). Out of a possible 1,000 points on the technical side of the equation, EDS received 567, while Bradford scored 680.1. As for pricing, EDS bid $390 million for the first year, versus Bradford's higher $457 million. However, since Bradford underbid EDS on the separate portion of administrative charges and won outright on the technical evaluation, Ashburn's committee considered its overall bid to be more attractive.

The evaluation committee presented its recommendation—that the contract be awarded to Bradford—to Hjornevik on June 10.

" 'Wow,' I thought. 'Man, this is Texas, and Perot is the biggest Medicaid contractor in the country,' " recalls Hjornevik, " 'and he is going to lose his home state contract.' I just knew the shit was going to hit the fan. So I decided to go and review every word and every number in the work done by the evaluation committee, because if we were going to go with this recommendation, we had to make sure we knew it inside out, and knew it was right."[23]

When Hjornevik told the evaluation committee he wanted to review their work, the committee was initially suspicious ("They thought I was going to make a fix for EDS," says Hjornevik). Hjornevik found the bids between the two companies were very close. In the meantime, both companies submitted revised bids. The new proposals raised EDS's technical score from 567 to 614, and also moved Bradford's from 680.1 to 687. Bradford also dropped its first-year bid to $417 million from its original $457 million. On July 14, 1980, EDS received notice that the Department of Human Resources had recommended that Bradford's overall bid was $20 to $50 million lower than the one from EDS and that the contract should be awarded to Bradford.

"I personally think that the major reason the contract went to Bradford," says Hjornevik, "is that since the evaluation committee was primarily composed of state employees who had been responsible for overseeing the existing EDS contract, there was a backlash against EDS. In the EDS environment, everybody dresses the same, they toe the mark, they know they are private industry, and there is a contempt for bureaucrats. EDS had never been monitored in any other state the way we watched them in Texas. And that caused a lot of friction with EDS people, the 'goddamn bureaucrats' type of attitude. So a lot of the people who were on the evaluation committee just felt they had not been treated right by EDS."[24] "There is no doubt about it, they didn't like us," agrees Ken Riedlinger. "One of the rules is that you never piss off your customer. We treated them like, 'If I want something out of you, I'll kick it out of you.' That was not an untypical style of Alberthal [EDS chief of health care] and his boys. That's how we treated them, and they did not want us to win."[25]

Riedlinger was also convinced, and remains so today, that members of the evaluation committee "had been paid off."[26] It was that belief, which Perot shared, that prompted EDS to wage one of its most aggressive battles, digging up anything that tarnished Bradford's reputation. Riedlinger and his team arranged a blitzkrieg of press stories questioning Bradford's financial stability, its competence on other state contracts, whether it had potential conflicts of interest with some financial analysts, and charges that an anti-Perot bias fueled its Texas supporters.[27] Ron Sperberg, Riedlinger's assistant, leased a jet and brought a New York state senator to Texas to complain to the press about what he deemed Bradford's horrendous performance on its New York Medicaid contract. Through Gary Fernandes's connections in Washington, EDS uncovered a two-year-old federal investigation into questions over Bradford's handling of a navy contract and then leaked it to Dan Dorfman, a nationally syndicated financial columnist. Riedlinger's most important discovery was Michael Diem, a New York health care bureaucrat who claimed a Bradford executive offered him a $185,000 bribe. That was also released to Dorfman, and put Bradford further on the defensive. Mike Snyder, then a reporter with the Dallas NBC affiliate, did an investigative television series that accused Bradford of industrial espionage and influence peddling. "I found Snyder, I tutored him, I lived with him," says Riedlinger. "I traveled with him and helped to set up the key interviews. I acted as their agent on that story; I ran them."[28]

Perot himself publicly attacked Bradford's competence. He termed their New York Medicaid work "primitive" and charged that "they're doing in New York what we were doing ten years ago" and that they were "totally unequipped to handle the job."[29] He did not even have anything good to say about Bradford's chairman, Peter Del Col—"I wouldn't hire that guy to clean out the chicken house."[30] EDS also started a whisper campaign around the state capital that bribery may have been involved in procuring the winning bid. Perot later publicly charged that Bradford vice-president Sol Seltzer was the "guy who does the payoffs."[31] When outside experts were brought in and verified that the conclusions of the Department of Human Resources in its bid evaluation were accurate, Perot implied that the experts were themselves tainted.

Perot's anger was fueled by twin conspiracy theories. In one, he suggested that the granting of the contract to Bradford was a conspiracy hatched by the state evaluation committee. His convoluted thesis was that the committee had selected Bradford knowing it was incapable of administering the contract, so that when Bradford failed, the state bureaucrats would once more have a reason to take over the Texas Medicaid data processing. The second theory was that the state workers on the evaluation committee conspired to pick Bradford since a new contractor would probably require a larger monitoring staff, thereby ensuring work for the state bureaucrats.[32] Perot further charged that Assistant Attorney General David Young, the legal adviser to the DHR staff, acted "in concert" with the staff to pressure the commissioners into supporting the Bradford bid. "Why is he [Perot] after me?" asked a bewildered Young. "I'm just a struggling state employee."[33]

While Perot's effort was public, Riedlinger and his team took their battle underground. He not only employed private investigators, but even used EDS workers to check the backgrounds of the DHR committee members who had recommended that Bradford be awarded the bid. Bradford executives were also investigated.[34]* "There were so many dirty people involved on Bradford's side," recalls Riedlinger, "that we started videotaping them—where they went after work, who they went to. They liked to drink Chivas and screw expensive women. We knew the prostitutes, we knew the names, we interviewed the prostitutes after they were done with them in a hotel. We had videotapes of them going and coming into motels. We had all kinds of stuff like that. At one point, we were set to trap a guy at a motel in Pennsylvania. We were going to have videotapes and holes in the walls. We had three rooms, and we were going to knock holes in the walls on the two outside rooms, and have cameras from

* During the 1992 campaign, Tom Luce, Perot's attorney and then campaign manager, told Larry King that in the Bradford matter, "I didn't hire any private investigators." That was true. But Luce was the wrong one to ask. The lawyers were not involved in the dirty work. "Luce was a goddamn Boy Scout," said one executive.

two sides film this guy accepting money. It was a sting operation."[35]* But when Claude Chappelear, EDS's general counsel,
heard of the plan he did some research and discovered that
recording conversations in Pennsylvania required the consent of
both parties. At his insistence, that operation was abandoned.
But others, less ambitious, continued. "I know we videotaped a
lot of people," recalls Riedlinger. "We interviewed a lot of people. We spent a lot of money." According to Riedlinger, some of
the Bradford executives realized they were under surveillance.
They "were scared to death," he says.[36]† "Do I know where the
smoking guns are?" Perot asked rhetorically when talking to a
reporter in the midst of the battle. "Yes."[37] "This was major
league hardball," recalled Austin attorney Frank Ikard, who represented Bradford.[38]

---

* When discussing the possible sting, Riedlinger's team tried to devise a way
to record the meeting. They discovered they were not the only ones at EDS using
surveillance equipment. In a meeting with Perot's assistant Merv Stauffer,
Riedlinger and EDS executive Ron Sperberg asked for assistance. "We went and
told Stauffer what we wanted," recalls Sperberg. "He was pretty noncommittal.
'We know this sounds like the movies,' we told him, 'but what do we do?
Somebody said we need a wire, what is a wire?' Stauffer said something to the
effect of, 'Yeah, I know what you are talking about.' 'Well, how do we get one?'
And I will never forget what Merv's answer was. He said, 'Oh, we have that technology.' And Ken [Riedlinger] said, 'Let's get it.' Merv said, 'Both of them are
being used.' " On another occasion, Stauffer had Riedlinger wear a wire in a
meeting with another competitor.

† According to Riedlinger, some of the surveillance taping was done by EDS
employees, but most was done by private investigators. As for an incident like
the one in Pennsylvania, where Riedlinger refused to do it because he believed it
to be illegal, he says, "It probably just passed by and wasn't done, but it also
could have been something that Merv Stauffer would have taken up." According
to Riedlinger, the Bradford situation was not unique, and similar clean and dirty
teams were used on other state bids. For instance, in 1982, when EDS lost a
Massachusetts contract to System Development Corp. (SDC), it again employed
a no-mercy approach that included intense lobbying, public relations control,
and litigation. Perot also hired a former FBI agent, now an Austin private investigator, Joe Wells. According to one person close to the investigation, SDC was a
"pet project" of Perot's, since its president had been one of his naval academy
classmates. Tailing and taping were again used, a mistress of one SDC executive
was interviewed, and at one settlement meeting an EDS lawyer warned his SDC
counterpart, "Wait until you see the videotape."

The Bradford people were not the only ones intimidated by EDS's tactics. The same happened to state employees on the evaluation committee. (For some, the fear of Perot and EDS has evidently lasted. When I tried to telephone former evaluation chairman Dr. Arnold Ashburn, he got very excited, said that he did not want any more problems, asked if I was taping him, and then refused to speak to me any further.) "We were tailed and knew it," recalls one of the state employees who had been on the evaluation committee. "Our phones were bugged, we were certain, because in the beginning we would say something over the phone, in confidence, and the next thing we knew, someone from EDS would be repeating that to one of the commissioners. There were lawsuits filed, and they had gotten several state agencies to investigate us. It was really terrible."

One EDS executive involved in the Bradford fight says that Perot told him to "nuke the three commissioners" by gathering personal information that could be used against them. "Perot thought that the DHR commissioner, Chapman, could have been touched by the Bradford people, and he also wanted me to go after him," he says. A great deal of information was also gathered on the chairman of the DHR board, Hilmar Moore. Moore denies that Perot ever pressured him, but does admit that "Perot assembled an amazing team that covered everything you could imagine on Bradford—things on the company, the individuals, their background—and when you checked it all out, they were right. They warned us about going with Bradford. It had looked like an even playing field, and then Perot showed us how it wasn't. He did some job. Better than the CIA, or any of those, could have—he showed us what was really going on behind the scenes. . . . I would never want to be on the wrong side of a battle with Perot."[39] After his meeting with Perot, Moore lost confidence in both DHR commissioner Jerome Chapman and his deputy Wesley Hjornevik. They both resigned.

At EDS there was little doubting the zeal Perot applied to the conflict. One evening, Perot walked into Ron Sperberg's office. Ken Riedlinger and Tom Luce were also there. Perot turned to Sperberg. "What are you going to do when this is all over?"

Sperberg initially thought it was a trick question. "I guess I will go wherever you guys want me to go. I will go back to what I was doing before."

"Do you know what I am going to do?" Perot asked.

"No, what's that?" asked Riedlinger.

"I am going to kill those guys [talking about Bradford], then I am going to bury them, and then I am going to dance on their graves until the stench gets so bad I can't stand it."[40]

Bradford tried, in vain, to slow the onslaught of EDS-generated bad news by placing full-page ads in a dozen Texas newspapers and *The Wall Street Journal* setting forth its position "to try to make the public aware of what is happening." By October 1980, Perot had obtained a temporary restraining order blocking the final signing of the Bradford contract. On October 24, at a televised DHR board meeting, Perot presented much of the damning evidence he had gathered about Bradford's problems. He also produced an EDS employee, Glen Self, who dazzled the board and the audience with his mathematics, purportedly showing that EDS's bid was actually lower than Bradford's. He furiously scribbled a series of formulas across a large board. "And when he finished," recalls Perot, "he stood there with a marker, because he was writing with a marker, not a piece of chalk, and he turned to the state, and said, 'Here, you take it. If I am wrong, explain to me how the formula works.' They didn't touch it. Then he turned to Bradford, and he said, 'You take it, and tell me,' and they didn't move. And then the state commissioners just went crazy, and said, 'Hey, wait a minute.' . . . To say that Bradford was incorrect on that one would be a real understatement."[41]

At the end of October, the DHR board hired the Touche Ross & Co. accounting firm to conduct a $100,000 ninety-day review to recommend "which is the lowest and best bidder." Touche Ross finished its work early but named no clear winner. It found no conspiracy among the DHR staff, but equivocated on several major issues, allowing both Bradford and EDS to claim that the report supported their contentions. A week later, on January 16, 1981, DHR board member Terry Bray read a prepared statement, which said in part that the board had made "an honest mistake" in awarding the contract to Bradford. He said that "the board has determined that it is not possible to determine the lowest and best bidder. Because of that, the board cannot legally contract with either bidder." Both bids were thrown out. The result was that EDS kept the contract for an interim eighteen months. Dr. Arnold Ashburn, the chairman of the evaluation committee, was moved to a nondescript job in a different department. Texas paid Bradford $3.1 million for the costs it had incurred in the losing battle. (Perot later demanded that EDS also be reimbursed for its expenses, since he had to fight to win back his contract. When Texas denied his request, he tried to submit them as administrative costs to the federal government, but they were also rejected there.)

The following year, *Texas Business* assigned respected journalist Hugh Aynesworth to do an extensive story about the EDS-Bradford fight. Perot got an advance copy. "We should never have let him see it," recalls Bill Smith, then the magazine's managing editor. "But we relented because he kept bothering us so."[42] After reading the draft, Perot called Brux Austin, the magazine's editor in chief. "He was charming and polite, but very upset with the story," recalls Austin. "He kept saying there were a lot of errors, but never pointed any out. 'It is the tone of the story,' he kept saying. He was upset about the wording in the sidebars about his background, very, very concerned about his image. I read it carefully and thought it was very positive, but he did not like anything remotely negative. One conversation lasted an hour, another half an hour. I had never encountered a CEO of his stature that sensitive about his image." Perot told Austin to have the story rewritten. When informed that the press run was finished, he offered to pay for a second run. His offer was declined.[43] A couple of days later, Tom Luce, accompanied by two EDS vice-presidents, arrived at the *Texas Business* offices. "They were no-nonsense type of guys," says Austin. "They gave us a loosely veiled threat of a lawsuit, that the article could be libelous. They were very unfriendly."[44]

When the new bidding for Texas's Medicaid contract was put out by the state in 1982, no other company challenged EDS.

"Every competitor was afraid of EDS after the way it crushed Bradford," says a state employee who served on the evaluation committee. "It would have been a waste of time," concluded the president of an EDS rival, Computer Science Corporation.[45]

"Good guys don't necessarily finish first," said Perot, "and the world is not a fair place."[46]

TEN

Memorial for the Dead

Since his 1969 trip to Vietnam and his work on behalf of POWs and MIAs, Perot had become a champion to many returning veterans. During the Ford and Carter administrations, Perot, who thought a tribute to the veterans was long overdue, tried to generate interest in a war memorial.[1] Texas congressman Ray Roberts, in charge of veteran affairs, was intrigued. However, the discussions did not go very far, since Carter was not enthusiastic. Perot let the idea rest.

In April 1979, the idea of a memorial resurfaced. Several thousand people attended Vietnam Veterans Week, an annual gathering in Washington, D.C. One of those present was Jan Scruggs, a working-class high school graduate who had joined the army in 1969 and was wounded during his first tour of duty in Vietnam. "I remember Scruggs standing up out of the blue at this meeting," recalls Bob Doubek, a veteran and lawyer. "It was completely out of context, but he proposed building a memorial for the veterans. Some people had no reaction. Some were negative, saying that a memorial was not what we were about, and that we should instead concentrate on getting more benefits. But for some reason, the idea hit home with me. I went up to meet him after the meeting and gave him my business card. He called me up, and I took him on as a client at half price."[2] Scruggs and Doubek established a not-for-profit corporation. The following month, Scruggs rented a room at the National Press Club and held a press conference announcing the formation of the Vietnam Veterans Memorial Fund (VVMF). By July 4, the fund had collected only $144.50. "In 1979, even my friends thought I was off the wall," recalled Scruggs.[3]

Nevertheless, Scruggs and Doubek, together with a third volunteer, Jack Wheeler, a Yale lawyer and veteran who had worked on the Southeast Asia memorial at West Point, met regularly and petitioned members of Congress to introduce legislation authorizing a site. "Wheeler worked out of the army and navy clubs, and he knew a lot of people," says Doubek.[4] "See, we had decided early on," says Scruggs, "that Perot had gone about it the wrong way. He thought all you had to do was to get the president behind you and everything else fell in place. Since we had no money or influence, we thought the way to do it was to get the U.S. Congress to give you a site, and then, with that, you could go and raise money."[5]

Unwittingly, the trio had picked a good moment to make their pitch. Because so much time had passed since the end of the Vietnam War, Congress was ready to consider a memorial as a symbol of closure of the divisions that had split Americans. In August 1979 Senator Charles Mathias, a Maryland Republican, agreed to introduce by year's end legislation providing land for a memorial. Two months later, in October, Senator John Warner, a Virginia Republican, agreed to help raise seed money. And when, on Veterans Day, Senator Mathias actually introduced the legislation to provide land in a prime location—two acres on the Mall, the long rectangular strip of greenery that stretches from the Capitol through the Smithsonian Museum to the Washington Monument—the press finally took notice. Doubek remembers that "individual contributions of ten to fifteen dollars started coming in."[6] A few days before Christmas, Senator Warner and his then wife, actress Elizabeth Taylor, hosted a fund-raising breakfast at their home. Warner invited defense contractors, and they listened intently as Scruggs talked incessantly about the memorial. At the end of 1979, eight months after incorporating, the fund had only $8,000, of which $2,500 had come from the Veterans of Foreign Wars and $1,000 from Senator Warner. Two weeks into January, Grumman Aerospace gave $10,000, enough to begin direct mail fund-raising.

"As part of the direct mail effort, we were advised to form a logo and make a national sponsoring committee with prominent names," recalls Doubek. "Perot's name came up, along with Roger Staubach, Willie Stargell, Bob Hope, Carol Burnett, et cetera." Letters were sent out in January 1980 to these celebrities, but the printing deadline was short, and hasty calls were made.

One night, Doubek called Perot and was put through to him. He explained what they were doing, and Perot asked, "Well, you aren't a bunch of kooky Vietnam veterans, are you?"

"No, we are lawyers, pretty sober guys."[7]

Perot then told Doubek about EDS's policy of hiring Vietnam veterans and about the memorial he had proposed under Carter, a large monument with fifty pillars for the fifty states. From his description, it sounded to Doubek like the Lincoln Memorial.

"Well, what is it going to look like?" Perot asked.

"I don't know," Doubek replied. "We are going to have a competition."

"Well, I don't want to support anything unless I know what it is going to look like."[8] Though Perot did not let his name be used for the sponsoring committee, he asked Doubek to call him once they had selected a design.

When Doubek told the fund's executive board about his talk with Perot, Scruggs asked for the telephone number. "I called him, and at first we talked about everything but the memorial," says Scruggs. "I was the only person that built a relationship with him over dozens of calls, talked about reminiscences during the Vietnam War, ideas he had for series of programs during the war, and other matters."[9] Based on Scruggs's request, Perot agreed to contribute $10,000, but asked that his name not be used and that he not get involved any deeper. Still, Scruggs occasionally called, keeping him abreast of the legislative progress.[10]

The legislation passed Congress in late June 1980, and the White House set the signing for July 1 in the Rose Garden. The night before, two EDS executives flew to Washington and met with Doubek, Scruggs, and the fund's public relations consultant, Ernie Wittenberg. They carried a last-minute request from Perot—he wanted his name mentioned in President Carter's remarks, and was willing to later field calls from the press about the memorial.

"We said it was impossible for us, the night before, to insert something into the president's speech," recalls Doubek, "especially something as far-out as this. The EDS people did not seem too pleased."[11]

The day after the Rose Garden event, Scruggs called Perot, who suddenly seemed no longer interested.* "He [Perot] stated that he really was too busy to get involved right now with the memorial," says Scruggs, "but that what I should do is call Robert McNamara and Melvin Laird, since they were the ones who sent us to Vietnam, and that they would be great candidates for raising the money needed to build the Vietnam memorial."[12] Despite Perot's dismissal, Scruggs stayed in touch with him.

The fund had decided to host a competition to select a design for the memorial. For a fee of $20, any citizen over the age of eighteen could enter. The submissions would be judged by a panel of eight internationally recognized experts in design. To ensure that they would have some empathy for what American servicemen experienced in Vietnam, the eight panelists were required to read a rather extensive list of books written by veterans.[13]

Scruggs called Perot and asked for his help in funding the competition, and after initially hesitating, Perot informally told Scruggs to "send the bills to him as they come in."[14] The registration closed at the end of 1980, and the final designs were submitted by March 31, 1981. The following month, after more urging from Scruggs, Perot agreed to donate $160,000; he warned, however, that he "did not want to see a 'flower power' memorial."[15]†

After the competition had closed, all 1,421 designs were displayed in a large hangar at Andrews Air Force Base (each was identified only by a number, to preserve the anonymity of its designer). The eight judges were brought to Washington on Sun-

---

* The Vietnam Veterans Memorial Fund had a form called a VVMF Call Report, which was a sheet of paper that was supposed to be filled in immediately after an important conversation. It listed the date of the call, the other person in the conversation, and the subject matter, and then had space for a summary of the talk. Many quotations or descriptions of conversations in this chapter are based upon those Call Reports, maintained at the Library of Congress.

† Perot's gift was the largest individual contribution, but it accounted for less than 4 percent of the almost $9 million eventually raised.

day, April 26, and by Friday they had agreed on a winner. The design was by a twenty-one-year-old Yale University architecture student, Maya Ying Lin. It was a radical departure from traditional memorials, with two long walls of polished black granite, meeting in a V, set low into the ground, and with the names of the dead chiseled into the walls, in the order they had died (some critics thought the V shape represented the peace sign flashed by antiwar protesters). There were no statues, flags, columns, or plaques. The public reaction was initially mixed. The architecture critics of *The Washington Post* and *The New York Times* wrote good reviews, yet the *Chicago Tribune* panned it. While two of the most prominent veterans' organizations, the Veterans for Foreign Wars and the American Legion, started raising funds for it, many rank-and-file Vietnam veterans hated it. And then there was Perot.

"The phone call I will never forget was on Friday, May 8," says Scruggs. "Perot called me and wanted to know more about it. I told him it was a wall of black granite, sunken into the ground, and you could walk down and see all the names. He got very quiet, then said, 'Jan, I've got to tell you, I think you made a serious mistake.' "[16] On May 13, Perot called Scruggs back. "Your design," he said, "is great for the 57,000 who died, but not for the 2 million who came home. I've enjoyed helping you, but I'm folding my tent now. I'm not coming to D.C. on Memorial Day to speak [he had previously agreed to be the keynote speaker for a May 25 celebration], because if somebody in the press asks me, I will tell them I don't like it. I never lie, but I'll never tell anyone that I don't like the design."[17]*

* Most of Perot's charitable gifts—nearly $120 million to a wide variety of causes—have been without incident. But his disagreement over the Vietnam memorial is not the only time his philanthropy has clashed over the aesthetics of a project. When the navy asked him to underwrite its war memorial in Washington, Perot was told it would feature an enlisted man. He liked that. But when given a preview, he disliked the sculpture. "This guy really had the most feminine face," recalls Perot. "And I said, 'I have met a lot of sailors in my life, and they are not going to like the face.' " Perot proposed that admiral Arleigh Burke, then chief of naval operations, have final approval. To get Perot's $1 million gift to underwrite the design, the navy agreed.

Separate from memorials, Perot has withdrawn pledges from other charitable organizations where he had a disagreement. Among others, he pledged $8 million to the Dallas Arboretum and Botanical Society and had given $2 million

Scruggs continued to write and call Perot, trying to persuade him to stay involved, unaware that Perot had decided to embark on "an eighteen-month crusade to try and satisfy the living veterans."[18] In May, Scruggs sent him a special award the Vietnam Veterans Memorial Fund had intended to present for his contribution—"I had hoped to give this to you on Memorial Day, but apparently that opportunity will not materialize so I am sending it to you through the mail."[19] Perot did not acknowledge the award. In June, Perot refused to sponsor a Dallas VVMF fund-raising luncheon to which he had previously committed. In July, Scruggs sent Perot refined drawings of the design, telling him, "Ross, this design really is magnificent. . . . I hope you can accept the memorial for what it is. When it is built you'll be proud of your role in this endeavor."[20] Perot was not convinced, however, and refused to call other business leaders to encourage them to help the memorial. He also further complained to Scruggs about the design. He didn't even like the advertisements run by the fund, finding them "depressing."[21]

In November, Perot again called to say that he had been inundated with letters from veterans, all of whom criticized the design. "Ross Perot dislikes the design more every day and is really teed off that he helped us out," Scruggs wrote in his notes.[22] Meanwhile, Scruggs kept sending Perot positive newspaper cuttings and reviews, trying to persuade him the design was a good one.[23]

Not only did the clippings not persuade Perot, but he suddenly became an active opponent of the design. By December 1981, Perot called Scruggs and told him to "stop plans for the memorial." Most veterans hated it, he said, and warned that "in 30 days we will have a big controversy on our hands."[24] Perot offered to change the design and fund a new competition, and claimed he

---

before he became disenchanted that the society had not planted thousands of trees around a lake or instituted his suggestions for elaborate security to prevent crime. He not only refused to give the additional $6 million, but also unsuccessfully demanded the return of his $2 million. In addition, the naval academy had difficulty over his pledge to an alumni hall when Perot was given a tour of the planned site and someone mentioned a basketball court, which he evidently thought did not make the center serious enough.

could quickly get the approval from the Fine Arts Commission.[25] Before Scruggs could do anything, he received a call from Mike Finesilver, an Associated Press reporter. Perot had told the reporter that the design was a "trench and hole in the ground" and that he intended to pay for a Gallup poll to publicize the reaction of veterans. Now the controversy was out in the open.

Perot was not the only one pressing to change the design. Others included Tom Carhart, a veteran who had unsuccessfully entered the design competition; James Webb, author of the bestselling *Fields of Fire*, about the war (and later a secretary of the navy); and Milton Copulos of the Heritage Foundation. Webb held a press conference, where he introduced the sketch of a competing design, all white, aboveground, and with a flagpole at the vortex.

Perot also initiated his own press campaign. He dubbed the design a "tombstone" and claimed he had talked to thousands of veterans, and that few liked it—"They think it is an apology, not a memorial," he scoffed.[26] And again, he threatened to sponsor an opinion poll. In December, he came to Washington with two Gallup representatives and met with Doubek, Scruggs, and other fund officers. The fund presented its own polling expert, who protested that it was not fair to conduct a poll about an architectural design based only on a photograph. But Perot was insistent. That meeting forced Doubek to seek a compromise. He appealed to Senator Warner, who proposed to host a mediation for the two warring sides.[27] Perot agreed to forgo any action until the Warner meeting.[28]*

It was scheduled for the last Wednesday in January, the twenty-seventh. Doubek and Scruggs expected it to be small, with only Warner and three representatives from each side of the issue.

* Beyond the fight over the design of the memorial, Doubek had also sought Warner's help to counter a string of damaging rumors about the design committee. One report charged that one judge, Garrett Eckbo, was a Communist. He had been mentioned in the McCarthy hearings, and Eckbo said the "accusations are, of course, a deliberate smear and a throwback to the bad old days." Another judge, Grady Clay, was chastised for not having any military service. In fact, he had served four years during World War II. Other innuendos, less specific, circulated throughout the capital corridors that several other judges were antiwar sympathizers.

Instead, ten days before the meeting, the fund began receiving calls from veterans' organizations from around the country. "It turns out that Perot was inviting people," says Doubek, "especially people not friendly to the design."[29]

On the day of the meeting, before it started, Perot demanded to see the architect's model of the memorial. Perot and some of the POWs went to Doubek's office to see it. "It was like Perot brought a bunch of people into your living room and he said about your couch, 'Hey, you ever seen anybody have a couch that ugly?' " recalls Doubek. Some of the POWs were also confrontational, questioning the fund members about their combat experience. "It was as if they were treating us like a bunch of Communists," says Doubek.[30] The gathering to see the model was a warning that the Warner meeting might also be confrontational.

Later that day, so many people showed up that Senator Warner had to move the meeting from his office to a Senate hearing room. "Perot walked in with about forty-five people," recalls Scruggs, "and roughed us up. It was very hostile."[31] "They all stood up with little three-by-five cards and gave prepared spiels about how bad they thought it was," says Doubek.[32] The arguments continued for nearly five hours. Then General Michael Davison (a former West Point commandant and commander of army forces in Europe) stood up.

"We have been fighting all day. We have an unconventional design, and some like it, some don't. What about a traditional heroic statue, stirring and patriotic, looking at the memorial?"

"I love it," said Perot. "We must find a statue the veterans love."[33]

Everyone shook hands and the controversy appeared over.

However, the truce was short-lived. "Some of the most radical people on Perot's side began lobbying that we should not commence construction until a statue had not only been designed but had received all the approvals," says Scruggs. "And they still wanted Perot's Gallup poll."

The groundbreaking was scheduled for March 1, 1982. But in January, Secretary of the Interior James Watt surprised the Vietnam Veterans Memorial Fund by threatening to postpone it unless a modified design, taking into account the critics' concerns, was resubmitted for his approval. Perot followed Watt's announcement by reiterating his willingness to finance a public-opinion poll.[34] A temporary compromise, including the flagpole and the building of a statue, was submitted to Watt, and he allowed the groundbreaking to proceed (the statue, inscription, and flag placement were all subject to the approval of a separate panel of four persons, split evenly between advocates and opponents of the Maya Lin design).

Before the groundbreaking, General Davison called Scruggs. "Jan, there is a little problem," said Davison. "Ross Perot has called me and asked for all the books and records of the Vietnam Veterans Memorial Fund. He believes that, as a contributor, you should give them to him and he has a right to audit and inspect every financial transaction that you made throughout the history of this project."[35]

Jim Webb and other opponents of the design had approached Perot and told him that the fund was "really grossly misusing money."[36] Perot had raised the audit issue with several people other than Davison, suggesting that the fund volunteers were, at the least, "inartful businessmen" and that Scruggs's brother-in-law had done the fund's last audit (that was wrong), and complaining at length that the Vietnam memorial was not the private domain of the fund but belonged to every American and that he, Perot, was "all-American."[37]

In notes of a conversation with General Davison, Scruggs wrote, "H. Ross seemed to be chomping at the bit. . . . We discussed [the] fact that Perot is raising the issue of an audit. He did so at the meeting and to [Ed] DeBolt. If he does so often enough, he will have people believe something is amiss. I told Gen D the facts (i.e. we have a big 8 firm do one annually)."[38]*

Perot indicated to General Davison that if he had an adequate say over the design of the new statue and its inscription, together with the placement of the flagpole, he would drop the issue.[39] But the fund would not agree to that, and Perot did not attend the

* The fund's attorneys, Williams & Connolly, researched whether Perot, as a substantial contributor, was entitled to review the books and records of the fund. They concluded he was not.

groundbreaking. (Perot later told Scruggs that he had not received an invitation in time, but only a photocopy of one.)

A month later, Perot spoke to Jack Wheeler and told him that the "VVMF is rude and arrogant," and again demanded an audit, for which he would pay. Wheeler's notes of the conversation indicate that Perot, who said he was "surrounded by counsel," was "angry personally, and will launch a frontal attack, and will not exclude the possibility of suing the VVMF."[40] Two days after that telephone conversation, Perot wrote to Wheeler, formally seeking a "detailed audit of receipts and disbursements by the Vietnam Veterans Memorial Fund. . . . I have routinely audited other organizations that I have given money to over the years."[41] The fund actually selected an independent committee of prominent businessmen to examine its books. The committee found no problems, but Perot was not assuaged.

At the same time, *60 Minutes* started researching a segment about the Vietnam memorial, which was scheduled to air about the time of the memorial's dedication. When correspondent Morley Safer interviewed Perot on May 3, Perot criticized the fund and told Safer that it only accepted the statue and flag compromise because it feared his Gallup poll. Yet the following day, when Perot called Scruggs and was friendly, Scruggs was wary. He had now been warned about Perot by Elliot Richardson, who had gotten to know Perot through the EDS Medicare contracts when he was the Nixon administration's secretary of health, education, and welfare. Richardson told Scruggs, "Perot is strictly a publicity seeker to whom money means nothing. Perot never feels that he gets enough public recognition for being a great guy."[42] Cyrus Vance, the secretary of state when Perot had his escapade in Iran, thought that the only way for the fund to deal with Perot was to ignore him.[43]

Yet in June, Scruggs tried to pacify Perot by writing about how well the design for the statue was proceeding ("The figures of the three American servicemen are a brilliant work that will make Vietnam veterans feel proud").[44] However, the statue, Perot's sole concern a few months earlier, had now taken a backseat to his demand for an audit.[45] That same month, Perot told General Davison that he was ready to sue to get the fund's records. Scruggs learned that Perot had approached officials from the Disabled American Veterans and asked if they would join in a lawsuit to gain access to the fund's financial records. They declined.[46] That prompted Scruggs to tell Elliot Richardson that the fund's "relationship with Mr. Ross Perot continues to be just as erratic as ever [and that] he stepped up his intimidation."[47] Richardson called Perot to see if there was any room for compromise, but reported back that he felt Perot wanted to go "fishing" through VVMF's records.[48]

During a June 1982 luncheon with General Davison and Scruggs, Perot alternated between tough talk of an audit and suggestions that he might sponsor part of the upcoming November National Salute to Vietnam Veterans. The fund thought that if Perot was wavering between being an enemy and a friend, they should encourage the truce. Both Scruggs and John Wheeler sent conciliatory letters. Wheeler, who had earlier been told by Perot, "If I don't get what I want, I can wipe you out," wrote, "For any share of [my role] in such anger, I apologize to you deeply."[49]* Scruggs said, "I feel that you have never been properly thanked for your support, but we are all very appreciative of your help."[50] In addition to the letters, the fund thought it might have pacified Perot by having its accountants, Peat Marwick and Mitchell, again review its books and records.

Perot ignored the peace feelers. He now said he knew of instances in which funds had been improperly disbursed and that he considered the Peat Marwick and Mitchell audit to be "very skeletal." He repeated his demand for an audit with an accounting firm of his choice, and further insisted that an EDS employee be sent promptly to get into the "nitty-gritty" with the Peat Marwick auditors.[51] Perot complained that the fund only looked out for itself, whereas he said he was "interested in helping the 2.7 million guys who served in Vietnam."

"I am through with your letters," Perot told the fund's Richard Radez. "Now you boys up there in VVMF get your act together and come back to me in a few days, telling me that I can talk to

---

* Perot has since denied threatening Wheeler by saying he could "wipe you out."

your auditors."[52] Radez suggested further discussions. Perot then angrily wrote to the fund's board of directors, warning, "It is not in VVMF's best interest to force this request into the legal system and make both the inspection and the results a matter of public record."[53]

The fund, trying to avert litigation, agreed to meet with Perot's representatives.[54] On September 17, 1982, several Vietnam Veterans Memorial Fund directors, including Scruggs, accountants from Peat Marwick and Mitchell, as well as lawyers from Williams & Connolly, met with EDS vice-president and general counsel Richard Shlakman and Michael Sanders, a tax attorney retained by Perot.[55] While saying that Perot had talked generally about "improper disbursements," the two EDS representatives claimed he had not told them any specifics, and they refused to put his charges into writing so that the Independent Audit Committee could investigate them. Shlakman advised the VVMF representatives that Perot routinely subjected the charities to which he contributed to thorough accounting checks.[56] As Scruggs recalled in a memo about the meeting, "Mssrs. Shlakman and Sanders could provide no evidence, but stated that Mr. Perot was 'single-minded' on this issue and always got what he wanted. . . . The meeting ended with Mr. Shlakman informing the VVMF that Mr. Perot was prepared to go to court if necessary."[57] That same day, Williams & Connolly wrote to Shlakman, reiterating its client's position that the "VVMF will not accede to it [the audit] simply because it comes from a substantial contributor. Neither will it succumb to the facile argument that unless the books and records of VVMF are opened there 'must be something to hide.' There is nothing to hide. . . . We have heard little or nothing from Mr. Perot except peremptory demands."[58] Four days later, Shlakman's response was to call the fund's lawyers to say that if Perot's demands were not satisfied, he had authorized a lawsuit that "would be highly publicized resulting in adverse publicity for the VVMF."[59]

The following month, the dispute became a national issue. The *60 Minutes* segment on the memorial ran on October 10, 1982. The Fine Arts Commission had approved the flag and the statue (done by Washington sculptor Frederick Hart, who had finished third in the design competition for the original memorial), but their exact placement were still in doubt. When Morley Safer raised the possibility of moving the statue and flag a hundred yards from the memorial, Perot said that if the flag was not literally drilled into the center of the memorial's walls, he would "jump in with both feet." He then drew the next battle line: "If anybody ever even raises that point and tried to change that, it is the worst kind of bad faith, it is the worst kind of double-dealing. And if that should even begin to occur, I will intend to spend whatever time, money, and energy is necessary to see that people keep their words, because we owe that to the Vietnam veterans. And I'm going to have a lot of powerful allies."[60] The next day, Perot released the results of a private poll he had conducted. Saying the design was a "slap in the face" to veterans, he told the press that 67 percent of those surveyed disliked the design. The sampling was not, however, a canvassing of the almost 3 million veterans. Instead, only POWs were questioned, and of the 587 contacted by the pollster, 265 responded.[61] The results nevertheless received extensive press coverage. Three days later, Perot and Scruggs appeared on *Nightline*.

"I guess one of the few truly courageous things I have ever done in my life," recalls Scruggs, "was when Jeff Greenfield from *Nightline* called. 'We would like you to go on and debate Webb or someone on the other side.' 'I will go on *Nightline* on one condition, that the other person be Ross Perot,' I told him. Since he had turned this into a vendetta, since he had accused me of being a crook and everything else, I wanted the world to know exactly what was going on, and that I was not afraid of him."[62]

On the show, Scruggs called Perot an "enemy" of the memorial and attacked Perot's survey, saying, "We have had his poll reviewed by polling specialists, and quite frankly it's not worth the paper it's printed on. He violated every scientific principle. It was not a random sample. He used a bad artist's conception. The questions were loaded. I sincerely doubt that anyone can do a Gallup poll on a memorial that they've never seen."[63] Perot, though clearly angry, kept saying that "my feelings don't matter," and that, instead, "the only thing that's important is how the fighting men feel about this memorial."[64]

The following month, Perot extended a peace feeler. He asked an acquaintance, businessman Joe Allbritton, a member of the fund's Independent Audit Committee, to satisfy himself that VVMF's books were properly maintained. Perot said that if Allbritton gave him assurances before Veterans Day (November 11), the matter would be closed.[65] Allbritton uncovered no problem in the fund's books. Yet Perot, apparently not mollified, did not attend November's National Salute to Vietnam Veterans, highlighted by the widely covered dedication of the Vietnam Veterans Memorial. (To exacerbate matters, the souvenir program listed $171,500 as coming from the Dallas Community Chest Trust Fund, an umbrella organization that included the Perot Foundation, but omitted Perot's name.)*

Although the site, with the granite wall, had been dedicated, the precise placement of the statue and flag remained unresolved. In December, Secretary of the Interior James Watt received a proposal from the fund for the placement of the statue and flag. Watt, however, wanted more alternatives, and the fund sent two more plans to him in January 1983. Watt did not immediately forward the proposals to the Fine Arts Commission. Scruggs felt the delay was because Perot was working behind the scenes to get the placement he wanted. Sensing that Perot was outmaneuvering them on this final issue, Scruggs appealed directly to President Reagan's chief of staff James Baker, Representative Morris Udall, and Vice-President George Bush to move Watt along. In early February, Watt finally submitted the three proposals to the Fine Arts Commission.†

To Scruggs, Doubek, and the rest of the fund leadership, it appeared they had successfully avoided a final confrontation with Perot. But that feeling of victory was short-lived. In February, when Watt sent the proposals to the Fine Arts Commission, Terry

---

* An IRS agent served the VVMF with a summons during the November celebrations, saying that serious allegations of financial impropriety had reached the IRS. Following an extensive audit, the IRS found no irregularities.

† Craig Fuller, Bush's chief of staff, was instrumental in encouraging Watt to submit the proposals. It was one of the first instances in which George Bush, unwittingly, crossed Perot, who had been hoping for Watt to delay until Perot could build enough political support for his favorite proposal.

O'Donnell, one of the fund's lawyers, received a telephone call from Roy Cohn, the New York lawyer who had started his career as counsel to Senator Joe McCarthy in the House Un-American Activities committees of the 1950s and had subsequently carved out a reputation as a well-connected, if somewhat notorious, litigator. In that initial conversation, Cohn said he represented some substantial contributors to the Vietnam memorial and that they wanted financial information "as to what funds were raised and in what manner and on whose authority they were expended."[66] "Cohn was the type of lawyer you used if you wanted to cause the other side grief," says an attorney who knew him well. "Roy enjoyed being nasty, and that's what his clients paid him for."

Although Cohn initially refused to identify his clients, the fund and its supporters immediately suspected that Perot had initiated the inquiry. Upon hearing of Cohn's involvement, Elliot Richardson warned Scruggs, "He [Perot] is a mean man, and he has hired a mean lawyer."[67] Chuck Bailey, a former political consultant to the fund, suggested it issue the following press statement: "Tens of thousands of Americans have contributed an average of $17 each to build the Vietnam Memorial. Mr. Perot has cost our organization hundreds of thousands of dollars in bad publicity and other costs. He is using Joe McCarthy tactics against us now. It is said that we have had to use other people's money to fight with an eccentric millionaire for the past year and a half. He is an angry man. His millions of dollars failed when he tried to build a Vietnam memorial in Washington years ago. Now he simply wants to harass the Vietnam veterans who succeeded where he failed."[68] The fund, after considerable debate, decided the press release was too inflammatory and did not release it. But they were under pressure, since news of Cohn's involvement was not a secret and rumors about possible misuse of funds were more prevalent during the spring of 1983.[69]

Cohn, for his part, soon denied that Perot was his client, saying it was instead a Houston veteran, John Baines. However, Cohn told former secretary of state Cyrus Vance that his impression was that Perot was paying the bill and that Perot was angry at VVMF more than he was concerned about obtaining an audit.[70] The fund later obtained a copy of a letter from Baines, sent to another person helping on the Cohn matter, John Stensland, a veteran associated with the San Antonio Vietnam Veterans Leadership Program. "I was assured I would be reimbursed if I carried the banner on the crusade," wrote Baines. "I will notify Roy Cohn that I was misled and ask for my money back if I am not reimbursed."[71] Perot has denied he was ever going to pay Cohn, and during the presidential campaign in 1992, Perot produced a letter in which Baines claimed that he (Baines) was Cohn's client. However, Richard Shlakman, EDS's general counsel at the time, has said that Perot hired Cohn.[72]

The fund, at a specially convened meeting, reiterated its refusal to allow any special audit. Cohn was quiet until late June, when he again demanded an audit, prompting another refusal.[73] (The new expenses incurred with Cohn meant that the fund's costs in defending itself against the continued requests for an audit now "far exceeded" Perot's contribution.[74])

Four months later, Carlton Sherwood, a reporter for a local Washington, D.C., television station (WDVM-TV), broadcast a blistering five-part series, raising questions about the fund's finances. Later, a ten-year acquaintance of Sherwood's, David Christian, said that Sherwood had been a longtime opponent of the memorial, calling it a "black gash" and a "liberal memorial," as well as referring to designer Maya Lin as a "fucking gook."[75]*

Was Perot behind the television special? Sherwood denied it. He admitted that while he had spoken to Perot, "nobody came to me and said, 'Do this story.' "[76] The Sherwood piece prompted congressional attention and a General Accounting Office (GAO) audit. The GAO conducted a widespread inquiry, not only reviewing the fund's books and records, but also interviewing its critics. After five months, on May 24, 1984, the GAO released its report, concluding that it "found that the Fund's financial operations had been conducted in a proper and legal manner. The Fund's receipts and disbursements have been properly accounted for and reported and prior audits have been conducted in accordance with profes-

---

* Sherwood left the television station shortly after the broadcast to work for the *Washington Times*. He was arrested on a complaint filed against him by the fund's Jack Wheeler for secretly trying to tape-record Wheeler in his home while researching the story. The charges were dismissed by the attorney general's office.

sional standards. The GAO also investigated a number of specific allegations regarding the Fund and found no evidence of any improper or illegal actions." The GAO report evidently thwarted Roy Cohn's clients. The fund did not hear from him again.

In November 1984, Ronald Reagan hosted a large ceremony at the Vietnam memorial for the dedication of the flag and the statue. Perot, although he had carried the argument on their placement and design, did not attend. The Vietnam Veterans Memorial Fund had earned his lasting enmity. A few months after the GAO report, he told an acquaintance at an air force gathering that it was a "whitewash." He suggested that the fund had abused its public trust and that it would misuse any remaining money left in its coffers.[77] When Scruggs wrote him in 1984 requesting an interview for a book he was preparing on the monument, Perot had his secretary send a letter claiming he could not help "due to commitments as Chairman of the Select Committee on Public Education in Texas."[78]

In 1992, the tenth anniversary of the dedication of the memorial, Scruggs invited Perot to the celebration. In a letter, Scruggs wrote, "the time has come to put aside the past differences that we have had over the memorial."[79] Perot refused to attend. "He looks upon this as a personal defeat," says Scruggs.

But Perot does not see it that way. "I never made any allegations," he said. "The Vietnam veterans made the allegations. I said, 'Let's get an audit and clean it up.' We eventually got an audit and cleaned it up."[80] When asked why so many veterans are enthusiastic about the memorial today, Perot does not hesitate to take the credit: "Because it has the flag and the three men on patrol. That made the difference. The men on patrol changed it. They [the veterans] are all happy."[81]

ELEVEN

The Detroit Invasion

In late 1983, Texas governor Mark White (who had been the state's attorney general during the EDS-Bradford battle), asked Perot to chair his Select Committee on Public Education (SCOPE), a panel to suggest reforms. The state was ranked forty-fourth out of fifty in educational achievement, and the high school dropout rate was one of the highest in the country. Perot said he was doing it for the people of Texas: "If I really thought the public did not want a better school system, I would do something else. I could be on a yacht somewhere."[1]

As opposed to his antidrug campaign, where he talked directly with law enforcement agents, medical personnel, and even addicts, on this new crusade Perot did not spend his time speaking with teachers and students. Instead, he hired consultants, decided what he thought was best for Texas education, and then went to the business community and citizens' groups to sell his plan. His research team, led this time by his lawyer and friend Tom Luce, developed the proposals (they became the core of House Resolution 72). They included keeping classes from kindergarten through the fourth grade to no larger than fifteen children and reducing the average class size in other grades from thirty-one to twenty-two students; starting prekindergarten services for children from disadvantaged families; having schools stay open from 7:00 A.M. to 6:00 P.M. for on-site day care; initiating merit pay for good teachers; and developing achievement tests for students.

His first target was the state's twelve thousand football coaches, who were of almost reverential interest in many small Texas towns built around high school football. "I thought I was living pretty good until I found a school system that had towel warmers and towel coolers for the football team," said Perot.[2] He criticized high school teams that had "playbooks as complicated as the Dallas Cowboys'," noted sarcastically that losing coaches either "get fired or [are] made a principal," and said he intended to visit small towns and ask the residents, "Do you want adult entertainment, or do you want your kids to learn?"[3] Angry parents and football coaches sometimes demonstrated at Perot's appearances, and sported bumper stickers: WILL ROGERS NEVER MET ROSS PEROT or I DON'T BRAKE FOR PEROT. But it was Perot who coined the phrase that came to represent the thrust of his reforms—"No pass, no play": meaning students had to maintain passing grades in order to participate in extracurricular activities.

Perot also went after teachers, saying the only people who get "paid extra for staying alive" are seniority-based teachers.[4] "The dumbest folks in college are studying to be teachers."[5] As far as he was concerned, four out of five newly graduated teachers were "incompetent," and he proposed literacy and competency tests. That prompted the largest teachers' union to walk out of talks with him.[6] "He did not want to negotiate," says Annette Cootes of the teachers' association. "We bore the brunt of his witticisms, and he can be a funny guy, and all he did was dismiss us as flat-earth people."[7]

Without the backing of the large teachers' associations or unions, Perot set about to push his ideas through the legislature by spending over a million dollars to hire prominent Austin lobbyists, including those who worked for the teachers and opponents of the reforms.[8] "All the good, expensive, high-powered lobbyists don't have anything to do," said Perot. "We hired them. The ones we didn't need we hired defensively just so no one else could get them. We couldn't have won without them."[9] "In the state of Texas, if you want to get a statute passed, if you want to get laws passed, if you want to get things done," said Eddie Joseph of the Texas High School Coaches Association, "you hire the right lobbyist, and he did that because he hired them all."[10] Raymon Bynum, the chief of the Texas Education Agency, recalled that the Perot lobbyists seemed to be everywhere. "I couldn't leave my office to go to the Capitol. Certain individuals would show up and might even walk into a senator's office."[11]*

Teachers, principals, and school administrators criticized Perot's bill as expensive and ineffective. But Perot was in no mood to compromise—"the most important thing is to get down in the ring and slug it out and don't back off," he said.[12] According to Republican state senator John Leedom, even Governor White, who had appointed Perot, thought he might be going too far, but was unable to rein him in.[13]† "He has a way of ridiculing the experts," says Leedom. "It is part of his style."[14] Governor White admitted that Perot's "style was polarizing—it put us in a posture where we were unable to make some compromises with teachers and coaches."[15]

Yet Perot's caustic style engendered little legislative opposition. One of his few opponents was Senator O. H. "Ike" Harris. He recalls sitting in the Senate chamber, about to start a crucial debate over the reform package, when he received a telephone call. It was from his banker, telling him to vote for the Perot package. "Ross, that was my banker," Harris said as he hung up. "He tells me he wants me to vote for your bill. Looks like you got to him." Perot, who denied instigating the banker's call, gave a tight grin, while others in the packed Senate hall laughed. Harris still voted against Perot, and his banker did not abandon him. "Ross has chairman-

---

* Perot's attitude toward lobbyists changed when he was running for president in 1992. Then, he condemned the deleterious effect of lobbyists, saying, "They'll have their lobbyists come to Washington with their six-figure incomes and tickle Congress behind the ear and try to maintain the status quo. They have done a good job so far and they are really hurting this country."

† Leedom says that Perot threatened to publicly embarrass White unless the governor backed him fully. White, who was later sued by Perot over a business deal gone bad, has refused to comment on the issue of pressure, saying only that he fully backed the reforms. But some close to the former governor say Perot threatened to take White on publicly if he failed to go along with the package in its entirety.

of-the-board syndrome," concluded Harris. "He figures, 'I've got more stock than you, so you gotta go with me.' "[16]

Perot has admitted that the fight for the reforms was not always easy. He had to play "pure hardball," he said. "It wasn't pretty, but we got it done. That's the way it works down here."[17] "When I went to see him before the vote," says Senator Leedom, "I talked about some of the concerns I had over the bill. It was like talking to the wall. After I voted against it, I lost my spot on the education committee. So did everyone else who voted against it. I know plenty of legislators who were not supporters of the bill, but they were intimidated by Perot's machine and afraid of going against him. He makes a contest out of everything, and people are afraid of getting crushed if they are on the wrong side."[18] Governor White, defeated in the 1986 election, later blamed the hostility generated by Perot's efforts as a "significant contribution to my defeat."[19]

In 1984, Perot got his House Resolution 72, a sweeping package that he claimed would revolutionize the state's education system, through a special session of the Texas legislature. (However, one of his most significant alterations, the appointed state school board, was later rejected by voters.) Despite Perot's hyperbole, the results were not dramatic—eight years later, when he ran for president, Texas had only moved up one notch, to forty-third among the states. Today Perot blames the way the laws were implemented. "This broke down," he says. "My job was to put in the law. That doesn't mean anything. Implementing them is what counts. They didn't execute it the way they should have. I had no involvement after the law was passed."[20]

Yet Senator Leedom says that the bill itself was the problem. It led to an early exodus of teachers, significantly undercut discipline by curtailing a principal's ability to suspend students, and created onerous paperwork. "Even 'No pass, no play' didn't work like intended," says Leedom, "since students took easy courses to ensure they didn't fail, instead of challenging themselves with more productive classes. Perot, without listening to those who had spent their lives in education, forced through, under the name of reform, a bill that we are still trying to correct."[21]

Although Perot worked against candidates who later tried to undo part of his bill, and education reform stayed one of his pet projects, his main attention in 1984 was diverted away from public service and back to his company. There, he would soon have to decide whether to sell EDS.

By 1983, EDS had overcome its earlier malaise and was again a strong performer. Contract signings were at a new high, the company had a record number of employees (over 13,000), revenues were up nearly a third, and profits were up a quarter to almost $60 million. Mort Meyerson was also trying to shift the company away from government work to more private data processing for *Fortune* 100 companies. He concentrated on a negotiation with AT&T that could have resulted in a massive contract for processing all of the phone company's long-distance telephone service (the AT&T contract would have been worth a billion dollars a year and would have doubled EDS's workforce almost overnight). But by year's end, the AT&T deal had been lost.

The following spring, a new opportunity unexpectedly developed. John Gutfreund, one of the major players at the New York investment house Salomon Brothers, had flown to Dallas to tell Perot that General Motors was interested in acquiring EDS in a friendly merger. Was EDS for sale? Perot, who owned 46 percent of EDS's stock, could have killed any potential suitor's interest with a firm no, but he left the door open to Gutfreund's question.

Two weeks after the first meeting, Perot and Meyerson flew to Detroit and were given a helicopter tour of the enormous GM sites. "We flew from the airport to the test track and then flew over three factories, all of which were bigger than anything I had ever seen in Texas," recalls Meyerson. "After the test track, we flew to their headquarters and saw eight other factories. I had never seen anything that had millions of square feet under the roof, and thirty to forty thousand employee cars in the parking lot. The sheer physical size of GM was an inducement. Ross and I thought, 'If we can paint masterpieces on an eight-by-twelve-inch piece of paper, imagine what we can do on something a hundred feet by a hundred feet.' "[22]

Roger Smith, the chairman of GM since 1981, made a persuasive pitch to the EDS pair. Smith liked Perot when they met. He later told an aide, "Ross is a GM kind of guy."[23]* Smith assured Perot and Meyerson that EDS would retain considerable autonomy, that GM needed its data processing skills in order to modernize, and that his plan for the future of automobile manufacturing involved a greater dependence on computer technology, which would allow EDS to become a partner in GM's future vision of the auto marketplace. An EDS alliance with GM, with its 750,000 employees and $84 billion in revenues, was tempting. GM annually spent $3 billion just on data processing, three times the entire revenue of EDS. Perot thought he could double EDS's size while also streamlining the world's largest corporation. He did not think the GM bureaucracy would hamper him, and of course, as a result of the buyout, Perot and the EDS executives stood to make small fortunes. Smith, on the other hand, was convinced that EDS was the ideal complement to his high-tech plans for remodeling GM, and moreover, that he could control Perot.†

By May, word of the GM interest in EDS began leaking out to the financial markets. Although Meyerson denied anything was under way when asked point-blank by financial columnist Dan Dorfman, on May 16 Dorfman's column said that EDS was in "exploratory merger talks [with a] giant U.S. corporation."[24] EDS's stock, which had been trading in the range of $28 to $30 a share, with a daily sales volume under 50,000, jumped to almost $36 on the Dorfman rumor, with volume exceeding half

---

* While Smith had methodically worked his way up to the top of the corporate ladder, Perot was much more the self-made man and potential street brawler. Smith, who prided himself as a "thinker," came from an old-line family that included a relative who had signed the Magna Carta. Perot, in 1984, spent $1.5 million to buy a signed original (one of four) of the Magna Carta, and loaned it to the National Archives (he was so pleased with the restoration work done on the document by the rare books curator at the University of Texas that he later bought a $15 million collection of rare books for the university—with the catch that the school had to eventually repay him).

† Smith was evidently not worried by a warning from Ed Pratt, a GM director and chairman of the Pfizer Corporation, who had served on the Corporate Advisory Board to the Vietnam Veterans Memorial Fund. Pratt had advised Smith that "Perot is a bulldog and has very little restraint."

a million shares.[25] (Perot was later suspicious that the GM negotiating team might be playing havoc with EDS stock by improper trading, and he assigned two EDS security men to tail the GM negotiators after one session. Salomon Brothers' Gutfreund was furious about Perot's "ridiculous suspicions" but did not say anything for fear of throwing the delicate negotiations off balance.)[26]

Within a week, several reporters had identified the suitor as General Motors, and Perot and Meyerson acknowledged they were in preliminary talks. The talks almost collapsed in late May, when Smith let loose with a stinging rebuke about the dragging negotiations. It was at this time that Perot replaced Mort Meyerson as the chief negotiator on the deal with Bill Gayden, the former chief of EDS World. Gayden soon made a prediction to a group from GM: "If it happens, it's going to happen on June 27. Somehow or other, the great events of Ross Perot's life always take place on his birthday."[27]

"Roger Smith had taken Ross up to the mountain and showed him the promised land," says investment banker Felix Rohatyn, who served on the EDS board at the time of the sale. "Perot thought that he and Roger were going to revolutionize the automotive industry. They were going to computerize the process from the time the customer bought a car—from the first part that was ordered to the car that rolled off the line. And that was unrealistic. Even if Roger Smith wanted to, he couldn't deliver it, because his division chiefs were just too powerful. I warned Ross, when he was thinking of the merger, that I had real reservations, that I thought it was like merging with the Department of Agriculture."[28] Perot and his executives thought they had protected themselves by ensuring as much independence as possible. "The terms of the agreement said we would be an autonomous unit," recalls Mort Meyerson. "We negotiated those specific things in there, and not by accident. We would set the compensation of our people, and we would select the auditors."[29]

On June 12, 1984, Roger Smith, having obtained the approval of the GM board, sent Perot a twelve-page summary agreement to sign. It offered to pay $44 a share in cash for EDS stock, and also to create a new class of stock, GM class E shares, which would be held by Perot and other EDS executives and would pay dividends tied to EDS's performance. GM would own 100 percent of EDS. Perot, who normally abhors memos and written correspondence ("Everybody knows you can't write me a memo. . . . I can't talk to a memo"), sent Roger Smith a long fax with questions and comments about the buyout.[30] The two traded notes for the next three days, with Perot trying to up the buyout price and carve out as much independence as possible. Smith, eager to close the deal as rapidly as possible, agreed to many of Perot's requests.

On June 27, Perot's fifty-fourth birthday, he called a meeting of EDS's twenty-eight officers and directors. He explained the deal to them and said, "I will do what you guys want to."[31] Then he left and Meyerson took charge. Most felt that Perot had decided to sign the GM deal no matter what they said. While Meyerson recalls that there were no dissenting opinions, others disagree.[32] "Ross pretended he didn't know where we were going," recalls one of the senior vice-presidents, "but that was bullshit. It was presented to us as a very general opportunity, but none of us knew the details of what it would be like with GM. In typical Ross fashion, he had kept this so compartmentalized that only he knew how it all fit together. Even though we didn't know all the issues, a number raised hackles." Gary Fernandes said he was troubled by making a quick decision in that meeting, and there were possible risks to being bought by a corporate giant like GM. "Most of us did not want to sell," recalled Les Alberthal. "We didn't see any net benefit."[33] "It was going to get done since Ross wanted it," says Ken Riedlinger. "It's that simple."[34] Later that day, as Bill Gayden had predicted, Perot signed a memorandum of understanding with GM.

Perot had pulled a coup. GM paid $2.55 billion in cash and stock for EDS. In less than two years, EDS would zoom from 15,000 employees to 40,000, and from less than $1 billion in revenues to $5 billion. Perot personally pocketed $930 million in cash, and received 5.5 million shares of the newly created GM class E stock (worth another $700 million, guaranteed by GM, if held for seven years).* And Smith had, in fact, given EDS greater autonomy than any other GM subsidiary. He told Perot, "If anybody shows up in Dallas with a GM procedures manual, I want you to shoot them."[35]

"At the time, everybody was excited," says Riedlinger. "It was an opportunity to rape an elephant. There was never any feeling that we were bought. No one felt as though they were going to work for GM, and Ross told us directly, 'Don't anyone, for even a moment, think we were sold.' We thought it was just a way to get the world's biggest customer, and we were approaching GM just like we did the government—big, fat, dumb, and rich."[36]

Perot joined the General Motors board. A handful of EDS executives were sent to Detroit. Meyerson and Perot chose to remain in Dallas and sent Ken Riedlinger to run the GM account. On June 28, 1984, Roger Smith and Perot held a joint press conference, each praising the other, the deal, and their companies. As the details of their deal were being ironed out by lawyers, the two executives were enjoying what would prove to be a short honeymoon.

---

* GM and EDS crafted the value of the class E stock so that any money earned by Perot was taxed at the lower rate for capital gains and not as ordinary income. It saved Perot millions of dollars in taxes. "The deal with GM was the only way Perot could ever cash out of his enormous EDS stake," says Riedlinger. "Perot could never have sold his EDS shares while still running the company, or the price of the stock would have plummeted. So a buyout was the only alternative." Other EDS executives also did well from the agreement. If the class E shares were held seven years, Meyerson would have over $100 million in holdings, Bill Gayden $45 million, and Ken Riedlinger and Les Alberthal $25 million each.

TWELVE

---□---

"The Tar Baby"

General Motors' data processing managers had no idea what the acquisition of EDS meant for their division, except that Smith had given their operations a vote of no confidence. Under the terms of the agreement still being hammered out by the lawyers, EDS would absorb nearly 10,000 GM computer experts and data processors. While most averaged annual salaries of $50,000, they considered themselves every bit as good as the new millionaire workers arriving from EDS. There was also the real possibility that their automatic salary increases and generous benefits would be traded for less compensation and leaner pensions in the EDS subsidiary (Smith had first suggested that GM workers who moved to EDS remain covered by GM's pay scales and benefits, but Perot vetoed the idea). They had also heard of the EDS boot-camp mentality. "EDS is a harsh culture," remarked Perot. "It's not for everybody and never was supposed to be."[1]

When Alex Mair, the group executive for GM's technical staffs, was told that EDS workers had arrived to take an inventory of the building's computers and were putting EDS tags on them, he exploded: "No one from EDS is going into the computer room, and no one will put EDS property tags on anything."[2] At the first meeting of GM's fifty top data processing managers with Mort Meyerson and Ken Riedlinger, they were told that everybody in GM's computer operations would be working for EDS. The response from one GM executive was "Bullshit!"[3] For five hours,

the GM managers challenged the EDS pair. "We were flabbergasted by our reception," recalls Riedlinger.[4] Once, Alex
Cunningham, chief of North American car operations, interrupted
Meyerson and Riedlinger's standard talk, saying, "It will be a cold
day in hell before I'm going to help pad the pockets of a bunch of
rich Texans."[5] When Gary Fernandes called on Bob Murphy, the
vice-president in charge of GM's car-loan and home financing
division, Murphy told him, "I don't know why you are here. I
don't need you here. Do whatever you have to do, but don't
bother me."[6] Riedlinger, more visible in the day-to-day operations
than Meyerson or the others, received a barrage of personal
harassment, including death threats, slashed tires, and "Dear Nazi
Riedlinger" notes. Perot assigned EDS security to him.[7]

"The deal had been done too quickly by both sides," concludes
Riedlinger. "It was also done at the highest level, Ross and Roger,
and that was a mistake. The people who had to implement it had
been left out."[8]

EDS exacerbated the problems. GM workers sensed that
Meyerson and Riedlinger treated them as merely another customer, not as if the company had just paid $2.5 billion to buy
EDS. The pair were considered condescending, and dismissive of
GM solutions for data processing. "The feeling was 'You fellows
make the cars, and leave the computing to us,' " recalls one GM
manager. There was even talk of filing a lawsuit, or obtaining the
aid of the United Auto Workers union in organizing the white-
collar workers. Riedlinger's reaction was to send a vitriolic letter
announcing there was "no place for a union" in EDS, and that
those seeking labor's help were a "small number of . . . disgruntled [people]." The response to that letter was so angry and widespread that Riedlinger soon had to apologize.*

---

* Some instances in which a transfer to EDS caused havoc for GM workers
quickly spread around GM and heightened the anxiety. One employee, a month
short of reaching his thirty-year retirement level, was transferred to EDS and lost
his retirement benefits. Another worker, who happened to be an amateur weight-
lifter, was spotted by Perot on a tour of the GM facilities. Perot spoke to him,
and moved him to the health and fitness division. Two months later he was fired.
"Out without any overlapping benefits, insurance, severance pay, nothing," the
worker recalled. "Over twenty years of my life blown away."

Under Meyerson and Riedlinger's guidance, dozens of GM data processing centers closed. The closings did not always result in the expected cost savings. When the Fisher Design Center was closed, EDS moved most of its workers to new sites in Texas and Michigan. The Fisher Center cost GM $2 million a year to operate, but costs inflated under EDS to $3 million.[9] EDS's work was also not up to par as it grappled with the size and complexity of GM. Initially, computer systems were down more often under EDS, parts were ordered and never used, and the new equipment was often costly and complicated to use. There were also new problems—thousands of dividend checks were sent to the wrong employees, the wrong beneficiaries were put on insurance policies, and some employees were dropped from medical coverage. Dr. Robert Frosch, the chief of GM's research labs, had more computer science Ph.D.'s in one of his departments than in all of EDS. He concluded that EDS did not have the necessary experience in robotics or computer aided design and manufacturing, and he managed to exclude them from his department for two years. Increasingly, some people derisively referred to EDS as an acronym for Ever Diminishing Service.

Another contentious issue was EDS's hiring policy. It often staffed jobs with many more employees for the same amount of work. "We used to do this job with thirty-six people," said one GM data processor. "Now EDS has eighty-six people here, and we still can't get the job done."[10] "The truth is that EDS has been a nightmare," said a senior engineer at an Indiana truck assembly plant. "They [EDS] just don't understand the technology at all. Their method is to move in quick and throw people and money at the problems."[11]

"I was told by Mort to hire ten thousand people immediately," says Riedlinger. "It was a hiring frenzy, but we didn't need them by a long shot. However, since we were having trouble arranging long-term fixed-price contracts with GM, they were going to pay us our costs plus a small profit. Mort wanted our costs inflated as much as possible, and told me, 'If that's the way GM wants it, we will bury them with people.' "[12] Riedlinger had arrived with only 240 workers, dubbed "the first wave" by Perot. Within one year they hired nearly 17,000 employees and added over 100 class-rooms to teach systems engineering.*

Despite these difficulties, neither Smith nor Perot was particularly concerned. Smith had expected that his entrenched bureaucracy would respond slowly to the EDS acquisition. Perot, on the other hand, considered the early EDS arrivals at GM a frontal assault on unfriendly territory but thought that eventually the GM resistance would subside. There were, however, several minor incidents that bothered Perot during the first few months. GM had announced EDS's latest earnings, something Perot felt should come only from him as EDS chairman. He was also "very angry," according to Riedlinger, that GM refused to give the new class E stock the trading symbol EDS. When Perot wanted to pass out copies of one of his favorite books, *Leadership Secrets of Attila the Hun*, at a dinner to celebrate the launch of the Saturn line of cars, Roger Smith's office told him that it was not appropriate and he could not bring the books. "I was the one who had to call Mort and tell him they would not allow the books," recalls Riedlinger. "Ross was unbelievably angry."[13] "Ross had not been told he couldn't do something in a very long time," comments another EDS executive.

But there were many things he could do, and he quickly showed he would not be a typical director. "For example," says Perot, "they gave a board member a new car every ninety days. I upset them every time I turned around. I said, 'I don't want a new car every ninety days. Why should I have a new car every ninety days? I should know what a real car is like.' They wanted to give me a specially put-together car that would be trouble-free for ninety days. I said, 'No, I want to go to a dealer, buy my own car with my own money, shop for it, and work with the dealer's mechanic when I have trouble."[14]

Roger Smith had already eaten with Perot in the EDS cafeteria when visiting Dallas, commenting that the food was good. Perot needled him about being out of touch with his own workforce: " 'Roger, if you ate in your cafeteria, the food would be terrific

---

* A common joke that made the rounds at GM was, "How many EDSers does it take to change a lightbulb? I don't know—they aren't finished hiring yet."

too.' "[15] At the Saturn dinner, Perot gently jabbed his GM counterparts and UAW representatives by bragging about how the
EDS vocabulary did not have the words "management and
labor."[16] In a *New York Times* interview, Perot said, "If you want
to get an elephant to move, you have to know where the sensitive
spots are."[17]

A more significant problem was over the question of how much
control Perot would have in setting the compensation of his top
executives. Meyerson had an agreement with Perot, prior to the
GM transaction, that promised him 1 percent of EDS's profits. In
the previous year, that had translated to $712,000 for Meyerson,
before stock options and bonuses. Now, with much larger income
and profits because of the volume of GM business, Meyerson's
salary would rival or surpass Roger Smith's, something GM's
directors considered unthinkable.* Moreover, Perot wanted to set
aside 20 million shares of class E stock to use as incentives for
EDS workers. Smith told Perot that he thought the compensation
was excessive.

While that issue simmered, Perot attended his first GM board
meeting in the summer of 1984. He was not assigned to the critical finance or executive committees, but rather appointed to the
unimportant public policy subcommittee. Perot resented it, especially since he was the largest shareholder on the board.

"My first question as a director of GM was 'Are our pension
funds fully funded?' " recalls Perot. "I always kept mine over-
funded. They said, 'We have three.' I said, 'Why do we have
three?' Executive, white collar, blue collar. 'Well, are all three fully
funded?' One was. Need I ask which one?"[18]

"They just couldn't imagine what proactive would mean," comments Meyerson. "They never had a board member ask questions

---

* The issue of compensation was not Meyerson's only problem. Smith had not
followed through on an early promise of naming him a GM vice-president. And
other, smaller affronts illustrated how poor the relationship was. Meyerson was
never invited to the homes of other GM executives, or asked to socialize at corporate events. Whereas all GM executives had heated garages to park their cars
in (where they were shined and serviced daily), Meyerson was told there was no
space for him. He dutifully told Perot of all the slights, but Perot, though perturbed at the treatment of his most trusted lieutenant, stayed out of the fray, only
occasionally calling Smith to urge nicer treatment.

like him. All of a sudden they have this guy down at the end of the table, asking in a Texas twang, 'Hey, why are we doing that?' "[19]

The EDS and GM alliance remained uneasy, though the compensation issue had not yet come to a head. In early 1985, Smith asked Perot to evaluate whether GM should invest in Comau Productivity Systems, a U.S. subsidiary of Fiat that specialized in automation for auto assembly lines. Perot met with Comau executives, heard their pitch, and told Smith that investing would be a terrible idea. GM ignored his recommendation and bought 20 percent, further irritating Perot.

Perot was in a mood to allow his EDS executives assigned to the GM account to be more aggressive. Meyerson confronted Roger Smith in March 1985. There was no teamwork between the companies, he said—"EDS people are abused and belittled wherever they go."[20] Smith contended that part of the problem was Riedlinger, whose style was too abrasive.

"You look pretty smug, like a guy betting his job," Smith told Riedlinger at a capital budget meeting. "You might be out on the street looking for a job tomorrow."

"I bet my job every day," Riedlinger replied.[21]

After hearing about the exchange, Perot called Riedlinger later that day to reassure him. "Whatever happens," Perot said, "you will always have a job with me."[22]

On Monday, April 29, 1985, EDS held its annual meeting in Dallas. The board now consisted of Roger Smith and the GM executive committee members, as well as EDS officers and Perot (the EDS side held a one-vote majority). Riedlinger, responsible for the EDS presentation, snapped at Smith when challenged about EDS's hiring policy. Meyerson, who thought Riedlinger had gone too far, confronted him after the meeting. "You've led EDS into this swamp," Riedlinger yelled at Meyerson. "Now you figure out how to get us out."[23] The two continued their argument in a private room. The tension that had built up around the difficulties at GM had taken a toll and strained their friendship. Riedlinger had not slept in two days, and had just spent six hours making the presentation to the EDS board.

"Mort was angrier than at any time I had known him in eighteen years," recalls Riedlinger. "I wasn't even sure over what. And

I was totally calm. Almost too exhausted to fight. Finally I said, 'I have been screamed at by Perot, and Smith, and now you. I have had it. Why should I put up with this? Take your job and shove it.' As I started to walk out, Mort said, 'I will give you until tomorrow morning to call and apologize.' "[24] The following morning, Riedlinger called Perot, who informed him that Meyerson was on his way to Detroit and that "things had been worked out."[25] "I waited all day and never heard from Mort," says Riedlinger. "Then I heard he had held a company meeting and told everyone I was gone."[26]*

The shake-up at EDS was overshadowed that same month when General Motors posted a 34 percent drop in profits from the previous year. Its sales plummeted, reducing its share of the important luxury car market. The Cadillac division was especially hard hit. "It was so bad that the Cadillac dealers demanded a summit meeting," Perot says, "and no one in General Motors wanted to go, so they asked me if I would go. I spent all day with them, and they were telling me how bad Cadillac was." Perot insisted on a special study to highlight the problems with the Cadillac line. The GM board was not enthusiastic. "I finally even had to offer to pay to have it done," he recalls, "because everyone at General Motors was dragging their feet, and then they [finally] did it out of embarrassment. It showed that the Cadillac customer thought the car was junk, the Cadillac dealer thought it was junk, the Cadillac mechanic who worked on the car at the dealer thought it was junk—the factory workers, it was a depressing experience to put it together eight hours a day—the engineers who designed it said

---

* When Riedlinger tried to come back to EDS, Meyerson rejected him, and Perot, who had always promised him a job, put him off ("Perot reneged on the only thing he had ever committed to me on," says Riedlinger). Finally, in the fall, Riedlinger went to work for Ford. Perot feared he might try to steal some of EDS's managers and had an EDS house counsel send him a warning letter. "I know where the skeletons are at EDS," Riedlinger told the lawyer, "and I have the maps to find them. Think about that before you start threatening me with legal action." Riedlinger did not hear again from anyone at EDS. Yet today he shares the mixed feelings about Perot expressed by many of the former executives I spoke to. "I like Ross. He saved my life a couple of times. But I also hate Ross. Yet I voted for him. And I would probably go back to work for him tomorrow if he asked."

it was junk, but if General Motors would get out of the way, they could build a good car. Then we got up to the head of Cadillac and they thought it was a pretty good car. Then we got to the four-teenth floor of General Motors [the executive floor] and they said it was the finest luxury car in the world—totally disconnected from reality. . . . Well, we shook a lot of trees."[27]

The GM directors did not like lectures from Perot about the auto business. David Davis, editor of *Automobile* magazine, thought that GM's executives were tolerant of Perot, considering that "every time you heard him say something about cars, it was so dumb and naïve, you'd wince."[28] But Perot thought his exper-tise extended even beyond the auto industry. He persisted in ques-tioning the possible acquisition of Hughes Aircraft, for which Roger Smith had prepared a $5 billion bid. The 73,000 Hughes scientists and engineers were another part of Smith's high-technology revolution. But Perot's doubts forced Smith to send a large GM team to Dallas in midsummer to answer questions about the proposed deal. Perot still did not give Smith his endorse-ment, instead saying he would think about it.

In August 1985, the long-simmering issue of setting the com-pensation for EDS executives finally came to a head. Perot wanted to give 20 million additional shares of the new class E stock to his officers. That would cost GM another $300 million. Meyerson's salary, excluding bonuses, was up to $851,000, higher than any-one else's at GM (later Perot would try to increase Meyerson's salary to $1.9 million, further aggravating the situation).* Perot, having always determined the compensation for his officers, took for granted that he would still have that power under GM, and was annoyed that Smith had delayed the decision for nearly six months. Yet GM viewed the EDS requests as pure greed. Smith finally told Perot he could not give the class E shares as extra com-pensation. Instead, Smith offered an alternative worth about one tenth as much ($34 million).

---

* Perot always bragged that he set his own salary at $68,000 a year in 1968 and never raised it. GM executives later fumed at that gesture. "Anybody who's got $3 billion, and you know that 10 percent of that gets you $300 million a year in the bank, and he says he's only going to take out $68,000?" said Jack McNulty, a GM vice-president. "It's almost dishonest. It's pandering to people's ignorance."

Perot invited Smith to Dallas, saying, "I think you're making a huge mistake by stopping our stock options. . . . But if you're determined to do this, then I think you ought to come to Dallas and explain your thinking to everyone."[29] The trip was a setup, because EDS management, unwilling to listen to Smith's rationale, planned to attack him for what they considered a breach of his original agreement. Tom Walter, EDS's chief financial officer, challenged Smith's numbers. Bill Gayden, the president of EDS World, suggested that the GM chairman had not been forthright and told him of a friend who had had a heart attack because GM's treatment was so poor. "When Roger Smith came to Dallas," recalls Gayden, "*ambush* is not a bad word. We were coached. This was not something unplanned."[30] Short scripts had been prepared for the key officers. "Roger launched into an uncontrolled rage at the people in the room," Perot recalled.[31] Smith almost walked out (Meyerson had previously told Riedlinger that "Roger Smith is exactly like Ross in his darkest moments.")[32] "We were stunned," Perot claimed.[33] To make matters worse, Perot lectured Smith. "I took Roger aside and told him he couldn't be chairman if he was going to act like that."[34]

When an angry Smith returned to Detroit, he was adamantly against the EDS stock bonus plan, and since the power to issue the incentive shares rested solely with the GM board, the matter was closed. But Perot was also fuming, because Smith had overridden him in front of his executives.

Outside management consultants were now hired to try and smooth the relationship between GM and EDS. And Tom Luce, EDS's outside counsel, flew to Detroit to meet GM's corporate counsel and senior vice-president Elmer Johnson to see whether there was anything in the contract or agreements that might help resolve future clashes like the compensation issue. But Perot was not in a conciliatory mood. In a letter to Smith on October 23, he demonstrated how deep the divide was between them. "In the interest of GM you are going to have to stop treating me as a problem and accept me as a large stockholder, an active board member, an experienced businessman. . . . In our relationship I will support you when I believe you are right. I will tell you candidly when I think you are wrong. If you continue your present autocratic style, I will be your adversary on critical issues. I will argue with you privately. If necessary I will argue with you publicly before the board and the shareholders. You and others at GM may think that I will simply get frustrated and go away if you continue to make life unpleasant enough. You need to understand that I cannot leave because of my obligations."[35]

Perot did more in his letter than merely state his willingness to challenge Smith, something unheard of on the GM board; he also attacked Smith's style, often in terms remarkably like those many EDSers have used to describe Perot himself. "You need to understand that your style intimidates people. Losing your temper hurts GM. Your tendency to try to run over anyone who disagrees with you hurts your effectiveness within GM. You need to be aware that people are afraid of you. This stifles candid, upward communication in GM. You need to know that GMers at all levels use terms like 'ruthless' and 'bully' in describing you."[36]

Although Smith was enraged by Perot's broadside, Luce and Meyerson, together with Elmer Johnson, were able to defuse the situation. Perot was appointed to serve on a committee whose stated goal was to devise a strategy to produce "world-class quality cars at the lowest competitive cost." GM agreed to devise a fair pricing agreement for EDS services, and it confirmed EDS's choice of vice-president Kenn Hill as the replacement for Riedlinger.

Two weeks after Perot's letter to Smith, the GM board gathered in New York for its regularly scheduled meeting. Luce had warned Perot not to be too strident in his opposition to the Hughes buyout. But Luce knew that Perot had become difficult to control once he saw the relationship with GM as a contest.

Perot asked for permission to address the board. He read a lengthy speech that castigated GM for its drop of market share ("Clearly, we are doing something wrong") and cumbersome organization ("Senior management is too isolated from the people"). He not only provided his ideas for solving them, but again spoke out firmly against the Hughes acquisition.[37]* Smith sat

---

* Just as GM had issued class E stock when it bought EDS, it intended to issue class H stock for the Hughes purchase. Some industry analysts thought Perot opposed the Hughes acquisition because he feared it would dilute the value of his E shares.

grim-faced as Perot addressed the board as if his ideas should supplant the chairman's as the best way to run the company. When the board voted on the Hughes deal, Perot cast the only no vote—the only time a director had ever voted against a Smith-backed proposal.

When the proxy disclosure statement for the Hughes purchase was sent to GM shareholders the following month, it noted that the GM board had approved the purchase, "with one director dissenting." The rift between Perot and Smith was finally public. There was now an undercurrent on the board that Perot should be removed as a director. "I told them to try it," Perot recalled. "I had more shares than all the others combined, so go ahead and try. I love a good fight."[38]

Behind the scenes, problems were growing. Smith had promised that EDS would receive long-term fixed price contracts for its data processing work. While negotiating those, both sides decided that all interim work would be billed at EDS's cost, plus 9.5 percent. However, GM wanted access to EDS's books, not only to provide necessary records for various government agencies, but also to ensure its costs were not overstated.[39]* Some GM executives charged that EDS had overcharged GM by upward of $1 billion during its first year.[40] It was the same issue on which Perot had taken such an adamant stance with the government over its Medicare and Medicaid work when he steadfastly refused to open EDS's books. This seemed quite different, since GM owned EDS, yet Perot still refused, pointing to a clause in the buyout that he could select the company's auditor. "See, I was just pursuing the autonomy that was guaranteed in writing," Perot later said.[41]

As word of the impasse spread in the financial community, the price of class E stock fell by 20 percent. A consultant hired by GM had already recommended that the only solution was to get rid of Perot, and quickly. But the GM management thought the advice too severe, and that a compromise could be had short of ending

---

* GM also wanted to see EDS's books, since the accounting firm of Peat Marwick had suggested twenty-one corrections to EDS's 1985 accounting, which EDS refused to make. Moreover, GM auditors had discovered an additional sixty-two mistakes, mostly clerical errors or understated revenues. In any case, the sloppiness added to GM's interest in seeing the EDS books and records.

the relationship. But Perot saw little improvement, especially when Meyerson told him that in meetings with GM managers, the three major areas of contention remained EDS's lavish compensation, charges of exorbitant prices for services, and complaints of delays on data processing jobs. Finally Meyerson, fed up with the obstacles he encountered at GM and humiliated by a public tongue-lashing he had received from GM's executive vice-president Don Atwood, flew to Dallas and handed his resignation to a shocked Perot in the spring of 1986. "It's clear GM isn't going to keep its part of the bargain," Meyerson told Perot, "and I'm not going to participate in the dismemberment of EDS. I've put too much of my life in it."[42] Although Perot managed to talk Meyerson into staying on temporarily as vice-chairman, the two had to decide quickly on a replacement president of EDS. Riedlinger, who would have been a candidate, had self-destructed. Senior vice-presidents Gary Fernandes and Les Alberthal were the remaining contenders. Perot liked Fernandes, a smooth and very personable executive, but Meyerson preferred Alberthal. Though Perot thought Alberthal to be colorless and too much a technocrat, he was finally persuaded by Meyerson. Alberthal became only the third president of EDS under Perot.[43] Tom Walter, the chief financial officer and one of Perot's most trusted executives, had recently had a bout with cancer and also resigned his post.

On May 5, at a GM board meeting in New York, Perot, still fuming over Meyerson's departure, warned Roger Smith that he would no longer compromise his principles for the sake of harmony. According to Smith, Perot told him, "You can try and terminate me but I will start World War III."[44] Two days later Perot sent Smith a three-page letter-agreement, seeking Smith's signature to twenty issues Perot demanded be resolved. It all came down to a single line: "I will run EDS, just as I ran it before GM acquired EDS."[45] Smith's response, which ignored the specific contents of the May 7 diatribe, prompted another Perot letter, on May 19. Now he warned Smith that "therefore, in the absence of any clear understanding between us, I will run EDS and when we disagree, we are going to have whatever size fight is necessary, between us, with the board, or in full public view to get the matter resolved. Your other option is to try to terminate me, in order to get rid of a nuisance. I want to make sure that you and every member of the GM board understand the magnitude and length of the fight that would result from such action. It would last for years and would be terribly disruptive. . . . The final resolution, if you want to get rid of me, is to handle the matter on a businesslike basis and buy me out. In my judgment, this would be a serious mistake for GM, but if that is what you want to do, it does reduce the issue to business terms."[46]

At a May 28 dinner in Dallas, Perot and Tom Luce met GM's Elmer Johnson. They remember the substance of their talks that night very differently. According to Johnson, he pursued the idea of a buyout and Perot was willing to consider it at $48 a share for his class E stock. Perot and Luce deny they spoke about a buyout at that meeting. (Later, that issue became critical to EDS employees who thought Perot had planned only for his own comfortable exit from GM and had abandoned them.)

With no acquiescence from Smith, and no offer of a buyout that he liked, Perot acted on his earlier warning that he would expose their disagreement to "full public view" (interestingly, speaking up within EDS against the corporation was a fireable offense). He began by giving *The Detroit Free Press,* the *Los Angeles Times,* and *The New York Times* biographical interviews (to *The New York Times* he said that what had been printed about his life was "half truth, half myth," and to the *Los Angeles Times* he was adamant that "nothing, nothing, nothing" would ever prompt him to run for public office). He peppered the interviews with potshots at GM.[47] Next, he gave *The Wall Street Journal*'s Doron Levin a broadside against GM's and Smith's inefficiencies, providing most of the information only as background and not for attribution.[48]* In some instances, he allowed his name to be used: "It

---

* Levin eventually wrote a book about the EDS-GM fight, *Irreconcilable Differences,* published in 1989. It was sympathetic to the EDS viewpoint. "It should be," says Ken Riedlinger. "Levin used to sit up at the EDS headquarters, and he would route drafts around to each of us, and each of us commented on them. We would see each other's notes. That book was pretty good. It sounded like people I knew. The only way things are sometimes not accurate is that sometimes Ross creates things in his imagination, and after he tells a story forty or fifty times, he really believes it."

takes five years to develop a new car in this country. Heck, we won World War II in four years."[49]

"He wanted to stir up the pot, and he considers himself a master manipulator of the media," says one EDS executive who worked with Perot on his anti-GM policy. " 'I can manipulate any story if you put me in front of it,' he would tell us. He is very good at knowing how to get his point of view into the press, and after he softened GM up enough with what appeared to be straight journalistic stories, then he would jump in." During one of the off-the-record briefings Perot provided journalists at his Dallas headquarters, he launched into a diatribe against Smith. When one reporter asked whether Perot feared that Smith might physically impose his authority by ordering GM security people to let the auditors into EDS sites, Perot reminded the journalist that EDS controlled all of GM's computers, telephones, and information files. Essentially, if Smith got nasty, Perot could pull the electronic plug on GM.[50] He ended that same conference by saying about Smith, "I realize I'm asking for something that is a little unrealistic. A guy who is fifty-eight years old and looks you in the eye and lies to you consistently isn't likely to change. But I've got to try. Roger is stuck with me. He has touched the tar baby."[51]

Perot's new tactics made Les Alberthal's task of integrating EDS into the GM bureaucracy almost impossible. "To be constructive, to help the situation," Alberthal later said, "you wouldn't go out to the press and do the things he was doing."[52] "GM, more than any organization, likes to deal with things in a private setting," said David Cole, a longtime auto industry observer. "They are very tough on themselves internally. . . . But you don't take those criticisms outside. Ross never learned that."[53] The press's reaction to the unusual public rift was to speculate that Perot was interested in Smith's job—something Perot denies, but which EDS executives are split over to this day.[54]

Smith tried to defuse the situation. "Ross didn't say those things," he told one reporter when confronted with Perot's quotes.[55] "I don't want to antagonize him," Smith said to those who urged him to fight back.[56] He told *The Wall Street Journal* that Perot was merely trying to "encourage us along the lines of

Strongly disciplined and competitive, young Ross Perot excelled in everything from delivering papers to earning Boy Scout merit badges. Above, a six-year-old Perot poses with his sister, Bette; at right he is with one of his horses, Bee, and his dog Shep; below is his Texarkana Junior College graduation photo, taken at age eighteen. *(Photos courtesy of Ross Perot)*

As a midshipman at the U.S. Naval Academy, Perot cleaned boilers and met presidents. Below, a proud senior class president stands with his parents, Gabriel Ross and Lulu May, and his sister, Bette, on graduation day in 1953. *(Eisenhower photo courtesy of the Dwight D. Eisenhower Presidential Library; other photos courtesy of Ross Perot)*

In 1956, after a four-year courtship, Perot married twenty-two-year-old Margot Birmingham. "I knew that I wanted to be around him," Margot said of their first meeting. "Life was exciting when he was there." *(Courtesy of Ross Perot)*

In 1962, after five years as a star salesman at IBM, Perot started his own computer services firm, Electronic Data Systems (EDS), working out of an office he shared with Texas Blue Cross. EDS boomed after the advent of Medicare in 1965. *(AP/Wide World Photos)*

EDS went public after six years, gaining almost 50 percent in value on its first day. Overnight, the thirty-eight-year-old Perot was worth $230 million, and just a year and a half later, his net worth had ballooned to more than $1.5 billion. *(Courtesy of Ross Perot)*

Perot loaned Richard Nixon several EDS workers for the 1968 campaign, and soon Perot was frequently talking to Nixon aides, as well as the president himself. Eventually, most of the government officials with whom he dealt soured on him, charging that he failed to come through on many promises and proposals. *(Courtesy of the Nixon Presidential Papers, National Archives)*

In 1969 Perot personally tried to take a planeload of Christmas gifts for American POWs into Southeast Asia. In Anchorage, he oversaw a volunteer effort to repackage the goods into thousands of small parcels in order to satisfy a last-minute North Vietnamese demand. *(AP/Wide World Photos)*

When two EDS executives were arrested by Iranian authorities in 1978, Perot enlisted Colonel Bull Simons to lead a team of EDS volunteers to try to rescue the two men. Here, Perot and Simons arrive in Dallas after the controversial mission. *(Courtesy of Ross Perot)*

In 1984, Perot received over $900 million when General Motors purchased EDS. Soon Perot's clashes with GM's chairman, Roger Smith (left), became so nasty that GM had to buy Perot out in 1986, at a cost of another $742 million. *(AP/Wide World Photos)*

Perot briefed Reagan and his chief of staff, Howard Baker (far left), on POWs and MIAs when he returned from Vietnam in 1987, but he was distressed to find national security adviser Frank Carlucci (second from right) and General Colin Powell (far right) also in attendance. "Once I saw those national security guys there, I knew it was a waste of time," says Perot. *(Courtesy of the Ronald R. Reagan Presidential Library)*

Perot and his son, Ross Jr., in front of a map detailing Ross Jr.'s real estate holdings in the Dallas–Fort Worth area. The younger Perot, backed by his father, built a commercial airport, Alliance, on the vast Perot acreage in North Texas. *(Courtesy of Ross Perot)*

Perot, shown here joking with reporters, promised to run for president in 1992 if volunteers put his name on all fifty state ballots. He then shocked everyone in July by withdrawing from the race, later blaming Republican dirty tricks for forcing him out. When he reentered the race in October, the Democrats and Republicans unexpectedly let him join the presidential debates. Below, Perot spars with the other candidates at the second debate, in Richmond, Virginia. *(Photos from AP/Wide World Photos)*

Vice-President Al Gore made a surprising showing against Perot in 1993 in a nationally televised debate over a free trade treaty with Mexico (NAFTA). Perot came off as testy and unprepared—and he now suspects that Gore may have been fed questions or answers through a hidden earpiece. *(AP/Wide World Photos)*

Although many political commentators wrote Perot off after the Gore debate, in 1995 he committed himself to a multimillion-dollar effort to create a new national political party. At a 1992 Texas rally, he held up a bumper sticker that followers saw as a promise. *(AP/Wide World Photos)*

what we want to do," and told *Fortune* that Perot was not "critical-critical," but rather "helpful-critical." But the conciliatory words from Smith did not ameliorate Perot's anger. In October, *Business Week* published a cover story ("Ross Perot's Crusade") that continued Perot's sharp barbs at Smith and GM.[57] There was growing sentiment in Detroit about ways to get rid of Perot. When Meyerson approached Smith in the late summer with an idea of selling part of EDS to AT&T, Smith saw it as an opportunity to solve his problem. After two months, the talks led to a dead end when it became apparent that AT&T erroneously thought Smith was so desperate to be rid of EDS that it could buy the company cheaply.

Perot discussed possible solutions at several meetings with his top lieutenants. At one, with Mort Meyerson, Les Alberthal, Jeff Heller, and Gary Fernandes, Perot briefly discussed a proxy fight to unseat Smith and the rest of the GM board. The group decided it would be too fractious and unlikely to be successful. (Roger Smith and GM were so concerned about this possibility that a board member and several lawyers visited the investment firm of Drexel, Burnham, supposedly Perot's backer on the takeover, and warned they would not leave without a major fight.) Then Perot talked about a possible shareholder suit, alleging that the GM board was "violating securities regulations."[58] "The bulk of the options were ideas brought to the meeting by Ross and Mort," Alberthal later recalled in a sworn deposition, "and they included such things as going out on strike and shutting down General Motors. There was a generalized term of nuking them, whatever that meant."[59]* Fernandes expressed "shock" at the idea of "pulling the plug." Alberthal and Heller feared that trashing GM would also ruin EDS, since no corporation would use EDS's services if they crippled their largest client because of a dispute with Perot. Alberthal resented Meyerson's arguments that "if the senior officers wouldn't go to war . . . we really didn't have the

---

* During the 1992 presidential campaign, while Perot refused to comment on whether he ever proposed the "nuke 'em" strategy, Mort Meyerson claimed, "It was said in the heat of battle—there was never any serious plans to implement these things." "It was deadly serious," says an EDS executive familiar with the meeting. "Ross did not joke about things like that."

strength or stomach to be leaders." Flushed red with anger, Alberthal walked out of the room. "There was no way I could support the kind of actions they were talking about."[60] "It was a first at EDS," recalls one of the meeting's other participants. "No one had ever walked out on Ross before." "Few of us thought Ross was serious about getting things done at that point," says a former executive. "Ross had been stymied at GM and had been looking for a way out. He was just as happy we couldn't agree on anything, because that gave him the perfect excuse to look out for himself." Perot, on the other hand, blames his fellow executives for the indecision at the meeting. "They just didn't have the stomach for it," he later said.[61]

Without the unified support of his own top management, Perot again started thinking about bailing out. In late October, Tom Luce once more approached Elmer Johnson about whether GM might be interested in buying Perot's stake.* Luce seemed in a rush when he met with Johnson, and for good reason. On January 1, 1987, a tax-reform package passed by Congress was set to take effect. According to Johnson, Luce said that if Perot delayed past the end of the year, it would cost him $50 million in extra taxes.[62] Johnson knew that Perot's constant attacks on GM had created too hostile an atmosphere to continue the relationship. "I have never seen a guy who likes to fight as much as he does," Johnson later said. "I understand fighting for a cause. But I don't understand getting real personal and vindictive."[63] Johnson agreed that a buyout was worth pursuing and promised Luce he would promptly bring it to Roger Smith's attention.

With only two months to make his most profitable deal, Perot kept the public pressure on Smith. In a November issue of *Ward's Auto World,* a highly respected trade magazine, he delivered his strongest public attack on Smith and GM, which was increasingly

---

* Luce says he came up with the idea on his own and never cleared it with Perot before talking to Johnson; that issue later became critical in a lawsuit. Executives familiar with the relationship between Perot and Luce believe it is impossible that Luce would ever have broached such an important matter without getting marching orders from Perot. "It's just not the way the relationship with that law firm worked," says Ken Riedlinger. "Luce would never have risked that. It is unimaginable."

personal in tone. Saying, "I'm looking for results—I'm not looking for love," he told the magazine, "I'd get rid of the fourteenth floor [the executive suite]. I'd get rid of the executive dining rooms. I would urge the senior executives to locate their offices where real people are doing real work."[64]

Smith was frustrated that Perot had successfully cast himself in the press coverage as a corporate reformer trying to overthrow an imperial GM hierarchy that had surrounded itself with the trappings of great wealth while forgetting about its core business. "Ross has an office that makes mine look like a shantytown," a perturbed Smith later told *The Detroit Free Press*. "He has Remingtons; he has a Gilbert Stuart painting hanging on the wall. Nobody runs around saying, 'Get rid of Ross's office.'" "They went nuts when I criticized their chauffeurs and executive dining rooms," countered Perot. "That was like criticizing the flag and motherhood to them."[65]

The normally taciturn Smith also tried more substantive criticisms, telling reporters that "Ross doesn't have a very deep knowledge of the industry. With fifteen thousand parts and regulations on everything, it's a complicated business. You can't just skim across this pond. Look at reorganization and Saturn. We did those things long before we knew how to spell Ross Perot."[66] But Smith was colorless in the press game, with Perot staying far out ahead with his folksy barbs. "The first EDSer to see a snake kills it," Perot told one reporter. "At GM, first thing you do is organize a committee on snakes. Then you bring in a consultant who knows a lot about snakes . . . then you talk about it for a year."[67]

On November 11, Luce brought Perot a draft of a buyout agreement he had negotiated with Elmer Johnson. There was a blank space where the price was supposed to be listed. "Tom, these guys are indulging in games," Perot said. "I'm not going to talk about this without a price."[68] GM did not want to give a price unless Perot agreed to refrain from further criticism of Smith and GM, would not compete with EDS in the computer business for five years, and would agree to place the money GM paid for his stock in escrow for a specific period of time, in order to ensure that Perot would stay silent about the real reasons for his departure. Perot rejected it. He knew, from his days of watching his father trade horses in Texarkana, that the person who needs the sale the most will eventually pay the price.*

Luce and Johnson returned to negotiations. Senior EDS executives who had worked closely with Perot over the years did not know about the talks. "We were all working our tails off figuring out the best way to deal with GM," says one of Perot's top officers, "while Ross had Luce up there negotiating his way out. At best it is disingenuous. At worst, it's deceptive. How could he do that? It was so devious."

But Perot saw nothing wrong with secretly proceeding with the talks. "I just kept making obscene demands and they kept agreeing to them," recalled Perot.[69] Luce and Johnson quickly had an outline for a new deal. Perot would retain the title of "founder" of EDS, and initially would be allowed to keep his office at the company's headquarters in Dallas. He could not compete with EDS or hire anyone from it for at least eighteen months, and then only for nonprofit work (Perot erroneously thought that many of EDS's top executives would come back to him after the eighteen-month restriction passed). After thirty-six months, Perot could return to the computer services business without any restrictions ("I can't believe they [GM] could have been so dumb as to write the contract that way," Perot later said).[70] Both sides agreed, under a possible penalty of $7.5 million, to refrain from publicly criticizing each other. However, if any shareholders filed suit over the agreement, GM agreed to defend Perot and indemnify him against any adverse judgments (dozens of suits were eventually

---

* Although Perot seemed calm and confident to his GM counterparts during the negotiations, his own employees noticed that his temper seemed more volatile. One flare-up took place in November 1986 at the opening of the first of four data centers in the Washington, D.C., area. Many on the GM board, the Virginia governor, and a number of local politicians came to the opening ceremonies. Just before the reception started, Perot called over Paul Chiapparone (one of the two EDS executives jailed in Iran) and the head of EDS's Government Services Group. In a voice loud enough to be overheard by several bystanders, Perot said, "What's that? What's that!?" He was frantically pointing to cubes of sugar in small bowls on the tables. "Well, they are cubes of sugar," Chiapparone told him. "Well, where the hell are the bags?" Perot yelled. "How stupid can you be?" "I was nearby," recalled another executive, "and you could not believe how Ross lost it and chewed out Paul. He was shaking with anger. He used to try and avoid anything like that in public. We all looked at each other. He was losing it."

filed by disgruntled shareholders). Perot was banned from launching a hostile takeover bid for GM for five years ("I was happy to do that since I had no interest in taking over General Motors," said Perot).[71] Most important, GM agreed to pay Perot $61.90 per share for his class E stock, then trading at $33. Perot demanded that three close associates be afforded the same buyout—Mort Meyerson, Bill Gayden, and Tom Walter. GM agreed. The terms meant that Perot, who had received $930 million in cash for selling EDS to GM just two years earlier, would receive another $742.8 million to leave. Even Perot thought the deal was so generous that the GM board would reject it. "I really thought the board would tell Roger he was out of his mind," Perot later commented. "It was the dumbest deal I ever heard of. I found in the negotiations that they'd agree to anything on the business side no matter how ridiculous."[72] "I must admit," says Felix Rohatyn, whose investment firm, Lazard Frères, had been hired to advise Perot, "GM gave us terms that were very hard to turn down. When you negotiate with someone who gives you everything you ask for, after a while it carries on a dimension of its own."[73]

Perot was right in that there was dissension on the GM board when its members were canvassed by Roger Smith about the buyout. At a meeting at the Regency Hotel in New York on November 30, nine directors and the special committee on EDS debated the buyout for five hours. Some, like former GM board member Murph Goldberger, thought Perot's antics were outrageous precisely so he could force GM into such a buyout. They viewed his actions as simple "greenmail" and instead suggested firing him. One director, John Connor, advised that the GM board wait for Perot to "self-destruct." But the majority backed the buyout, agreeing that even with its generous terms, it was essential to remove an irritant as large as Perot.*

The board was encouraged by information that showed that if GM could free itself of Perot, the original concept behind the alliance could thrive. GM managers were reporting that the EDS

---

* "I talked to some General Motors people," Caspar Weinberger told me, "and when they paid $750 million to get him out of the room, quite a few of them believed it was quite a bargain."

arrogance of the early days had largely disappeared. Moreover, performance had improved as EDS and GM got used to each other. EDS had engineered new techniques that were saving GM almost $200 million a year in its health care costs by the fall of 1986. A massive EDS installation of a half-billion-dollar telecommunications network was proceeding on schedule and budget.

The buyout agreement was a closely guarded secret, even within EDS and GM. Les Alberthal did not find out about it—or that he would be the new chairman of EDS—until November 25, when he returned from a business trip to London. He had an urgent message waiting from Mort Meyerson. When he called, Meyerson told him, " 'I think we have an agreement whereby Ross, myself, Tom Walter, and Bill Gayden are going to leave, and you need to call Don Atwood [GM's vice-chairman]. . . . He's going to talk to you about stepping in and running EDS."[74] On November 30, the EDS officers met with Luce, who explained the agreement. No copies of the agreement were made available for review (EDS general counsel Claude Chappelear thumbed through Luce's copy while Luce gave his presentation).[75] Perot dropped in to tell them, "Good luck, Godspeed. If you have any questions, I would be glad to help you."[76] "It was everyone's impression, mine included," Les Alberthal later testified, "that the deal had been done. Ross had sold out. There was a tremendous amount of emotion around that. There was a lot of discussion that was interpreted by the other officers as being Ross's attempt for the officers to make the decision to clear his conscience."[77] Although Perot wanted the senior EDS executives to approve the buyout, he did not want them concentrating too carefully on the inflated buyout figures for him and the three employees he had decided to take with him. For instance, Gary Fernandes was in London when Luce sent him the consent form to sign as an EDS director, but without a copy of the agreement. Fernandes called Luce. "I was not inclined to sign the deal," he later said. Perot called "very shortly. . . . It was basically a one-way conversation," recalled Fernandes, "for Ross to point out the positive things about the contract. . . . Sometimes with Ross you don't get much of an opportunity for a response."[78] Perot said to Fernandes, "Don't you trust me? I am the fiduciary for all the shareholders." Fernandes relented. Alberthal, who as president acted on behalf of EDS, did not see a copy of the agreement until he signed it at Tom Luce's office, on a Sunday afternoon.[79]

On Monday, December 1, 1986, the GM board formally approved the buyout. In Dallas, Perot was pacing back and forth in his office. He called in Bill Wright, his head of public relations.

"What are the troops saying?" Perot asked.

"They say you are a cut-and-run artist," a grim-faced Wright said.

"They don't understand."

"Well, then, you should explain it to them," Wright answered.

"They don't understand, it should never have gone this far. I'll tell you what I am going to do. I will escrow the money. That's what I will do."

Merv Stauffer then walked in. Perot asked him the same question about what the troops were thinking. Stauffer was noncommittal. Perot then called in Tom Luce, who said, "We are close to signing—let's do it."

"I am going to sign it but escrow the money," Perot told him. Luce, who was near Perot's desk, turned ashen and, according to others who saw him within minutes of the encounter, was "slack-jawed."

"You can't do that, Ross," Luce told him. "I gave my word and you gave yours."

"Well, that's what I am going to do."

"What are you going to do about the stockholders?" asked Wright.

"I am going to pound them and see if they rise up."

According to two of the executives waiting to see Perot, Luce left the meeting and went to the seventh-floor bathroom, where he became ill.

Another executive came into the office. "Ross was like a wild man," says one who was there, "running around his desk, flailing his arms. In twenty years, I had never seen him like that."

Perot turned to his colleagues. "He [Luce] did everything I wanted. Every time I sent him back and told him to ask for more, the crazy bastards gave in, and now I have to sign it."

"Would you rather take over GM?" asked Wright.

"Hell, no, the auto business is in the tank."

When Elmer Johnson called Luce at mid-morning and asked whether Perot was ready to sign, Luce said, "Elmer, Ross wants the [GM] board to approve it and Roger to sign it before he puts his name on it. I think he needs a little more time."

"Nothing doing," Johnson replied. "I'm not presenting this to the board on a hypothetical basis. Either he signs the papers now or nothing is going to happen."[80] Within half an hour, Johnson called to determine whether Perot had signed the agreement. He had not. Perot told Luce that he was still convinced that one of the GM directors would realize the buyout was "ludicrous" and would stop it. But within a few minutes Johnson called again, this time to report that the GM board had approved the agreement and that Smith had signed it. "You're kidding," Perot said to Luce. He finally signed.[81]

Three quarters of a billion dollars was wired from a GM bank account in New York to Perot's Dallas account. Vague and conciliatory press releases, prepared by GM, were simultaneously issued for both Perot and Smith. Except for the top executives at EDS, the final announcement shocked the workforce. Many had heard the rumors but could not believe that the man who had founded EDS, and whose personality was so closely identified with it, would accept any amount of money to walk away. "The spiritual leader of the company had, in the eyes of the employees, sold out and walked out," said Les Alberthal.[82] Some had been personally assured by Perot that he would not leave. "On an airplane returning from a trip, I had asked him directly if he was going to sell out," recalls one executive. " 'It's a Chinese fire drill,' he told me. 'Just a lot of people running around. No, I'm not selling.' "

Before the day was over, Perot went downstairs at the EDS headquarters and met a group of reporters. He handed out the following press release:

At a time when General Motors is:

—closing 11 plants,
—putting over 30,000 people out of work,

—cutting back on capital expenditures,
—losing market share,
—and having problems with profitability,

I have just received $700 million from General Motors, in exchange for my Class E stock and notes. I cannot accept this money without giving the GM directors another chance to consider this decision. This money will be held in escrow until December 15, in order to give the GM directors time to review this matter and the events that led to this decision.*

If the GM directors conclude that this transaction of December 1 isn't in the best interests of GM and Class E shareholders, I will work with the GM directors to rescinding the transaction.[83]

"I've alerted the stockholders," Perot later said, "that if they accept this, then they deserve what they get."[84] The first reaction of GM directors and lawyers who had worked on the buyout of Perot, upon hearing of his press statement, was disbelief. Smith was enraged and called Elmer Johnson out of a meeting, demanding to know, "What the hell is going on?"[85] Ira Millstein, a senior partner at GM's primary New York law firm, Weil, Gotshal and Manges, called Luce to demand an explanation but was told he had gone home for the day and could not be reached. When Luce, who was paid $2 million by Perot after the buyout, spoke to Elmer Johnson, he swore he did not know what Perot planned to do.[86] Alberthal, who had seen Luce before he left, recalled that "he was white. He was very, very upset because it made a blow to his integrity."[87] Johnson sarcastically remarked, "The first time I knew Ross had a conscience was three minutes after he got the money."[88]

To add to the rancor, Perot held a press conference later in the day. When asked if GM was paying him all the money just to get rid of him, Perot quipped, "I would hope not. My philosophy

---

* In 1988, in testimony in a lawsuit, Perot explicitly stated that he placed the money in escrow for at least two weeks. Yet those familiar with the transaction say that Perot never placed the money in escrow, and that an escrow account did not even exist. "I was never so flabbergasted as when I saw Ross say, on a witness stand, that he had escrowed the money. It's just not true," says a former colleague.

is 'To know me is to love me.' " Perot called the deal "morally wrong" and dubbed the payment "hush-mail," saying that GM had paid him to be quiet because they did not like his criticisms. "Don't ask any questions that will cost me too much money," Perot smirked, but he added that if GM tried to enforce the $7.5 million penalty clause, he would happily "write them a check." Although some reporters seemed incredulous, Perot was adamant that he had agreed to the buyout not for the money, but just because it was the only way to get the buyout into the public arena.[89] In his scenario, the uproar over the buyout would force GM shareholders to throw Smith out as chairman. What he failed to mention to the press was that it was Luce who had first approached GM about a buyout. Perot instead cast himself as someone unwilling, but virtually forced, to accept the GM offer. "It seems incomprehensible that they want to spend this much money here," Perot said. "Seven hundred million would buy a brand-spanking-new car plant."[90] To the consternation of the GM directors, Perot's attack on the buy-out as a lousy and unwarranted investment only encouraged the filing of shareholder suits, all of which GM had to pay for under the terms of the agreement. "I have to live with myself," Perot said. "Why should I take this money? It would be morally wrong. I don't need it."[91] (Yet the day the deal closed, when GM was fifteen minutes late in transferring the $742 million from New York because of a computer glitch with the bank, Perot had Tom Luce on the phone demanding to know where the funds were.)[92]

An additional irritant to the GM executives who later saw Perot's widely reported comments was his emphasis on the part of the agreement allowing him to start another firm after eighteen months. Smith and the GM directors were infuriated, since Perot was essentially telling his employees to wait eighteen months until their stocks vested and reminding them they could then leave to join a future Perot company.

By the end of the first day the agreement was public, the GM board, responding to Perot's suggestion that it reconsider its action, voted unanimously to confirm the agreement and sever its ties to Perot.

Within days, Perot accelerated his attacks on GM. To *Newsweek* he claimed that GM's decision to award year-end bonuses was "exactly as though the generals at Valley Forge in our revolution had decided to go out and buy new uniforms for themselves when the troops were fighting in the snow barefooted." To ABC he said, "I just don't want to be part of an organization that's closing plants [and] laying people off."[93] GM briefly thought of trying to enforce the $7.5 million penalty clause against him, but quickly decided it would only bring more attention to the still-festering event. Soon Perot suggested that without his leadership, EDS would not flourish. Investment analysts shared the same fear. But instead, without the friction caused by the Smith-Perot battle, it thrived.*

As the year drew to a close, Perot and Smith had one more encounter, before the Economic Club of Detroit. Perot had accepted an invitation, several months earlier, to give a speech, and Smith had agreed to introduce Perot. The night before his appearance, Smith discussed putting some one-line jabs at Perot into his introduction but decided not to, since he did not "want to provoke him."[94] Instead, Smith was cordial, while Perot kept his speech, and subsequent television and radio interviews, focused on a theme of the general malaise of U.S. industry and how it could better compete in foreign markets. He also reinforced the notion that GM had thrown $700 million "at a guy who didn't want it."[95]

---

* When Perot left in 1986, EDS had $4 billion a year in revenues. By 1995, Alberthal had increased its income to over $10 billion. Profits have set records for nine consecutive years. EDS's reliance upon government business, and its GM work, has dropped steadily each year. The workforce has doubled from 40,000 at Perot's departure to over 80,000 today. GM class E stock was worth $22 billion in 1995, compared to the $2.5 billion GM paid for it in 1984. "EDS's success has been like a knife in Perot's heart," says one of the executives who stayed with the firm. "He really thought we would fold up without him. The fact that we did better than ever after he left must tell him something. Ross had gotten to the point where making everything into a confrontation was a detriment." What irritates EDS executives is that the company is still referred to as "Ross Perot's former company" at a time when they believe their stellar performance should have ended any association of his name with the firm. In June 1996, EDS was once again an independent company.

In the question-and-answer period that followed Perot's talk, someone asked him if he would consider running for president, with Lee Iacocca of Chrysler as his running mate. "Boy, they think they have controversy now. Between the two of us, that'd be one way to get President Reagan off the front page. We'd stir up more trouble than we could ever solve. Poor old Sam Donaldson would probably spin out and turn into ashes in thirty seconds." Even Roger Smith allowed his first smile of the day at the mention of Perot running for president.

THIRTEEN

□

Missing in
Action

When Perot left GM near the end of 1986—barred from establishing his own business for eighteen months—he again became involved in one of his favorite public-policy issues: questions over the fate of POWs and MIAs.

During a trip to Southeast Asia in April 1970, Perot has said, he was given an intelligence briefing at the U.S. embassy in Laos by the CIA station chief, Larry Devlin.* He was shown a large wall map that pinpointed where American planes had been shot down and was told the CIA had the capability to track POWs in Laos. Tom Meurer, Perot's assistant, remembered Devlin saying that the CIA had located twenty-seven men in caves northeast of Vientiane.[1][†] Perot became convinced there were American prisoners held in Southeast Asia, particularly in Laos, who were not officially accounted for on U.S. government lists.

---

* When Perot testified before the Senate Select Committee on POW/MIA Affairs in 1992, Frances Zwenig, one of the committee aides, says that she asked him not to disclose the name of the CIA agent in his public testimony, since the committee had gone to pains to keep it classified. "He did not answer me, but he clearly understood the point," she recounts. "Then he went before the committee and named Devlin in the first couple of minutes." Perot has "absolutely no recollection" of Zwenig's request. Moreover, he says that Devlin was sitting in the row behind him, and most people at the hearing knew who he was.

† Devlin, under oath to congressional investigators in 1992, said, "I don't recall having ever met with him [Perot] personally." The American ambassador at the time, G. McMurtie Godley, also under oath, said, "I don't recall Mr. Perot

When the war ended in 1973, North Vietnam released 591 men, fewer than had been expected. Ten of the returned prisoners had been captured in Laos but had subsequently been transferred to North Vietnam. No prisoners came out of Laos at the end of the war. The Communist Pathet Lao were not formal signatories to the peace agreement between the United States and Vietnam, which mandated a release of prisoners. Perot was suspicious because a Pathet Lao representative had told him on one of his trips that there was a list of captured Americans. He was also incensed by the American government's own contradictory actions and statements. In late March 1973, the Defense Department secretly considered air strikes to force the release of any remaining prisoners. But two weeks later, the official position was that "there were probably no more live Americans loose anywhere in Indochina."[2] Indeed, Richard Nixon had said that "all our American POWs are on the way home." Yet the Pentagon, two months after the homecoming, listed 1,303 Americans who did not return.*

Perot believed that the government had abandoned any American survivors in Southeast Asia, although initially he thought domestic scandal had distracted officials from the core issue. "We left the POWs because of Watergate," he says.[3] Later, he thought more nefarious and callous motives prompted some officials to deny the existence of POWs and, in his opinion, cover up the truth. "So those are the patterns," he told me. "The thing that bothers me is the principle that you don't send men into combat and leave them. . . . If there is only one [alive], the principle remains the same, and if he dies when the plane lands in the

---

ever visiting the embassy." Godley did not remember a map like the one Perot described. "A map like that [is] worthless. . . . The idea of tracking POWs is . . . [a] pure figment of imagination . . . it's a lot of bullshit," said Godley. However, a review of the statements from witnesses shows that Perot and his associates did meet at the U.S. embassy and were briefed, probably by Devlin.

* By 1980, the MIA number had increased to 2,500, as those previously listed as Killed in Action/Body Not Recovered were added to the count. Government officials persistently scoffed at the idea that U.S. servicemen might still be alive in Southeast Asia. It was not until 1992, before a Senate Select Committee, that three Reagan administration officials admitted that it was possible that 130 to 135 prisoners were still alive when U.S. forces withdrew in 1973, but that it was almost certain they had not survived the intervening years.

United States, the principle remains the same—we have an obligation to bring them home."[4]

Perot's certainty that live Americans were still in Southeast Asia
fueled his actions over the years. "Perot's basic conversation with
me," recalls Ann Mills Griffiths, the executive director of the
National League of Families, a grass-roots organization aimed at
drawing attention to the POW issue, "was: 'I don't care about
bones [the forensic identification of remains to resolve some MIA
cases]. You can take care of that. I only care about live prisoners.'
Ross never grasped that the two issues are symbiotic and sup-
portive of each other. If you get remains of a guy you thought was
alive, you have impacted directly on the live prisoner issue and
count. Ross never got that."[5] "Dead men tell no tales," Perot
quipped to one reporter.[6] "Without live prisoners, he would probably lose interest," admits Richard Childress, a former army lieutenant colonel who was on the National Security Council (NSC)
under Ronald Reagan.[7]

On his own, Perot had tried to determine whether any POWs
were alive or not. His search officially started in 1973, in the middle of the du Pont crisis for EDS, when Perot sent Bull Simons and
Tom Meurer to Laos to see whether they could find a trace of anyone alive. "We paid four people," recalls Meurer, "including Vang
Pao, a Meo general [who was also on the CIA payroll], and some
of his hunters; a Miss Hanoi, who ran a brothel in Vientiane, who
was running dope and was an old friend of Bull; and we had a
doctor in Vientiane who was doing a lot of work with high-
ranking Lao officials; and a Eurasian who knew Bull from 1962."
Simons and Meurer financed a small team to trek into the Thai
and Laotian panhandle, wander among the indigenous tribes, and
seek news of captured Americans. After two months in the jungle
terrain, the team reported back. "It turned out that by 1972, the
North Vietnamese had put such a priority on capturing POWs,"
says Meurer, "that the pressure was too much for the local people.
So if somebody was shot down and survived the fall through the
jungle canopy, then they had to get to water. And a villager would
see you, since there are only so many trails in there. Then you
were picked up and executed."[8] Simons and Meurer reported their
findings to Perot.

"He said to me, 'Look, I've sent my expert Bull Simons, and no one's alive.' " says Ann Mills Griffiths. "And he basically disappeared from the POW issue for the next five to seven years."[9] But in early 1979, after the rescue of his two executives from Iran, Perot was deluged by soldiers of fortune and scam artists seeking his money, usually to buy purported evidence of living prisoners or to finance expeditions to Southeast Asia to search for MIAs. A few who beat their way to Perot's door were individuals of questionable credibility, spinning complex tales of drug-running, CIA assassination plots, and elaborate cover-ups. Some of these stories must have intrigued Perot, because instead of throwing these people out of his office, he listened, and over several years became the fiscal source of last appeal for a fringe element of the POW/MIA affair.

"People kept calling Ross, I know that," says Ann Mills Griffiths. " 'Ross, we know there are prisoners alive,' they would tell him. People off-the-wall would go to him with that because they knew he was interested in live prisoners. Every nutcase, everybody claiming to have information, all found their way to him."[10]*

A couple of months after the Iran rescue, General Eugene Tighe, director of the Defense Intelligence Agency, asked Perot to finance a private effort to determine whether any U.S. prisoners were alive.[11] In April, at Tighe's recommendation, Perot summoned "Bo" Gritz, an ex–Green Beret turned soldier of fortune. Gritz, now a right-wing survivalist who conducts paramilitary training sessions at his Idaho compound, arrived at Perot's office, where he joined Bull Simons (Simons, who was supposed to plan the operation, died the following month, prompting Perot to tell Gritz he "was the only one left"). "He [Perot] instructed me accordingly," Gritz testified in a Senate investigation into the POW/MIA issue. " 'I want you to go over there and see everybody you have to see, do all the things you need to do. You come back and tell me there aren't any American prisoners left alive. I don't believe it. And I'm not interested in bones. I am going to plan this operation and you're going to execute it.' "[12] Perot's support for

---

* Griffiths, who has worked with Perot on the POW/MIA issue for almost twenty years, says Perot is a "tremendous patriot who is unfortunately about as self-centered as can be. He doesn't care about the fundamental principles."

Gritz, however, was evidently more moral than financial. He and Gritz have recently said the only payment was a return plane ticket.*

But others working on the POW issue believed, at the time, that Perot had financed Gritz. When Gritz visited Ann Mills Griffiths at the National League of Families, he boasted of his newfound backing from Perot. "Gritz had people with him sweeping the office to make sure we weren't bugged, and speaking buzzwords and in code," says Griffiths. "To the vulnerable people we were at that time, and to the uninformed populace, Gritz can be very persuasive."[13]

As opposed to the 1973 Simons/Meurer expedition, which concluded that no live prisoners were likely left in Southeast Asia, Gritz's team returned convinced that POWs were detained by the North Vietnamese. He even suggested that a refugee who claimed to have seen forty-nine POWs in a camp north of Hanoi be made "available for interrogation by electronic and chemical means."[14] Perot agreed and telephoned General Tighe, trying to get the refugee brought to Dallas for questioning. When Secretary of State Cyrus Vance finally rejected the idea, Gritz testified that Perot told him to return to Asia to get "more convincing evidence."[15] Gritz again led patrols into Laos, and claimed that one of his units came across thirty U.S. POWs at Nhommarath, Laos. Without any supporting evidence, few believed Gritz.

By 1981, Gritz had a new plan under development, Operation Grand Eagle, in which he wanted to send small covert teams to Laos to film the supposed POWs. Perot dangled the possibility that he would provide as much money as necessary to bring out a live prisoner, but would not risk any funds until Gritz was certain of his proof. "Perot was always willing to pay the ransom," said

---

* In 1981, EDS spokesman Bill Wright said that Perot had given Gritz a "minor amount" of money to cover his expenses in going to Laos. In 1990, apparently at Perot's request, Gritz swore in an affidavit that Perot only paid for his plane fare home. But Perot has flip-flopped over the question of financing covert missions to Southeast Asia. In 1985, *The Detroit Free Press* reported he had paid for twenty "secret" forays to free POWs, none of them successful. In 1986, he told the *Chicago Tribune* that he had financed an elaborate private spy network that bribed Communist officials for information about POWs. Several years later, the ever changeable Perot told another reporter that he had never financed any such projects, as he still insists today.

Gritz, "but only after we had our arms around them and he had them."[16] Part of Gritz's four-man unit assembled in October 1981. The squad did go to Thailand, and again into Laos, but did not uncover any evidence of live prisoners.

By this time Gritz's credibility had been challenged. After one of his expeditions, Gritz, with great fanfare, produced bones he claimed were those of some MIAs. They turned out to be chicken bones ("I know a chicken bone," Gritz argued in his defense once he was unmasked. "I eat a lot of Kentucky Fried Chicken. . . . I am certainly not qualified to make serious judgment calls on identification, but I can distinguish between bird and human bones.")[17] On another trip, he videotaped Burmese opium warlord Kuhn Sa and his assistants spinning an incredible tale of how U.S. intelligence agents and government officials were involved in the drug trade to the exclusion of searching for POWs. Part of it involved an Australian bank, the Nugan Hand, that supposedly laundered the CIA's worldwide drug profits and had defrauded investors out of millions of dollars. Michael Hand, an ex–Special Forces soldier and one of the bank's partners, had disappeared with some of the firm's money; his partner, Francis Nugan, was shot to death. Several ex–CIA contract operatives who had worked for Air America were on the payroll.

One of Kuhn Sa's aides identified Richard Armitage, an assistant secretary of defense responsible for overseeing the POW/MIA issue, as one of the people who handled the drug money for the Nugan Hand bank. The allegations on the videotape could have easily been proven false with a little checking. For instance, there were charges that Armitage, a decorated naval veteran of four tours of duty in Vietnam, was a prominent narcotics trafficker while stationed at the U.S. embassy in Bangkok from 1975 to 1979 and that, prior to the fall of Saigon, he had been in an illegal partnership with CIA agent Ted Shackley. In fact, Armitage had never been assigned to the U.S. embassy in Bangkok and had not lived there during those years. Instead, he was stationed in Washington, and for half that period was an administrative aide to Senator Bob Dole. He never even met Ted Shackley during that time.

Yet, back in the States, Gritz showed the videotape to Perot, who did not know that the sensational charges were false. Nor did he know that Gritz had personal reasons for tarnishing Armitage's reputation. It was Armitage who exposed Gritz's "MIA remains" as chicken bones, and who also stopped him from selling a ring that Gritz claimed to have recovered in Laos to an MIA family. To Perot, the Gritz tales called for further investigation. It was possible, he thought, that the reason American intelligence was not looking for POWs was because it was involved in the narcotics trade in Southeast Asia.

Perot's renewed interest in POWs and MIAs was also fueled by Bobby Garwood, a marine private captured by the North Vietnamese in 1965 and finally released in 1979. Upon his arrival in Bangkok, instead of being treated as a hero, Garwood was arrested and charged with aiding and abetting the enemy. (Perot was so intrigued at what Garwood might say about his captivity that he offered to the Defense Intelligence Agency to have his EDS secretaries transcribe the government's interrogations of Garwood.)[18] A court-martial found Garwood guilty. Speaking with an unusual Vietnamese accent that he acquired in captivity, he received tremendous press coverage, often telling contradictory stories. In a 1984 article in *The Wall Street Journal,* for the first time he said he had seen other Americans in Vietnam while he was imprisoned.

Garwood's story was the eyewitness account for which Perot had been waiting. He telephoned Robert "Bud" McFarlane, then Reagan's national security adviser. "You've got to get our guys out of there," Perot urged him, saying that he considered the Garwood article proof that MIAs were alive. "Put an offer on the table. If they say no, double it, and if they say no, double it again. Soon, they will say yes. I will take some of the returning prisoners with me and sort out the deserters on the ground." On another call, he reached the National Security Council's Richard Childress. He told Childress that "he thought monetary incentives or ransom would be responded to by the Vietnamese." His offer was $1 million for each POW returned.[19]*

* Childress later gave Perot a one-on-one briefing at the Pentagon about U.S. policy on POW/MIA negotiations. Perot has denied meeting Childress or ever talking to him about ransoming the hostages: "If I have met him, it was just to shake hands." "He may not remember the calls or briefing," says Childress, "but he was the first billionaire I ever dealt with, so it was pretty memorable for me."

Some activists now wanted Perot to head a commission to investigate the MIA issue. On Capitol Hill, Perot had found a soulmate in a Republican congressman from North Carolina, Bill Hendon, who believed there was a widespread government conspiracy to cover up the truth about the prisoners. Hendon, despite six previous government inquiries that had concluded there was no evidence of live prisoners, proposed that Congress authorize the "Perot Commission on Americans Missing in Southeast Asia."

Perot was disdainful of commissions.* He called Childress at the National Security Council. "He wanted me to know, and to tell other people, that the commission was not his idea," says Childress. "He wanted the White House to know he really wasn't interested."[20] Perot told a reporter that he would be willing to head the commission only "if both houses [of Congress] want me to do it, the president wants me to do it, and there's no controversy surrounding it."[21] "It was never anything I initiated, sought out, or had an interest in," said Perot.[22] A congressional committee voted down the Perot commission.

In May 1986, General Leonard Peroots, the new director of the Defense Intelligence Agency (DIA), asked Perot to join a POW/MIA task force headed by former DIA director General Eugene Tighe. Peroots knew of Perot's suspicions about POWs and thought he would provide balance to the committee.[23] "I said no," Perot recalls, "because we know we left men behind, you are not going to do anything about it, so it is a waste of everybody's time."[24] Instead, Perot suggested ex-POW and war hero General Robinson Risner as his replacement.[25] Peroots agreed to take Risner, who acted as Perot's proxy. Privately, Perot grumbled to sympathetic journalists that he feared that no matter what the Tighe commission did, a conspiracy of silence in the press would muzzle the results.[26]

At the same time Perot turned down the Tighe commission, he heard from fellow Texan George Bush. "Bush came to me," recalls

---

* Perot was already on the president's Foreign Intelligence Advisory Board, a general policy group that was supposed to give advice on intelligence issues. It did not deal specifically with POW/MIA issues. When he resigned from the policy board in 1984, he told another board member, "All you people do is talk, talk, talk and write reports no one reads."

Perot, "and said, 'To give all this credibility, you've got to get involved.' I said, 'Only if President Reagan asks me to.' "[27] Bush suggested that Perot speak to the president directly. Perot approached Reagan at a social reception and briefly told him of his continuing interest in the POW issue. Reagan thanked him for his efforts and said he always appreciated Perot's help.

"Do I have your promise that if I bring hard evidence to you, you will follow up?" Perot asked Reagan.

"Yes," the president told him.[28]

Perot took that answer as a mandate. By the autumn of 1986, he told *The Dallas Morning News* that "the president and the vice-president asked me to dig into this issue—go all the way to the bottom of it and figure out what the situation was—then come see them and give them my recommendations."

"I did not have the impression from my conversations with President Reagan that there was such an assignment," said national security adviser Frank Carlucci. "So if there was such an 'assignment,' it would have been as a result of Ross Perot's inter- pretation of a casual conversation."[29] "Ross got it into his head that Reagan had asked him to find out if there were any MIAs," says James Cannon, a Perot friend who also happened to be the deputy chief of staff to Senator Howard Baker, White House chief of staff. "I have had years in the White House, and people that talk to the president imagine they hear what they want to hear."[30] "Reagan was especially vulnerable to that type of approach," agrees Boyden Gray, the White House counsel. "Any president in a receiving line is going to be as nice as possible. It is just crazy for any person to think they are going to be deputized on the basis of a receiving line, without anyone there to record what was said."[31] Perot bristles at the idea that the conversation was only a passing exchange at a social reception. "President Reagan, face- to-face, asked me to," he insists.[32]

In any case, not long after his conversation with Reagan, Perot heard from the administration. This time it involved two ex– Green Berets, Major Mark Smith (known as Zippo for having ordered a napalm attack on his own position) and Sergeant Melvin McIntire, who said they had seen a 240-minute video- tape showing thirty-nine POWs linked together with slave collars, digging for gold in a mine somewhere in Southeast Asia. The two ex-soldiers had traveled to Beirut and Singapore to meet a British con man, Robin Gregson (alias John Obassy), who showed them the only copy of the tape and was willing to sell it for $4.2 million. George Bush had learned of the tape and telephoned Perot to see whether he might help. "I was asked by our government to pursue this thing, to get the tape if it existed," said Perot, "and I said, Fine, it's a long shot, but I'll be glad to do it."[33] Meanwhile, Gregson, who had earlier convictions for fraud, was jailed in Singapore for defrauding an Indian businessman of $45,000. Perot paid for Mark Smith and his lawyer, Mark Waple, to travel there. Gregson said he could not arrange the deal to get the tape unless he got out of jail. Waple arranged for Perot to pay $45,000 to the Indian businessman, who dropped his complaint, thereby freeing Gregson.

"A few days later, he [Gregson] called and said, 'I am ready to come,' " recalls Perot. "He wanted me to buy him a plane ticket. And I said, 'No. For what I am paying you, you can buy your own plane ticket.' 'Well,' he said, 'it was worth a try.' "[34]

According to Perot, the U.S. government then bungled the operation. Gregson flew to Washington, where he evaded federal agents who tried to arrest him. He then called Perot and threatened to kill him, thinking Perot had set him up. "I convinced him I hadn't," says Perot. "He just disappeared. The last I heard he was in Beirut having knee surgery. Before that he had been to the West Coast to try to sell a movie to someone."

Gregson later said that he burned the tape, and accused U.S. authorities of covering up the truth about POWs. To most observers it looked as though the entire event had been nothing more than a scam, but Perot is still not certain whether or not the tape existed. "The fact that we have one American, a Special Forces major [Mark Smith] who says he has seen the tape," Perot persisted, "makes it more than just some bogus thing floating out there in Asia."[35]

Now Perot was more certain than ever that Americans were alive in Southeast Asia, and angry that "the government had botched it beyond belief."[36] He was also upset with Bush, saying the vice-president's office had reneged, in the middle of the incident, on a promise to reimburse him. General Leonard Peroots had called Perot to tell him of the change.

"We said we were going to reimburse you, but there has been a policy change, and we won't."

"Well, Lenny, who made that decision?" asked Perot.

"I don't know."

"Surely his mother thought enough of him to give him a name when he was a baby, so I want to know who it was. I want to talk to the vice-president."

"He is out of the country."

"Well, have him call me the minute he gets back."[37]

Bush did not call Perot. "So I had to call him," says Perot, "and he expressed surprise at the whole thing." Privately, Perot blamed Bush for either instituting the change of policy or not being strong enough to have fought against it.[38] Perot was so frustrated with his dealings with government officials that he now thought some of the them knew about live prisoners and did not care. Perot, in fact, told a reporter, "My biggest disappointment is that we never got all the prisoners back from Vietnam. I know there are still guys over there, but we need proof. These guys in Washington are sitting on their hands about the MIAs. We know they're there, they know they're there, everybody knows they're there."[39]

Several months later, in the fall of 1986, Bush decided that the way to quiet Perot's accusations was to give him access to classified DIA files on the POW/MIA issue. "Bush's people didn't want any more problems with Perot," says Childress. "They figured that any logical person would go into the files, see how much better this administration was investigating the subject than anyone ever had, and would quickly conclude there was no conspiracy."[40] General Peroots agreed. The DIA established a separate office for Perot to read reports on sightings and other sensitive material.[41] He again claimed that he only agreed to look at them because Bush "assured me that both he and the President" would take action if there were any evidence of live prisoners.[42]

Perot reviewed the files over several months. But now that he had access to the government's classified papers, he suddenly feared for his safety. He said that two CIA men had told him he could quietly disappear, and they had even mentioned his children as possible targets.[43] "If I'm killed, my will is written so that the bulk of the estate goes into the fight, the fight to get back our men, and the fight to expose what was done to keep them in Communist jails," he told Monika Jensen-Stevenson, an author who agreed with his views. "So my death won't benefit anyone."[44] He also became fearful that the FBI was investigating him. He called FBI director William Webster and told him, "Don't snoop behind my back." "Don't be paranoid," said Webster. "We're not running any investigation."[45] Perot thought Webster too decent to know about the secret investigation he was confident was being conducted against him. Later, he told a Senate panel that "they [probably the NSC] were tape-recording my conversations."[46] On one occasion, as Perot was returning to his Washington hotel after reviewing some of the POW/MIA files, he thought he noticed people watching him from a suite across from his. He immediately left the hotel by the emergency stairs and checked into another. After that incident, each day he would return to the first hotel, wait until what he was convinced was a surveillance team settled in across from him, and then surreptitiously slip out to the second hotel. Perot also tried to lose the surveillance by driving around Washington in a battered Volkswagen ("a perfect disguise," he once bragged).[47]

Soon after he began reviewing the files, he told a reporter off the record, "When you look into the prisoner cover-up, you find government officials in the drug trade who can't break themselves of the habit."[48] And even as he studied the government files, he also became receptive to the stories of conspiracy theorists. David Taylor, a BBC producer based in Washington, told Perot about Jim Badey, an Arlington, Virginia, detective who supposedly had denigrating information about assistant secretary of defense Richard Armitage.[49] Perot called Badey, a respected investigator on Asian organized crime, on a Sunday at his home. The two met, together with a reporter from Jack Anderson's column, Donald Goldberg, at Perot's suite at the Madison Hotel (in the 1992 campaign, Perot incorrectly claimed that Badey had approached him).[50]

Badey brought with him a one-inch-thick file. From that file, Perot learned that Armitage had, in 1984, written a character recommendation, on Pentagon stationery, for a Vietnamese woman,

Nguyet O'Rourke. She was a Washington, D.C., restaurant owner about to be sentenced for operating an illegal football pool. Armitage knew O'Rourke from his active duty days in Vietnam, where she had also run a restaurant. Perot thought the letter was proof that Armitage was naïve about his Vietnamese connections, or it might even indicate a link to the criminal world, since Badey suggested that O'Rourke was rumored to have ties to Asian gangs. Moreover, the file included three photographs that looked like an amateurish attempt to either embarrass or blackmail. Each showed the same naked Vietnamese woman, near a bed and dresser. On the dresser, in the center of each photograph, was a framed picture of Armitage, posing with the woman.

Perot told Badey and Goldberg that "I'm looking at this POW issue, and Armitage is in the way. He's evil."[51] He questioned the detective and reporter for five hours, taking notes. Before the meeting ended, Badey gave the file to Perot. Soon, Perot evidently felt the information needed a wider audience.

"We were sitting in his Dallas office for an interview," recalls journalist David Remnick, who did two extensive profiles on Perot in the late 1980s. "He began to talk with that frightening certitude that a conspiracy buff gets. He had lots of things to say about Oliver North, about how the Reagan administration was always trying to drag him in and that he was always the savior. Then he turned to a name I was only vaguely familiar with— Richard Armitage. Why he was talking about him I had no idea [Perot assured a reporter in 1992 that Remnick had raised Armitage's name].[52] He started in on how Armitage was all these terrible things, how he was involved with women. And then he walked into a small room off his office. He came out with several photographs. There was an Asian woman in a bleak room, and some picture in the background that Perot said was Armitage. He showed me this with great conspiratorial satisfaction—what struck me was not the content so much but the tone. He really thought he had something in those pictures."[53]

But Badey's investigation had been narrowly focused on a single question: Did the Vietnamese have any potential blackmail information on Armitage that might affect his duties in the Defense Department? Perot later claimed that he merely "gave it

[Badey's file] to the appropriate law enforcement authorities, walked away from it. Now, that is not chasing down information on someone."[54] But Perot did much more follow-up investigation than he has acknowledged.

One day, while watching television, Perot saw Daniel Sheehan, counsel to the radical left-wing Christic Institute and a believer in a gigantic conspiracy spanning several decades that involved, among other things, POWs. It centered around drug dealers, intelligence agents, and government leaders, in what Sheehan termed the "Secret Team." In Sheehan's convoluted theory, Armitage was only one of hundreds of insidious government conspirators in the cabal. Perot called Sheehan (Perot later incorrectly said that Sheehan had first approached him).[55] He told the Christic Institute's counsel, "I heard you've got all kinds of important information about some really bad actors. I've gotten wind of the same stuff, and we need to talk about it."[56] Sheehan was pleased that someone of Perot's stature was willing to listen to his accusations. He soon had an opportunity to make his case face-to-face with Perot. After Perot gave a lecture at the naval academy in the fall of 1986, he took Sheehan to Dallas in his private plane for a debriefing. Altogether, Sheehan and Perot spoke on six occasions about "how profits from drugs and arms financed covert wars in the name of American national security."[57]

Perot also listened to Scott Barnes, a soldier of fortune and inveterate storyteller who was part of Bo Gritz's first team to Southeast Asia. Again, as in the case of Arlington detective Jim Badey, it was the BBC's David Taylor who told Perot about Barnes.[58]*

Perot called Barnes shortly after Taylor's recommendation. Barnes told Perot that Armitage was not only intimately involved with the Australian-based Nugan Hand bank but also with the Hawaii-based investment firm of Bishop, Baldwin, Rewald,

---

* Taylor had met Barnes while investigating a story that partly involved allegations of drug smuggling by intelligence agencies. He considered Barnes reliable. Perot also had another reason to give Barnes some credibility. When he had asked General Eugene Tighe about Barnes, Tighe said he had spoken to Barnes, and that Barnes surprised him by describing, in detail, the "most secret briefing room of our embassy in Thailand." "What does that mean?" Perot asked Tighe. "That just means that he has been around something," replied Tighe.

Dillingham and Wong. Bishop, Baldwin's chairman, Ronald Rewald, unsuccessfully tried to defend himself against fraud charges by claiming his company was really a CIA front. (While there actually was a retired CIA agent on the payroll, the defense did not work, and Rewald is serving an eighty-year sentence for fraud.) Barnes told Perot that the CIA had assigned him to kill Rewald and that the government official who was a key player in this and other nefarious plots was none other than Richard Armitage.

Both Sheehan and Barnes had taken the original information that opium warlord Kuhn Sa and his aides gave Gritz and had expanded it into much more colorful and byzantine stories. Perot was so taken with the information from Sheehan and Barnes that he put in a call to William Casey at the CIA and requested the Agency's files about Nugan Hand, the Rewald case, and Jerrold Daniels.* Casey ignored Perot's call. Perot then wanted the Senate to take Barnes's testimony. Admiral Bobby Ray Inman, the CIA's former deputy director and a fellow Texan and friend of Perot, unofficially made his own inquiry at the intelligence agency. He concluded that Barnes's charges were worthless. When briefed by Inman, Perot refused to believe him, saying, "I knew they would keep you in the dark."[59]†

In October 1986, shortly after he started studying the government's classified files on POWs and MIAs, Perot went to hear General Tighe testify about the results of his task force study. Tighe appeared before the House Committee on Foreign Affairs

---

* One of Barnes's stories was that Jerrold Daniels was his partner on a supposed CIA mission to Laos, where he says the Agency ordered him to kill MIAs. Daniels later died in Thailand of carbon monoxide poisoning from a faulty gas water heater in his house. However, Barnes claimed that Daniels was murdered by the CIA. Perot was suspicious, and not certain that the corpse buried in Daniels's hometown of Missoula, Montana, was really him. He hired an investigator and even considered exhuming the body, but decided against it because Daniels's "mother [had already] gone through an awful lot."

† Barnes was gratified that Perot trusted him. During the 1992 presidential race, he told Sidney Blumenthal of *The New Republic* that he expected Perot to "clean out" the conspirators once he became president. "He will get tough on this top brass involved in dope dealing. Generals, admirals, assistant secretaries of defense, they don't want him in. . . . They better look out. Colin Powell would be history. It goes directly to Bush. We know that. . . . He did nothing to get the POWs home. There's a cover-up. The evidence is overwhelming."

(the so-called Solarz Committee, named after its chairman, Stephen Solarz [Democrat–New York]). Seeing Perot in the back of the hearing room, Solarz asked him to make an extemporaneous statement. Claiming that "I am not looking for this job," Perot told the committee that there was "overwhelming evidence" that Americans were held in Indochina against their will.[60] When Solarz asked Perot if he would provide the names of people who could help the committee on the issue, Perot refused but said his sources would be willing to testify if subpoenaed.[61] Solarz offered to subpoena them. "I would have to ask them," Perot countered. Solarz then offered him the chance of providing the names confidentially. Again, Perot declined.

While he was not ready to disclose his information about POWs to the Solarz Committee, he was not so reticent about talking about the data he collected on Armitage. In October 1986, he decided to take it directly to George Bush and demanded that Bush force Armitage from office. The vice-president told Perot he was certain that the allegations were wrong but that if Perot wanted to pursue them, he should take them to "the appropriate authorities."* (In a letter declining a formal interview, Bush told me he recalled "a vicious assault by Perot on Rich Armitage . . . hatred of Armitage is what came out.")[62] Perot also surprised Bush by raising the possibility that two of Bush's four sons might be involved in the Iran-contra scandal. Perot says an unsolicited Drug Enforcement Administration agent brought him the information.[63] The Christic Institute was another proponent of the theory that Bush's sons were connected to Iran-contra. "George, as one father to another," Perot told the vice-president, "a DEA agent told me this, and it is not my mission to be involved in this. I just want to let you know."[64]†

---

* Perot also had little success with Bush's staff. Marine Lieutenant Colonel Terry Mattke, a Bush aide, spent a month searching for evidence of the cover-up conspiracy Perot was certain existed. When he finally reported that there was nothing to support the theory, Perot "stood up and walked down the hall arguing with me and trying to intimidate me, saying, 'You're obviously not doing your job if you can't get better information than this.' " Poking Mattke in the chest, Perot told the surprised colonel that he was "part of the problem."

† In a handwritten addition to his 1986 Christmas note to Perot, Bush thanked Perot for the information and said his sons were "all straight arrows, uninvolved in intrigue." Perot and Bush interpreted that thank-you differently. To Perot, it

The stories about Armitage had gotten so bad (Jack Anderson did four scathing articles on Armitage) that he offered his resignation to Secretary of Defense Caspar Weinberger. Weinberger would not accept it. "Richard Armitage was one of the best people I ever had in the Defense Department," recalls Weinberger. "Perot spread as much poison, as much untrue poison, about Armitage as possible. It was absolutely despicable."[65] When Armitage called General Peroots, who had also heard Perot's allegations, he asked the DIA chief: "Why? Why is he [Perot] doing this to me?" "I don't know," a bewildered Peroots told him. "I just don't know."[66]

In late October, Armitage's secretary called him to say Perot was in the Pentagon on separate business. Armitage was determined to confront Perot personally and ask why he was attacking him. "It wasn't right that he was making these charges without talking to me," says Armitage. "He has been saying a lot of terrible things about me behind my back, and I thought he should have the decency to say them to my face."[67] At Armitage's request, Perot agreed to see him.* They met, together with a military assistant to Armitage, in a small bare-walled office dominated by a single mahogany desk.

"You're saying all these things about me," Armitage remembers telling Perot. "I'm no saint, and I've done some things with women in the past, but I've resolved all of that with my wife. But these charges of crimes is outrageous. It's not true in any way."

Initially, Perot didn't answer. Then he quietly said, "Some people think you are dirty."

"I am not resigning."

"I think you're compromised," Perot told him.

---

was proof that the allegations were substantive and taken seriously by Bush. But Bush, in a response to the author's written questions, said the "mention of my sons involved in running arms to the Contras [was] a totally false and malicious allegation." He says that he only thanked Perot since he was grateful to Perot "for tipping me off to such slander."

* Armitage was startled in 1992, during the presidential race, when Perot appeared on the *Today* show and took credit for initiating the meeting: "The first thing I did after I got the file [from Badey] is to talk to him [Armitage]. I said, 'Look, I was given this. I don't know anything about it. But if this is true, it is very compromising to you.' "

"Compromised with who and why?" Armitage shot back. "With the Vietnamese because I had four years of combat there, or with my family? It can't be. I've worked that out. The POW/MIA families support me."

"You are compromised," Perot insisted.[68]

Armitage remembered leaving the meeting "perplexed."[69]

A month later, Perot went to see William Webster and urged him to open a formal investigation of Armitage. Perot gave Webster a file prepared by Christic Institute chief Daniel Sheehan. Later, when questioned about that file, Perot insisted he had never read it before passing it to the FBI. "It was too long [to read]," he claimed. "I just handed it to the Director. . . . the part I remember all had to do with drug dealing in Central America, and some weapons shipments and drug shipments coming back. I didn't have time to get into it, but just on the off chance that it might have some validity, I passed it on."[70]* When the FBI conducted its own investigation, it found the charges to be baseless.[71] (About the same time, Perot, in his hotel suite at the Four Seasons in Georgetown, spent two hours questioning an FBI counterintelligence agent to discover whether the Bureau had thwarted an earlier investigation into Armitage.)

Shortly after he had taken the Sheehan file to the FBI, Perot confronted national security chief Frank Carlucci. He tried to convince Carlucci that Armitage was compromised, but Carlucci would hear none of it. "You have the wrong man in Armitage," Carlucci remembers telling Perot. "He's clean. You should drop it." Instead, Perot repeated the allegations about Armitage and

---

* Much of the information Perot had received about Armitage from Sheehan was the basis of a lawsuit filed by the Christic Institute, against several retired military and intelligence officers, in Miami in December 1986. Among other charges, the suit alleged a rogue intelligence operation to sell cocaine to raise money to buy arms for the contras. Federal district court judge James King threw the Christic suit out of court in 1988, and accused Sheehan, the institutes's general counsel, of lying under oath and "abuse of the judicial process." He ordered that Christic pay $1.2 million in legal costs to the defendants. Author Leslie Coburn later repeated many of the same charges in her book *Out of Control*. Armitage brought legal action that forced the publisher to paste a sticker bearing the true facts on the offending pages in 500 copies already in the stores and to destroy more than 6,000 in the warehouse. When Armitage asked his lawyer if he should sue Perot, his attorney told him that Perot's wealth was too great: "You don't have arms long enough to box with God."

insisted the "government was all screwed up on this issue." He demanded that Carlucci remove Armitage from the POW/MIA matter.[72] "The consequence of that meeting is that Perot decided never to speak to me anymore," said Carlucci.[73]

Although Perot no longer spoke to Carlucci, he did continue to confront others with expanding charges about Armitage. He told Howard Baker's assistant, Jim Cannon, that Armitage was tied to a Department of Defense scandal involving bribery and Egyptian arms sales.[74] To Craig Fuller, Bush's chief of staff, he complained that Armitage was in the arms business with Eric von Marbod, a former director of the Defense Securities Assistance Agency.[75] To journalist Mort Kondracke, Perot, off the record, said Armitage was "as corrupt as they come" and "up to his ears" in Iran-contra.[76]* As the stories expanded, Bush tried to soothe Armitage's feelings, telling him not to worry, and that Perot was merely "a loose cannon."[77]

Perot has always denied that he played an important role in promoting the Armitage stories. "I have never said a word to anybody about drugs and weapons and Armitage," he told *The Boston Globe* in January 1987.[78] Nevertheless, the press was beginning to connect Perot to Armitage. *Time* reported that he was investigating "the alleged links between ex–CIA agents Thomas Clines and Theodore Shackley, retired Generals Richard Secord and John Singlaub, Iranian-born businessman Albert Hakim and other former and present Government officials going back to the early 1960s. . . . A far more curious target is Richard

---

* Perot, who had provided ransom money to Oliver North in failed efforts to win the release of American hostages in Lebanon, had his own dispute over Iran-contra with North. North, in his book *Under Fire,* reported that Perot visited his lawyer, Brendan Sullivan, in December 1986 and said, "Look, why doesn't Ollie just end this thing and explain to the FBI that the President didn't know. If he goes to jail, I'll take care of his family. And I'll be happy to give him a job when he gets out." In contrast, Perot says he first approached White House officials Don Regan and Mike Deaver to ask whether they had any problem if North told the truth. "If he will tell the truth, I will provide him with lawyers and support and what have you," said Perot. Regan and Deaver encouraged Perot to make that offer to North, whom Perot then called. "Ollie, you can get this whole thing over with in a few days, as opposed to dragging it on for months and distracting the country. That is the proper thing to do." Perot recorded that conversation, and the tape supports his version.

Armitage, a man widely respected for his integrity and effectiveness."[79] In a broad-ranging 1987 interview with *Barron's* magazine, primarily about the GM debacle, Perot did not speak specifically about Armitage but instead expounded on his belief in widespread government conspiracies. "This whole Iran arms deal–contra thing," he said. "It is the same team of beautiful people selling arms around the world. This is not a new experience for them to be selling arms at a profit. I mean, some of them got caught once, in Australia [the Nugan Hand bank]. They got caught again in Hawaii [the Rewald case]. Edwin Wilson got put in jail. And if you go back and follow the trail, these guys have been working together since the Bay of Pigs. And yet now, suddenly, it is all coming into focus. And we will clean it up."

Perot decided to take direct action to circumvent what he considered the government's efforts to block his quest to uncover the truth about POWs and MIAs: He would visit North Vietnam and meet directly with government officials. The issue of whether Perot went to Vietnam on his own initiative, possibly interfering with government policy, or whether he traveled at the behest of the administration is a hotly contested one. Internal administration documents show that in the spring of 1987, just prior to Perot's trip, administration officials vigorously debated whether he should go, with most deciding it would be a mistake.

The official who was selected to be the administration's contact with Perot was James Cannon, Howard Baker's deputy chief of staff. "I was just about ready to leave government service in late February or early March," recalls Cannon, "when Baker came in and said, 'We've got a problem here with your friend Perot.' " Perot had made his displeasure with the administration clear by canceling his $2.5 million pledge to the Reagan library. "Reagan has offended him," Baker told Cannon. "Bush has offended him. And I have offended him. Now it's your turn."[80]

Cannon, a former aide to Governor Nelson Rockefeller, knew Perot from his EDS/Medicaid work in New York. The two had a cordial relationship, and Cannon was one of the few administration officials who liked the Texan. When Cannon called him, Perot reiterated that while Reagan had asked him to help out on the POW/MIA matter, various people, including Armitage, had tried to block his efforts. "He was very upset," recalls Cannon.[81] Perot, because of security concerns, refused to meet Cannon at his White House office. When they did get together, Perot complained about being "jerked around by candy-ass non–decision makers."[82]

"Basically, I had to figure out what to do—not to get the pledge of money back, but to defuse it," says Cannon. "We didn't want this man mad."[83]

On March 21, a Saturday, Perot called George Bush and said, "I am shutting down my operation." Bush, in a three-page typed memo of the call, described Perot as "frustrated," and said that he had "detailed a litany of gripes," and affirmed he had canceled his multimillion-dollar pledge to the Reagan library.[84] Again, Perot complained about Armitage, and told Bush he was "severing all ties with the Reagan administration." Wrote Bush, "He feels he has been badly treated by all (although he didn't say so, I think he means me too)."[85]

Perot did not tell Bush that he was planning to leave for Vietnam within twenty-four hours. The same day that Perot and Bush spoke, Colin Powell officially advised Cannon that "it is not wise for Ross to go. . . . Our policy interests not served by Mr. Perot's interests at the moment."[86] There was now a consensus against Perot going to Vietnam.

But according to Perot, Howard Baker approved his trip. Perot cites a March 19, 1987, memo in which Baker told Perot that the "president feels that you can go to Vietnam unofficially and as a private citizen, on the conditions outlined . . ." says Perot, "There's no question that Howard Baker cleared me to go on that trip as a private citizen." However, Baker, who wrote to me in response to written questions about the issue, says that among the "conditions" he had discussed with Perot was that he should not go unless the Vietnamese government lived up to a promise it "apparently made to Mr. Perot that he would see a live POW. . . . I did not know of Ross Perot's trip to Vietnam until his return. . . . I do not believe anyone in the Administration 'approved' the Perot trip in 1987, nor were we aware that he had gone until he returned."[87]

Actually, one person was aware that Perot had left—Jim Cannon. "Was he authorized to go?" says Cannon. "No. But on a Saturday night [March 21], I got a call at home from Perot, and he said, 'I am on my way.' He went on to tell me that he had decided on his own to go to Vietnam, to go to Saigon, that he had been in touch with 'my people.' . . . He loves conspiracies. It's his nature, I think. I believe he said he was sending his private plane somewhere else as a decoy, and he was on his way in another plane [under another name].* He wanted me to know this, because he said, 'You can tell the President or Howard [Baker], but I don't want NSC to know. They might try to stop me, even by creating "an accident" that would kill me. Don't forget, I've dealt with that bunch before.' I could not have stopped him on the night he called to say he was going. He was not calling for advice, he was calling to merely inform me that he was leaving."[88]

Cannon says that while Perot told him that he could inform Reagan or Baker about the trip, he did not. "The next week, Baker did not ask me if I heard from Perot, and I never told him," says Cannon. "The only two people who could have asked Ross to go to Vietnam were Reagan and me, and I didn't ask him, and I know Reagan didn't."[89]

However, Perot, for his part, is adamant that he did not even tell Cannon that he was leaving for Vietnam. "I did not tell Jim Cannon I was going before I went," contends Perot. "I was on my own and I felt the best thing to do was just to float over there and get back. . . . I am dead sure I didn't tell anyone in Washington. . . . See, they wanted me to go. They wanted me to go, and I was working on a task force for him, a one-man task force for the president."[90] According to Perot, when he returned, Cannon was so shocked that he initially refused to believe that Perot had visited Vietnam, since he knew nothing about the trip, but Perot had the record of his Pan Am flight and photos of himself with Vietnamese officials.†

---

* Perot had filed a flight plan for his private jet for one day after he actually left. He later told a reporter that he was certain the government was monitoring him. "They have enormous surveillance resources, as you know," he said.

† "Perot bragged that he had met with high-ranking officials who had never before spoken to Americans," says Richard Childress. "They were the same officials I had dealt with for the previous six years."

"The reason this entire issue is so important is that Perot was a loose cannon in Vietnam on his own, discussing everything from economics to advisers," says Richard Childress. "It would have been disastrous if the Vietnamese had perceived Perot as an official representative. He tried to take over the negotiations by portraying himself as being close to the president and vice-president. He was running his own foreign policy."[91] There was brief discussion in the administration about whether Perot had violated the Logan Act, which makes it a crime for a private citizen to conduct foreign policy, but the quick consensus was that the act was unenforceable. Yet administration officials were deeply disturbed by Perot's trip. "He was more than an irritant," says Frank Carlucci. "He could hurt policy. It was very unhelpful."[92] "It became a problem," said Colin Powell. "We had a policy that was firm. The Vietnamese were marvelous negotiators, and they were constantly trying to find seams and ways around this policy. . . . We were concerned that the Vietnamese were going to try to achieve in an indirect means [through Perot] what they couldn't achieve by a direct means."[93] Powell was especially concerned because Perot was willing to offer potential economic benefits to North Vietnam, something the administration was against. When the National Security Council sent Richard Childress to Hanoi two months later, in May, he found the Vietnamese had a "strikingly different attitude" and were more difficult on key issues. Childress said he felt the change was "related to the Perot visit."[94]

Meanwhile, on his return, Perot wanted to discuss the results of his trip to Hanoi directly with the president. According to Colin Powell, he was "fairly insistent," and a meeting with Reagan and Howard Baker was set for May 6.[95] Perot prepared a seven-page report on his trip, and also drafted a proposed statement for Reagan to issue publicly, confirming that "some months ago, I asked Ross Perot to look into the Vietnam POW/MIA issue, get to the bottom of it, and make recommendations to me about what the U.S. should do to resolve it."[96] (Reagan did not release it.) When Perot arrived, he was dismayed to see that, in addition to Reagan and Baker, Carlucci and Colin Powell were there. Perot thought he had a "clear understanding" that only Baker and the president were to meet with him. "Once I saw those national security guys there," he says, "I knew it was a waste of time."[97] Perot had wanted to get his message directly to Reagan in the hope that the president would then "stand up to the staff." "But he had been pretty well programmed before I got there," says Perot.[98]

Reagan spoke to Perot from index cards prepared by Carlucci and his staff. "The theme was 'We only need one foreign policy,' " says Carlucci. "We had told the president that Perot was a strong personality and he had to get his points across firmly and quickly. He did that."[99] Reagan thanked Perot for his efforts, but told him that future work on the POW/MIA issue would be coordinated only through General George Vescey, about to be appointed a special liaison to Vietnam. Perot sat and listened politely. At one point, Reagan read one of the index cards twice. After the meeting, Perot bitterly complained to Howard Baker that he had been ambushed by Carlucci and the National Security Council, who he was convinced were only concerned about protecting their own reputations in case live Americans were found in Southeast Asia.[100] When he returned to Dallas, he was fuming, talking openly about Reagan's reliance on cue cards and how "futile" the meeting was.*

Following his brush-off by Reagan, Perot went back to George Bush, suggesting that he might offer to buy all of Cam Ranh Bay as a form of ransom. Bush rejected it. What about offering $1 million per prisoner? Again, the Bush office said no.† Feeling as though he were getting nowhere, Perot told Bush, "Well, George, I go in looking for prisoners, but I spend all my time discovering the government has been moving drugs around the world and is

---

* Reading a cue card twice was evidently not unheard of for Reagan. "A friend of mine, an ambassador, took the foreign minister of a minor European country in to see Reagan," Jim Cannon told me. "He read one card twice. The foreign minister was not fazed at all."

† Perot denies ever offering any kind of ransom for MIAs. "I'll buy you the biggest steak in Texas if you can find one shred of evidence that that's true," he told a reporter in 1992. But government officials like the NSC's Richard Childress confirm that Perot wanted to buy MIAs, and Perot even discussed it with some outside of government. "He called me up," recalls former detective Jim Badey, who had provided Perot the original file on Armitage, "and said, 'Remember, let your sources in the Vietnamese community know I'll give $1 million for every prisoner returned.' "

involved in illegal arms deals. . . . I can't get at the prisoners because of the corruption among our own covert people."[101] Perot told Bush that other officials around him were not corrupt but merely incompetent. As for Bush himself, Perot told friends in Texas that he was "weak." "The animus was certainly directed at Bush," recalls James Cannon. "He [Perot] used to tell me that Bush was a wimp, and all of that."[102]*

"People get 'Potomac fever,' " says Boyden Gray, Reagan's counsel. "What I think is that once Perot got inside, saw what it is like to have power, it got to his head. It goes beyond POWs and MIAs. Then it became a contest of who swung the biggest club in Texas."[103]

The administration had had enough of Perot and his conspiracy theories. Bush, with the backing of Caspar Weinberger, Frank Carlucci, and Colin Powell, cut Perot off from any further involvement. "I was appalled at Perot's paranoia," says Carlucci. "His seeing of plots where there were none, creating situations that don't exist, his ability to distort facts."[104]

Despite his fight with the administration and the controversy caused by his March trip to Vietnam, Perot maintained a relationship with the North Vietnamese, but this time through Harry

---

* Perot later focused on personal matters with Bush. For instance, Perot and his lawyer, Tom Luce, paid $10,000 to a Washington lawyer, Berl Bernhard, to investigate a $48 million tax deduction obtained by Pennzoil, which was chaired by J. Hugh Liedtke, Bush's oil partner in the 1950s (Bernhard says he only gathered public documents). Perot thought that effort might uncover a "mini–Teapot Dome" scandal, and later tried, unsuccessfully, to interest *The Washington Post*'s Bob Woodward in doing a story. Perot and Luce also investigated two private investments that Bush had made during the 1970s. The two thought one of the deals had questionable tax implications, and in the other, Perot claimed one of Bush's co-investors "maybe had a cocaine habit." Even as late as 1991, Perot was looking into possible Bush wrongdoing. When the wife of an imprisoned navy captain called Perot and told him that her husband had flown Bush on a spy plane to Europe as part of the purported "October Surprise" (a conspiracy theory that the release of the Iranian hostages was deliberately delayed until after the 1980 presidential election), Perot sent investigators to interview the inmate. But on the day the Perot team arrived, the inmate suffered a heart attack, precluding any interview. Perot is still suspicious about that incident. "The guy was out and back in the jail the minute we left town," he says.

McKillop, who had worked for Perot since 1986 (he was an ex–Braniff Airlines employee who accompanied Perot on his 1969 trip to Southeast Asia). Perot authorized McKillop to travel to North Vietnam, seven times during the next five years.[105] (A Vietnamese spokesman claimed it was thirteen visits).[106] "I didn't send him," claimed Perot. "They [the North Vietnamese] would invite him."[107]

McKillop cleared each trip with Perot before making it, and then briefed him on every return. He had nearly fifty meetings with North Vietnamese officials in charge of various ministries, including tourism, transportation, heavy industry, and agriculture. In 1990, McKillop brought back a letter of intent addressed to Perot and signed by the Vietnamese minister of foreign affairs suggesting that Perot could be the business agent for numerous industries ranging from computers to oil and gas development. The letter said that "compensation to agent to be mutually agreed upon by both parties based on effort and investment."[108]

When the letter of intent became public in the 1992 presidential campaign, McKillop and Perot quickly said it was meaningless. "I have no interest in doing business in Vietnam. . . . It's just something that fell out of the sky," Perot told investigators for the Senate Select Committee on POW/MIA Affairs. "Today, see, I will get at least 100 unsolicited business offers from all over the world. . . . I don't think I ever read it. He [McKillop] told me about it. . . . It was just an unfortunate mistake that he made in ever accepting it."[109] When asked about McKillop's meetings with Vietnamese officials responsible for trade and commerce, Perot claimed, "I don't know anything about them."[110]*

Yet, to the same Senate Select Committee investigators, McKillop exhibited a tremendous lack of recall when it came to specific discussions, especially connected to the supposed mission of his trips, POWs and MIAs. During his deposition, he answered, "I don't know," "I'm not sure," "I don't recall or remember," or

---

* McKillop said he insisted that the letter of intent state that it was being drafted "in anticipation of the normalization of relations." In 1993, Ross Perot, Jr., visited Vietnam to look into business opportunities, including the possibility of upgrading Hanoi's airport. When President Clinton moved to normalize diplomatic relations with Vietnam in 1995, Perot was unusually quiet.

"I have no knowledge," 176 times.[111] When asked about the substance of conversations with Vietnamese leaders, McKillop often said he could not remember even meeting with the officials listed on his itinerary. Pressed about any progress on POWs and MIAs in a midsummer trip in 1990, McKillop said, "I would have to answer that I have no recollection of what took place specifically, whether I made any visits to anybody or anything."[112] (In contrast, when asked about whether he had discussed business developments, he was surprisingly specific: "No. I recall positively there was not.")[113]

A Vietnamese government official, Le Van Bang, told American reporters that Perot and McKillop had promised money, medicines, and other humanitarian aid, with an eventual goal of developing commercial trade. Perot again adamantly denied it.[114] He even suggested that the Vietnamese had deliberately tried to sabotage his run for the White House in order to curry favor with the Bush administration.[115]

Perot's fallout with the North Vietnamese, coupled with the disregard in which the Bush administration held him, left Perot with virtually no allies for his efforts on POWs and MIAs. After twenty years, his quest to find live prisoners ground to a halt.

FOURTEEN

---□---

"*Vacuum It Up*"

Back in Dallas in the late spring of 1987, Perot was blocked, by the terms of the General Motors buyout, from starting a new company until June 1, 1988. He had moved out of the EDS building but rented a suite of offices in a tower directly overlooking his former headquarters. He busied himself by investing in oil and gas operations, a chain of wholesale clubs, and several high-tech start-ups, and even invested $20 million in a new undertaking by Steven Jobs, one of the co-founders of Apple Computer.

In early June, his daughter Nancy, a favorite of Ross's, married attorney Clay Mulford. That same month, to much local fanfare, Dallas's symphony hall marked its halfway point in construction. Perot had given $15 million toward the $82 million project, with the stipulation that it be named the Morton H. Meyerson Symphony Center, after his longtime business associate.*

Not everything that greeted Perot after his return to Dallas was good news. One of Perot's favorite provisions of the Texas school

---

* Meyerson, a classical music aficionado, was a member of the commission to raise money for "a world-class hall" for Dallas. Perot made the pledge shortly after the $742 million buyout from GM. Although the gift was for Meyerson, Perot became involved in the design. "Ross Perot looks at his philanthropy as an investment," says George Schrader, one of the officials involved in the hall's construction. Others who dealt with Perot over the symphony hall said he "was difficult to work for," brought in his own consultants, and "kept meddling nonstop." Meyerson is credited by most with having kept Perot focused on the more important and less contentious issues.

reform bill he had pushed through the legislature in 1984—an appointed state board of education as opposed to an elected one—was under increasing assault. In the coming months, Perot spent more than a million dollars in a failed effort to stop the voters from returning the board to its old status.[1]

Then, in documents produced for the Iran-contra investigation, it came to light that Perot had been involved in three failed efforts to free American hostages in the Middle East, all requests that he insists were "authorized at the highest levels of government." (In 1985, Oliver North persuaded Perot to give $200,000 as a ransom deposit, meant to win the release of Beirut's CIA station chief, William Buckley. Perot sent Jay Coburn, an EDS employee posing as an oil tycoon, to Canada with the money. Buckley was killed by terrorists, and an informant absconded with the funds; later that same year, North convinced Perot to give another $100,000 deposit for the release of American hostage Peter Kilburn, and Coburn again delivered the money but returned with it when the deal fell through. And in 1986, Perot dispatched Coburn to Cypress with $2 million in another effort to free Kilburn, but it was not successful and Kilburn was later killed by his captors.* On all the trips, Coburn carried a letter on White House stationery intended to help him in case of trouble.)

Perhaps what irritated Perot the most was news that EDS had posted another record quarter of revenues and profits (the second consecutive one since he had left). Now, with EDS as General Motors' most profitable business, the financial press ran stories saying that the question of whether EDS could survive without Perot had been resoundingly answered—SCORE ONE FOR ROGER

---

* According to Lieutenant Colonel Robert Earl, North's deputy, North had wanted Perot to wire the $2 million to a bank account. Then North intended to divert the money for the contras, something Perot had already rejected. Having already lost $200,000 with North, he instead sent the money with Coburn.

Five years earlier, in 1981, Perot had been involved in yet another ransom effort. The Joint Chiefs asked Perot to deliver $500,000 to Italy—in under an hour—to free Brigadier General James Dozier. Although Perot made the money available, it was never used, because Dozier was released by his Red Brigade kidnappers.

SMITH was one headline in *Forbes*.[2] "Ross was fuming as those stories broke," recalls a colleague. "It just made him more determined that when the time came for him to form his own company, he was going to go after GM and change their cheery tune."

Yet the issue that dominated most of Perot's time during the late spring and early summer of 1987 was a political and business battle in Fort Worth. This fight was over whether the city should annex 5,358 acres of Perot-owned land, most of it near the little farming town of Haslet (population 700), where Perot wanted to build a 9,600-foot runway as the centerpiece of a new airport called Alliance.

The Perot strategy was brilliant and simple. Despite the presence of Dallas–Fort Worth International Airport and the smaller Love Field, he saw an opportunity to entice major corporations to use a new airport as a supply base and a hub for commercial air shipments throughout the South. If Fort Worth annexed the land, it would start collecting taxes on the undeveloped parcel, but Perot would benefit because the city would have to build water and sewage connections and provide emergency and basic services. Moreover, if the Federal Aviation Administration (FAA) approved the airport, the federal government would pay 90 percent of the cost of construction. Fort Worth would contribute the remaining 10 percent, and Perot offered to donate 418 acres (valued at $18 million) on which the airport could be built. Because of the way that gift was arranged, Fort Worth could use the value of the donated land to pay for its 10 percent share of building the airport.

The land in question was owned by the Perot Group, the expanding real estate holdings of Perot, his son, and other members of the family. In addition to the more than 5,000 acres the Perot Group wanted Fort Worth to annex, it had also bought another 11,000 acres in the same area.* Its large holdings now completely surrounded the proposed airport site. If that airport

---

* The Perot family started accumulating the property, which cost over $100 million, in the fall of 1984. Rick Salwen, the EDS in-house counsel who helped Perot on the war on drugs, left EDS in 1986 to work full-time for the Perot Group. He coordinated many of the purchases. In 1989, he sued Perot for $250 million for breach of contract over oral representations he said he had received from both Ross Sr. and Ross Jr., promising him ownership interest in one of the

were built, Perot's adjoining land would be ideal for development, by major manufacturers or local industry, and even for residential subdivisions to service the new workforce. The value of the Perot property would quickly multiply.

In an arrangement so complex, there was a series of approvals to obtain at every government level. The first step was the annexation of the property, because without that the FAA would not be interested in financing the airport. Initially, that decision was in doubt because even the most conservative estimate was that to extend essential services to the Perot land would cost the city $50 million over five to six years.[3] But the Perot Group gave the city strong incentives to agree to the annexation. Not only would it donate the land for the airport itself, but it also promised to pay $14.5 million toward the new streets and utilities that the city would have to build. Perot also put up $2 million toward the city's costs for engineering studies.

The Perots also aggressively lobbied the Fort Worth city council, which was responsible for making the annexation decision. The Alliance Airport project was ostensibly the bailiwick of twenty-eight-year-old Ross Perot, Jr. "Ross was very emphatic that this was Ross Jr.'s project," says Robert Bolen, the Fort Worth mayor who voted for the annexation, "but privately there was no question when we met with him that Dad knew what was going on, his resources were involved, and he was tutoring him as they went along."[4]

The Perot Group used some of the most effective lobbyists in Austin and Washington, not only to move the Fort Worth city council toward a quick decision, but also to obtain the freeway permissions and rights of access needed from the Texas Depart-

---

partnerships formed for the property purchases. While the suit was pending, on January 11, 1990, Pat Horner, then president of Perot's new company, called the chief financial officer of Dell Computer, Donald Collis, the company to which Salwen had gone after leaving Perot. Horner told Collis that the litigation between Perot and Salwen would soon get nasty, and that there was denigrating information about Salwen, including evidence Perot purportedly had showing that Salwen (who was married) had a mistress (Salwen later denied it). The suit was settled out of court for an undisclosed amount. When the issue became public during the 1992 campaign, Perot denied that he had attempted "to intimidate [Salwen] with information of a personal nature."

ment of Highways and Public Transportation; the extension of utility improvements from neighboring governments; and, of course, FAA approval. "Because of who he was and the money he had," says Steve Wollens, a state legislator, "he could coordinate, consolidate, and move into action a hoard of lobbyists to provide an infrastructure to make Alliance work. An enormous infrastructure had to be built around it. It wouldn't have happened unless it was Ross Perot."

"Now, I worked with Ross and his people probably more than anyone else, and 90 percent of the time we were on the same side," says Mayor Bolen. "The 10 percent of the agitation came because he could move faster than we could. And I said, 'Ross, just because you can get things done instantaneous in Washington and Austin doesn't mean it works that way here.' The fact is that he had more people and lobbyists to work on certain things than we did. It took us longer to do things than them. So the only time we had any real difficulty was when he would say, 'Bobby, you're just not moving fast enough, let's get this done.' And that's Ross—when he gets focused on something, he is like a bulldog."[5]*

Garey Gilley, a city councilman, admits that Perot "put a lot of manpower and resources" into persuading the council, and "his people were constantly at city hall. He probably didn't need to push so hard."[6] "They were a tremendous team," recalls Bolen. "They not only could throw resources and money at it, but they could also put manpower on it. If they wanted eight lawyers on it tomorrow, they had eight lawyers on it. We had one or two lawyers in the our entire legal department that were swamped with forty-eight other things."[7]

On September 15, 1987, the city council voted to annex the land, the largest municipal annexation in Texas history. Undisclosed at

---

* During July 1987, in the midst of the Fort Worth considerations for Alliance Airport, newspapers ran stories that Perot was thinking of a 1988 presidential run: "H. Ross Perot is telling everyone at high levels of high-tech circles he's going to jump into the Democratic presidential sweepstakes . . ." Perot was evidently so furious at George Bush that he briefly considered mounting a challenge. But by early 1988, he had lost the fervor, reiterating, "I do not have the training to run for president." Still, other candidates spoke about Perot. Christian-right leader Pat Robertson, then running for the Republican nomination, announced he would appoint Perot secretary of defense.

the time of the vote was that at least one of the council members had a passing business relationship with the Perots. Councilman William Garrison had netted almost $180,000 from a partnership that sold land to Ross Perot in 1985. That property was part of the parcel that Fort Worth annexed. When the information became public, Garrison claimed he did not know Perot was the buyer. He said he had deposited his $179,443 check without examining the accompanying papers—"I probably had other things on my mind."[8] Councilman Garey Gilley was hired to survey a 1,300-acre site the Perot Group acquired in 1989.[9] Although city council members are prohibited from accepting gifts, there is no ban on their conducting business with a company or person that has matters pending before the council.

While the annexation effort was under way the Perot Group sought approval for freeways and an infrastructure of roads that could feed the new airport.* The effort at the Texas highway department was successful. State legislator Steve Wollens recalls that Perot gave him a helicopter tour a couple of years later: "I was shown all these highways, and I was shocked. I was just blown away. There were all these highways built in nowhereland. You don't get this by just having a nice personality. It takes a lot of muscle to get the Texas highway department to spend an enormous amount of money on an infrastructure like that. It was very impressive."[10†]

But the most controversial approval in the Alliance deal was at the federal level. The Federal Aviation Administration, which had been interested in building an industrial airport in North Texas for several years, was not in favor of the Perot proposal because it was too ambitious. The FAA wanted a simple industrial cargo airport, with a runway and control tower costing no more than $5

---

* In late 1986 and early 1987, the Perot Group bought thirteen parcels of land around a strip of land they were donating to the state for the future highway (the strip was approximately 400 feet wide by 11 miles long). Using multiple trustees and title companies so that Perot's name did not appear on the purchase documents, the Perot Group bought several thousand acres surrounding the soon-to-be-built freeway. Once again, Perot thought that if Texas built the road, his adjacent property would increase in value.

† Between state and federal monies, some $70 million has been spent on roads and highways over the Perot land connected with Alliance.

million (Perot wanted a more elaborate complex costing $25 million). Also, the FAA thought that the Alliance proposal concentrated too much on servicing corporate clients, and as a result did not satisfy requirements that a new airport serve the general public. But Perot largely bypassed the regulatory agency by enlisting the aid of Speaker of the House Jim Wright (whose congressional district included Fort Worth). The Perots met with Wright and took him on a helicopter tour of the Alliance site. Wright then tacked a two-paragraph grant into a $600 billion stop-gap spending measure designed to keep government agencies and programs running. One newspaper referred to Wright's move as "that late-night, secret, pork-barrel scramble."[11] Wright dealt directly with House Appropriations Committee chairman Jamie Whitten, Sr. (Whitten's son, Jamie Jr., was a partner in one of the Washington lobbying firms retained by Perot). The December 1987 amendment set aside $25 million in federal funds to build the airport on the donated Perot acres.* Ross Jr. and his wife made a $5,000 contribution to Speaker Wright after the amendment passed.[12]

Alliance Airport was finished in two years, a remarkably short time for a complex project that required regulatory approval at three levels of government (many experts had estimated it could take ten years).[13] Once it was completed, Fort Worth had to select a company to manage the Alliance project. Two groups competed, the Perots (under the name Pinnacle Air Services) and Reed Pigman, a businessman who ran a fuel concession at the smaller Beacham Airport.

"Both of our bids went before the city manager's office," recalls Pigman, "and I started hearing feedback that they liked my proposal and it looked like I would be chosen. Then, for some reason I don't know, the city asked for more information from both of us. I submitted more, and Perot submitted a plan whereby he would be giving a $12 million facility to the city. Suddenly the city said, 'We like Perot's offer better.' The Perots were offering a 40,000-

---

* The costs kept inflating. Two years later the federal government had spent $31 million, and by 1992 topped $51 million. By then, the Perots asked the FAA for more money to rip up the old runway and build a longer one capable of handling jumbo cargo planes; by 1995, the federal government had put in more than $70 million.

square-foot administration building, with a 20,000-square-foot aircraft hangar, and a fuel farm. At that point, I said, 'You win.' There's no way I could give a facility like that to the city. I didn't have deep pockets."[14]

The battle between Perot and Pigman was reported in the local press. Perot did not always like the coverage, especially by Fort Worth's premier paper, the *Star-Telegram*. The paper's editor, Richard Connor, said that Perot called on July 31, 1989. The newspaper had run a story the previous day implying that Ross Jr. had been using political muscle to win the contract before the city council. "He [Perot] had begun the conversation," Connor later wrote, "by asking whether he was on a speaker phone, whether anyone was listening and whether the conversation was being taped." He began by complaining about the paper's treatment of Ross Jr., but then he suddenly asked "who were we to be scrutinizing them, when our own house was not in order." Perot told Connor that the *Star-Telegram* "was being compromised. . . . He said he was certain I was aware of a relationship between one of our employees and a city official." Connor, assuming Perot meant a sexual relationship, replied that it was irrelevant, and there was no proof of it. "It was at this juncture that he referred to photographs he said proved his charge. . . . Never, in more than 20 years in this business, had anyone suggested anything so seamy, so mean-spirited, when complaining about a newspaper. . . . It makes one wonder who else was phoned during those days and what kind of pressure was brought to bear on the decision makers."[15]*

Four months later, the management contract came to the city council for a vote. Perot's attorneys had drafted the agreement. In the more than fifty pages of small print, there was a clause that gave the Perots the contract for two hundred years. "They thought no one would pay attention and they could get their wish list

---

* When Connor's story broke in 1992, Perot issued a written statement denying the incident. "Mr. Connor's account of our conversation is incorrect, except for the part stating that I did call and complain about the accuracy of a story. I made no comments of a personal nature about anyone." Perot told me the Connor article was "not true" and that it had made him angry. "Things like that happen and you just sit there and marvel at it," Perot says. "This was just something he made up."

through the city council," says Pigman.[16] Two city council members, Steve Murrin and Louis Zapata, raised questions about the one-sided terms. Pigman's lawyer threatened a legal challenge. Some, though, were sympathetic to a long term. "The Perot Group had invested millions and millions of dollars," says councilman Garey Gilley. "For instance, they paid out of their pocket all the engineering costs, they paid everything that would normally have been paid by the city of Fort Worth, as part of their matching grant. Perot funded all of that. There were no strings attached. So we were talking about what would be a reasonable period of time for them to recoup their investment."

But even Mayor Bolen had some reservations about the length of the management contract. "I said at one point to Ross, 'My God, Ross, the United States is only two hundred years old, and I'm not going to give it to you in perpetuity.' He laughed, and said, 'Okay, we will look at it,' which they did."[17] The city council backed off and gave Perot the contract for five years, at $1 a year. In return, the city agreed to absorb all losses from the airport's management. Alliance averaged $250,000 in losses during each of the next three years, prompting Fort Worth to solicit new bids from twenty-seven airport management companies. The city held out a carrot of a twenty-five-year contract. Under the new agreement, Fort Worth wanted the management company to absorb the losses and give the city part of the gross revenues. No one bid.[18]

After six months, Fort Worth discovered that the only company willing to take the risk was Ross Perot's Pinnacle Air Services. Now Perot offered to shoulder up to $1 million in losses, while the city granted him the first option to build and operate terminal buildings and hangars, all constructed at city expense. Also, Perot and the city would split all profits over $1.5 million a year. The six-member Fort Worth Aviation Advisory Board unanimously recommended that the city council reject the Perot offer. "I do not feel that the Pinnacle proposal will result in any revenue to the city," said advisory board member Bob Hullet.[19] Nevertheless, the city entered into the contract with Pinnacle.

Now, with a long-term management contract guaranteed, the Perots began to reap the benefits of Alliance's success. The first major tenant, American Airlines, bought some of Perot's land for

$17 million. American had been looking nationwide for an aircraft repair facility, and was induced to establish the facility at Alliance after it was partly financed by $500 million in a municipal bond issue and American received a ten-year tax abatement.[20] The Drug Enforcement Administration paid nearly $2.5 million for 12.5 acres ($4.30 a square foot for land for which Perot had paid $.50 a square foot). That purchase had been recommended by Thomas Kelly, an aide to the DEA director and the former agent in charge of the Dallas office. Kelly left the DEA before the actual purchase was made and temporarily went to work for Ross Sr. in early 1990.

In late 1993, Federal Express chose Alliance as its cargo-sorting hub. It was one of the most sought-after airport contracts, worth up to $300 million.[21] The Perots received even better news from a Commerce Department decision establishing one of the nation's largest foreign trade zones on fifteen square miles of land surrounding Alliance.[22] The decision affected half of the Perot holdings and allowed companies to import and export products cheaply by paying greatly reduced tariffs.* The Commerce Department action had the added benefit of kicking in millions of dollars in tax benefits for the Alliance owners, under a 1991 state law that granted the tax breaks wherever a trade zone was approved.† Analysts now estimate that the Perot Group, over the next two decades, could make a profit of $1 billion on its Alliance property.[23]

While the Perot Group was handling the Alliance project, Perot himself became the center of a raucous public debate in Dallas over the police department. At the beginning of 1988, after three

---

* Such a designation allows companies to import parts without paying tariffs until a completed product is assembled and ready for sale. If a product assembled in a foreign trade zone is then sold in the United States, tariffs are often lower. As for foreign parts, if they are imported into the zone, assembled into a complete product, and then exported, no tariff is paid.

† The trade zone split Ross Sr. and Jr. over the issue of NAFTA (North American Free Trade Act). Ross Jr. was strongly for NAFTA, with its liberalized trading rules and elimination of tariffs, whereas his father made it a cornerstone of his post-1992 election polices. It was over the NAFTA issue that Perot debated, and showed poorly, against Vice-President Al Gore in November 1993.

officers were killed in the line of duty, Perot, a strong booster of the force, began holding "listening sessions" with the police. As a result of speaking to, he says, 1,800 of the 2,400 city's police officers, he began a campaign to chastise the city for not adequately supporting the police. He also freely gave out advice about how to run the department. After a tour in south Dallas (a black ghetto riddled with crime and drug problems), Perot told a reporter that the "Jamaican drug dealers go around with firepower something like the Delta team would have. And we send police officers in there." His solution was to cordon off south Dallas for a one-night covert operation and send in hundreds of police to "vacuum it up"—search every dwelling and person on the street and confiscate the drugs and weapons.[24] Perot advocated infrared tracking devices that might pinpoint drug locations in a neighborhood.* He also told James Ragland, a former city hall reporter for *The Dallas Morning News,* that police should "just go in there [high-crime neighborhoods], cordon off the whole area, going block by block, looking for guns and drugs." When asked if that did not present a constitutional problem, Perot retorted, "Look, I'm sure 95% of the people who live there would support this."[25†]

The chief of the Dallas Police Association, Monica Smith, liked Perot's ideas. "It really would solve the problem if we could go in there and take all the guns and all the firepower out of there," she said. "We were wondering about the legality of it and how many judges would oppose it. . . . The same so-called leaders who come

---

* When Perot was called for jury duty in 1988, he was struck from the prospective panel by defense lawyers after expressing strong support for the death penalty. He said that he thought the justice system spent too much time "looking after criminals" instead of "law-abiding citizens," and that if a psychiatric defense was used, he would not give it any weight since he considered that "just close to faith healing."

† At the time that Laura Miller, the reporter, published Perot's comments, he did not object. The following year, on an October 25, 1989, *Today* show, Perot reiterated the same ideas, stating, "You can simply declare civil war, and the drug dealer is the enemy. At this point, there ain't no bail. You go to POW camp. You can deal with this in straight military terms . . . we can apply the rules of war." In the 1992 campaign, he often said that cleaning up the drug problem "would not be pretty." However, when his earlier comments were discovered, he accused Miller of a "flight of fancy," and suggested to other journalists that they should investigate her. "How much do you know about Laura Miller?" he asked.

out against everything would certainly object and see it as racist. They say everything is racist. I don't know, I think it has possibilities, but I think it has to be worked out."[26] As for Perot's suggestions of using high technology against criminals, Smith said that the police and Perot had agreed to investigate whether "there is a way to detect chemicals in the air and pinpoint that to a house in a particular neighborhood." Smith added, "Is that legal? Can you obtain a warrant?"[27]

Perot also backed a referendum to disband the Citizens' Police Review Board, often viewed as a safeguard against police brutality, especially in the inner city. Black and Hispanic community leaders were incensed. He was accused not only of insensitivity, but even racism. "He went to one side and made up his mind and that was it," said Domingo Garcia, a Dallas city councilman active in police issues. "I don't think he has any concept of crime or the social ills of the inner city."[28]

Perot bristled at the criticism. He met with Hispanic city leaders but made little headway.[29] To the editors of the *Dallas Times Herald,* he argued that it was actually certain minority leaders who created an atmosphere of racial hatred by criticizing the police. He said he had only agreed to help the Dallas police because he was convinced there was a complete absence of racism on the force. "It bothers me to have spent 20 years of my life and tens of millions of dollars trying to help the minorities in this state and get the kind of reaction I'm getting right now. I never expect anybody to thank me, and nobody ever did. But I sure as hell didn't expect to get my teeth kicked in [and be called] a racist."[30] Perot told the newspaper editors that he would spend $100,000 for a poll to measure the attitudes of city officials and the police, in order to find out "what people think we ought to do."[31]

Soon, he blamed the Dallas city council for not aggressively backing his solutions. "The city council makes the General Motors board look informed," Perot said.[32] On another occasion he said they were "brain-dead." But a story that soon appeared in the Dallas papers had Perot on the defensive. The previous year, Perot's twenty-five-year-old daughter-in-law Sarah was stopped in north Dallas by a motorcycle policeman. Two other policemen stopped by moments later. When writing a ticket, one of them, Billy Powell, saw a pistol inside the car. Carrying a handgun in a car was a class-C misdemeanor in Texas, punishable by a maximum sentence of one year in jail and a $2,000 fine. Yet, according to Powell, they decided not to charge Sarah, since her father-in-law had been a longtime supporter and financial backer of the force.[33] Sarah, however, thought the policemen had harassed her and complained to her father-in-law. Perot then called the chief of police and said the officers involved had a choice: They could meet with him, or Sarah would file a complaint against them for abusive treatment. The three policemen, Billy Powell, Gene Keith, and Steven Solaja, arrived at Perot's office and were shocked to get a tongue-lashing, with Perot actually accusing Powell and Keith of sexually harassing his daughter-in-law. Powell later told a Dallas reporter that Perot "belittled them. He chewed them out. He made fun of the way they looked. Then he dismissed them."[34]

When the story was revealed, Perot refused to comment. "I am not going to tell you. It is irrelevant to anything." Perot told me that the policemen had been "beyond rude. . . . These two guys were nothing to write home about, they were an embarrassment to the police force. What I was really mad about is that no Dallas police officer should ever act like that. . . . They got the word."[35] Perot said that faced with the same situation, he would handle it the same.[36]*

Dallas county commissioner John Wiley Price was so angry over the incident that he filed a formal complaint with the police department's internal affairs division asking why the police had failed to cite Mrs. Perot for the pistol. "Does a person's financial standing or connection to relatives with considerable financial clout routinely influence how or whether the laws of our city are enforced?" asked Price. He was also upset with Perot. "Here is a guy who was on a personal crusade against a citizen's review board, summoning police officers to his office."[37]

While the public debate continued, Perot says he stayed on the issue "even though it was unpleasant."[38] Together with his attorney Tom Luce, he privately negotiated with the Dallas city man-

---

* The third officer, Steven Solaja, later signed a statement supporting Sarah Perot's version of events.

ager, Richard Knight, to reinstate the citizens' review board. Those talks resulted in the board losing most of its power to subpoena witnesses and independently investigate charges of brutality. Luce later claimed that if Perot and he had not done those negotiations, the public would have eliminated the board entirely.[39] That did little to calm the anger of many black and Hispanic community leaders. "To say Perot is resented in the black community is a gross understatement of the way people feel," said Peter Johnson, director of the Southern Christian Leadership Conference.[40]

But beginning in the spring of 1988, Perot moved beyond the local controversy surrounding the police. On June 1, under the terms of his buyout with General Motors, he could start a company, but only for nonprofit purposes for the first year and a half. He could also hire employees from EDS at will. At General Motors, most executives thought Perot was unlikely to start a new company, since he could earn no profit. Yet, as they had in the buyout, they underestimated him. Ross Perot had some surprises ready for his old nemesis GM, and his soon to be new foes at his former company, EDS. The fight with EDS was about to begin.

FIFTEEN

Free the Slaves

On June 1, 1988, the first day permitted by his GM buyout agreement, Perot announced a new data processing and services company—Perot Systems Corporation. "Starting Perot Systems is fun," he later said. "I consider business fun."[1] The limited partnership formed to fund the new company was called Here We Go Again.[2] Perot had struck an ingenious arrangement with the U.S. Postal Service. ("The Postal Service came to me—that is why we formed the company," says Perot.)[3]

Initially, Perot Systems would conduct a study and make suggestions for improvements and cost savings at the post office, which had a $38 billion budget. Postmaster General Anthony Frank was hoping for savings of $4 billion a year. For the study, Perot would receive $500,000. Then, for the first eighteen months (while limited by the GM buyout to not-for-profit ventures), Perot Systems would be paid only its costs. After that, it would receive an undetermined share of the Postal Service's savings. Potentially, the contract could last for ten years.[4] *U.S. News & World Report* ran a cover story, typical of much of the early press commentary: "Super Patriot: Ross Perot—How He'll Make his Next Billion."[5] "It was as though he had found the second coming of Medicare and Medicaid," says a former colleague who stayed behind at EDS.

Perot had begun planning for his post office coup in January 1988, when he had frequent conversations with several senior

EDS executives. He told them he would soon be starting a new company and asked whether they wanted to join.[6] One he spoke to in April was Paul Chiapparone, who had been rescued from Iran. Chiapparone decided not to join Perot's new firm and reported the conversation to EDS's chairman, Les Alberthal.* It put the company on alert. Perot's intentions were a serious concern. By the terms of the GM buyout, Perot and the few executives who left with him in 1986 were the only ones who could hire EDS employees and have them start working immediately for a new computer services company (but for that exception, EDS employees were prohibited from working in the same field for three years).

Within a couple of months, Perot had narrowed his initial selection to eight EDS executives. He met with them at the L'Enfant Hotel in Washington. They included lobbyist DeSoto Jordan; Pat Horner, president of the government marketing division; Ross Reeves, a vice-president in information services; Bruce Heath, vice-president for the GM account; Gary Wright, president of the government technology division; John King, general manager for all federal business; Meryl Smith, vice-president of the government systems group; and Donald Drobny, president of EDS communications. Perot believed the hotel and his meeting were under surveillance by EDS (they were not).[7] To induce the eight to come to his new company, he offered each 2 percent of the firm's stock. Perot owned 40 percent, and fully funded the start-up costs of $20 million. "I gave voting control of the company to the people who would build it," he says. "You don't find that very often in capitalist America."[8] He told the group that his goal was to earn $100 million in profits in ten years and then go public at ten times the earnings, $1.5 billion. If his plan was successful, each of the eight stood to make $30 million. It clinched the deal.†

---

* Perot was so furious that Chiapparone did not join Perot Systems that the following year, when there was a dinner celebration for Chiapparone and Gaylord marking the tenth anniversary of their rescue from Iran, Perot refused to attend.

† Perot Systems, as a private company, does not have to disclose its annual revenues or income. However, Perot told me that after seven years, "it is twenty-five times as big as EDS was when EDS was seven years old." In the year 2000, Perot expects that it "will be the size EDS was when I sold it to GM."

On May 28, the Friday of Memorial Day weekend, Perot called Les Alberthal to tell him that he would announce his new venture on June 1. When Alberthal asked how many EDS employees he was taking with him, Perot refused to say.[9] It was clear to both men that some longtime EDS workers were soon going to be faced with a quandary of choosing between loyalty to the corporation and personal fealty to Perot. "The message I got," Alberthal later said, "was that his mind was made up, he was going to do this; he had checked it out legally, and if I did anything, it was going to a David and Goliath war, and EDS would lose."[10]

Alberthal and most of the top EDS management had worked with Perot for over twenty years and were familiar with how tough he was as a competitor. The issue Alberthal now confronted was whether he would stand idly by while Perot took employees, or have the courage to fight back. "In the end, we had put our hearts and souls in EDS," says one of the company's senior executives. "We were not going to allow Ross to destroy it."

EDS opened a two-pronged attack on the Perot Systems deal with the Postal Service. They first approached Congressman Jack Brooks, a Texas Democrat. He had earlier authored a bill that required competitive bidding for government contracts. Brooks quickly demanded that Postmaster Frank cancel the Perot contract and submit it for other bids. The second EDS front was to file a formal complaint, on June 16, with the General Accounting Services Board of Contract Appeals, also protesting the lack of competition. Postmaster Frank, fresh from the private sector when he negotiated the deal with Perot, had ignored the advice of senior Postal Service aides that avoiding the contractual regulations would cause a furor in Washington.[11] "It was a sweetheart deal and absolutely stupid," said Judge Cyrus Phillips, a prominent former member of the Board of Contract Appeals.[12] Senator Carl Levin (Democrat–Michigan) introduced a nonbinding resolution to ask the Postal Service to delay the contract while it was studied. "This is a very, very sweet deal," said Levin, "unlike any contract any of us have ever heard of."[13]

"Perot was furious at the criticism," recalls a lawyer who dealt with him at the time. However, publicly, he tried to airily dismiss

EDS's actions to obtain a rescission. "I called these guys before it started and said we can't have a war because it won't hurt me," Perot said. "And it really will hurt EDS. . . . Gosh almighty, I can't believe those are my boys."[14] But it was clear now that EDS was the enemy. At Perot Systems, Ross distributed a document to new and prospective employees in which he boldly announced, "By the end of our business careers, Perot Systems will be the largest, most respected and most profitable company in the computer services industry."[15]

But as EDS increased its effort to block his postal contract, Perot's reaction became sharper. "How would you like to be competing against a nonprofit company?" he asked a *Dallas Morning News* reporter. "If you have the overhead that EDS has, it gets a little brutal to compete. It will be like turning a bunch of bulldogs loose on a bunch of poodles."[16] At EDS, many employees who admired Perot as the founder and motivator of the company could not believe that suddenly he was using the same language about them that he had used for years about competitors. Perot warned EDS about trying to compete with his new company: "Competitors have got scars on every part of their body from competing with me. I don't blame them for not wanting to compete with me again."[17] "He's like a captain abandoning ship," said Bill Wright, the EDS press spokesman and Perot's longtime friend. "He is in his lifeboat and he is angry because the ship won't sink."[18] But to Les Alberthal, Ross had not changed "a bit. . . . It's just a different battle and a different war."[19]

Soon Perot tried a different tactic, portraying his company as the underdog in a battle with a much larger corporation. But he still wanted to give the impression that it was not bothering him very much. "It's like watching my life repeated before my eyes," he said. "In 1962 when I started EDS, IBM organized a five-man team to put me out of business. That was like being in all-out nuclear war. This is like a light, spring shower."[20] According to Perot, EDS was trying to "crush the new company with politics and legal maneuvering."[21] By June 25, three weeks after starting Perot Systems, he charged that EDS was using "harassing tactics" against him, and declared the "fight is on."[22] "I am mounting a huge war," he told a reporter two weeks later.[23] Even Ross Jr.

noticed that his father had focused on a new target. "He needs challenges," said Ross Jr. "[EDS] is his biggest, newest mountain."[24]

But the press, normally kind to Perot, did not accept his new spin. Editorials spoke out against the Postal Service contract and criticized him for engineering a greedy deal. The management newsletter *Gallagher Report* gave Perot its worst-executive-of-the-month award. "Corporate monkey wrench goes to PSC [Perot Systems Corporation] chief Ross Perot for sweetheart no-bid contract with the USPS [United States Postal Service]."[25] In Washington, Postmaster Frank was under increasing criticism for having struck a non-negotiated deal. On July 10, he temporarily suspended it, prompting Perot to say that if General Motors and EDS "want war, we'll give them war. . . . It's time to let my gorillas loose to go looking for bananas now. It's no more Mr. Nice Guy."[26] On August 5, the Board of Contract Appeals voided the Perot–Postal Service contract. Five days later, Postmaster Frank tried to mollify a Senate panel by suggesting that the proposals Perot Systems developed would later be competitively bid.*

Perot barely had time to plan his next move before EDS stunned him by seeking a preliminary injunction against Perot Systems in Fairfax, Virginia, on September 27, 1988. EDS's suit claimed that Perot had violated the terms of his GM buyout.† Perot said that EDS had "opened the Pandora's Box," saying its officers must

---

* In the middle of the fight over the postal contract, Merv Stauffer, Perot's longtime personal assistant, left the Perot Group and returned to EDS. Stauffer was the EDS officer who coordinated almost all of Perot's extracorporate and special assignments. "Merv had just had enough," says an EDS executive who spoke to him on his return. "He had a higher tolerance than most of us, but eventually Ross just burned him out. He was fried when he came back to us."

† The action was filed in Virginia state court after long deliberations by EDS counsel. According to one of the lawyers involved in the original decision, there were four options. Texas was struck from the list because "there are elected judges and we couldn't trust Ross." In Washington, D.C., they could not satisfy the jurisdictional requirements. Rockville, Maryland, where Perot had done some of his recruiting of EDS employees, was high on the list as a possible site. But Fairfax, Virginia, where Perot Systems was headquartered, was chosen because "we thought it had the highest caliber of state judges, and we did not smell a good old boy network." Three days after EDS filed in Virginia, Perot filed a suit against EDS in Texas, trying to preempt the Virginia case. He was unsuccessful.

have been "hallucinating" when they filed their "classically stupid" suit.[27] Alberthal later said that the decision to sue Perot was extremely difficult, since he worried about the "emotion of taking the founder to court. . . . [It] took a little bit of time to come to grips with that."[28]

The major issues in the lawsuit centered on the language in the simplified fifteen-page buyout agreement that Tom Luce and Elmer Johnson had quickly negotiated during the closing days of 1986.* Did Perot violate the clause that said he could not earn a profit by signing a two-part contract with the Postal Service, with the profits commencing after the December 1, 1989, deadline had passed? Had he violated his buyout agreement by talking to EDS employees before the June 1 deadline for forming a new company? Did the buyout prohibit him from hiring anyone from EDS for at least three years? And finally, for how long could Perot exercise his right to hire EDS workers?

Perot derisively called the issue of his right to hire EDS employees "free the slaves," meaning that at long last they could flee General Motors and return to him. He once said that "probably half the work force over a period of time might want to join us."[29] Only 65 out of 50,000 workers had switched to Perot, but EDS was still concerned. If there was no time limit on the hiring provision, Perot could raid the corporation in small numbers for years. Since the agreement did not specify a time limit, it was up to the court to decide what the parties had intended when they drafted the buyout.

"We are not going to be awe-struck or intimated by this action," said Perot. "This has nothing to do with a legitimate lawsuit, and it has everything to do with stopping our new company. They will fail. . . . The only reason they did this is they are getting their heads torn off in the marketplace." (At the time of the state-

---

* Part of the problem about the buyout agreement was that Tom Luce had been EDS's trusted counsel for almost twenty years when it was negotiated. At the time it was done, Les Alberthal testified, "I had no reason in my own mind to believe that he [Luce] was not representing EDS." In fact, Luce was also functioning as Perot's personal attorney, and the interests of Perot and EDS were not always the same. Although Perot's interests might not always coincide with EDS's best interests, Luce never recommended that EDS should retain a different counsel.

ment, EDS had not competed on, and lost, a single contract to Perot Systems.)[30]

Perot was represented by two of Wall Street's best attorneys, Tom Barr and David Boies of Cravath, Swaine & Moore.* On the issue of hiring away EDS employees, Boies argued the most aggressive position, that Perot and Luce had intended that the "free the slaves" clause should extend forever. Elmer Johnson, the General Motors vice-president and general counsel, testified that he would have called off the 1986 buyout negotiations if he had thought that Luce was asking for the hiring right in perpetuity. "We certainly didn't have time in two weeks to write a thousand-page document. It was [not] based on the assumption that the people I was dealing with had the ultimate, extreme Machiavellian deviousness that you think I should have assumed."[31]

As for the non-compete clause, Johnson said that Luce had led him to believe that Perot only wanted the ability to do charitable work, not to undertake new business ventures. "Mr. Luce told me . . . that his client could not live with an unqualified non-competition agreement," testified Johnson, "that Mr. Perot is a man of strong charitable interests. . . . He simply has to have an outlet for these activities that might involve a contribution of his know-how in the data processing field. And he said we've got to have a qualifier that permits him to engage in these charitable not-for-profit activities that are in the public interest."[32]

Les Alberthal confirmed Johnson's recollection. He testified that Luce told him explicitly, at the time he signed the buyout for EDS, that the only reason Perot could form a company after eighteen months was for "nonprofit public service kind of activities like he has done before. He [Luce] says, 'You know, like Texas War on Drugs and education reform.' "[33] Alberthal considered the non-compete clause critical because it was the only way he could be guaranteed enough time to try and create a new identity for EDS separate from the image of Ross Perot.[34]

On October 21, less than a month after the suit was filed, cir-cuit judge William Plummer signed a temporary restraining order

---

* The author was an associate attorney at Cravath from 1978 to 1980, work-ing under Tom Barr, but did not have any contact with matters for EDS or Perot.

against Perot Systems, prohibiting it from writing contracts in two parts or entering into any business relationship "that contemplates or calls for any profitable return."[35] The judge then scheduled the next stage of the proceedings, the hearing for the permanent injunction, for April 1989. That same week, in an interview Perot gave to *Fortune,* he showed that the lawsuit had not diminished his combativeness. "I'll rip their heads off," he said. He also boasted that he had hired away EDS's best "battlefield generals and colonels," and that of the 6,000 résumés he had recently received, most were from EDS employees.[36]*

In early November, while the suit was on hold in Virginia, Perot figured out a way to pursue business while still satisfying the court's injunction. He decided to go after one of EDS's prime contracts—its multiyear deal with Texas Medicaid. It was the same contract that had helped launch EDS's success in 1968 and over which Perot had waged such a hard battle with Bradford National Corporation in 1980. Perot submitted a "me-too" bid —he offered to run the program under the same terms and conditions that EDS proposed. Since Perot Systems was still technically in its nonprofit stage, he agreed to do the work at cost, which would save the state money. Moreover, because he was still allowed to hire EDS personnel at will, pending a final decision from the Virginia court, he offered to "employ all qualified EDS personnel currently working on the Texas Medicaid Program." Perot said he was doing nothing more than giving "the option of having the Medicaid work done in a non-profit foundation funded by Ross Perot for the benefit of the needy in the State of Texas." As with other competitions, he went on a full offensive. Perot hired Austin lobbyists Rusty Kelley and Buddy Jones, placed full-page newspaper advertisements seeking new health care employees, and produced copies of internal EDS memorandums suggesting that any embarrassing company files be purged. In the press, Perot even attacked EDS's profits on the Medicaid contract, saying that its 40 percent profit margin (the

---

* The only good news for Perot, in October, was that he sold his privately held oil company Petrus to the Australian energy firm Bridge Oil, Ltd., for $112 million.

same as the company had had when he was president) was "obscene."*

Despite Perot's efforts, EDS waged an even more effective campaign. The state let it retain the Texas Medicaid contract. "Ross couldn't believe it," says one of the former executives who remained at EDS. "Alberthal, Fernandes, Heller—all the fellows who now ran the company—had been trained by Ross. They were his boys. And while he knew they were good, he didn't think they could hold a candle to him. So he couldn't quite get over that they were beating him at his own game."

Perot's national profile was higher than it had ever been. In November and December, he was asked to go on a brief speaking tour. His first appearance, at the National Press Club in Washington, D.C., was well received. He covered a wide range of issues. At one point he said that Oliver North and national security adviser John Poindexter should be pardoned, since they were "bit players" who had chosen to "take a bullet" for higher officials. "They ought to sweep the decks clean," Perot urged. When asked if he thought top government officials knew of the arms-for-hostages deal, he dismissed the question with a wave of his hand. "They all knew."

Perot warmed to other subjects, like the growing deficit. "I think you [the media] were the dwarfs and wimps in the last campaign," he told the audience of reporters. "You let the politicians get away with murder. . . . [Americans] are living in this fantasy land beyond our means." He complained that the budget deficit

---

* At an impromptu news conference held outside the Virginia courtroom, Perot told reporters that EDS was driving employees into his arms by having instituted a policy of searching those who were working on the bid proposal for Medicaid. Bill Wright, the EDS public relations chief, heard Perot's comments and told a reporter that Perot had actually instituted the search policy in 1980 during the Bradford fight. When the reporter asked Perot for a comment, he yelled, "Who's the son of a bitch who said that?" When Wright walked over and repeated the statement, Ross changed his story: "That was Alberthal [then head of health care]," said Perot. "I would have fired him on the spot if I had known that." Actually, Perot had removed Alberthal from the Bradford fight because he did not think Alberthal was tough enough for such a dirty battle.

was being treated "like a crazy aunt we keep in the basement." He called on politicians to stop living in "a fantasy world" and to face the "harsh realities." Perot even gave one of the sound bites that would become a staple of his 1992 campaign: "It's our country, we own it. It belongs to us. We can make it anything we want it to be. We've got to start acting like owners . . . to demand the things that will give our children a better life." But when asked if he would run for president, Perot said no. "I think I'd be a fish out of water unless there was a crisis around," he said. "I am too results oriented."[37]

Others, however, were skeptical of Perot's protestations. *Texas Monthly* reporter Peter Elkind, in an extended profile in December 1988, wrote: "Listening to Perot, one expects a declaration of candidacy at any minute—so evident is his scorn for the dummies in Washington and his sense that he could do better." At Harvard, also in December, Perot again rang the alarms, telling the audience, "Our country is diseased with just doing enough to get by." Condemning the poor education system, the decline of manufacturing, and the scourge of narcotics, he tempered a fire-and-brimstone message with hope for radical change. "Whose country is this?" he asked the audience. "This is the core of my message. It's ours." When asked about the recent presidential campaign in which Bush defeated Massachusetts governor Michael Dukakis, he said, "They sounded like Lawrence Welk—'Wonderful, wonderful, wonderful'—and we bought it." Finally, a hand shot up in the third row. "So when are you going to run for president?" "I won't be running for anything," said Perot. "That's not my niche in life."[38]

But as 1988 drew to a close, Perot focused once more on business. On December 16, Postmaster General Anthony Frank announced that due to the delays caused by the litigation started by EDS, the Postal Service had officially terminated its cost-savings contract with Perot. As 1989 started, Perot began working with his lawyers, preparing for the hearing on the permanent injunction in the EDS lawsuit over the terms of his GM buyout agreement. The proceedings started again in April. The testimony was largely a replay of the preliminary hearing the previous October. During closing arguments, Tom Barr, Perot's attorney, no longer insisted that the hiring clause continue forever but suggested that it be limited between twenty and twenty-five years, "or their natural employable lives."[39] Taking a cue from his client, Barr said that General Motors had "over 900,000 people. Perot Systems has 184. I can't help it, Your Honor, but I have to compare this little group of 184 to the mob, the horde from General Motors and EDS to the small group of people at the Alamo."[40] EDS attorney David Fiske asked that the court have the "free the slaves" clause expire in eight months, in December 1989.[41] The judge's decision came from the bench the same day that closing arguments finished, on April 11, and was Solomon-like. He gave Perot five years from the signing of the buyout (until December 1, 1991) to hire personnel from EDS.[42] That meant that Perot had only thirty months to exercise his option, instead of the lifetime for which he had hoped. Further, the judge restricted the pool of employees from which Perot could hire to those who were at EDS at the time Perot left.

There was a sharp contrast between the litigants outside the courtroom immediately after the verdict. Perot walked out in a huff, refusing to talk to the press, his team of lawyers rushing to keep up with him. Les Alberthal, EDS's president, stood on the side, beaming. "We're ecstatic. It's a great day for EDS," said the normally quiet executive.[43] *The Wall Street Journal* called the verdict "a sharp setback for Mr. Perot."[44] Yet Perot, as he often does in looking back at a conflict, somehow sees it as a victory. "They [EDS] sued me for executing the rights I had," he says, "and I won in court."[45]

No sooner had Perot received the verdict in the Virginia courtroom than he heard some political news from Washington that upset him—George Bush had nominated Richard Armitage to be secretary of the army. To Perot, it was like having a red flag waved at him. On this occasion, the FBI had a chance to again investigate Armitage as part of its background check for his nomination. The agent in charge was Oliver "Buck" Revell, then the assistant deputy director of the FBI in charge of field investigations. To ensure that there could be no charge that the investigation was incomplete, Revell even sent FBI agents to Perot to "make sure we had all the information he had." Perot allowed the agents to review his file on Armitage. According to Revell, Perot sometimes called him "to make sure we were pursuing all the allegations."[46] The FBI "overturned every rock we could find," said Revell, "and concluded that none of the accusations had any basis. . . . There was absolutely no evidence of complicity in drug smuggling on the part of Mr. Armitage, or that he was covering up the existence of MIAs, or any criminal activity whatsoever. I have never found anything the Christics have said of any substance to be accurate. They follow an agenda that has nothing to do with the facts, and it's unfortunate that people give credence to this sort of stuff. I think the whole thing was unfair to Armitage."[47] At the same time that the FBI investigation ended, James Harmon, the executive director and chief counsel of the President's Commission on Organized Crime, concluded that Armitage had no "connection with, or knowledge of, underworld elements in the Vietnamese community."[48]

Although Armitage had been officially cleared of the whispered allegations, they continued to circulate. Perot talked to anyone who would listen. For instance, when House Intelligence Committee chairman Dave McCurdy traveled to Dallas to solicit a contribution for a new think tank, Perot "did go on at great length about what he thought was a connection between drugs and Mr. Armitage," recalled McCurdy. "He made it pretty clear that he thought this was a very, very serious problem, and he would do about anything to prevent Armitage from becoming secretary of the Army."[49] When McCurdy returned to Washington and told "top officials" about the Armitage rumors, "most everyone said," recalled McCurdy, " 'You've been talking to Ross Perot.' "[50] "This is the kind of a classic case of Perot's absolute contempt if you're crossing one of his certitudes," said General Jack Merritt, president of the Association of the United States Army.[51] "There's no there there," a frustrated Armitage later said. "Why am I being pilloried by this guy?"[52]

But the Armitage nomination had the bad timing of running into a dispute between Senator Jesse Helms (Republican–North

Carolina) and the Bush administration over whether Japan should be allowed to co-develop an American fighter aircraft, the FSX. Helms was against Japan's participation, and decided to use the Armitage confirmation hearings as leverage to move the administration closer to his protectionist stance. One of Helms's aides asked the Defense Intelligence Agency for information on Armitage and the POW/MIA issue. There were also warnings that all the earlier personal charges would be aired at the hearings.

On May 26, before the confirmation process had started, Armitage withdrew his name from consideration. "I couldn't put my family through that. All that garbage was going to come out in a public hearing," Armitage says, "and no matter how convincingly you dismissed it, some of the mud still might stick for the confirmation process. It's a different standard in Washington: 'Is the person too damaged to be effective in the job?'; not, 'Are the charges true or not?' He really did a job on me. I wasn't going to let Perot get the satisfaction of seeing me and my family twist in the wind."[53]

SIXTEEN

"Think Outside the Box"

It was not until August 1990, when George Bush began committing American troops to the Persian Gulf, that Perot reappeared on the national scene. He spoke to eight thousand people from August through September. In each speech, he questioned whether the president had the constitutional power to commit so many troops, asked if the nation understood the consequences of fighting a war for oil, and predicted enormous casualties if combat ever developed. As Perot later said, "We rescued the emir of Kuwait. Now, if I knock on your door and say I'd like to borrow your son to go to the Middle East so that this dude with seventy wives, who's got a minister for sex to find him a virgin every Thursday night, can have his throne back, you'd probably hit me in the mouth."[1]

And he kept hammering at the budget deficit, at a time when politicians felt most Americans did not care about or understand it: "We have just been so rich for so long, we think we can do anything we want to, and we'll have the money to come up with it." He blasted Bush for allowing the savings-and-loan crisis to balloon from "$50 billion to $500 billion," and when Bush raised taxes, Perot was one of the first on television asking, "Whatever happened to 'Watch my lips—no new taxes'?" "Our president blames the recession on the war in the Middle East," Perot said. "Don't be fooled. The recession is the result of ten years of gross excess spending and mismanagement in our country."

In November 1990, he was back at the National Press Club, delivering a speech that sounded increasingly like a campaign stump talk. During the questions period, someone again asked, "Isn't it time you run for president of the United States?" Perot still claimed he did not have the temperament, but he did urge, for the first time, that people stay in touch by calling him in Dallas or writing to him at a post office box.*

He started 1991 on the talk-show circuit. He used both the *MacNeil/Lehrer NewsHour* and *Donahue* to bang the drum on the budget, and to criticize the "Super Bowl mentality" about the Gulf War. For the remainder of the year, his message was constantly being refined to a more populist attack that focused on the lack of direction in Washington, the malaise gripping America, and the need for ordinary citizens to retake the country. These themes increasingly attracted the attention of many independent and disaffected political forces.

It was at this point that Jack Gargan, the head of THRO (Throw the Hypocritical Rascals Out), started talking to Perot and gave him a forum as the keynote speaker at the fall 1991 THRO gathering in Tampa. That speech electrified many in the independent political movement, and soon Perot had the first of what would be hundreds of conversations in which Tennessee's John Jay Hooker constantly urged him to run for president.

In the subsequent months, as Perot inched closer to opening the door to a draft as an independent candidate, his family remained ignorant of his intentions. When Perot said on the February 21, 1992, *Larry King Live* that he would run for the presidency if volunteers put his name on all fifty state ballots, Margot Perot was "stunned." The day after the King appearance, as he entered Perot Systems headquarters, Perot bumped into Sharon Holman, a fellow Texarkanan and former personal secretary. She was now in the real estate division, working with Ross Jr. "My, you surprised us last night," she told him. "Don't worry. It will have all blown

---

* Although Perot did not run for public office in 1990, his lawyer and friend Tom Luce ran unsuccessfully for the Republican nomination for governor of Texas. He finished third in a hotly contested primary. When Luce was left with a $953,000 campaign debt, Perot paid it off for him by year's end.

over by Monday," he replied.[2] But even without a toll-free number, his secretaries still logged several thousand calls from forty-six states within the first week. It was a grass-roots response that had not been seen in decades in national politics.

On March 4, Perot told CNN "I don't want to do the job [be president]."[3] The following day, volunteers qualified him on his first state ballot, Tennessee. It earned him front-page headlines in many newspapers and prominent television coverage, but the Perot people knew it was not a significant milestone. Tennessee was one of the easiest states in which to qualify, requiring only 275 signatures. The big test was coming fast, his home state of Texas, where 54,000 signatures were needed by May 11, just eight weeks away. "If Texas doesn't do it, then basically it's over," Perot said. "I would just send the word out that we didn't make it."

Clay Mulford, Perot's son-in-law and a partner in Tom Luce's law firm, was put in charge of figuring out the intricacies of the ballot petition process. "There is no instruction manual," recalls Mulford. "The rules are not clear. We were not even sure initially that we could get him on the ballot in all fifty states. So six to eight people from Hughes and Luce, working nineteen hours a day, were trying to figure this out, doing daily time lines—which state deadlines came first, when to have to select a vice-presidential candidate, and the like."[4] Tom Barr also assisted on the question of ballot access.

It turned out to be one of the most difficult areas of the incipient campaign. Every state has different rules, with the deadlines running from Texas's May 11 to Arizona's September 18. Some states only allow registered voters to sign petitions, while others say voters must reside in the county where the petition is solicited, and still others bar those who voted in a party's primary from signing any petitions. Some counties have arcane rules requiring that the signatures be in a certain color ink, or that the petitions be submitted in alphabetical order. The percentage of signatures required varies widely from state to state, and some of the largest states—Texas, California, and New York—have the most stringent requirements.*

---

* Richard Winger, an expert on ballot access, says, "Most of these arcane rules were started in the 1930s by the major parties, as a reaction to their fear of

Mulford, Luce, and Barr were sure that some of the rules—those requiring an independent candidate to go through an earlier and more rigorous process than a major party candidate—were unconstitutional. "But Perot did not want to challenge them," says Mulford. "He was either going to get on the ballot with the rules the way they existed or not. He didn't think he deserved to be on the ballot if he had to do it through a court challenge."[5]

At the urging of Tom Luce, a meeting was held on March 7 at the Hyatt Hotel at the Dallas–Fort Worth Airport. "I wanted to determine if it was legally possible for Perot to get on the ballot in every state," remembers Luce.[6] Jack Gargan attended, and he also paid for several others to be there, including Richard Winger, the nation's leading ballot access expert; Lionel Kuntz, co-founder of the Coalition to End the Permanent Congress; Chuck Perry, an expert on getting petitions signed and collected; and Rick Arnold, founder of a professional petition gathering firm. The Perot representatives included Tom Luce; Clay Mulford; Bob Peck, from Perot Systems; and several lawyers from Hughes & Luce and Cravath, Swaine & Moore.

The meeting lasted the entire afternoon. "We knew after that meeting that it could be done," says Mulford, "and we told Perot that it was possible for him to get on in all fifty states." Perot was concerned, however, that he might have to formally announce his candidacy—which he did not want to do—in order to get on some of the ballots.[7] The Federal Election Commission (FEC) also requires that a person file with it if he or she has raised or spent more than $5,000 for testing the waters about a candidacy. Perot filed that letter on March 13, but it received no publicity.[8]

In mid-March, when Perot was out of Dallas, Luce, Mulford, Tom Barr, and Lloyd Cutler, a prominent Washington lawyer (and

---

the growth of Communism. They wanted to ensure that no 'red' candidate could get on a ballot easily. And over the years they have usually tightened the rules to ensure there is less chance of an outside challenge. The United States is really one of the worst countries in this regard."

former counsel to Jimmy Carter) met at Luce's office. According to Mulford, they talked "about what the game plan would be." The consensus was that Perot should maintain a low-key approach and just master the ballot access process. "If he stayed very low in the polls," says Mulford, "and was not really noticed, he would not be a threat so none of the parties would try to keep him off the ballot. We thought it best if he kept a low profile and then, in August, come out, start raising the campaign, and then make the run. Our mistake was that we greatly underestimated the extent of the dissatisfaction in the country, and that Perot would soon start rising in the polls even if he didn't spend any money or do anything."[9]

Some of the discussion during those two days centered around possible vice-presidential choices, since nearly half the states required that the petitions contain a name, even if temporary, of a vice-presidential candidate. There was some division over whether Perot should select just a temporary stand-in (even Luce was considered for that role) or whether a final choice should be made early. Dozens of possibilities were briefly discussed, including, among others, Paul Tsongas, Bob Dole, Jeane Kirkpatrick, federal judge Bernadette Healey, General Norman Schwarzkopf, and businessman Lee Iacocca.

When Perot returned to Dallas from his brief holiday, Luce and Mulford met with him at the Crescent Club. They presented their preferred choices for vice-president: Peter Ueberroth, Colin Powell, ex-senator Warren Rudman, and Senator Al Gore. Perot liked Ueberroth the best. Ross's children were friends with Ueberroth's daughter, and Perot considered him a public-minded businessman, interested in civic activities. They shared similar political philosophies. Luce tried to discourage Ross from any commitment. "I told him it was way too early," says Luce. "You haven't even decided you are going to run, or that people have put you on the fifty ballots, and then you are going to say here is my vice-presidential nominee—this isn't right. Good gosh, it is a huge decision. Ueberroth sounds good, but he has never run for office before, and we didn't know anything about his background."[10] "But Ross thought Ueberroth was the perfect match," said one campaign insider. "Two 'can do' personalities, both without the stain of politics and ready to tackle and solve the country's biggest problems. It looked like a dream ticket."*

At that Crescent Club meeting, Perot completely agreed with the idea of maintaining a low profile, and, hopefully, staying low in the polls until late August. "There was, however, a very prophetic moment in the conversation," says Mulford. "We said this is the plan, unless somebody starts defining him in June, for example. Then we agreed we would have to change the schedule and have to define Perot ourselves. But that was our only concern."[11][†]

While Perot and his close advisers discussed strategy, the frenzied public enthusiasm to his potential candidacy was unabated. The pace of telephone calls to Perot Systems now approached nearly two thousand an hour. They were almost all from people wanting to know how they could help get Perot on state ballots. On March 10, which happened to be "Super Tuesday" and the Texas primary, Ross picked Sharon Holman and five other Perot Group employees to form a team to coordinate the phone operation and gain some direction over the volunteer organizations that were being formed in different states.[‡] "Things had really got out of control because of all the telephone calls coming in," recalls Holman.[12] Yet as newcomers to politics the group initially found the work enjoyable: "I can remember all of us were in one room, with folding tables and phones all over," Holman says, "and everybody talking at once, with the BBC, *The New York Times,* everybody calling in, it was such great fun."[13]

---

* The Ueberroth selection never materialized, even though the Perot camp pursued it by having Mulford meet him for dinner. Ueberroth was interested, but unknown to almost everyone in the campaign, Perot and Mort Meyerson personally made inquiries about him and eventually opted for a stand-in candidate.

† The Perot plan of keeping a low profile had to be quickly abandoned as Perot's poll numbers kept steadily climbing. "He keeps his own counsel in many areas," says one campaign insider. "I have often wondered if when Perot dropped out in July, he had in the back of his mind our early advice that he should not start the real run until the end of the summer."

‡ Included in the group were Mark Blahnik, Perot's personal security chief and man Friday; Mike Poss, Perot Systems' leading accountant; Russ Monroe, a CPA who did Perot's personal tax returns; Darcy Anderson, a former EDSer who worked in real estate development; and Darrell Lake, also in real estate.

Separate from the effort by Tom Luce and the lawyers, those six employees became the heart of the nascent campaign. They quickly established toll-free numbers, leased twelve hundred lines from the Home Shopping Network, and hired temporary workers to help manage the volume. (It was not announced that workers were hired; instead, they pretended to be volunteers until July, when Perot dropped out of the race.)[14] A computer specialist was brought from Perot Systems to take the scraps of paper with names and addresses of callers and create a database. It provided Perot with a mailing list larger than the Republican and Democratic lists combined.[15]

The other major assignment tackled by the six Perot employees was to try to establish control over the numerous state groups, which were composed of volunteers, each of whom often had his or her own idea of how Perot should become president. Volunteers, who had sometimes left jobs and spent their own money on founding state organizations and learning about ballot petitions, suddenly resented the "white shirts" from Dallas. "Part of that problem we created," admits Sharon Holman. "If you look back at campaign themes, he was saying, 'I am Ross, and you are the boss.' He kept empowering those people to have that feeling." In the ensuing months, tension mounted as a power struggle ensued between state volunteers who thought that Perot had empowered them and Perot employees, based in Dallas, who wanted state organizations to toe the line without questions. "The volunteers felt they were doing great," says Holman, "but we at the national level knew we had to find out what to do next."[16]

"Ross called me on March 10 and told me he had a team of 'young tigers,' " recalls Jack Gargan, "who will work with my volunteers so he will have a seasoned team by August."[17] But Gargan discovered that the "young tigers" did not want his advice on strategy, and they soon started telling him what to do. When Gargan was told that Tom Luce wanted him to close the Draft Perot office he had founded in Washington, D.C., he refused, and instead appealed to Perot in a letter: "Could you imagine how that would play to the press if it were ever found out that any of the grass roots headquarters were under the direction of Tom Luce? That is the dilemma of asking for a draft and grass roots support—you lose total control."[18] Later, Gargan wrote to Perot, dubbing his employees the "Dallas Mafia." He warned that "the press will get this story eventually. And it is your own group who are shipwrecking your campaign. Instead of a corps of young tigers they are coming off as a gang of young nazis. I think you need some urgent damage control here."[19]*

Gargan was not the only volunteer to feel that Perot's employees were trying to dominate the state efforts. "The Dallas people wanted control and forgot that we were volunteers," says Joyce Shepard, an early Perot organizer in New York. "They never quite learned that you can't fire volunteers. Perot had told us it was our country and that we should take control, but when we tried to take control of our own states, Dallas didn't like that." "I knew within two weeks that it was from the top down," says Marianne Garboff, a Perot volunteer who had been a state press secretary to Senator Eugene McCarthy in 1968. "Accounting firms and law firms started taking over the grass-roots operations. Perot just had no faith in ordinary people—that's why he had to control it."[20]

Although Perot wanted his Dallas operation to direct the movement in the states, he was largely unaware of the details of the early battles. He was instead involved in discussions about what type of campaign he might run if he joined the race. An eclectic group of advisers had started gathering in Dallas, primarily on Saturdays, and talking during the week by telephone. This small group included Mort Meyerson (who was skeptical that Perot would even make the run); Tom Luce; New York lawyer Tom Barr; Jimmy Carter's former campaign manager Hamilton Jordan, who was intrigued by the Perot phenomenon; Washington consultant Buzz Miller; and Jim Squires, the former editor of the

---

* Sometimes harsh fights erupted between the paid Perot representatives from Dallas and the volunteers who had originally started the state organizations. Among many others, Pat Clawson was forced from the leadership in Virginia ("This is the only campaign that ever ate its young."); and John Opincar, a key organizer in Austin, was eventually forced out, largely over a fight about the type of software that could help organize the volunteers. In the Opincar fight, as in some others, anonymous death threats were received, and Opincar was so frightened that "I started sleeping with a gun on the floor." Later it was discovered that the backgrounds and credit histories of several volunteers had been investigated without their knowledge.

Chicago Tribune, who had met Luce while teaching at the Kennedy School at Harvard. "We only brought in guys who thought the same way," says Squires. "And we decided to run an unconventional campaign that by its very nature pointed out the weaknesses in the system. We didn't want a press plane. We wouldn't do commercials that were emotion-based. We wouldn't take litmus-test positions. No photo opportunities. And no contributions."[21]

On March 18, Perot gave a speech, "We Own This Country," at the National Press Club, that reflected the new strategy. Carried live on C-SPAN, it had a finely tuned message playing to voter dissatisfaction. It received one of the highest ratings in the network's brief history. The Dallas phone bank was swamped with calls after his speech. Following that talk, Perot went on his first extended media blitz as a potential candidate. Within a week he did dozens of shows, including *This Week with David Brinkley, 60 Minutes,* and another *Larry King Live.* On *Donahue,* he posted his 800 number for the first time. MCI later said that eighteen thousand calls hit at the same moment, and over a quarter million came within the hour.[22] Free television, especially in such large blocks of time, was not something offered by the networks in earlier races, nor was it sought by the candidates.* Perot was changing that perception at an early point in the campaign. But he also reminded the other candidates of his ability to finance a campaign when he told the *Los Angeles Times* on March 20 that he was prepared to spend between $50 and $100 million on a presidential run. *The New York Times* published its first national poll, conducted the last week of March, showing that Perot would get 16 percent of the vote in a three-way race with Bush (44 percent) and Clinton (31 percent).[23]

On March 31, Ross announced that he had picked his old friend Admiral James Stockdale as his vice-presidential candidate. Half the states required the name of a vice-presidential candidate in order to collect petitions, and Stockdale agreed to do it only under the con-

---

* Gary Hart, the former Colorado senator and presidential candidate in 1984, said that he "would have died" for a two-hour appearance on the *Today* show or *Good Morning America* during his campaign.

dition that someone else be selected before the election. A prisoner for seven years, Stockdale was the highest-ranking naval POW of the Vietnam War, and was considered by those who knew him well as a bright and reasonable man. Tom Luce's argument of selecting an interim candidate had prevailed, in part because all of the states would permit Perot to substitute his final choice later in the year.

Perot now asked Luce to become his campaign manager. Luce, who had been helping Perot since early March, had strong ties to the Republican party and had also just started a new business separate from his law firm. He had hoped that Perot would not ask him to make the association a formal one. "I was a longtime friend of George Bush's, I had great respect for him, and I thought highly of him as a president," recalls Luce. "But when Ross called and said, 'I need to ask you a personal favor. I need you full-time, I need your help,' it was actually pretty simple. I was hoping it wouldn't happen. But Ross had given me my first big break as a lawyer. I was very loyal to Ross, we were close friends, and he basically put it on a friendship basis."[24] Luce abandoned his new business venture and announced his appointment as campaign manager on April 16.

The first outsider to be hired was Jim Squires, the former *Chicago Tribune* editor. Squires had been out of the newspaper business for three years when he came aboard as press secretary. When he arrived, there were over twenty-five hundred backlogged calls from the media. "Tom Luce called me when he began to be deluged with the calls from the press and he didn't know how to deal with them," says Squires. "And everyone was very uptight and concerned about the fact that they were getting demands, hundreds of phone calls. They were overwhelmed. 'So please come down and sort it out,' he asked me. And all I could do was very basic kind of stuff. If you get ninety-six phone calls in one day from one conglomerate, which ones do you return? That's all I did when we first started."[25]

Yet Squires himself answered very few of the calls from reporters. "His attitude was that he hated the press," says Sal Russo, one of the most experienced Republican campaigners, who later became part of the Perot effort.[26] Squires kept a large stack of phone messages piled on his desk and often boasted of how he refused to call back reporters. His hiring, although taking the pressure off Luce, did not do much to help win friends in the media. However, he did help Perot in dealing with clashes with the press. For instance, on April 10, when Perot gave a speech to the American Society of Newspaper Editors, he had a bristling confrontation over the issue of his membership in an all-white country club.

"And Perot's initial response," recalls Squires, "was that he was not going to resign from the country club, and he told me a million reasons why. And my response to him was, 'That's fine, I understand that, and in fairness, you probably shouldn't have to resign, because you are not a racist. I'm not even sure the country club is racist. But here's the key point. If you don't resign from that country club, you will still be answering that question in October.' That he understood, so he did it. And the fact that he understood it and was willing to make that type of concession told me he was willing to play a little bit, compromise enough to be a player."[27]

A week later on NBC's *Meet the Press,* Tim Russert grilled Perot over his figures on the budget. Although Perot publicly held his ground, he was actually infuriated, and afterward called Luce and Squires to tell them he intended to quit.

"I had only been there a few days," remembers Squires. "Tom and I were in his office at the time. Perot said, 'The hell with this, I don't need this.' We talked him out of dropping it." The show also gave Squires an insight into Perot. "He would never, never admit that he made a mistake or that he was wrong about something. For instance, on that particular day, he had some figures which had been given to him by someone. Russert was trying to show the figures were wrong. Perot would not acknowledge that someone else had given him the figures or that they could be wrong. He just wanted to say, 'You are trying to do me in.' "

Although Squires had only briefly been on the job, he realized that Perot was certain to have more clashes with the press. "Getting to know Perot, you could tell things like this could happen," says Squires. "It was very obvious from the beginning that he couldn't exist in close proximity to the press because he could not behave the way politicians do, in the sense of being 'on' all the time. Then, combine that with the fact that he is impulsive, and forceful—I think if you were a bulldog trying to stop him, you couldn't do it—he would just run right past you. That's what made him high in the polls, and it was also the problem area. Oh, man, you knew it was going to come."

But any problems Perot had with the press were quickly overshadowed by his rising poll figures. Two days after his appearance on *Meet the Press,* a poll conducted in Texas showed that Perot's popularity was growing: He now led in that state (35 percent to Bush's 30 percent and Clinton's 20 percent).[28] Within a week, a national poll by *The New York Times* showed Perot up sharply from the previous month, to 23 percent, just 5 percent behind Clinton.[29] *The Washington Post,* a day later, showed Perot at 30 percent, in a dead heat with Clinton, and just 6 percent behind the president.[30] In California he was ahead of Clinton and tied with Bush.[31] Perot's surprising strength nationwide convinced both the Democrats and the Republicans that he would not merely fade away.

In late April, the entire campaign—as yet officially unannounced—was moved from Perot Systems headquarters to a glassed-in second-floor office in a modern high-rise off LBJ Freeway in Dallas. It was a sprawling space, capable of handling a much larger campaign staff. Some of the rooms were filled with long tables of phones, manned by volunteers and temporary workers. Security was also better at the new site, befitting Perot's concerns.

On April 26, a Sunday, just two weeks before the Texas petition deadline, Perot made his first "campaign" appearance at a picnic at a local park. On May 11, the Texas deadline, over 200,000 signatures were turned in at the state capital, Austin. It was another reminder to both major parties of the momentum the Perot movement had gathered in such a short time. Through April, Perot had spent nearly $2 million, almost all of it on the petition drive. There was no advertising—and no need for it—because of the remarkable amount of free television time.

Perot's populist, anti-Washington message had a powerful impact on many voters. He appealed across a broad political spectrum when he harshly denounced the Republicans' handling of the

economy and the enormous deficit created under the Reagan and
Bush administrations. Balancing the budget and eliminating the
deficit became his central themes—he promised to solve the deficit
"without breaking a sweat." On trade and commerce, he complained about the decline of American industry ("I would put the
guts of the blame for the economy in terms of the people who run
the companies"), while honing nationalistic attacks on Japan and
Europe. He ridiculed the corrupt practices of bureaucrats and
politicians ("They are picking our pocket. . . . The guys in
Washington work for us. They are our servants"). He demanded
that campaign finance laws be overhauled. Perot was often short
on specifics, but he promised vast changes at a time when voters
thought part of the system needed fixing, even if they were not
certain of what the remedy should be ("Take health care—we will
take it apart," he promised). But his ideas—including the politi-
cally unpopular position of imposing a fifty-cent-a-gallon gasoline
tax increase to help pay off the deficit—were often innovative.
Meanwhile, on social issues, he did not fit the stereotype of the
conservative Southerner. He was, in fact, pro-choice on abortion
("Yes, it's a woman's choice"); for gay rights ("We are a country
of individual rights, and it's that simple to me"); in favor of gun
control ("I can't believe the gun lobby wants the crazies to have
machine guns"); and for increased AIDS research ("Now, we've
got to really blitz that and get it done"). This unusual mix of political positions found a target in a large, alienated segment of the
electorate who felt frustrated by a general malaise that seemed to
grip the country. The people attracted to Perot were hard to define because they were so diverse. George McGovern and Jesse
Jackson Democrats mixed with Ronald Reagan Republicans at
Perot gatherings. They were tired of business as usual in Washington, and Perot had sent a clear message that he was eager to
change it. He was the only candidate who offered hope for fundamental change to those voters dubbed by some journalists the
"radical center" or "anxious middle."

In May, Perot freed himself entirely from any concerns about
his business so he could focus full-time on the growing interest in
his campaign; Mort Meyerson agreed to run Perot Systems. But
Perot Systems quickly took a backseat, even for Meyerson, who

soon left to join the campaign.* "I wanted Mort there full-time," says Luce. "I valued his judgment. He knew Ross. I knew Ross had confidence in him, trusted him. I went and besieged Mort. And Mort was kind of like I was—if he had his druthers, he would have preferred staying on the sidelines."[32]

Yet, even with the addition of Meyerson, the small group still felt overwhelmed. "We were working from daylight to midnight and doing only what we could do," recalls Squires. "No one was going home or sleeping. And finally, Tom and Mort, who were the only insiders, basically concluded that Tom could not do it by himself. This is really the key to 'Are we going to run, can we win, are we serious?' So we tried to bring in professionals who were willing to run an unconventional campaign with us."[33]

The emphasis was on the unconventional aspect. "One of the things that Perot had told us over and over again," said Sharon Holman, "was that we should always think outside the box. That was something that was very important to him . . . that we should never do things just because that's the way they had always been done."[34]

While the search quietly began for outside professionals to help the campaign and while Perot continued climbing in national polls, the press began scrutinizing him more closely. The first negative stories broke, including one that Perot, who was portraying himself in the campaign as a Washington outsider, had in fact been a Nixon administration insider (May 8, *The New York Times*); the accusation by newspaper publisher Richard Connor that Perot had tried to pressure him over negative coverage by suggesting there was a sexual relationship between a reporter and a city offi-

---

* Meyerson, who was independently wealthy from his years at EDS, had not gone back to work for Perot when the two left GM in December 1986. Instead, he served on a number of public projects, philanthropies, and various corporate boards of directors. "It's not as much fun to do the same thing the second time around," he had told a friend in describing why he had not gone to Perot Systems. Some were surprised when he accepted the chairman's position at Perot's firm in 1992. Several who know Meyerson believe that he had had some bad investments. In any case, Perot offered him a deal he could not refuse (a percentage of Perot Systems, which, if it went public, could be worth tens of millions of dollars).

cial (May 9, Fort Worth *Star-Telegram*); and the disclosure that Perot had tried to get out of the navy two years before his tour of duty had expired (May 23, Associated Press—"That one really bothered him," recalls Sharon Holman).[35] The Republicans also started attacking him publicly. White House spokesman Marlin Fitzwater called Perot a "monster" and said he considered him "dangerous and destructive."[36] Marilyn Quayle said, "I think it's pretty sad when someone can capture the imagination of the country with money and no policy."[37]*

Yet the negative comments did not dent Perot's popularity. In the midst of the coverage, he had finally taken the lead in national polls, 33 percent to Bush's 28 percent and Clinton's 24 percent.[38] The media started referring to the upswing as "Perotmania." Some prominent personalities either supported Perot or flirted seriously with the idea of jumping from their own parties to him. Among them were *60 Minutes* executive producer Don Hewitt's wife, Marilyn Berger; New York investment banker Felix Rohatyn; writer Shirley Lord; and celebrities Katharine Hepburn, Clint Eastwood, Willie Nelson, and Cher.

By the end of May, Perot had mastered the art of campaigning almost exclusively on television. Not only had he made additional appearances on *Larry King Live,* the three network morning shows, and the Sunday political programs, but he had also exploited the smaller shows—*Tom Snyder, Talk of the Nation, Coast to Coast,* and others. Even his three speeches—at the National Press Club, the American Newspaper Publisher Association, and the American Society of Newspaper Editors—were all broadcast on C-SPAN. The campaign only provided reporters with a schedule of upcoming television appearances, sometimes with merely

---

* When recalling the attacks three years later, Perot told me, "Oh, forget about the Quayles; you are talking Miller Lite there. I'm talking about heavy-weights. The first person to attack me—and I was just amazed by this—to levy a direct attack, a person who I had never in my life said anything but beyond positive things about, was Mrs. Bush. And all I had ever said is that she was the kindest lady. And I never said an unkind thing about Bush, and all the attacks came from the other side. But as the propaganda hits, I did this [run for the presidency] because I was upset at Bush."

a day's notice. "He's a television candidate, period," concluded David Brinkley.[39]*

Keeping his message simple, and spicing the shows with his own brand of down-home Texas humor, he was a fresh face in a sea of candidates who normally were reserved and shied away from candor, controversy, or color. That he was not well versed in all the issues initially worked to his advantage. Polls showed many people liked it when Perot was asked on *Larry King Live* if Bush should go to an environmental conference in Brazil and he replied, "I don't know a thing about it." When asked on *Evans and Novak* if the federal government should fund abortions, he said he had not "spent ten minutes thinking about it." And the public liked it when Perot stood up to reporters. On one occasion, "Lisa Meyers [of NBC] put a microphone in my face," recalls Perot, "and nearly knocked my teeth out, and asked me, 'Have you ever used dope?' And I said, 'No, why, have you?' She wouldn't answer. 'Ever cheat on your wife?' 'No, ever cheat on your husband?' I didn't know if she was married or not. And I thought, Boy, this is weird. This is weird."[40] Reporters joked about the backlash. On *Meet the Press,* Tim Russert had been hard on Perot's deficit-reducing numbers, but Perot had refused to budge. *The Wall Street Journal*'s Al Hunt later said, "Back in April, he [Perot] was at 22 and 24 percent in the polls. Russert beat up on him and now he's at 34."

Perot first stumbled with the press on a May 29 Barbara Walters interview on *20/20.* Intended by the Perot camp to introduce Margot Perot to the public for the first time, the show instead highlighted Perot's statement that homosexuals should not be appointed to the cabinet. "I don't want anybody there that will be a point of controversy with the American people," he told Walters. "It will distract from the work to be done."[41] There was an uproar from gay rights activists. Within days, Perot had "clarified" his position and backed off.

---

* Perot bypassed some opportunities for television exposure, most notably after the Los Angeles riots that started on April 29, following an acquittal of white policemen in the beating of a black motorist, Rodney King. Perot did not fly to Los Angeles because he did not want to be seen as a regular politician. Charles Black, a consultant to the Bush-Quayle campaign, later said, "The Clinton campaign, the day the L.A. riots began, was seized with the terrifying

Despite bumps like the Walters program, a high-water mark for the yet-to-be announced Perot campaign came on the day of the critical California primary, June 2. Although he was not on the ballot, exit polls showed that if Perot had run in either the Republican or Democratic primary, he would have defeated the winners, Bush and Clinton. David Gergen, a *U.S. News & World Report* editor, summed up the feelings of many when on the *MacNeil/Lehrer NewsHour* he said, "If the election were held next Tuesday, Ross Perot would be elected. . . . The only person who can beat Ross Perot is Ross Perot."[42] Perhaps in part to ensure that Perot would not defeat himself, Tom Luce made a surprise announcement the day after the California primary: Two leading campaign managers, Republican Ed Rollins and Democrat Hamilton Jordan, had officially joined the effort. Rollins would run the campaign on a day-to-day basis, while Jordan would concentrate on long-term strategy. To many commentators, it seemed like a brilliant move, the essential component that would empower the campaign to make a successful run at the White House.

---

thought that Ross Perot would get in his own plane that afternoon and fly to Los Angeles and that he'd win the election right there." But "Ross thought it would be political grandstanding," said Tom Luce.

SEVENTEEN

Enter the Professionals

When a decision was made to hire professionals, Perot's inner circle was initially inclined to hire only Hamilton Jordan, the Democratic consultant, who had attended some strategy sessions during April. Although Luce and Meyerson liked the forty-seven-year-old Jordan, they were not certain he was the right choice on his own, since he had been out of politics and had not run a campaign in twelve years. By mid-May, as Perot's poll numbers skyrocketed, Meyerson began actively pushing for balance by hiring a Republican consultant to work with Jordan. "I thought that if we went with only one or the other," recalls Meyerson, "we would have been labeled as Democrat or Republican, and I thought the only way to avoid that was to hire one from each party."[1] Soon the Republican list narrowed to forty-nine-year-old Ed Rollins, who was credited with Ronald Reagan's successful reelection effort.

Jim Squires, however, argued against hiring Rollins. "I told Mort and Tom that Eddie is the antithesis of Perot," says Squires. "He is all professional, he is big-time, he loves the press, is a spin guy, and Perot is an anti-spin guy. So it's like mixing oil and water. I think he is very smart, and he is well connected, but he is not for Perot. He was the worst choice. Fellows like Eddie are really out to convince the press how smart they are. They take credit for everything. What you needed with Perot were a bunch of self-effacing anonymous guys who wouldn't take credit for anything, who would hide in the woodwork and do what they could do. And Rollins was just the opposite."

Luce also had mixed feelings about Rollins. "I was concerned about him being a leaker and about his judgment," he says. "Early on, I read where Ed Rollins said he turned down a million-dollar offer to be campaign manager for Ross Perot. That was before I ever met with him."[2]

Meyerson, however, was a strong Rollins booster. "I had met both Rollins and Jordan and was quite impressed with both," he recalls.[3] His argument that both were necessary to give the campaign balance prevailed. When Luce and Meyerson presented their decision to Perot, he agreed. "They [Luce and Meyerson] were two people I knew, that I trusted," says Perot, "and I was busy on the road, so I left it up to them."[4]

Jordan was anxious to join the campaign. Yet, just as the Perot team was divided on Rollins, so Rollins himself had not made up his own mind as to whether he would accept the offer. His wife, Sherrie, was in the Bush White House as one of eight presidential aides, and he feared that if he worked for Perot he could lose substantial Republican business in the future. But after several weeks of being courted by Meyerson and Luce, Rollins was inclined to accept. On Memorial Day weekend, Rollins joined Luce and Meyerson for a conference at Jordan's office in Nashville. There, the two professionals divided their campaign responsibilities.

"We had each managed campaigns and knew you couldn't run it by committee," recalls Rollins. "So I said, 'I am happy to let you manage it if you want to, or I will manage it.' Ham said, 'I am not current, I haven't run a campaign in twelve years. You know the game, you know the players, you are better equipped to do it.' There was no power struggle."[5]

Neither Jordan nor Rollins had yet met Perot. Both agreed to fly to Dallas the following weekend to make sure the chemistry was right. Before that happened, on May 28 a story broke in *The Wall Street Journal* that scooped the Perot campaign's announcement about the hiring.[6] Rollins, by his own admission, was the source for the story.[7] Perot was furious, since if there was one thing he could not tolerate, it was leaking information to the press. He wanted to cancel the meeting with Rollins, but Jordan spoke to

Rollins, who apologized and said it would not happen again.[8] Perot was temporarily placated.

Before meeting Perot, Rollins and Jordan again met with Luce and Meyerson. There, according to Rollins, "we told them a final time what we needed to do to run a modern-day campaign. They didn't have a primary, they didn't have a political party, so to make up the difference, we talked in the neighborhood of a $150 million budget. It was important that they begin an advertising campaign in June or July, and run it through the summer, to define him, since no one knew who he was. The potential with Perot was real, and the potential to win, given the unique set of circumstances in 1992, was very real. We were both very insistent that we did not want to be part of anything less than that, because it just wouldn't work."[9]*

However, Luce and Meyerson deny that Rollins or Jordan ever mentioned such a large sum. "Neither mentioned $150 million, never," Luce says. "No way. That statement is not true. If it had been mentioned, it would not have stopped the conversation, but I would have remembered it, and I would have thought that was crazy. Ross Perot didn't get to be a billionaire by giving people blank checks."

Instead, Meyerson and Luce tried to impress on the two professionals that they needed advice on how to run an unconventional campaign. Luce remembers saying, "You must understand that this will be an entirely different presidential campaign than has ever been run, and if you think you are going to prepare cue cards for Ross Perot, forget it."[10]

Rollins and Jordan wondered whether Perot might still veto their hiring the next day.[11] Yet, when they finally met for five hours, Perot was gracious and likable. "He was in his sales mode.

---

* Although $150 million seems large compared to the approximately $70 million spent by each Republican or Democratic candidate, it is not an easy comparison to make. The major party candidates get the equivalent of tens of millions of dollars of "soft money" in expenditures by their party organizations. Also, the multiday party conventions, receiving widespread television coverage, are worth several million dollars in free advertising. Many professional consultants believe that an independent candidate must spend at least twice the amount of "hard money" (that reported to the Federal Election Commission) as the Republican or Democratic candidate.

He agreed to everything," Rollins remembers. "We put the $150 million figure on the table. 'I will spend whatever it takes,' Perot said. 'I have never swam halfway across the river.' He said all the right things."*

Rollins was impressed by Perot. "There was a Reagan quality to him and a Nixon quality to him, the two presidents I had worked for. The Reaganesque quality was when he spoke of Americana and POWs. He started telling some of his great stories about these POWs, and he had obviously done some wonderful things. The Nixon part was the paranoia, the sort of 'They are out to get me.' I can't tell you precisely what it was, but there were little things that warned me even then about his paranoia—this whole thing, 'The Republicans are out to get me, the opposition research,' and all this horseshit. Then we spent some time talking about my wife [a Bush aide]; he was very concerned about that."[12]

Perot also said several things that led Rollins to believe that Perot had had him investigated prior to the meeting. "He talked about my health, and no one really knew much about my health," says Rollins. "I had a stroke in 1982. He talked about my first marriage, and said, 'You've already had one failed marriage; we wouldn't want you to damage this one.' No one, anywhere, knew about my first marriage. It happened before I came to Washington, it wasn't in the clips, you would just never have found it in the Lexis/Nexis clips. No one thought of me as someone divorced."[13]

But Perot told Rollins and Jordan they could run a campaign that might change political history. They left feeling comfortable with their decision to come aboard. They were not aware that Perot was not especially impressed with either of them. Less than a week later, Rollins further dampened any enthusiasm Perot may have had when he appeared on a Sunday morning television show talking about his new job. "He didn't clear that with Perot first," says Jim Squires, "and Perot was on the phone chewing him out

* Perot denies that Rollins put a $150 million figure on the table. "That's not at all true," says Perot. "No chance. I never even considered spending 100 million. [If he had said that] it would have raised a warning flag about his judgment. . . . If he thought he had to spend that much, then maybe he shouldn't come, because I wouldn't spend that much."

and critiquing his performance immediately. And he said something on TV that got Jesse Jackson all riled up, and Jesse was calling Perot. Perot was all out of joint."[14]

"Rollins ignored direct instructions," says Luce. "He had agreed not to go on television. Then he goes right on and purports to speak for Ross Perot. Ross said, 'I am not going to have Rollins speak for me when he doesn't know me from Adam. He doesn't know what I think. He doesn't know what I say.' Rollins's first strike was the *Wall Street Journal* article, strike two was that he went right back on television after we had gone through this with him again, and strike three was Jesse Jackson."[15]

It almost made Perot feel that he had made a mistake by agreeing to any professionals coming aboard. "I should have said absolutely no [to their hiring]," he says. "Within three days after he [Rollins] was on board, I felt it was a serious mistake and wondered if he was really on board to represent me."[16]*

Perot's uneasiness worsened when the first professional, Charlie Leonard, arrived in Dallas the week of May 25. Leonard, a young adviser at the political consulting firm of Sawyer-Miller, had been the campaign director for the House Republicans in the 1990 elections. He was coming aboard at the urging of Rollins, and cut his own deal with the Perot group. Luce wanted him to become the political director, in charge of the state field operations. Leonard's mistake was being too aggressive in his first meeting with Mark Blahnik, Perot's personal security chief and man Friday, who had been responsible for the field operations. Leonard thought he was in charge of Blahnik, and at a meeting ordered him around as if he were a new assistant.

"Blahnik was like a deer in headlights, completely overwhelmed," says Leonard. "But he didn't want to give it up, because he couldn't give it up since he was working for America's hero, Perot, the man who always said, 'Never give up.' "[17]

Blahnik, instead, went to Perot and complained. "Charlie Leonard made Mark Blahnik mad," says Jim Squires, "embarrassed

---

* Meyerson, in a telephone call to Rollins, later told him that he had considered the possibility that Rollins was a "double agent" for the Republicans. When I asked Perot if he thought Rollins could have been a plant, he was firm: "Of course. A plant? No team could have been that destructive by chance."

him, hurt his feelings, and berated him. That was like chewing out Ross's son. It was the end of Leonard having any responsibility in the campaign."[18]

"Luce called me in the next morning," recalls Leonard, "and says, 'What's the problem with you and Mark? He is steaming mad because he said you bullied your way around here for the last two days, gave him a hard time, and you keep getting in the way of getting his job done.' "[19]

A couple of days later, Mort Meyerson called Leonard into his office. It was the first time they had met. He told Leonard the run-in with Blahnik was a serious problem and that "Ross would like me to fire you. I would have no problem doing that." Leonard responded, "Even without knowing the facts." "Yes," said Meyerson, "even without knowing the facts. They don't concern me. But I don't want to do that. We have to figure out how we will get around this."[20] Leonard finally agreed to be deputy campaign manager, focusing on the operations and campaign budget.

Soon after the flap with Leonard, some of the other professionals recruited by Rollins and Jordan began coming to Dallas. Sal Russo and Tony Marsh, two of the Republican party's most experienced media consultants, got there on Friday, June 5. Russo had been a former Rollins business partner and would be his chief deputy, concentrating on campaign strategy and issues development. Rollins arrived full-time the following day. June 7 was the arrival of Bob Barkin, a media strategist who had previously been the managing editor at *The Washington Post*. None of the new consultants had any idea of the early tempests. Nor were they initially aware that many of the volunteers who had flocked to the Perot effort feared that their arrival would further stifle the grassroots spirit and turn the campaign into a traditional one.*

Perot, only days after they were hired, tried to downplay any excitement about the professionals, as well as reassure his core

---

* There was political naïveté not only among the volunteers, many involved in a political campaign for the first time, but even among the Perot Systems employees who formed the core of Perot's inner circle. "By June, when they started," recalls Sharon Holman, "I was so green I had done nothing more than cast my vote. I had never heard of Ed Rollins before. I had never seen C–SPAN before."

supporters, in an interview with CNN's *Morning News.* "Tom and Mort felt it would be wise to get the two best people in the business. . . . [but] this will not be a conventional campaign. What we're trying to do is get the talent in here to make sure we can deliver on my commitment to run a world-class campaign. They will not be my handlers. They will not get me up in the morning, dress me, give me words to say, tell me what to do and where to go. That's not their role. Their role is to bring the experience of what's involved in the massive campaign, in terms of getting it organized, and making it work."[21]

The day of Rollins's arrival, he had scrawled two words on a blackboard: HOPE and KOOK. "This is our challenge," he told Charlie Leonard. "Depending on what we do here, is how Perot will emerge from this campaign."[22] That night Leonard and Rollins had dinner. "Charlie started to tell me the horror stories of what had happened that week, and it emphasized to me that this thing might be going nowhere," says Rollins. "I had bad vibes from that first day." He could not easily get answers from Luce and Meyerson about what Perot wanted to do. Perot often would not talk directly to the professionals, but instead only through his trusted aides.

"And nobody really had the ability to go to Ross and talk to him straight," says Joe Canzeri, a Republican advance man who came to the campaign in early June. "The only two who could do it were Meyerson and Luce, but they had the least campaign knowledge."[23] There was also a problem in that Meyerson admittedly had no interest in politics. At a dinner party at his house (a multimillion-dollar converted power plant filled with modern art), Meyerson hosted Rollins, Leonard, Russo, and Canzeri. Perot was riding high in the polls.

"What do you think of this?" Leonard asked Meyerson.

"Not much."

Leonard, knowing that Meyerson considered himself a Renaissance man, interested in philosophy and history, rephrased the question: "I mean, the campaign, the perspective in terms of politics and this moment in history."

"I could care less about politics," Meyerson told him. "I rarely read a newspaper and I don't vote."

"You are kidding me," said a startled Leonard. "You've got to be joking."

"I'm not kidding."[24]

"Meyerson was just brusque and cold," recalls Sal Russo. "It was more than he just couldn't be bothered; he actually seemed hostile."[25]

But while the professionals had early complaints about the Perot team, Luce and Meyerson were also displeased with their new consultants. "I thought Ed and Hamilton did a disservice to Ross," says Luce. "They had no campaign plan. Ross Perot is a very businesslike guy. He kept saying, 'Give me the plan.' And I would tell them, 'Guys, that is not the way you deal with Perot. You must give him a specific proposal. He is not going to give you a blank check. You must give him a proposal.' "

But there were actually several early suggestions by Rollins that Perot rejected. One was to send personal thank-yous to the people who had called in to Perot headquarters. "They had four to five million names, all volunteers who wanted to get out and do something for them," says Rollins. He told Perot that the campaign should mail a package to each volunteer, thanking them for their support, asking them if they wanted issue papers to give to their friends, and checking on whether they would make phone calls, put up signs, and other campaign jobs.

"You mean like the junk mail that comes across my desk?" Perot asked Rollins. "I don't read that crap."

"If it comes from you they will read it," said Rollins. "We will put a certificate in there, and they won't only read it—they will save it."

"What will this cost me?"

"Maybe fifty to sixty cents each."

"Well, that's just a waste of money, spending two to three million dollars. That's just a waste."

"But you would be getting three million people working for you," Rollins implored.

"I won't spend that type of money to say thank you. Forget it."[26]

But the more serious issue that immediately confronted Rollins and the rest of the professionals was to change the way Perot dealt with the media, which angered many journalists. Rollins told

Perot that in order to stem the tide of negative stories, it was best to feed the press some fluffier pieces so that they kept busy. The fact that Squires was largely ignoring media requests was another part of the problem. Rollins wanted to handle the press directly, but Squires kept that responsibility.

"That was a major mistake," says Rollins, "because Squires, who had been a young star at the *Chicago Tribune,* was bitter because he had been fired. He had this tremendous resentment toward television, the new press, and the modern campaign. He basically would leak shit to his buddies from the Watergate era and piss all over everybody else. The new generation just drove him nuts. And the whole idea of manipulating the press, which he considered people like me to want to do, was just so foreign to him. The reality of it is that they are going to write a story, and you basically have to get them to try and write your story. Squires didn't want to do that, nor did Perot."[27]

"It would have made my job a lot easier with the press if he [Perot] had played the game," says Sharon Holman. "I kept hoping that he would understand that it is a game."[28]

Almost all of the professionals thought Squires was wrong for the press job. "I liked him, but he was caustic," says Joe Canzeri. "A lot of reporters told me he was mean."[29] "He had a Nixonian contempt for the media," according to Charlie Leonard.[30] "Avoiding the media at all costs is not a plan," says Tony Marsh. "Since we had a candidate who was unique in American political history, that attitude squandered many opportunities to get our message across."[31] "Did Jim go too far?" asks Tom Luce. "Probably so."[32]

Yet the most important opinion belonged to Perot. He liked the way Squires dealt with the press. "Eddie Rollins thought I was too tough on the press because I wouldn't make them comfortable, feed them, spin them, and make them happy," says Squires. "Perot took this daily beating from the media, and then Eddie would tell him it's because you've got to feed the press like animals in a circus and all that stuff. A lot of that is right, and I didn't disagree with that, but it was counterproductive to what Perot wanted to do. The press was going to chew Perot up any way you dealt with them. Do you chew him long-distance, or do you chew him up close? It would have been a pipe dream to think you would avoid all that bad coverage—it would not have been a pipe dream if you had been a Democrat or Republican who had been one of them, who had been legitimized by them. But Perot—and I don't even think Eddie understood it—the Washington axis, the Elizabeth Drews, Bill Safires, the Katherine Graham group, basically thought Perot was a dangerous man. And Perot had a temper, he's a volatile kind of guy, and having the press in close proximity to him was inviting disaster."[33]

"Perot has a mistrust of the media in general," says former television anchor and friend Murphy Martin. "Rollins did not understand that."[34]*

Realizing he could not generate better stories by having Perot change his dealings with the media, Rollins then proposed that Perot start running television advertisements in June to counter the largely Republican efforts to negatively identify him. "When I went into public life," says Perot, "I had to be redefined [by the major parties] because the person they defined in private life would have been an attractive candidate."[35]

The problem was deciding when the commercials would run. "Everybody wanted to run television ads in June, to identify him, except for Perot," says Clay Mulford.[36] "Perot was convinced that elections are decided in the last thirty days," says Squires. "Voters don't pay attention until then."[37] Perot refused to budge, despite repeated entreaties from Luce and Meyerson. "I never succeeded in getting Ross to sign off on the strategy that I thought was winnable," said Luce. "I was pushing very hard to go on television, to define Ross before the Republicans could define him. . . . Perot had it in his mind that that approach was politics. . . ."[38]

Hamilton Jordan, as eager as Rollins to run early ads, put together rough cuts of some biographical segments in the hope of

* "They [the media] have an agenda," Perot told me. "They have their own candidate. They have a person they have to subtly endorse. The best endorsement is not an open endorsement. When the other candidates are being diminished by odd stuff—that is better than endorsing John Smith. Just say good things about John Smith for several months, chew up the other competitors, and John Smith is a natural."

convincing Perot that advertisements could be a valuable tool. When he made his presentation, Ross hated them, especially the way Margot appeared, and that his Annapolis days had been virtually ignored. Suddenly, Jordan discovered how volatile Perot could be. "Mort Meyerson and I came into the meeting late," recalls Rollins, "and Perot was yelling and screaming at Hamilton, calling him unprofessional and incompetent. Perot was really going nuts."[39]

Jordan went back to his office, where he had an anxiety attack. "I walked in on him," says Rollins, "and thought he was having a heart attack. 'Ed, I have never been talked to like this. Jimmy Carter and I had differences of opinion, but nobody has ever yelled and screamed at me and treated me like a piece of shit. I am leaving, I won't take it.' So I said, 'Ham, you have to do what you have to do.' "[40]

The next morning, Jordan told Luce he was leaving. He asked Rollins to leave with him, but Ed told him no, that he had formed a team and felt an obligation to them. By midday, Luce and Meyerson had talked Jordan out of resigning. "I didn't want to be seen jumping ship," Jordan later said.[41] He largely stayed away from the office for two weeks, calling Charlie Leonard two or three times a day for a briefing, and occasionally dropping in.[42] Even after his full-time return, the other professionals noticed that Jordan stayed quiet in most conflicts, instead using Rollins as his proxy. "He would stir the pot," says Tony Marsh. "He would get all of us anxious about something and then say to Ed, 'Ed, you are the guy who has to bring this up. You've got to go and talk to these people.' Then Ed would go in and say, 'This is all screwed up,' and Ham would stand there and be quiet."[43]

But Jordan's treatment convinced Rollins that he would rather leave than be spoken to the same way. His already fragile relationship with Perot was soon further strained. "See, I wouldn't take it," Rollins says. "When I started, I had told him I was not a yes man, but a street fighter who had worked for three presidents. 'I don't take any shit from anybody. I am going to tell you exactly what you need to hear, and you may not like it, but you have got to know it is what I think is best for you.' He told me that's what he wanted. It turned out, of course, that he didn't like it. A couple of times, shortly after the Jordan incident, he started yelling and screaming at me, and I said, 'Ross, calm down, and when you do I will be in my office.' 'Don't you walk out of here, Rollins.' 'Don't treat me like some employee. I work with people, not for them. And if you want me to work with you, then I will. But I am not going to be treated like one of your busboys here. If you want me out of here, then I'll leave, but I am not going to tell you that you are right when you are wrong.' "[44]

"But the key, by then," says Luce, "is that Rollins is out. Perot isn't paying one minute of attention to what he is proposing. Perot has already written him off within the first two weeks."[45]

Although Perot rejected ideas from Rollins and Jordan regarding press relations, he continued to field television producers' calls on his own and, without telling anyone else in the campaign, would suddenly fly off to appear on a show. One of the most frequent was the *Today* show, on which he appeared seven times, once for the entire two hours. "We would say, 'Where is Perot?' and then turn on the TV and find him on *Today,*" recalls Squires. "He liked the producer on that show, and would go on even though Katie Couric was one of those people that irritated him to the point where he could almost not handle it.* We were all telling him, 'Don't do this, don't do that.' But he would get a call from someone he liked and just agree to do the show or the interview on his own, and he wouldn't tell the rest of us. He thought that was better than paying for commercials. There was one producer on NBC who could always talk Perot into going on. And there were half a dozen others—Ted Koppel could always get to Perot, Jack Nelson from the *L.A. Times* could always get through, and so could Bob Woodward. And, of course, Larry King."[46]

"He did some of those shows so many times, and he was reaching a repetitive audience," says Murphy Martin. "And after a while, the hosts had asked him all the nice questions, so they started becoming more aggressive. As the shows got tough with him, he got into the mode 'They aren't going to get the best of me.' "[47]

---

* Couric's roommate in college was Ed Rollins's wife, Sherrie. "Ed kept telling Perot that Katie couldn't stand him," says Sal Russo, "and that he should forget trying to win her over. But he kept thinking he could."

Unaware of how little influence he had with Perot, Rollins continued generating new campaign ideas. For instance, Sal Russo and Tony Marsh had developed an elaborate concept for a national convention, a week-long extravaganza of people from all fifty states, punctuated with celebrities. Russo wanted to fill ten stadiums around the country on the same day, plus put another half million people in Central Park, and link all the sites through a satellite hookup. "Everyone seemed to like it," recalls Russo, "but a decision was never made. It just sat there, and no one gave us the go-ahead to pull it together."[48] "It wasn't just on the convention," says Marsh, "but also on issues like when and how we should formally announce his candidacy, and what about the vice-president. Perot would say, 'Let me think about it,' and then there was no answer."[49]

Although Perot paid little attention to the Rollins group, he did become preoccupied with the growing number of negative stories about him in the press. There were reports that he had investigated President Bush and his sons; that he used private detectives against competitors and employees; that he benefited at public expense over Alliance Airport; that he had threatened to "nuke" General Motors; and that he had blown up a coral reef at his Bermuda home so he could dock his boat nearer his house. "You could not believe the amount of time he would spend trying to track down the sources of those stories," says Rollins. "And the crazier the story, the more it bothered him. The coral reef made him go ballistic."[50] "It was easy to divert Ross, especially if you discussed his children," says Squires. "We couldn't get him off those issues."[51]

At times the campaign could be diverted by trivial issues. Liz Noyer, a Republican media consultant who arrived in July, was surprised at how much time was wasted on such issues. "For instance, reporters would call and ask, 'Does he wear boxers or briefs?' " she says. "Then there would be a two-hour discussion about it. 'Don't talk to this person, we are not allowed to talk about it,' or, 'You can't ask him about it.' Then Sharon [Holman] would talk to Ross about it, and then they wouldn't answer it. The amount of time wasted on a nonissue like that was the same as given every other issue—all issues seemingly had the same gravity, except that personal issues were the highest priority."[52]*

Rollins and Jordan were concerned that since Perot would not allow them to run a television campaign to promote his image, the unanswered press stories would be hard to counter prior to the election. In fact, Perot actually blamed the professionals for the poor press. He told them that he had received only good coverage before they arrived. "He didn't understand that it took a couple of months for the press to take him seriously and start the investigations that were now resulting in stories," says Rollins.[53]

Rollins brought in a prominent television adman from San Francisco, Hal Riney, in the hope of building a positive Perot image. Rollins and his team remained convinced that if Perot was shown the right material, he would go along with an early ad campaign. Riney had done the "Morning in America" series for Ronald Reagan, as well as the critically acclaimed series for GM's Saturn. He sent some film crews to trail five ballot petition rallies, and intended to cut scenes and interviews from those to create a series of advertisements that defined Perot by allowing average voters to say why they supported him. "We wanted these realistic, not some warm and fuzzy stuff that looked staged and manufactured," says Bob Barkin.[54] There were almost a dozen commercials planned. Barkin worked with Riney to develop a plan to run the commercials through the first night of the Democratic convention, in mid-July. Tony Marsh worked on his own media pieces, including a five-minute biography, and some commercials built around Perot's formal announcement.

Perot, meanwhile, wanted to see a detailed budget for the entire campaign. Charlie Leonard worked on it, and used the $150 million figure that Rollins considered critical. While preparing the budget, Leonard discovered that campaign spending was "out of control—they had no idea of what was going on."[55] He found that campaign workers were renting offices, buying computers, leasing phone lines, and hiring workers without checks and balances. "I knew how bad it was when we had a meeting of the field people,

---

* "The Republicans made a major tactical mistake in aiming their attack, and so much negative press coverage, on Perot in June," says Clay Mulford. "It allowed Clinton to go into hibernation, let him get off the defensive, and Hillary started baking cookies. By leaving them alone, the Republicans allowed Clinton to come back."

about forty of them," says Leonard. "My first clue was, we were at a hotel and took a break, standing in front of a bank of pay phones. They were all on their cellular phones. I went back and asked for the cellular bills, and we had a kid who had a $30,000 cell-phone bill in one month. I brought it to Mort Meyerson, and he flipped."[56]

Leonard, not wanting to upset Perot with too large a figure, devised the first budget so that some costs were hidden. Among them was the expense of the nearly seventy-five professionals who had come onto the staff by the third week in June. Another was the hiring of a pollster, former Pat Buchanan bean counter Frank Luntz. The pros needed polling data, and wanted Luntz to do in-depth focus groups in New York. Perot was against both, so although Perot knew Luntz worked for him, he did not want to know the specifics.*

Leonard's budget had general figures and categories, including $60 million for an ad campaign, $13 million for direct mail, and other large sums for regional phone banks, satellite uplinks, staff, and travel. It was presented to Perot by Luce, Meyerson, and Rollins in the second week of June. Perot hit the ceiling.[57] He wanted to eliminate some parts of the campaign (like the group working on issue papers) and wanted to know why other things, such as a fund-raising plan, were not included. Rollins thought it a poor idea for a billionaire to solicit contributions, but Perot wanted everyone "to get a little skin into the game."[58] "Perot had this feeling we were trying to rip him off or something," says Rollins. "It was very strange. And meanwhile, Luce and Meyerson, who said, 'Don't worry, we'll translate for you and get Ross's approval,' were useless on this one."[59]

Former EDS executives Bill Gayden and Tom Walter came in to help Leonard completely redraft the budget and put it in terms Perot would accept. "Gayden and Walter told me how nutty Ross is with money," recalls Leonard, "that he doesn't understand money, and he doesn't understand budgets. They said, 'Your work is thorough, but it's not the way to sell it to Ross.' "[60]

---

* Luntz conducted fifteen focus groups, and discovered that the more voters knew about Perot's stand on various issues, the more they liked him.

Instead of presenting Perot a budget for the entire campaign, they brought it to bare bones and calculated it for just forty-five days. Advertising was broken away from the main numbers and placed into its own category. Even without advertising, it was close to $40 million. Gayden and Walter pitched it to Perot, and got it approved.

Perot's antagonism toward the professional staff was growing. "You've got more damn desks in here than the Pentagon," Perot mumbled on one of his infrequent visits to the campaign floor.[61] "Perot used to be in the headquarters every day, and then started coming in less frequently," says Sal Russo. "He used to wander around, then he stopped that, and then he would just come in for meetings, and then he had the meetings at his office. He became more estranged and distant, almost on a daily basis. You could sense that things were going straight downhill. Plus the fact that every single day he was rejecting ideas one after the other. Every day it was a new batch of rejections. You couldn't get a decision made."[62]

Meanwhile, the professionals were increasingly bypassing Luce, the campaign chairman, and appealing instead to Meyerson for help in dealing with Perot. "Ultimately, we were all reduced to using Mort," says Squires. "We all agreed that Mort was the only one that could have any influence with him. Tom got really undercut and hurt during this campaign. Even Tom started relying on Mort."[63]

Not even Meyerson, though, was able to resolve the impasse over the question of the advertisements. Rollins took Ross Jr. to dinner and enlisted his help. Ross Jr. went to his father and tried to persuade him to accept Riney's ideas and start an early ad campaign. "All that happened," says Squires, "was that Ross chewed out Ross Jr. and banned him from the campaign and told him to stay the hell out of it. Ross Jr. didn't come back until the fall. And once you manipulate Ross's children, you are a dead man. Boy, they killed themselves."[64]

The professionals sat there daily with nothing to do. "The work area had no buzz," says Liz Noyer, "as opposed to any other campaign headquarters I had worked in. It was sterile—no camaraderie, and a general feeling that people were just spinning their wheels."[65]* They met daily, and continued planning an entire campaign, down to the schedules, appearances, and the platform and issues. The campaign had been mapped out through the end of August. Perot appearances were settled into early October. "We did it to occupy ourselves," says Bob Barkin. "That's how bad it was. Ed would say we were all going to get fired, and we would say, 'Please God, sooner rather than later.' "[66] Charlie Leonard had finished a twenty-two-page campaign plan. No one, outside the professionals, read it.

"We started to come to the conclusion that Perot was not the right guy, and if he got elected, he might do more harm than good," says Tony Marsh.[67] "We would get weekly summations of each candidate's electoral votes potentials," recalls Bob Barkin.[68] On Friday, June 25, Perot had 408 electoral votes. Barkin looked at Rollins. "My God, we are going to elect this guy president." Rollins did not even look up from his paperwork. "Do we really want to?" he asked.[69]

Outside the campaign headquarters, the negative press stories were slowly having an effect on the public's perception of Perot. Also, his testiness with reporters no longer seemed charming, but rather played into the hands of those who claimed he was not of presidential timber. Perot's negative ratings in the polls started rising, and his support softened.

In late June, Ruth Altshuler, a prominent Dallas philanthropist and Perot volunteer, sent a memo to Luce, Meyerson, Rollins, and Jordan. In it, she told them that Katharine Hepburn's agent had called, and Hepburn was about to resign from Perot's National Advisory Committee. The agent had asked Altshuler, "What's happening down there?" In the memo, Altshuler listed her observations:

* At the time of the campaign, she was known as Liz Maas but has now returned to her maiden name, following a divorce. When she interviewed for the job in Dallas, in addition to Meyerson and Luce, Perot also talked to her. He asked her if she was separated or divorced and if she could handle the job as a single parent (she had a three-year-old daughter). He probed into her earlier jobs with Peter du Pont and the Bush White House. "It was very uncomfortable," recalls Noyer. "The details and the types of questions he was asking me, they were way too personal and made me feel very uncomfortable. He made me feel ashamed of myself. I should have walked out then."

- Perot is going down the drain here.
- He is self-destructing.
- He is breaking people's hearts.
- It's disappointing, horrible, and shocking.
- Those who were for Perot are switching to Clinton.
- He should have new speeches.
- The commercials should be out now.[70]

"Actually, many of us were thinking, 'How do we get out of this?' " recalls Bob Barkin.[71] According to Leonard, "Hamilton was so stressed out that he couldn't come to work. He was like a whipped puppy."[72]

"I have been very sick once in my life," Jordan told Leonard, "and I lost a marriage. I am not going to let this thing do it to me again."[73]

As the atmosphere worsened, the professionals began to feel that the heavy security at the campaign headquarters might be directed against them. "We all thought our phones were tapped," says Charlie Leonard. "We heard clicking on our phones. There were always security people walking around. Blahnik told me that Perot would not have Secret Service protection because they all worked for the White House and the Secret Service was close to the CIA. I heard all the time from the Perot people that Rollins was a Republican plant. It got kind of spooky." (Leonard actually tried to obtain a device to check if the phone lines were tapped.)[74]

Sal Russo, who had been around every presidential campaign since the 1960s, could not remember any with such stringent security. "Every time you turned around you had to carry cards or talk to someone for permission to go anywhere."[75] "These guys with Ross Perot haircuts," says Bob Barkin, "and white shirts and polyester ties, and carrying cellular phones and walkie-talkies, would always be in the corner of your vision, walking around, lurking around. They never said anything. You always felt like you were being watched. Who knows what they did?"[76]*

---

* One Perot volunteer, Bob Penn, claimed that at least some of the Perot Systems employees were involved in computer hacking late at night at the headquarters. Penn said that voter and motor vehicle registration files from different

When Liz Noyer started working for the campaign during its final, tumultuous week, she found it was like "Fort Knox. I left some papers on my desk the first day, and the patrol left a note for me, 'For security reasons, your things were taken.' "[77]

At the end of June, Rollins decided to bring the unsettled issues to a head with Perot. He asked Leonard to give him one page on the major outstanding problems. Leonard turned in a single-spaced typewritten page with ten issues. Among them were "No Strategy," and "Decision Making Too Cumbersome."[78] Sal Russo prepared his own three-page sheet of issues that had to be resolved quickly.

Rollins thought Perot was at a critical junction and that the top priority was still to convince him that he had to start running advertisements, and almost immediately. Much to Rollins's frustration, Perot had begun relying for media advice on Murphy Martin, the former news anchor who had known Perot since the 1969 Christmas trip to Vietnam and now had his own media consulting business in Dallas. Rollins thought Martin was "clearly in over his head."[79] But Perot liked Martin and trusted his opinion.

On Thursday, July 9, Rollins and Riney met with Perot. Murphy Martin was there. Riney started presenting his concept for the campaign commercials, when Perot interrupted him.

"What does it cost to make one of these things?" he asked.

"Well, it depends. You don't just go out and shoot rallies," Riney told Perot. "First, you have a meeting and talk about concepts. Then you write a script, and then I bring in storyboards. At that point, we sign off on the concepts. Then we go out and shoot film and then take film and try and edit it. That's the way we do it. So it depends on all that goes into that."

"So you can't tell me then what one costs?"

"Well, we just shot fifteen commercials for Saturn, and it cost $12 million. So I would say the commercials you see on television are $400,000 to $800,000. The top-notch ones are a million to a million and a half."

---

states were being downloaded. He later told his story to the FBI and picked out pictures of the alleged perpetrators. The FBI gave him a lie detector test. Penn claims that the agents told him he passed the exam, but the FBI refuses to disclose the results, or its reasons for not pursuing the case.

"Well, that's ridiculous," said Perot, waving his hand as if to dismiss Riney. "That's not at all what I had in mind."

"But you asked me what a commercial could cost," Riney said, "and I am telling you."

"Could you make them for $80,000 to $100,000?"

"Sure, I could probably make one for that. It depends on what you want to create and what type of impact you want to have."

"Could you do one for $5,000?"

"If that's what you wanted. I could go down to a store, get a Betamax, shoot you, and that's it. Is anyone going to watch it or care? Probably not."[80]

Murphy Martin says that Perot had told him before the meeting that he intended to fire Riney. And now he did.

"Hal, I appreciate all you have done, but I don't think we need to go down this road any further. You are trying to put me in a Rolls-Royce and I want to be in a Volkswagen."

Then Perot turned toward Martin. "Murphy, what can you get local crews for?"

"Well, I can get them for $1,500 to $1,800 a day [Riney had told Perot his crews would cost up to $175,000 a day]. They aren't the Cecil B. DeMilles, but they are good."

Rollins and Riney were taken aback. "Riney's eyes popped open," recalls Martin. "Rollins tried to say that something could be worked out, but it was too late. The handwriting was on the wall for Rollins."[81]

As they walked back to their offices, a glum Rollins told Riney, "Tell your kids this is the day the Perot campaign ended."[82]

The day after Perot dismissed Riney, he left for Lansing, Michigan, where volunteers were to turn in the petitions that would place Perot on their state ballot. Squires had convinced Perot that it was possible to control the press coverage if the campaign developed specific issues for appearances like the one in Michigan. Lansing was the test case. Squires developed a theme (Perot always wrote his own speeches) for a car-producing state: "Japan should give us the same deal we are giving them, and we would make Detroit the number one auto city in the world again."[83] Squires ensured that a copy of the speech was given to the press beforehand, with the hope that subject would dominate reporters' questions.

At the end of a day of rallies with his volunteers, Perot returned to the airport. Joe Canzeri had arranged for the press corps to be on the side of the tarmac. Perot refused to stand on an X marked for him on the ground. He walked over to the reporters, expecting they would talk about the auto business. The very first question was from Morton Dean of ABC News, who wanted a comment about a *New York Times* story concerning Perot's policy on gays.* Perot was furious, wouldn't answer any more questions, and got on his plane to return to Dallas. He later screamed at Sharon Holman, bringing her to tears.

"That is the day it all came apart," says Jim Squires. "If you are looking for the incident or the time when the real Perot comes into conflict, a direct conflict, with the managed candidate Perot, it was on that tarmac in Michigan. And we were gone from that moment on. We didn't have a chance after that."[84†]

Perot was so angry that the next day, Saturday, July 11, he flew to Nashville on his own for a speech to the NAACP. Squires was accustomed to getting calls from Perot while he was en route to his next engagement, "but he didn't call that day," remembers Squires. "He was mad at Eddie and Mort and Canzeri, and he went off to Nashville and did his own thing."[85] In that speech, Perot referred to his black audience as "you people" and told them how they could help "your people." Although the NAACP and prominent black spokesmen like Jesse Jackson tried to play down the incident, it was an embarrassment that prompted Perot to issue a statement the same day from Dallas saying he had meant no offense.

"We sat around and watched the NAACP talk," remembers Charlie Leonard, "and it confirmed to all of us that this guy is just not going to listen to anyone. He is not going to let anyone write a speech. He is just going to keep doing it his way until he implodes. It was the final straw that broke the camel's back after twenty little

---

* Meyerson had issued a campaign position on including gays in the military that contradicted Perot's earlier stance. *The Wall Street Journal* and *The New York Times* prominently covered the difference.

† According to Sal Russo, who discussed the incident at depth with Canzeri, Perot "went berserk that the reporters could see the tail numbers on his plane. He acted like it was a state secret or something, and accused Joe of a major breakdown in security."

events that led up to it." Rollins turned to the group of professionals and said, "We've got to figure a way out of here."[86]

On July 10, the same day as the Lansing incident, Rollins had
submitted a memo to Perot listing three options: to run a proper
campaign; to continue his current pattern, in which case he did
not need Rollins and Jordan; or to quit. Meyerson responded to
Rollins's memo to Perot: "He is not going to do it your way, and
he is not going to quit."

On the Sunday, July 12, talk shows, there was considerable discussion that either Rollins or Jordan would soon leave. The next
day, *The Wall Street Journal* reported that Riney had been dismissed. Perot blamed Rollins for the leak. On July 15, Perot met
with Luce and Meyerson in the morning. When the two left
Perot, they went to a lunch they had scheduled with Rollins.
Rollins expected that either the meeting would result in a break-
through or he would be finished. Bob Barkin wrote in his notes:
"D-Day."

The purpose of the lunch was actually to fire Rollins. "I told
him," recalled Tom Luce, " 'Ed, you know, we're swimming
upstream. You're miserable. This isn't working. You're having no
impact. The campaign is in two armed camps. Perot will not listen to you. It's best if you leave.' "[87]

"It was not confrontational," recalls Meyerson. "Rollins did not
throw a temper tantrum. Instead, he said, 'You guys don't know
what you are doing, you surround yourselves with losers, you
don't get it. I am a professional.' We told him that we would work
something out with him but that we didn't want him going around
bad-mouthing Ross. 'We would not feel good about being nice to
you, helping you in your personal situation, if meanwhile you
turned around and lobbed grenades at us.' He understood that."[88]

When Rollins returned to campaign headquarters, he gathered
his staff together to tell them that he was finished. Within a few
minutes, the main area on their floor filled with security people. "It
was like the Gestapo had swept down on us," recalls Bob Barkin.
"It was incredible. One minute they weren't there, and the next
moment they had swept in and somebody was standing over each
of our shoulders. Rollins's secretary came running in, in tears, saying that some guy wanted to get what was in Ed's computer."[89]

"They came around and started confiscating people's papers and turning off computers," says Liz Noyer. "My computer had been turned off, and I wasn't at it. When I asked what had happened, some security fellow said I had been neutered. And they were trying to turn off some of the phones."[90]

Reporters were calling to obtain a comment on the rumor that Rollins was gone, but they could not even reach the answering machines. Charlie Leonard ran into Tom Luce's office, yelling, "This is an outrage!" Luce was genuinely surprised. As he tried to put a stop to it, Joe Canzeri walked up and down the aisles. Rolling a piece of paper into a makeshift megaphone, he barked, "They're boarding the buses for Buchenwald. They are taking us to Buchenwald." Tony Marsh stood on the side laughing. Jim Squires just glared from his office. Sharon Holman went over to Liz Noyer. "I am so sorry," she said. "It didn't have to happen. I am so sorry."[91]*

Perot initially seemed unfazed by the commotion over Rollins's dismissal. Later that day, he told Murphy Martin, "Now that we have gotten rid of the Pentagon, we can go to work."[92] That night, when Tom Luce and Mort Meyerson joined him for dinner, his calm veneer was gone. He was agitated, more than at almost any time they had known him. Perot "struggled with the decision of whether to stay in or get out," Luce remembered. He had a "catalog of reasons" for withdrawing, no one more important than another. Among those mentioned was his fear that the election would be thrown into the House of Representatives and his belief that the Republicans were waging a dirty-tricks campaign against him.[93] Perot was uncharacteristically indecisive. By the end of the evening, he announced that he had made up his mind. "I am going to get out of this thing," he told them. Nobody argued with him.[94] Although Luce was devastated, he hid his disappointment from Perot. Meyerson, however, felt "relief that we didn't have to continue going on the death march."[95]

---

* The day Rollins left, *The Washington Post* published a poll that showed Perot had lost his onetime lead over Bush and Clinton and, in a free fall, had dropped to third place.

The next day, Perot showed up to take over the microphone at Tom Luce's weekly press conference. He told a room of reporters, "Now that the Democratic party has revitalized itself, I have concluded that we cannot win in November and that the election will be decided in the House of Representatives . . . so therefore I will not become a candidate." He incongruously did not close down the operations in the states where petitions were still needed to put him on the ballot. In fact, he urged the volunteers to continue their work so "that both parties can know exactly who the people are who are so concerned about their country's failure."[96] Tom Luce had tears in his eyes. Afterward, Perot refused to address the volunteers. Luce spoke to them, and broke down during his talk. Many of the volunteers were weeping openly as reporters crowded in trying to get comments for their evening news feeds.

Perot had withdrawn from a race he had never officially entered.

EIGHTEEN

The Second Coming

Perot seemed genuinely surprised by the fury of his followers at his withdrawal. He was also chagrined by *Newsweek*'s cover, THE QUITTER, and newspaper headlines that trumpeted THE YELLOW ROSS OF TEXAS. There was a rash of stories about Perot's history of throwing in the towel if things did not go precisely his way (wanting out of the navy early, leaving IBM when it would not adjust his commission rate, and taking a buyout from GM when it refused to listen to his proposals). Within a day of withdrawing, however, he seemed to be keeping the door open for a possible return. Perot told Barbara Walters that he did not see reentering the race "unless I thought it was good for the country."[1] That night, on an appearance with CNN's Larry King, he refused to say that people should not vote for him. When King said, "You're still sort of hanging that leaf out," Perot responded, "That's the magic, Larry."[2] Halfway through the show, King felt that Perot missed running for office and that "if I had him on longer, I know I could have had him say he was getting back in that night."[3]

There were those around Perot who were not surprised that he so quickly questioned his withdrawal from the race. "I thought that if he dropped out, he would regret his decision within seventy-two hours," says Murphy Martin.[4] "A week or so after he withdrew," says Mort Meyerson, "I saw that he was thinking about coming back in."[5] When John Jay Hooker reached Perot within a couple of days of his withdrawal, he told Ross, "We need you. What happened?" "I'm still in the stadium," Perot told him. "I'm on the sidelines. I'm not in the game, but I am still here."[6]

Murphy Martin, for the remainder of the summer, continued assembling fifteen to twenty television commercials, "in case he [Perot] decided to get back in the race."[7] The campaign organization Perot had started in Dallas was not disbanded. The Dallas headquarters cut its phone bank from 72 lines to 48, and the paid staff in Dallas dropped from 178 to 35, but many of the hard-core volunteers refused to leave. Perot did not object when Meyerson returned to run Perot Systems and Tom Luce went back to his law firm (Perot blamed Luce for most of the foul-up with the professionals and refused to even talk to him, shattering a friendship of twenty years). Perot was now making his own decisions, unfettered by arguments with consultants or longtime friends.

He first wanted to ensure that though he was not a candidate, his issues stayed at the forefront. Within ten days of his withdrawal, *U.S. News & World Report* ran an extensive cover story on his economic plan, which Perot consultant John White had worked on for two months. And fortuitously, a paperback book Perot had been working on for months, *United We Stand: How We Can Take Back Our Country*, also about his economic plan, was published. While he contributed to its success by buying 100,000 copies, it sold well on its own, climbing to the top of the best-seller lists by Labor Day. His core issues still struck a responsive chord in the electorate, and that encouraged him.

He also must have been encouraged when, within days of his withdrawal, volunteers from all fifty states flew to Dallas, at their own expense, to urge him to reconsider. Although he rejected their entreaty, he did, however, agree to pay for their return to Texas at the end of July for a three-day meeting. There, Perot addressed the state representatives, and told them they should decide their own future. "It was the consensus that everybody wanted to go on," says Orson Swindle, a former POW and a friend of Perot's. "We talked of the twenty-four states or so where he was not on the ballot, and we asked if he would fund the effort in the remaining states and see where this can go. He agreed."[8] Perot decided to give $7,500 a month to each state chapter for a new organization, which the state representatives decided to call United We Stand

America.* When Swindle, who became the first president of United We Stand America, privately asked Perot if he would honor his commitment he had made on the Larry King show— that if his name was on all fifty state ballots, he would run—Ross said, "We'll see."[9] During the next seventy days, when Perot was officially out of the race, Federal Election Commission records reveal that he spent $11 million in maintaining petition drives and establishing state organizations that could be turned into campaign offices on a moment's notice (he spent more money in August, for instance—$4 million—than in any month in which he had actually been in the campaign).[10]

Meanwhile, both the Democrats and Republicans made efforts to win Perot's support. Perot would only consider it if one of the parties endorsed his positions, especially his economic plan. John White, who had helped Perot draft that plan, went to work for the Clinton campaign and also became an unofficial emissary there. Mickey Kantor, the Clinton campaign chairman, was a friend of Jim Squires and provided another Democratic link. On the Republican side, Perot was his own intermediary.

Neither effort started with much promise. As for the Republicans, Perot spoke to Bush, and then had two private meetings with campaign chief James Baker. Perot first demanded answers about what he believed were Republican dirty tricks directed against him. "They never came back with an answer," says Perot. "Now, when they desperately want your help, you think they would at least come back and lie and say no, say something."[11] That single issue, which was more serious than the Republicans realized at the time, stalled any progress.

The Democratic effort also started off rocky. "Carville [James Carville, a Clinton campaign consultant] called and offered me a job," says Jim Squires, "and Al Gore called and wanted to know what sort of job Perot wanted. That was the wrong way to approach Perot."[12] Finally, Squires opened negotiations with Kantor, trying to convince him that Clinton should adopt Perot's

---

* The name was almost the same as the one Perot had used for his Vietnam missions for the Nixon administration. However, the name United We Stand was now held by a gay and lesbian group in California, so Perot had to settle for United We Stand America.

positions. "Kantor tried hard to do it, and we thought it was going to happen," says Squires. "Clinton was close to Ross on many of the issues," says investment banker Felix Rohatyn, who was part of the Democratic effort to win Perot's support. "Ross could have stayed out if he wanted to, but I just don't think he wanted to."[13]

In mid-September, Perot and Clinton spoke on the phone but could not resolve the final 10 percent of disagreement between them. The major parties had begun to view Perot's reentry as likely. He was already on the ballot in forty-nine states by that time, and he reemerged into the public eye when he toured the areas in Florida damaged by Hurricane Andrew. When asked on C-SPAN about the increasing talk that he was planning an "October surprise," Perot said, "If the volunteers said, 'It's a dirty job, you've got to do it,' I will belong to them."

On September 18, Arizona became the fiftieth state to put Perot's name on the ballot. Almost immediately after, Perot issued a most unusual invitation to the Republicans and Democrats: He suggested they send emissaries to Dallas to meet his volunteers, so they could decide whether they wanted to support a major party candidate or instead wanted him to reenter the race. "I didn't think they would come," says Clay Mulford. Actually, both parties feared the meeting was, as Republican consultant Mary Matalin says, "a setup." They thought Perot intended to boost his public standing by showing how both parties had to answer to him, while citing the manifest sentiment of his volunteers as a reason to rejoin the race. Yet the parties agreed to the meeting, since their greater fear was alienating the substantial bloc of Perot voters.

On September 28, 1992, they trekked to Dallas. The Democratic delegation consisted of campaign chairman Mickey Kantor, investment banker Felix Rohatyn, Senators David Boren (Oklahoma) and Lloyd Bentsen (Texas), Congresswoman Nancy Pelosi (California), and civil rights activist Vernon Jordan. The Republican team included campaign manager Bob Teeter, Senators Phil Gramm (Texas) and Pete Domenici (New Mexico), housing secretary Jack Kemp, national security adviser Brent Scowcroft, and Mary Matalin. Perot gave each delegation two hours to present and defend its platform to his state leaders, followed by a press conference (the press was excluded from the actual meetings). Hours of national television coverage were given to the one-day convocation, with Larry King, who ran his show from Dallas that night, saying, "We've come to the mountain."[14]

The consensus was that the Democratic delegation made a much stronger presentation. "The Democratic one was thoughtful, prepared, and well planned," recalls Mulford. "The Republican presentation was the opposite, nonsubstantive. It was conclusionary. Their point was, 'As bad as they are, we aren't as bad.' "[15] Sharon Holman remembers that even the Republican attitude worked against them. "Mary Matalin's body language was terrible," she says, "turned away from the United We Stand people. She almost had a scowl on her face. The Republicans just looked like they were going through the motions."[16]

On the following day, September 29, Perot said that his 800 number had received 1.5 million calls urging him to run. No record was kept of how many called opposed to Perot's reentry.[17]

Two days later, on October 1, Perot ended whatever suspense was left. He announced that the volunteers "have asked me to run . . . and I am honored to accept their request."[18] At the press conference that followed, Perot showed he had lost little of his disdain for the press. "Have fun," he told them. "Get raises and bonuses, and play gotcha. I don't care." He refused to disclose any travel plans or campaign appearances. "We're not going to lay out strategy for you," he snapped.*

Perot did, however, have a concept for running his second campaign. There would be no professionals. The new guard com-

---

* Over the summer, Perot's anger at the press had increased as a series of stories broke about how his campaign had paid credit firms and investigators ($76,000 to just one company) to check the backgrounds of dozens of volunteers who were leaders in many of the state efforts. Those checks prompted the campaign to dismiss some of its state leaders, in often nasty internal fights that resulted in yet more press coverage. Some of the cases ended in litigation, and the FBI even temporarily looked into the issue to see if any laws had been broken (none had). In other instances, volunteers who were not affected by the background checks were still so infuriated with the notion that they resigned. Perot viewed the checks as necessary to ensure that the people who represented him at the state level did not have unsavory pasts, and he thought the press had overplayed the issue.

prised Clay Mulford as campaign manager and Sharon Holman as press secretary. Murphy Martin and Lanier Timerlin (a longtime friend and the owner of a successful Dallas advertising agency) became the media team. United We Stand America director Orson Swindle doubled as a television spokesman. Jim Squires gave advice from his Tennessee farm. Also, some of the young Perot Systems employees, like Mark Blahnik and Darcy Anderson, were back. Perot decided he would conduct his new campaign over television and not in the field. Within ninety minutes of his reentry into the race, he had bought a half hour from CBS ($380,000) and a prime-time slot from ABC ($500,000).

"The second campaign was a lot more fun for Ross," remarks Mort Meyerson. "It was free-swinging—no organization. He could do whatever the hell he wanted to. It was perfect for him."[19]

But Perot had done tremendous damage by his July withdrawal. The poll numbers after his reentry showed how far he had plummeted since the lofty days in May and June when he ran in a dead heat with Bush and Clinton. The day after he came back to the race, a national poll showed Perot at only 7 percent. His solution to those dismal numbers was to spend his money on infomercials, where in thirty-minute blocks he addressed single subjects, without any bells and whistles. His first show ran on October 6, five days after his return, and was titled *The Problems—Plain Talk About Jobs, Debt, and the Washington Mess*. He was insistent on the presentation—talk directly to a camera, armed only with a few charts and a pointer. It looked like a low-budget corporate training film, and most political professionals were skeptical that it would hold the public's interest. Perot had the last laugh. The first program, with Perot flipping through charts at the rate of one a minute, drew 16.5 million viewers, and actually beat the network competition in the Nielsen ratings, including a baseball playoff game. That success encouraged him to eventually run five infomercials during the campaign, including one expanded to an hour.

Also, under the gentle prodding of Lanier Timerlin, Perot finally agreed to a series of thirty- and sixty-second commercials that were as slick as anything Ed Rollins and Hal Riney had suggested. However, on these, Perot was involved in the message, editing, and script. He did not speak on any of them. They were instead filled with imagery (a powerful storm in one, a red flag in another, and a ticking clock in a third), and concluded with the words "The candidate is Ross Perot. The issue is leadership. The choice is yours." The first one appeared one week after Perot returned as a candidate. When Mulford suggested that he might want to mix some campaign appearances in with his television onslaught, Perot said, "Tell me a good reason to do that."[20] (It would be headline news when he did finally make a personal appearance, only nine days before the election.)

While Perot had bought himself a significant presence on television, the one opportunity that he knew could jump-start his campaign—appearing in the presidential debates—was not in his control. The two major parties had to invite him, and the Commission on Presidential Debates then had to approve his inclusion. The Republicans wanted Perot in the debates because they thought he would split the vote for change with Clinton. Mulford feared, however, that if Perot dropped too low in the polls, he might be excluded. But when the Clinton campaign provided Mulford a draft agreement between the candidates, it specified that Perot be included. Mulford did not wait for an official invitation. Instead, he sent letters to both Mickey Kantor and Bob Teeter "accepting" their invitation on behalf of Perot and Admiral James Stockdale, who was still his vice-presidential candidate.[21] It was too late for the major parties to back out. The commission, in a split decision, agreed to Perot's participation. "I was outside the system," Perot told me. "I marveled that they even let me in. I couldn't believe that the two-party system allowed me to participate, and I am sure they are sorry they did."[22]

While Perot crammed with his advisers in Dallas to prepare for the first debate—on October 11, at Washington University in St. Louis—he sent just three people to do the advance work (Bush had 350 people; Clinton, over 250). "I was the entourage," says Murphy Martin, who was the only person to accompany Perot to all three debates. "Coming from the airport we would have one unmarked police car, with no sirens. We stopped for lights. People would recognize him and he would roll down the window and talk to them while waiting for a light to change."[23]

Debate officials were startled that Perot not only refused a motorcade but that the car he used was a rental from Hertz. Perot arrived only thirty minutes before the start of the first debate. He says he learned that Clinton and Bush had "been there all afternoon, with their makeup on, leaning forward in the chairs, saying, 'I feel your pain,' literally. Rehearsing. So I had nothing to do, so I thought I would visit these guys. So I went in to see Governor Clinton and everybody kind of looked like a snake had crawled in the room.

" 'I just came in to say hello.'

" 'He's getting up.'

" 'Oh, is he taking a nap?'

" 'Oh, no, he is getting up for the debate.'

" 'Oh.'

"So I went over to see President Bush. And, of course, Jim Baker came out, and I couldn't get in the door. And we had a nice conversation, and I said 'I just came over to say hello.' "[24]

When Perot heard that neither Bush nor Clinton had agreed to shake hands when they entered the stage, he made it a point of walking up to them and vigorously shaking their hands. In the debate, he did well, mixing his quick wit with sharp answers. "I'm all ears," he said at one point, and when criticized for not having any government experience, he shot back, "I don't have any experience in running up a $4 trillion debt." The focus groups watching the debate for different pollsters found Clinton likable, but ranked Perot the best. Bush was a dismal third, coming off flat and without any direction. At one point in the debate, James Carville, who was watching it with other aides, remarked that Perot's performance was starting to worry him.[25]

Perot thought he had clearly won. "However, the real issue is how do the spin masters—not *their* spin masters—but how do the network announcers and all deal with it," says Perot. "And how does the press play the debate. I would be happier to live in a world where you watched the debate and then went off and talked about it and drew your own conclusion. But if you stay tuned, you will be told what to think. In wrestling, when one guy is lying there unconscious, you know the one standing won. Or a football game, you can look at the score. But a debate is a little more subtle."[26] The public evidently liked his performance. He jumped to 13 percent after that first encounter. Seventy percent of the respondents to a *Newsweek* poll said they would take Perot more seriously as a presidential candidate because of his performance.

Two nights later, Tuesday, October 13, was the vice-presidential debate. Admiral James Stockdale had barely been heard from before he took the stage that night in Atlanta, with Al Gore and Dan Quayle.* While Gore smoothly dominated the banter, Stockdale seemed lost at times, wandering away from his podium, uncertain of his answers. At one point, he had to have his hearing aid turned down. It was a painful ordeal to watch, and many post-debate commentators thought it would reverse Perot's mini-surge. But Perot helped himself two days later, in the second presidential debate, in Richmond, Virginia. It was watched by more than 90 million people, the highest-rated of the three contests.

"I was sitting in the room by myself," Perot recalls. "You go to the other guy's rooms, there were enough people there, just makeup people, to shake hands for thirty minutes. The makeup guy is there, the wardrobe master is there, the guy who practices the lines is there—they had a two-minute answer memorized for every question in the history of man. I had to just sit there for thirty minutes. I didn't have anything to do. I wandered behind the stage at one point and talked to the fellows there, and at another point went into the audience and made sure my children were okay and well seated."[27] When Perot went into the audience, there was momentary panic in the Bush and Clinton camps. Aides believed he was trying to gain an unfair advantage by working the crowds beforehand. They were particularly worried since the format of this debate was different from the first. This time, a moderator would direct questions from an audience of 209 uncommitted voters. Instead of standing behind podiums, the candidates would sit on stools, out in the open.

Perot was again good, but seemed somewhat uncertain. Rather than sitting, he leaned against the stool, appearing uncomfortable throughout the debate. Some of his answers sounded like prac-

---

* Perot's late reentry into the race made it impossible to substitute a permanent candidate for Stockdale. The deadline for substituting a candidate had expired in many states.

ticed sound bites. When he flubbed a statistic on one answer, that became the segment used by many news organizations. But Perot's performance still shone compared to that of Bush, who was again unconnected to the audience. Clinton continued to build on his first respectable outing. The postdebate polls showed Perot up slightly, at 14 to 16 percent.

The final debate was on Monday, October 19, in East Lansing, Michigan. "They had to come out from the same side of the stage," remembers Perot, "and they [Bush and Clinton] didn't want to look at each other, so they had to build a partition. And they stood there for ten seconds so they couldn't see each other. [I realized] this is theater, this is the magic act, this is the illusion. And it really doesn't have much to do with anything. . . . It was an act."[28] But Perot showed that he knew how to perform the act well. While Bush and Clinton were both in top form, Perot was at his mischief-making best, scoffing at both men's accomplishments and positioning himself as the real messenger of change. The four networks judged the debate close, with two declaring Clinton the winner; one, Perot; and one, a tie between Perot and Clinton. Again, national polls showed Perot creeping up, to 18 and 19 percent, while his negative ratings had dropped by half, from 63 percent when he reentered the race to only 33 percent.

With just two weeks left before the election, Perot had momentum. Bush was worried that Perot could deprive him of victory by stealing away some key states, such as their home state of Texas. Clinton fretted that Perot would split the vote for change and might let the Republicans sneak back into office. But Perot had made a decision in the third week of October that was to prove fatal to his revived ascendancy—he had arranged an interview with *60 Minutes,* to disclose his "real reason" for withdrawing the previous July.

On Sunday, October 25, he startled viewers of *60 Minutes* when he announced: "I received multiple reports that there was a plan to embarrass her [his daughter Carolyn] before her wedding and to actually have people in the church at the wedding to disrupt her wedding. I finally concluded that I, as a father who adores his children, could not take that risk."[29] Perot also charged that the Republicans were about to release "a computer-created false photo of my daughter Carolyn." He did not explain what he meant.

He did, however, tell *60 Minutes* that the sources for these stories were three people—one was a highly placed Republican (a "person I respect," said Perot) whom he has never named;* the second source was a "longtime friend" whom he also declined to identify (actually David Taylor, a BBC producer based in Washington, D.C., who had developed a close relationship with Perot over the POW/government conspiracy issues during a ten-year period); but he did name the third source: Scott Barnes.[30]

Understanding Barnes is the key to unlocking the mystery of why Perot really dropped out of the presidential race and what was behind the puzzling explanation he offered on *60 Minutes*.

---

* After his initial interview, Perot said there were two Republican sources, but still refused to name them. Published reports later named the two as Senator Bob Dole of Kansas and Representative Bob Dornan of California, but both denied they were the sources. An FBI official later intimately involved in the investigation says, "We could never find any evidence that he [Perot] had been warned about his daughter's wedding from anyone in the Republican party."

NINETEEN

---□---

The "Mystery Box"

Who is Scott Barnes, and how did he end up as the only named source for Ross Perot's belief that the Republicans were waging a dirty-tricks campaign against him? Eight years earlier, Barnes had given Perot information about Defense Department official Richard Armitage. At that time, the CIA's deputy director, Bobby Ray Inman, had told Perot that Barnes's information was useless. In fact, to many, Barnes's reputation was poor. "Among the hucksters, mercenaries and information peddlers who people the shadowy world of Vietnam POW investigations, Scott Barnes may be the biggest tale spinner of them all," was *Newsweek*'s assessment in 1992.[1] Even to Perot, Barnes is a "mystery box."[2] The one thing that is certain about Barnes is that almost everything in his past is enveloped in controversy.

Barnes entered the army for a three-year hitch in 1973, at the age of nineteen. He later claimed to be working with a military police intelligence group, and said the army had released him early as part of a coordinated plan for him to return to school and then work in the intelligence community.[3] Years later, when the military intelligence group said it had no record of him, the chief of the intelligence group did not remember him, and army documents showed that he was actually dismissed for failure to "meet acceptable standard for continued military service," Barnes has said it is all a deliberate effort to discredit him, and that his military records had been tampered with.[4]*

When Barnes turned to a law enforcement career, controversy followed him. Within two years, he was hired and fired from the police forces in El Cajon and Ridgecrest, California. El Cajon contended he had filed false police reports, and Ridgecrest said he had destroyed evidence and lied on the witness stand.[5] Barnes, unfazed by the dismissals, countercharged that both cities let him go because they feared his private investigation into police corruption.[6] (He sued the El Cajon police for $200,000.)

His assertions during the next few years were startling: Someone, he alleged, tried to kill him in July 1979; the next month, he said, he received $10,000 in the mail to kill Mafia chieftain Joe Bonanno, Sr.; he was arrested in October 1979 for grand theft by fraud, but was subsequently acquitted; in November 1979, Barnes said he was working for the Department of Justice on a Hells Angels investigation (the Justice Department denies he has ever worked for them, and information he provided to California investigators about the Hells Angels prompted a warning to state law enforcement agencies that he was an unreliable informant); he filed a civil suit against the Los Angeles police for the use of excessive force after they acted on an anonymous tip about a drug smuggler that fit his description (he later received a settlement on that, though the police came to believe that he himself had set up the incident by placing the anonymous call).[7]

Nineteen eighty-one was the year that he connected with adventurer Bo Gritz and was soon on his way to Thailand, where he became embroiled in the controversies over POW/MIA issues. Barnes later wrote that he had found live American prisoners in Laos and then received an order from the CIA: "If merchandise

---

* For almost every allegation against him, Barnes offers an explanation. For instance, he has the original of his release records from the military, and they do not reflect the derogatory language that appears in a photocopy made available by the Senate Select Committee on POWs/MIAs in 1992. He asserts that the FBI has investigated his claims and determined that his military records were improperly altered. The FBI has refused to comment.

confirmed, then liquidate."[8]* Upon returning to the States, Barnes regaled a writer from *Soldier of Fortune* with details about his "covert" mission, including how he entered Cambodia by swimming over a river. The result of those talks was an article ("Scott Barnes: My Favorite Flake") in which the writer criticized him, in part, since there was no body of water anywhere near where he said he crossed the border. Barnes then said he had actually crossed at a completely different location.[9] But that still did not explain how, on the day he claimed he swam the river, others said they saw him in the U.S. embassy cafeteria in Thailand.[10]

The same year Barnes met Gritz, he handed out business cards that showed him to be on the staff of Representative Robert Dornan, who was then chairman of the House's POW/MIA task force. "He never worked for me," said Dornan. "He faked my business card and put his name on it and was passing it around Bangkok."[11] (Barnes explained, "The Agency [CIA] figured it'd be a good cover to use Congressman Dornan.")[12]

In 1984, Barnes landed a job with the Hawaii Department of Corrections. One of the inmates in the prison where he worked was Ron Rewald, who had tried to defend himself against embezzlement charges by claiming he was a CIA agent. Barnes later wrote that the CIA told him, "Rewald must be killed," but he began to fear that the CIA intended to frame him for the murder.[13]†

It was Barnes's involvement with the Rewald case that would indirectly lead him to Perot. The man who introduced them was BBC producer David Taylor.[14] He was investigating allegations of intelligence drug smuggling under the guise of secret warfare, and the laundering of narco-dollars into unauthorized government operations, when he first met Barnes. He was impressed, especially with Barnes's knowledge of the Rewald matter, and told a

---

* Barnes boasted that he had taken hundreds of photographs of the prisoners, but said that the CIA destroyed them.

† ABC News broadcast Barnes's allegations about the CIA and Rewald on September 19 and 20, 1984. The CIA demanded a retraction, threatened suit, and filed an unprecedented complaint with the FCC. After its own investigation, ABC retracted the stories. Barnes then sued ABC.

fellow journalist that "he [Barnes] was for real."[15] Soon, Taylor recommended that Perot talk to Barnes.

"Now, the only reason Scott Barnes could ever have any contact with me," Perot told me, "was because David Taylor was the person who would talk to me and convince me that I should listen to this voice over the phone that I had never met yet."[16] That Taylor was the one introducing Barnes was significant, since Perot trusted Taylor completely. "David is very bright, very intelligent," says Perot. "David has one hundred percent recall, he is very crisp with his facts, he can give you four sources for every fact he brings up, and as you listen to David, it is almost like talking to a computer. He is fact, source, fact, source, and that gave David a great deal of credibility with me."[17]*

Perot started calling Barnes in 1984. On the first call, Barnes did not believe it was really Perot and hung up. Once convinced, however, that the call was not a prank, he spoke to Perot.[18] In that conversation, according to Barnes, Perot wanted information about "POW intelligence matters overseas." He was particularly interested in Ron Rewald.[†] "He also wanted information concerning drug smuggling," says Barnes, "and some arms dealings in the Golden Triangle."[19]

Over the next several years, Barnes says that Perot called between ten and fifteen times a year. Some of the conversations lasted over two hours. One of Barnes's three ex-wives (who did not want her name used in this book) confirmed to me that she answered calls from Perot about ten times a year. Perot protested to me that he only talked to Barnes once or twice a year.[20] "And I just felt that he was a person I felt sorry for, frankly," claims Perot. "He was a well-intentioned person, and I felt sorry for him."[21]

---

* Perot still stays in touch with Taylor, as evidenced by one of my conversations with Perot, in which he suggested I talk to Taylor further about Barnes. When I told him that Taylor was in London and unreachable, Perot said he would get him to call me. Finally, Taylor wrote me a letter saying he did not want to be interviewed further for my book. After Perot again called him in November 1995, Taylor consented to some conversations.

† In 1992, Perot was still trying to peddle some of the information about Rewald. He gave a copy of his file on the Rewald case to lawyers for the Senate Select Committee on POWs/MIAs who came to interview him before taking his deposition. "Take this for a slow, rainy afternoon," he told one of the attorneys.

As Barnes and Perot talked over the phone, they discovered things they had in common. Barnes had become a very close friend of Miriam Shelton, the first president of the National League of Families. Miriam's husband, Colonel Charles Shelton, was the only missing American still officially carried on the government's list as a prisoner of war (he was shot down on an intelligence gathering mission in Laos in 1965 and was later confirmed to be alive on the ground; for three years, U.S. intelligence sporadically tracked him in Communist hands, and then officially lost track of him). Perot knew Shelton, and considered her husband's case to be an important one.* Barnes also ingratiated himself with Perot by attacking Richard Armitage.

To Perot, Barnes's stories provided direct evidence of the POW/MIA cover-up he believed existed. He was not surprised by the peculiar situations Barnes claimed to have encountered. "One constant is that people who were in intelligence," says Perot, "who had access to this highly secret information, who ever talk about it publicly, a lot of weird things do happen in their lives."[22]

In 1985, Barnes traveled to Washington to tell his POW tale directly to the Defense Intelligence Agency (they refused to see him), and he stayed at Taylor's home.[23] While Barnes was in Washington, Daniel Sheehan, the general counsel of the Christic Institute, filmed several hours of Barnes talking about his POW missions.[24] Sheehan was another deep source for Perot (Sheehan refused to be interviewed for this book). Barnes claims the tapes were sent to Perot.

Although Barnes's statements were astonishing, he impressed both Taylor and Sheehan. His assertions about convicted investment banker Ron Rewald complemented Taylor's view, since Taylor had already told another journalist there was "no doubt" that Rewald's company "had been a CIA enterprise."[25†]

---

* When Miriam Shelton committed suicide on October 4, 1990, it was Barnes who called Perot and told him of her death. "Ross got kind of paranoid after her death," claims Barnes. "I no longer think he is stable," Barnes says with a laugh, "but I guess he would say the same thing about me."

† Taylor interviewed Rewald on several occasions, listening raptly to his unproved tales of CIA skullduggery. Rewald added to the allure by warning Taylor that he if broadcast what he heard, "your life's in danger."

In 1986, Taylor videotaped Barnes, this time under the influence of sodium amytal (the so-called truth serum, though the concept of truth serum is a myth; someone can lie under its influence, and if a person is inclined to lie, sodium amytal can actually facilitate the deception).[26] At the taping, Taylor was assisted by Mark Waple (the attorney who was involved with Ross Perot that same year over the sale of a videotape for $4.2 million that purported to show POWs being used as slave labor).* Under friendly questioning, Barnes swore to the POW events he would soon publish in a book. Later, when Barnes spoke to reporters, he sometimes produced a copy of Taylor's tape as evidence of his credibility.[27]

In mid-1986, Barnes remembers, Perot called him, angry. "The vice-president has removed my powers," said Perot. "He has removed my access, and I'm going to take care of him." Unknown to Barnes, Perot had approached Bush and other government officials with his charges about Armitage and had been rebuffed. Barnes says that Perot sent him to Bakersfield to do background investigations on an old George Bush connection to the Zephyr oil company. "It was then that I knew Ross was at war with Bush," Barnes says.[28] During this time, Barnes says, David Taylor arrived in California with money from Perot. "One time, David came out and gave me a thousand cash and said, 'Ross wants you to have this, you did a good job.' " (Barnes's going rate was $45 an hour, plus expenses. "Ross is my biggest client ever," boasts Barnes. "I had my house bricked one year, eighteen thousand bricks, a buck a brick, and they were Perot bricks—paid in cash.")[29] While Perot denies ever paying Barnes, Taylor admits "there was one incident, in 1987 or 1988, when Ross sent Barnes $200 or $300 to pay for an airline ticket for him to go to Washington State, so he could apply for a job. . . . It was in the context that Perot told me he felt sorry for Barnes, and he wanted to give Barnes an opportunity to start over."[30] Perot gave Barnes the money, says Taylor, also as a way of thanking him for his Washington testimony about POWs/MIAs.[31]

---

* The taping was part of an unusual affidavit submitted in an unsuccessful suit filed by some POWs against Ronald Reagan, and other ranking government officials, alleging a government cover-up.

In 1987, Barnes published his POW tales in a book titled *Bohica: A True Account of One Man's Battle to Expose the Most Heinous Cover-up of the Vietnam Saga! Bohica,* an acronym for "Bend over, here it comes again," has become a sourcebook for believers in POW conspiracies. However, a Defense Intelligence Agency review of the book concluded that in *Bohica,* "virtually every page is rife with total fabrications and misrepresentations. . . . *Bohica* is nothing more than a collection of his fantasies and the fantastic tales he has been peddling for years."[32] The National League of Families of American Prisoners and Missing in Southeast Asia published a research paper refuting significant portions of the book and concluding that "Barnes' illicit activities, including his authorship of *Bohica,* is exploitation at its most obvious, and worst."[33]

Reprinted in *Bohica*'s appendix of several hundred pages is everything from Barnes's personal phone book to résumés and miscellaneous letters he received from others. One of them was a February 27, 1987, letter written by David Taylor on BBC letterhead, addressed "To Whom It May Concern." It was a rather extraordinary personal recommendation: Taylor said he had known Barnes for three years and "found him to be an honourable and talented individual. I have checked into his background with numerous sources in Washington and have come to the firm conclusion that there are certain officials who, for their own protection, have attempted to discredit Scott. I have discussed Scott's case with H. Ross Perot in Dallas, and we both feel that a disservice has been done to this man. I think I speak for Ross when I say that we both hope that Scott will be given a chance to apply for employment and have that application considered on its merits and not on what an anonymous source may claim." Taylor concluded his letter by saying, "I certainly have no hesitation in recommending him for employment," and to "underscore my confidence in Scott," he revealed that Barnes had helped the BBC on several investigations.[34] (Taylor has since said that he never expected that letter "to see the light of day.")

In 1987, Barnes was under investigation by the Kern County district attorney's office in California. When one of the investigators, Walt Newport, noticed that Barnes had once listed Perot on a job résumé, he decided to call Perot to check further. In an internal case file, Newport summarized the conversation: "On July 31, 1987, Perot called me back and described Barnes as a true patriot interested in POW/MIA issues, as was he. Perot advised me of his financial assistance to the Bo Gritz mission. Although Perot stated he never met Barnes in person, he stated he knew Barnes to be truthful because when he would try to talk to his friends in Washington D.C. circles about Barnes and POW/MIA's, they would not talk to him about them and he thought they were concealing information from him."[35]*

On March 5, 1987, Barnes claimed that two assassins had tried, and failed, to kill him. He called David Taylor at 3:00 A.M. "David! David! You've got to help! They finally got me! My God, they're out there, David! They've stabbed me!" Then the phone went dead.[36] The police who responded to his call for help found him drunk, but he did have a knife cut in his stomach. Although he said he exchanged gunfire with one of them, only his shell casings were found at the scene, and the holes in the wire mesh of his screen door showed shots had come solely from inside the residence, casting doubts on the existence of another shooter. But Barnes also insisted that the second hit man, who stabbed him, attempted to nick the bottom of his heart: "I'd have bled internally because all you'd see would be a small external cut. It's a technique."[37] He later revised his story: The two hit men had been sent only as a warning; the shooter was a marksman capable of firing close to his head, while the knife wielder knew how to surgically cut him so that it was not lethal.[38] Taylor, however, was convinced that the attack on Barnes was further evidence of his importance and veracity.[39]

In 1988, Barnes had more tangible problems than phantom killers. He was arrested for illegally tape-recording his conversations with government officials. Barnes was convicted of twelve counts of wiretapping, on an operation that he claims "was for

---

* In *Bohica,* Barnes had also thanked both Taylor and Perot in the acknowledgments. "A special thank you to David Taylor of BBC, Washington, D.C., for uncovering and reporting the *Bohica* mission. You are a true friend of the POWs and of mine. To H. Ross Perot for your many words of encouragement and your efforts to get our men home."

Ross Perot."[40] It was Taylor, he says, who brought Perot-financed "state of the art surveillance equipment" to California. (Taylor only acknowledges buying Barnes a cheap suction-cup device, from Radio Shack, that could be used to record telephone calls, because "Barnes was making wild allegations involving gun-running, and I did say to him that I needed proof of this.")[41] According to Barnes, he was instructed to talk to government officials, usually ex–CIA agents Carl Jenkins, Tom Kleins, and Ted Shackley. During the conversation, he would try to shift the talk toward gun-running and covert operations. Of nearly forty hours of tapes, Barnes says he sent between ten and fourteen hours to Perot. (Perot dismisses Barnes's story as fiction.) The court was obviously not impressed with any excuse Barnes offered at the trial. He was sentenced to a year in prison, but served only 109 days (he did receive a favorable psychiatric evaluation while incarcerated). That same year, he was convicted of false imprisonment and disturbing the peace for assaulting and arresting a car repossessor.[42]

As he continued to move from one project to another, Barnes variously claimed to have been involved in civil defense, criminal intelligence, social work, nuclear weapons training, scuba diving, real estate, retail clothing, undercover investigations, and radiological inquiries. He told one reporter he was a freelance assassin for the CIA.[43] On one of his résumés, he listed having been an adviser to the White House on national security matters (it has no record of him) and said that he had access to secret information about military space projects. In 1990, he lost one of his career options when his private investigator's license was revoked.

Barnes says that during this time, 1987 to 1990, in addition to Taylor's being his contact to Perot, the Christic Institute's Daniel Sheehan also acted as a middleman. When Barnes traveled east, he often stayed at Sheehan's Washington house.

In 1991, Barnes had quit work as a social worker in Washington State when local officials began an investigation of his criminal history (he maintained he left after state agents visited him with "an intelligence memo that I was out to assassinate Saddam Hussein" and warned him, "It's probably in your best interest that you immediately resign and move out of Washington.")[44] In 1992,

Barnes landed a job, though it lasted only a few months, as the supervisor for child abuse investigations for a Native American tribe, the White Mountain Apache Nation, in Arizona.[45]*

By the spring of 1992, Scott Barnes and David Taylor were about to reenter Ross Perot's life, just as Perot was climbing in presidential public-opinion polls. They would be the central characters in the morass that Perot says prompted him to withdraw from the race. The Dallas police and the FBI soon became bit players to charges of grand conspiracy spun by Barnes and supported by Taylor.

---

* Barnes has continued to insinuate himself in unusual and high-profile matters. In June 1995, he sued Judge Lance Ito, of California superior court, claiming that Ito and two deputy sheriffs had conspired to have him wiretap the phones of O. J. Simpson's defense team and to eavesdrop illegally on the Simpson jury. "I got screwed by F. Lee Bailey," Barnes says. He also told Los Angeles reporter Rod Lurie that he was "involved" in the Heidi Fleiss (the so-called Hollywood madam) case but could not disclose what he was doing since it was "top secret." To other reporters, he said he has secret information that he cannot disclose on deceased White House aide Vincent Foster. "He's always calling with some crazy story," Don Hewitt, the executive producer of 60 Minutes, says. "He is a guy who, after an Oklahoma City bombing, you expect it to be Scott Barnes calling, that he knows someone who lives on a ranch and so on and so forth."

TWENTY

□

Dirty Tricks

The man Perot would eventually come to believe was at the center of a Republican dirty-tricks campaign against him was Jim Oberwetter, the chief of the Texas reelection campaign for George Bush. A prominent executive at Hunt Oil (he worked under Tom Meurer, Perot's friend and former employee), the forty-seven-year-old Oberwetter was a close personal friend of the Bushes' and a respected Dallas community leader. He had earned Perot's animus for gentle gibes he made to local papers after Perot's announcement on *Larry King Live* in late February 1992. And at the end of March, he was quoted in *The New York Times* as saying that Perot's liability in politics would be his inability to "take advice from somebody else."[1]

At a speech to the American Society of Newspaper Editors in Washington, D.C., on April 10, Perot was asked about Oberwetter's remark. "I get confused sometimes with 'bed wetter,' " Perot said. Then, in an unusually personal attack, he charged that Oberwetter was "a former White House staffer [who] got a bigtime job down in Dallas, Texas. This is a young guy that probably has trouble buying cat food, he's so inexperienced."[2]

"I told the press the next day," says Oberwetter, "that I hadn't been called that [bed wetter] since grade school. That showed up in the newspapers, and I was told that Perot was hotter than the dickens after he saw that one, because he thought it was a putdown."

A few days later, Oberwetter got his first telephone call from Scott Barnes. "He said he got my number from some reporter," says Oberwetter, "and said he had some material about Mr. Perot involved with POW/MIA things, where Perot had been off base." Oberwetter put Barnes off, telling him he was not interested. But a couple of days later, Barnes called again and repeated his offer of damaging information about Perot. Oberwetter says he was "very cautious and careful, and any call from a person I don't know is on a suspect list to begin with."[3] Barnes had left a telephone number, and Oberwetter called it "just to see if it was a ruse. It was some dress shop [Barnes's business, Jessica Lynn's High Country Fashions], and I hung up. Then things got quiet for a while."[4]

Unknown to Oberwetter, Barnes was now calling other Republican officials. In May, he tried to get in touch with Bob Teeter, the national chairman of the Bush-Quayle campaign, and Marlin Fitzwater, Bush's press spokesman. As he did with Oberwetter, Barnes left messages that he had important information to pass along about Perot. Fitzwater talked to him only once and showed no interest. Teeter, however, asked Terry O'Donnell, a partner at the Washington law firm of Williams & Connolly, to return the call on his behalf. O'Donnell was the former general counsel at the Pentagon. He had also been involved with the Vietnam Veterans Memorial Fund project when it had its bruising fight with Perot in the early 1980s.

"I did not know anything about Barnes when I called," says O'Donnell. "We had a long conversation. He said he wanted to be helpful to the Bush campaign and that he knew things about POW issues and Ross Perot. He mentioned Richard Armitage and said that he had information that Bush was going to be ambushed on CNN over an issue with Armitage. But the more I probed, the less reliable I thought he was. By the end of the conversation, I was convinced this fellow was a waste of time, and I closed the book on the matter."[5]

But Barnes, ever persistent, called O'Donnell several more times, sometimes catching him answering his phone directly. Once he left a message—"Urgent"—and O'Donnell returned the call, only to find the conversation was again useless. "I could not figure out what he was doing at the time," recalls O'Donnell. "It was apparent to me that he was playing a game, and I didn't know what his game was, but I knew I wanted nothing to do with it."[6]

Barnes was also tenacious enough to get through to David Tell, the Republican director of opposition research. Tell says that he expressed no interest in Barnes's information.[7]

Barnes did not tell David Taylor about his conversations with Republican officials until late April.[8] However, in Barnes's version, the Republicans had called him. Oberwetter was the first, he said. Barnes claimed they wanted compromising information about Perot and asked him to tell them what he knew about Perot and POWs and MIAs.* Barnes recalls that Taylor was "very excited" by this news, and told Barnes that Oberwetter "was Bush's number one man and Perot's number one enemy."[9] Taylor, of course, personally knew of the bad blood between Perot and Bush over the POW issue. He knew that Senator Bob Kerrey was planning a special hearing during the summer about POWs and MIAs and that Perot was one of the invited witnesses. Taylor hypothesized that since Perot had had access to many of the government's classified documents about the POW issue, he might have collected information that could embarrass Bush and other top administration officials. Therefore, when Barnes told him that Republican officials were seeking damaging information about Perot, it made sense to Taylor. The Republicans might go to extraordinary lengths, Taylor thought, to discover what explosive information Perot had and what he might disclose at the upcoming Kerrey hearings.

By early May, Taylor had convinced the BBC to let him interview Perot as part of a segment for the evening newscasts. Because of his conversations with Barnes, Taylor also thought this simple news interview could expand into an explosive story.[10]

---

* In 1995, when I interviewed him, Barnes claimed for the first time that his calls to the Republicans had actually been initiated by Taylor and Perot, who told him that Bush was out to "get Perot." Barnes maintains that before he ever called Oberwetter, he received a call on his private line from a man who identified himself as Jim Oberwetter (a caller he now realizes was an impostor). "Oberwetter" told him he had just finished reading his book, *Bohica,* and said he had some questions about Ross Perot and POWs.

In mid-May, Perot met with Taylor for his BBC interview. For the first time, Perot learned of Barnes's charges about the Republicans.[11] That trip also gave Taylor an opportunity to verify whether Barnes's primary claim—that he was talking to Jim Oberwetter—was true. Taylor had arranged an interview with Oberwetter by claiming that he was doing a general documentary about the American presidential race. He then told Barnes to call Oberwetter during that interview so that Taylor could film Oberwetter's reaction. When Taylor arrived at the Hunt Oil offices for his May 13 meeting, he was kept in the reception area for a few minutes and then taken by a receptionist to Oberwetter's office. As Taylor and his film crew neared the office, he heard the last seconds of a conversation. "I can't talk," said Oberwetter. "I have British television outside." During the interview, Barnes did not call. Afterward, Taylor called him and asked why not. "I did call, and you were there, weren't you?" Barnes told him. "How did you know I was there?" Taylor asked. Barnes responded, "Well, he told me you were outside."[12]

"I was surprised," says Taylor, "that the head of the Republican campaign was talking to Barnes about anything." Taylor and Perot thought that snippet of a conversation confirmed Barnes's claim that he was regularly talking with Oberwetter and other Republican officials. Barnes added to the allure by suggesting that he had called Oberwetter on a private number (he had not, and Taylor did not check the existence of such a number).[13] Moreover, if either Taylor or Perot had asked Barnes for his telephone bill, they would have discovered that Barnes's May 13 call, at 11:10 in the morning in Dallas (just as Taylor walked into the office), lasted less than one minute. It was also the only call from Barnes to Oberwetter's office that month.[14]

During the next several weeks, Barnes and Taylor continued speaking by telephone. In early June, Barnes said he was in touch with more important Republicans, including Bob Teeter (Barnes did reach Teeter, briefly, one time).[15] Although he only had Barnes's word for the calls, Taylor was impressed. "He was no longer talking to flunkies," says Taylor. "If I can't get through to Bob Teeter, what on earth is Scott Barnes doing getting through to Teeter? . . . What the hell was going on?"[16]

The Democratic convention started on Monday, July 13, and Taylor covered it for the BBC. During the next three days, he received several telephone messages at his hotel from Barnes. He was too busy to return the calls. Perot later told *60 Minutes* that it was during those three days that he received a "call from a person who I respect who said that there was a plan to have a computer-created false photo of my daughter Carolyn that they were going to give the press shortly before her wedding to embarrass her."[17]

Perot was undoubtedly referring to Scott Barnes. At the time, Barnes claimed that two Republicans (one of whom he identified as a staff assistant in opposition research, Joe Deoudes) had shown him thirty-five fake photos of two of Perot's daughters, Carolyn and Nancy, each in compromising lesbian-related situations. Many of the pictures were, Barnes contended, set in the parking lot of a country club frequented by the Perot family. When Barnes was unable to reach Taylor, he telephoned Perot's office and passed the information to one of his secretaries.[18] On Thursday, July 16, Perot dropped out of the presidential race.

Taylor did not return Barnes's calls until Sunday, July 19. That was the first time he learned about the photos.[19]

Barnes now, incredibly, admits that no such pictures existed and that he concocted the story. But he insists he did so on explicit instructions from Perot himself, so that Perot would have an excuse for his withdrawal from the race.[20] It is hard to imagine, though, that Perot, so concerned about the privacy and security of his family, would encourage anyone to circulate such a story. It is likely that both Perot and Taylor believed the pictures existed, although they never asked to see copies.[21]

Yet Perot gave *60 Minutes* a second reason for his withdrawal. "I received multiple reports that there was a plan . . . to actually have people in the church at the wedding to disrupt her wedding."[22] At the time he dropped out of the race, Perot told several close associates about his fear that the Republicans would disrupt his daughter's wedding. But both Barnes and Taylor insist they were not the source of that story. "The wedding allegation is strictly from Ross," says Barnes. "The first time I heard about the wedding was on *60 Minutes*. It did not come from me."[23] "You see," says Taylor, "Barnes never mentioned the wedding to me at all. I know he made no reference to the wedding, because when I heard Perot say it on *60 Minutes,* my first reaction was, 'Well, I wonder where he got that from.' "[24] Perot refuses to identify any sources.*

Although Perot was out of the race, Barnes was not finished with his rather startling tales. When he spoke to Taylor on Sunday, July 19, in addition to telling him about the alleged photos, he revealed that the Republicans wanted him to gain access to Perot's office in order to wiretap certain phones. To support his tale, he produced a floor plan of Perot's Dallas office, together with several telephone numbers, and faxed them to Taylor (who, in turn, sent a copy to Perot).[25] His new assignment, he claimed, was to get enough information to ensure that Perot did not reenter the race. (Like the story of the composite photo, Barnes now insists that Perot had given him the floor plan, as well as the list of telephone numbers.)

Perot did not initially believe Barnes's latest story, since he did not recognize the telephone numbers. "Then I went back to the telephone switchboard," recalls Perot, "and the lady said, 'Those are for your financial matters.' This guy [Barnes] had things that some guy who was broke in Arizona couldn't get."[26] Some of the numbers were direct lines Perot used to call his children.

In late July, Barnes told Taylor that he had traveled to Mexico at the request of the Republicans and there had met two unidentified men who offered $150,000 to wiretap Perot's office. (Actually, he had gone to Mexico for a friend's bachelor party.)[27] He soon called Taylor and played a tape of a conversation in which an unidentified man asked him to bug Perot's phone lines and warned him "to keep your mouth shut."[28]

Perot received a copy of that tape the next day, courtesy of Taylor. After playing it, he called Taylor.

"David, I just listened to this thing. What do you make of it?"

---

* According to Mickey Herskowitz, who co-authored Governor John Connally's 1993 autobiography, Connally was told by Richard Nixon that there were plans to conduct a dirty campaign against Perot, including spreading a false rumor that his daughter was a lesbian. This story was removed from the final draft of Connally's manuscript. Perot says, though, that Connally was not one of his sources.

"I don't know," Taylor said. "What about that telephone number?"

"Well, that is a number in my system. I am going to talk to someone called Jim Siano, and he is going to be contacting you."[29]

James Siano was a former FBI agent (he had been in charge of counterintelligence at the Dallas office) who had done some private investigative work for Perot.[30] Perot hoped Siano might be able to make sense of Barnes's allegations.

Perot sent Siano to visit Taylor at his home in Leesburg, Virginia, on Sunday, August 2. They talked on Taylor's rear porch for nearly five hours. "He [Taylor] had checked all this out," recalls Siano. "And as far as he was concerned, there was a lot of credence to this."[31]

Perot had left for a vacation in Bermuda, but he spoke to Siano by telephone. They debated, says Siano, whether "Barnes and Taylor could be working together on something." But Perot insisted that these were strong allegations that should be pursued.[32] When Siano suggested taking the matter to the FBI, Perot resisted, evidently concerned because the agent in charge of the Dallas FBI office, Oliver "Buck" Revell, had been responsible for the FBI investigation that had resulted in a complete exoneration of Richard Armitage.[33]* Instead, Perot directed Siano to the Dallas police, and personally arranged an appointment for him with the chief of police, Bill Rathburn.

Meanwhile, Barnes was busy in Arizona. He told David Taylor that his Republican contacts were about to provide him with bugging equipment, a prepaid ticket to Dallas, and a hotel room near Perot's office.[34] As a result, Taylor, with a cameraman in tow, planned to fly from Washington to Phoenix on Tuesday, August 4.

---

* While Revell, now retired, cooperated in research for this book, the FBI officially refused to provide any information or to allow the author to speak to any active agents who had been involved in the case. Revell, who had been the supervisor in charge of the Dallas office (1991–95), says that he received a call from Perot about once every two months, often on "matters completely unrelated to him." Revell often pushed Perot off to the assistant special agent in charge of the office, Tom Rupprath. On one occasion, after a particularly busy period of receiving calls from Perot about POWs, Revell asked, "Are you a social worker?" Perot did not like the gentle gibing.

There he would rendezvous with Barnes and follow him to Texas, planning to film him for his BBC documentary.

Barnes now admits that he drove to Phoenix (an hour from his home in Prescott) before Taylor arrived in Arizona and he picked up a box containing surveillance equipment at an electronics store on Bethany Home Boulevard.[35] He then proceeded to Phoenix's airport, Sky Harbor, and placed the box in a rented locker.[36] However, when Taylor arrived, Barnes lied, telling him instead that his Republican contacts had given him the number of a locker at Sky Harbor. With Taylor watching (and filming clandestinely when in public places), Barnes opened the locker and retrieved the box. Taylor later videotaped the surveillance equipment (he thought it unusual that "there was a diagram inside the box of how to put all the equipment together, with a little line on the bottom that said 'Batteries Not Provided' ").[37] That same evening, Taylor also filmed Barnes picking up a first-class ticket from the Continental Airlines desk.[38]*

Earlier that same day, in Dallas, James Siano kept the appointment with Chief Rathburn that Perot had made. Rathburn asked two of the department's top officers—Captain Rudy Diaz, executive assistant chief, and Captain Eddie Walt, commander of special investigations and intelligence—to join him.

Siano told them Perot had vetoed the idea of going to the FBI, since "George Bush would know about it in fifteen minutes."[39] He said that the Bush reelection committee was trying to tap Perot's phones to get incriminating information in case he decided to run again for president. After urging the police to undertake an investigation, Siano said that Perot had authorized him to offer financial and technical assistance if the investigation proved too costly or complex.[40] Very quickly, however, the three police officials agreed that the case was beyond their jurisdiction, and they declined to pursue it.[41]†

---

* The ticket was eventually given to the FBI, which will not disclose whether it ever traced who paid for it.

† Although the three officials were polite in rejecting Siano's request, privately they were not as kind about the story he presented. Walt believed it could be "a case of extreme paranoia." Diaz thought "it was a weird story," while Chief Rathburn later deemed it "bizarre."

"It was a given that we would incur Perot's wrath for saying no," says Walt.* The same day the police said no, Perot sent Siano to the FBI. There he met with his former colleagues at the Dallas office. Buck Revell listened as Siano again made his presentation. The difference between the FBI starting the investigation or not was the involvement of David Taylor. "Taylor's work and confidence in Barnes put it over the top for us," says Revell. "It would have been very unlikely that we would have gone ahead with Barnes alone."[42] Late on the afternoon of August 4, he gave the go-ahead for an undercover agent, using the alias George Allen, to be present when Siano met Taylor and Barnes. Perot would stay informed of developments through Siano.

On August 5, Barnes and Taylor flew into Dallas on a Continental flight from Phoenix. Upon arriving, Barnes tried to check into the Sheraton Park Central, but his reservation had been moved to the nearby Marriott, across from Perot's office. The hotel had been prepaid, and Barnes did not receive a bill.† That night at eight o'clock, Siano, FBI agent Allen, and Barnes and Taylor met in a room rented by the FBI at the Sheraton. Siano introduced Allen as a telephone engineer hired by Perot to assess the bugging equipment Barnes had brought from Phoenix.[43]

Barnes announced that he had a meeting set with Jim Oberwetter for the next day, and that he would offer Oberwetter a chance to buy nonexistent audio tapes (Barnes actually just intended to show up at his office and try to talk his way into a meeting). To bolster Barnes's credibility with Oberwetter, Perot

---

* On Monday, November 2, 1992, only days before the presidential election, Perot held a massive rally for his volunteers at Reunion Arena in Dallas. Perot wanted police protection at the rally, and asked that neither Walt nor Diaz have anything to do with providing security. Although Perot and the city manager at the time, Jan Hart, deny that this request was made, the three police officials are insistent, and one remembers Clay Mulford as being the one who transmitted the Perot demand.

† Taylor says that the hotel clerk told him that Barnes's reservation had been canceled by Mike Thomas, of 1050 15th Street, Washington, D.C. The address was that of the Bush-Quayle campaign headquarters, and Mike Thomas was an alias Barnes used for Joe Deoudes, a twenty-three-year-old staff assistant he had spoken to on several occasions. Taylor again believed the information bolstered Barnes's story.

had decided to cooperate with an FBI request that he tape several innocuous telephone conversations with some business colleagues. These would be supplied to Oberwetter as "proof" that Barnes had successfully installed telephone taps on Perot's phone lines.

For Taylor, this was an unexpected opportunity. He wanted to film any Barnes and Oberwetter meeting. "I remember the FBI finally said that Oberwetter would have to come outside into the plaza, and that was great for me," recalls Taylor, "since I could not go into the building because there was an expectation of privacy inside." The FBI raised no objection to Taylor's filming the undercover sting.

At 6:00 A.M. on Thursday, August 6, Perot taped several short conversations with associates.[44] Perot then had Siano take the tapes to the FBI. George Allen, the FBI agent, then brought them to the Sheraton, where he met with Taylor and Barnes. Although he had time to play the recordings for them, the Bureau later claimed there was no time to wire Barnes for his meeting with Oberwetter. As a result, it would have to rely on only Scott Barnes's recollection of what was said.[45] Nor had the Bureau, at this stage of the investigation, finished a complete background check on Barnes (on whom it has a large file), identified the two men who met Barnes in Mexico, found the source of the money for his airfare or hotel, or located the source of the surveillance equipment he had picked up in Phoenix.

Jim Oberwetter was in the midst of a difficult campaign in Texas for George Bush. Now that Ross Perot had withdrawn from the race, it would be easier for Bush to carry his home state against Clinton. On Thursday, August 6, Scott Barnes was one of the last people on his mind. He had not heard from him since the two conversations in April.

Around 3:30 P.M., a man identifying himself as Howard Parsons appeared at the reception desk on Oberwetter's floor at Hunt Oil in downtown Dallas. He said he was from the Bush national campaign headquarters and did not have an appointment. Oberwetter checked his calendar, saw he was not expecting a visitor, and then tried for the next half hour to reach someone in Washington who knew the unexpected Mr. Parsons. He did not reach anyone who could answer his question. Soon, the receptionist again called Oberwetter. "He's acting awfully nervous. Would you kindly come and get him?"[46] Oberwetter went to meet his visitor, not knowing that "Howard Parsons" was actually Scott Barnes.

"I have some very important political information for you," Barnes said.

"Okay, I will bite," answered Oberwetter. "What is it?"[47]

But Barnes would not tell him in the reception area, suggesting they go elsewhere. When Oberwetter started to walk toward his office, Barnes said he would also feel uncomfortable speaking there and instead wanted to go outside. Oberwetter hesitated, but then agreed. Outside the skyscraper, there is a landscaped garden with a reflecting pool, running water, and several benches. They sat on the bench closest to the building. Oberwetter was so nervous that when he saw a woman fiddling with a pack of cigarettes, he wondered if the pack hid a tiny camera. "I then thought this might be a setup," recalls Oberwetter, "but I didn't know for what."

Taylor's crew filmed the entire meeting (the FBI later unsuccessfully tried to have someone read the lips of Barnes and Oberwetter from the video).* An FBI agent parked in a car half a block away took still photographs of the meeting with a 300mm telephoto lens. Barnes told Oberwetter that he had brought wiretap recordings of Ross Perot discussing his upcoming testimony before the Senate Select Committee on POWs/MIAs and that it was explosive. Although the offer sounded vaguely familiar, Oberwetter did not immediately connect it to his April conversations with Barnes.

"I am not interested in anything you have," said Oberwetter. "Perot is out of the race."

"Well, he might get back in."

"He's going to do whatever he does whether I take what you've got or not. I don't want what you have."

---

* Taylor provided a copy of the video to Perot (who denies having it), the FBI, and Senator Tom Harkin (Democrat–Iowa). Taylor knew Harkin from having done an earlier documentary about his candidacy. Lorraine Voles, Harkin's press secretary, said Harkin had returned the tape to Taylor soon after receiving it, and that "he did not watch it." The BBC, which has the original video, refuses to release it.

"But you don't know how good it is unless you hear it," urged Barnes.[48]

After eighteen minutes of fending off Barnes's solicitations, Oberwetter had had enough. He stood up, and the two of them shook hands.

Barnes asked Oberwetter a final question. "Is there anyone I can give this information to?"

"Yes. Give it to the editors at the Fort Worth *Star-Telegram*. They don't like Mr. Perot there. Mr. Perot has a picture of one of their reporters in a compromising position with someone from city hall, and they have written about that. So take it to them."[49]

With no one to challenge his version of events, Barnes told the FBI that Oberwetter did not want to buy the Perot tapes before first consulting directly with President Bush.[50]

When Perot learned of the meeting between Oberwetter and Barnes, he saw it as further evidence that the Republicans were involved in dirty tricks against him. He called Buck Revell to find out what the FBI intended to do next. At FBI headquarters in Washington, urgent meetings were convened between senior Bureau and Justice Department officials. The unanimous conclusion was that while Barnes's credibility was "questionable," the fact that Oberwetter met with Barnes, coupled with Taylor's "corroboration," provided enough justification to proceed further.[51] In the Dallas office, there was no hesitation whatsoever. "Everyone thought it was the next Watergate, and were all caught up in it," says an FBI official close to the case. Perot was informed of all the developments that night.

On Friday evening, August 7, George Allen called Barnes, who had returned home to Arizona, and asked him if he had spoken further with Oberwetter. Barnes surprised Allen by saying that he no longer wanted to be involved, and provided no explanation.[52]

While the Bureau's official position is that Perot did not know about, or influence, its next move, he did show an inordinate interest in the investigation. Perot called on Saturday, says a senior FBI source in the Dallas office, and was patched through to Buck Revell's house by the weekend duty agent. Later, he spoke to Stephen Largent, the supervisor of the Public Corruption Squad, as well as case agents John Kubinsky and Henry

Garcia. Kubinsky got so tired of Perot's calls that he stopped returning them.

Revell and the FBI leadership in Washington had given a go-ahead to the undercover agent, George Allen, to make a final attempt at ensnaring Oberwetter. That same day, Allen proceeded to Oberwetter's office. Disguised as a cowboy and wearing a ten-gallon hat and flashy ostrich boots, he used the name Bob Watson. Shortly after 5:00 P.M., Kim, Oberwetter's receptionist, called him and said, "Jim, there is another one out here. No appointment, but he is insistent to see you."

This time, Oberwetter asked Hunt Oil's security chief, Wilbur Rainey, to accompany him when he went to the reception area. When Oberwetter told the visitor (whom he later referred to as "Cowboy Bob") that he would talk to him right there in the lounge, Allen said he would rather go someplace else. " 'My God,' I thought," says Oberwetter. " 'This can't be happening again.' "[53] Oberwetter took Rainey and Allen to a side office. The FBI agent was wired, and what follows is based on that transcript.[54]

Cowboy Bob told Oberwetter that he was "an associate of Mr. Scott Barnes," and he then opened his briefcase and produced a tape that he said was a recording of a Perot conversation from a tap on his phone lines.

"I was hired to do this," said the undercover agent, "and it was my understanding from Mr. Barnes that you wanted him to do this."[55] Oberwetter denied it, and when told that Joe Deoudes, a worker on the Republican opposition research committee, had wanted the tapes, Oberwetter said, "They would *never ask* somebody to do what you have suggested [emphasis in original transcript]."[56]

Cowboy Bob seemed confused, expecting that Oberwetter would be happy to receive the tapes. "Do you want to receive this tape or anything like this?" he asked, somewhat quizzically.

"Of course not," Oberwetter told him firmly. Then Oberwetter became more aggressive, telling the undercover agent, "I'm serving as chairman of the president's campaign in Texas, and I smell an effort to embarrass the president and to ruin me, and that means lawsuits. . . . There is mischief afoot."

The FBI was stunned that Oberwetter did not want the tapes. The Bureau had completely accepted Barnes's tale that the Republicans, and especially Oberwetter, were anxiously awaiting wiretapped conversations of Perot. Now they realized Barnes's story was false. "By the end of that day," says an FBI official in the Dallas office, "there was already finger-pointing going on."

Belatedly, the following day the FBI decided to try and get to the bottom of the story. By this time, Buck Revell thought that, in addition to Barnes, Taylor "was culpable. I believe that he knew the story was false when he came to us."[57]

The FBI sent agents, identifying themselves as such, to interview Oberwetter, Barnes, and Taylor. Barnes stuck to his same story—that the Republicans had recruited him to wiretap Perot's phones and that he was not sure why Oberwetter had refused the tapes at the last minute. During his interview, Barnes received a frantic phone call from David Taylor, who was nervous because two FBI agents were at his Washington office. When he hung up the phone, Barnes turned around to the two agents and asked, "Any guarantee of immunity?" They said no.*

To Ross Perot, the collapse of the FBI investigation was a great disappointment. He had dropped out of the race, ready to pin it on Republican dirty tricks, and was confident that Barnes and Taylor had kicked off an inquiry that would lead to arrests, indictments, and public humiliation for those who had conspired against him. The FBI came to the conclusion that it had been had by Barnes, but Perot remained convinced that the Republican dirty tricksters had merely escaped detection. In a few months, he

---

* A final strange footnote to the story is that on September 28, as the FBI investigation into Barnes and Taylor continued, Barnes was suddenly on his way to Vietnam with Phil Huff, another veteran. Barnes's passport confirms the trip. The tickets were issued by a local Prescott, Arizona, travel agency and paid for in cash. According to Barnes, Perot sent him to Vietnam, ostensibly to follow up on MIA issues, but "what he really wanted to do was to have me out of the country while the race was still on," asserts Barnes. After the two men had been in Vietnam for three weeks, Huff's daughter had a serious accident in Arkansas, and they returned to the States. "Ross was furious when I came back early," claims Barnes. "He thought I would be over there through the election." The FBI later talked to the travel agent to determine how Barnes, who had no money, could afford to travel to Vietnam unless someone paid his way. They evidently never discovered who paid for the trip.

would try to personally expose them on *60 Minutes,* in the court of public opinion.

But the interview did not turn out as Perot hoped. It was confrontational. *60 Minutes* had been unable to find any corroboration for a Republican plot. On camera, Buck Revell acknowledged that the Bureau's investigation had uncovered no evidence of dirty tricks. When correspondent Leslie Stahl confronted Perot with that statement, he claimed it was the first time he had ever heard that conclusion, and said, "We've got a squirrely situation in the FBI if that happened. Sounds like it's politics to me. [The FBI] can't talk to me, but they talk to *60 Minutes.* Don't you find that interesting?"[58]*

The public reaction to the show was bad. Polls showed that many thought it revealed a tendency for Perot to draw conclusions before he had all the evidence, and it revived unfavorable images of his bent for conspiracy theories.

The press had a new story and relentlessly pursued it, not allowing Perot to get back to his core issue, the deficit. The day following the *60 Minutes* broadcast Orson Swindle, Clay Mulford, Sharon Holman, and Ross Perot, Jr., tried to handle a flurry of questions about the incident at a packed press conference. Suddenly Perot, who had been listening to the news conference on his car radio while driving to work, arrived, angry at the sharp questions being asked of his son.

"Black Sunday was followed by blacker Monday," recalls Swindle. "I was at the podium answering questions. Some reporter said, 'Well, what does Mr. Perot think of that?' And I said, 'I don't know, I will ask him.' Somebody else said, 'Why don't you ask him, he's over there.' I had the damnedest look on my face. I thought, 'Oh my God,' and he just walked into the room and right up to the microphone. It was like he walked into a trap. The press nipped at him and he responded in kind, and he didn't look presidential. It was catastrophic."[59]

The *60 Minutes* episode stopped Perot's momentum dead in its tracks. Within five days, his rating in one poll had flip-flopped

---

* But Buck Revell says he had told Perot that he thought the charges against the Republicans were baseless. "That's my criticism of Ross on this matter," says Revell. "I told him there was nothing there, and he still continued. That was upsetting."

from a positive 56–34 to a negative 44–46.[60] Not even a series of public rallies turned the tide.*

Still, on Election Day—Tuesday, November 3—Perot's $65 million campaign paid off in 19 percent of the vote. It was the best finish by an independent candidate in a presidential election since Teddy Roosevelt in 1912. Perot's vote totals were remarkably consistent in all fifty states, especially considering that he had campaigned personally in only a few. He pulled more than 20 percent of the vote in thirty-one states, and over a quarter of the electorate in nine. Moreover, exit polls showed that 40 percent of the electorate would have voted for Perot if they had thought he had a chance to win. "That means he could have won," says third-party expert and pollster Gordon Black. "And that is the only question of the exit poll that the four networks did not report on election night." Largely because of that, Perot is convinced he could have won. "The Republicans elected Clinton in 'ninety-two by a nonstop propaganda campaign, saying, 'Don't waste your vote on Perot.' . . . People were talked out of their vote."[61]

As the election results came in, Perot held a party as unconventional as his campaign. The lasting image was of a smiling Perot, dancing with Margot to the tune of Patsy Cline's "Crazy." "That was their [the Republicans and Democrats] central theme," says Perot with a twinkle in his eye, "that I was crazy. But the thing that drove them crazy was when I took that as my theme song. The devil made me do it."[62]

---

* At one of the rallies in California on the last weekend of the campaign, Perot railed against the press, which he was convinced had so damaged him. He made the crowd so angry that, following his talk, some tried to overturn a satellite truck, and reporters were actually afraid they would be harmed.

TWENTY-ONE

□

Back in the Game

Many political commentators thought Perot's 1992 campaign would be his one and only entrance into the public arena and that the unique set of circumstances (extremely high public dissatisfaction with government, and two weak major-party candidates) was unlikely to be repeated in 1996. Perot, though, was not content to merely focus national attention on the deficit and get 19 percent of the vote. Instead, he settled back in Dallas and plotted a slow reentry into the debate on national issues. He was encouraged by many of the volunteers and his core supporters, who did not view the 1992 election as the end of the crusade, but rather asked the question "What do we do next?" Initially, Perot's attention was directed to his not-for-profit, nonpartisan United We Stand America. Organized in all fifty states and incorporated in every congressional district, it was fueled by his enormous lists of callers and volunteers from the 1992 campaign.* Although some activists wanted United We Stand America to become a third political party, Perot instead envisioned it as a "watchdog" organization that would lobby for deficit reduction

* Based on his 1992 votes, Perot thought he could get as many as 20 million members, at $15 each. Perot claimed that in the first twenty-four hours, 400,000 joined. But Perot, who promised to release the membership numbers by the end of 1993, never has. The bulk-mail figures from the Dallas post office show that United We Stand America peaked with slightly more than a million members in 1993 and dropped steadily after that.

and campaign finance reform, and could also be the swing vote in elections.

After the election, the national staff of United We Stand America consisted of Perot Systems employees and paid workers from the campaign. The board members were Perot, Clay Mulford, and Perot's accountant, Mike Poss. Perot Systems officer Darcy Anderson was executive director. Most of the funding (estimated as high as $1 million a month) came from Perot. Orson Swindle, who had been the director during the campaign, thought the organization should be based in Washington, not Dallas, and configured like a more traditional issues group, such as the Heritage Foundation. When Perot did not agree, Swindle resigned.[1]

In February 1993, Perot broke his low profile with a public speech in Maine. "They in Washington just don't get it," he told the audience. "You and I get it. I don't understand a $25 million inauguration at a time when people are hurting."[2] It was a message to Washington that Perot had not gone away, but few in the Beltway were yet listening.*

Perot's speech in Maine was actually the start of a multistate trip intended to boost the United We Stand America membership rolls. But all was not well within his organization. Almost two dozen state leaders complained that they were unable to get their own membership lists from Dallas and that they were prohibited from endorsing local candidates. Others griped that expenses were not reimbursed by headquarters. A number of state leaders appeared on television shows to criticize the extent of control from Dallas (on NBC's *Dateline* and ABC's *Nightline*, both in May 1993). Some quit, and others were pushed aside. A third of the new directors were military veterans, and a growing percent-

---

* There was even little interest in the aftermath of the Barnes/Taylor/FBI sting. At the start of 1993, Barnes sued Perot in Arizona, asking for unspecified damages and charging that Perot had promised to take care of him if he helped on the sting. In March, Barnes dropped the suit, but he soon filed another suit in Texas with similar allegations. While he also dismissed that one, he did not give up. Two years later, he wrote to Perot, again demanding payment for his 1992 services. Perot's attorneys have now threatened Barnes with court sanctions. Also related to the unsuccessful sting, in March 1993 the House Judiciary Committee held hearings into the aborted affair, but only Barnes, Oberwetter, and a senior FBI official, Dennis Aiken, testified. Little new was learned.

age were placed on the Dallas payroll. Those who dissented were sometimes stripped of their membership or banned from local meetings.[3] There was little room for different views in United We Stand America, and the Dallas headquarters set an agenda that was to be strictly adhered to by the state organizations. Several disgruntled ex-members filed lawsuits. Those who abandoned United We Stand America referred derisively to the new hierarchy and its remaining members as "Perotbots."

Perot was not concerned about the complaints, viewing them as merely the normal growing pains for a new organization. "Part of organizing from the bottom up is you will have disputes," he said. "You will have turf battles. People will be displaced. It's just people being people."[4] Perot was more concerned with finding an issue to champion that would unite his followers and give him a national platform.

"We had a poll done in 1993," says Clay Mulford. "It showed widespread support for campaign finance reform." Mulford took several leaders of United We Stand America and met with Clinton aides Mac McClarty and George Stephanopoulos, as well as Senate leaders George Mitchell and Bob Dole and Speaker of the House Tom Foley. Mulford wanted the political leaders to back legislation on campaign finance reform, and although they appeared interested, nothing concrete resulted from the meetings.

Mulford used the poll figures, and the failure of the Republicans and Democrats to act, to encourage Perot to make campaign finance reform the centerpiece of his new message. But Perot, by this time, wanted to concentrate on the fight over NAFTA (the North American Free Trade Agreement, a free trade treaty with Mexico that four previous presidential administrations had failed to pass). Perot was opposed to the treaty, convinced it would cost American jobs as U.S. companies utilized cheap Mexican labor. Mort Meyerson, Ross Jr., and Orson Swindle were all NAFTA supporters, but that did not deter Perot. Third-party expert and pollster Gordon Black told him, "It will put you against the entire *Fortune* 500. They will go after you personally. Your own constituency doesn't care about it, and is not united on it."[5] But Perot had made up his mind—NAFTA would be his central issue.

By mid-1993, Perot had appeared at more state rallies than he had during his presidential campaign—fifty rallies in twenty states, and more than one hundred by year's end. He hammered home his NAFTA arguments at almost every stop. He also did a circuit of national television shows, appeared before Congress to testify about NAFTA, and continued to buy thirty-minute blocks from NBC for future infomercials. His favorable poll ratings had jumped sharply since the election, from 44 percent to 66 percent.

In his second book, *Not for Sale at Any Price,* published in 1993, Perot attacked NAFTA and again laid out his economic proposals. As it climbed onto the paperback best-seller lists (number two on the *New York Times* list), he decided that NAFTA deserved a book on its own and rushed one out (*Save Your Job, Save Our Country: Why NAFTA Must Be Stopped—Now!*). His first thirty-minute block of prime-time television (which aired on CNBC on October 30, 1993) was devoted to NAFTA. His efforts were having an effect, with polls showing that the number of people against the trade treaty was growing. *U.S. News & World Report* said Perot "may be the most important force in American politics," and reported that 45 percent of the respondents to its poll would consider voting for him for president (up 15 percent since Clinton had taken office.)*

But just as Perot derailed himself in the 1992 campaign, first by withdrawing and then by giving the inopportune *60 Minutes* interview, he again made a strategic choice that would not only

---

*In the fall of 1993, Perot was summoned to a private meeting of top Republican party leaders. He thought they were prepared to discuss NAFTA and campaign finance reform. "I had to be up there [Washington] on business," he says, in recounting the remarkable incident, "so I said, 'Fine, I will come and see you.' They wanted to meet in a hotel meeting room. I show up, I walk in—you are not going to believe this—after what they did to me in '92, they asked me if I would give a million dollars to do dirty tricks against the Democrats in 1994. And the dirty-tricks guys were all there, spring-loaded to tell me all the dirty tricks they were going to do. And I said, 'Fellows, I am amazed that you would even want me to be in this room and know who these people are. And certainly I will not be part of this.' I got up and walked out. That's the system, and it is a sad commentary." Perot will not disclose the names of those at the meeting, and in 1996 told a similar story to a reporter from *The Washington Post,* without disclosing which party had asked him for the contribution.

reverse his newfound momentum but tarnish public judgment about him for a considerable time. He agreed to a two-hour debate with Vice-President Al Gore, to be carried on CNN's *Larry King Live* in November. The decision to debate Gore looked like another great move for Perot. It confirmed his national importance, and it seemed certain that Perot, with his quick wit and sharp one-liners, would maul Gore, whose intellect is often masked under a plodding style. But the White House was some 30 votes short of the 218 needed to pass the NAFTA agreement in the House of Representatives, and gambled that a strong showing by Gore could make the difference.

Before the debate, Jim Squires received information from a friend in Tennessee (the home state of both Squires and Gore) about how Gore intended to rankle Perot in the debate. Squires sent Perot a one-page memo with specifics. "That memo told him exactly what Al Gore would do," recalls Squires. "We knew they would go after Ross Jr., we knew they would go after integrity, because that is what would get him mad."[6] Although Squires wanted to plan a debate strategy, Perot was unconcerned by the report. Squires had to settle for half a dozen conversations with press secretary Sharon Holman.

Two days before the debate, on Sunday, November 7, Perot revealed to a crowd of three thousand anti-NAFTA crusaders in Tampa that the FBI had just alerted him that a six-member Cuban hit squad had been sent to murder him. "The organization is a Mafia-like group in favor of the North American Free Trade Agreement," Perot told the stunned rally. "I am willing to stand up here like a clay pigeon if you will write your congressman."[7] It turned out that there was a basis for what he said. An Albuquerque "tip line" had received a call on Saturday night from an anonymous source. The caller claimed to have just been released from a Mexican prison, where he had heard that an assassin squad "would take out" Ross Perot. The tip line passed the information to the FBI in Los Angeles, which in turn passed it to the Dallas police. "It could be totally legitimate," said the FBI's Buck Revell. "It could be a hoax. There's no way of verifying these things."[8] Again, the press treated the story as another example of Perot reaching wild conclusions without enough supporting evidence. The Tampa speech was his first real gaffe since the campaign, and it set the stage for what would be a dismal confrontation with the vice-president.*

On the day of the debate with Gore, Perot traveled to Washington with Sharon Holman.

"Sharon, what do you think they will go after me on tonight?"

"What they always do—your kids."[9]

On Tuesday, November 9, Perot and Gore squared off, sitting in chairs less than two feet apart, positioned behind a low desk. In what was to be the most watched show in cable TV history, Gore took command early. He remained calm in tone and manner, even as he accused Perot of misdeeds. Gore charged that Perot opposed the trade deal because he stood to profit personally (from the family's Alliance Airport), chastised him for using numerous lobbyists in Congress to win personal tax breaks, and challenged him to open the books on his financing of the anti-NAFTA campaign. The attacks threw Perot off stride and provoked increasingly tart responses. "You're lying now," Perot snapped at Gore. "What are you talking about?" At another point, he accused the vice-president of using "phony numbers." His one-liners came off largely as sarcasm instead of wit. "Are you listening? Work on it." Perot was clearly bothered by what he considered Gore's interruptions, at times refusing to proceed unless Gore stopped or Larry King enforced the rules they had agreed upon before the debate.

Even Perot's closest associates offered no excuses for his performance. "I was stunned by that debate," says Mort Meyerson,

---

* Perot is still infuriated at the way the story of the Cuban assassins played out. An FBI agent had told him the Bureau took the threat seriously, and as a result, assigned extra security to him in both Tampa and Washington. "In the press clippings," Perot told me, "I was [portrayed as] paranoid, crazy, so on and so forth. . . . It is a specific example that how something that comes from the FBI, you can twist it, manipulate it, get it distressed all over the place—look at the facts, and then look at the twist, and the twist bears no resemblance to the facts." Perot said that the FBI had a copy of the caller's voice on tape. "Guess who it was? . . . Scott Barnes pulling stunts again. The fascinating thing is I guess there is nothing you can legally do to the guy." When I confronted Barnes, he admitted the FBI had interviewed him about that call, but denied that he made it. "I heard the tape. It was some Hispanic with a heavy accent. Do you really think that if they had a tape of me, they wouldn't have arrested me? I don't have many friends in the FBI."

"because I knew that Ross was aware of what they [Gore and his advisers] would do."[10]

The press was merciless. Typical comments charged Perot was "weird" (Orlando *Sentinel*) or "a whining, mean-spirited distorter of fact" (*Arizona Republic*).[11] A Gallup poll, taken a week after the debate, showed Perot's favorable rating had plummeted, from a 66 percent favorable rating in June to 29 percent, close to the same figure that had haunted him after the *60 Minutes* story.[12] NAFTA passed the House, and Clinton signed the agreement by year's end.

At first, Perot blamed himself for his poor performance. "After he had been a disaster, he called me the next night," remembers Jim Squires. "And for the first time in our relationship, he said 'I'm sorry, I didn't listen to you.' He just couldn't help it. He told me he knew what they were doing, but when he sat there, 'I couldn't help it.' "[13]

However, Perot has since developed another explanation, and it involves a rather astonishing theory about why Gore may have done so well: "And if you want the ultimate education on the NAFTA debate," Perot contends, "watch it again, and watch Al Gore's ear. And there is something glistening in his ear. They boasted about it after the debate, and I said, 'Oh, that couldn't have happened, that is just Washington talk.' Then someone walked in and said, 'Watch this,' and they showed me this piece where you could see this thing glistening in his ear. Then, to make a long story short, look at where the questions, just listen to the questions in the NAFTA debate. Count the number of times he was allowed to interrupt me in midsentence, which was a clear violation of the understanding that that would not happen. They had really pressed, before the debate, for his handlers to come out and surround and talk to him at every commercial. They wanted to have a huddle. And I said, 'No, that's goofy, he knows what he wants to say, and I know what I want to say, so we don't need any handlers.' Well, if you freely allow a person to interrupt you in a two-person debate, I think if you count them you will find it is thirty times.

"And at every break, I would say, 'Larry, I would appreciate it if you would let me finish the answers to your questions and not be interrupted, because that is what we agreed to.' Well, he would go right back to it, and Larry probably felt that he [Gore] was the vice-president of the United States and you just couldn't say, 'Hey, sucker, you're interrupting.' I didn't notice it [meaning the ear-piece]. Watch the debate and you will see that thing twinkle. And the only reason that somebody on my team looked at the film again was that was the word on the cocktail circuit. See, this is where they are so stupid. Let's say you've pulled that off, and let's say you were being fed good answers, or good questions, or you name it, don't boast publicly about it because that is cheating. See, the news should have been, 'They cheated.' Maybe it was an ear-ache, who knows [he laughs]. All I know is that you can see it twinkle. It was right at the bottom of the ear."[14]*

By the end of the year, 1993, Perot's poll ratings had dropped to an all-time low of 22 percent. Syndicated columnist George Will concluded that the best result of the debate was that it unmasked Perot's real character. Many, like Will, thought Perot was finished as an effective public figure. "The Beltway was wrong to dismiss Perot after the Gore debate," says Gordon Black. "He has the resources and does not have to solve the problem of running. He can communicate to the American people, on his terms, in his way, at his leisure."[15] "People counted Perot out too quickly," says Larry King. "He didn't get as far as he did by rolling over and playing dead. I never thought Ross would stop being a player. And what makes him able to come back, and such a great salesman, is that he still doesn't know he lost the Gore debate."[16] King was evi-dently right. Perot told a reporter in early 1994 that his debate with Gore "had no impact on the NAFTA vote."[17]

After NAFTA, he returned to Dallas and focused primarily on United We Stand America. He hired a new executive director, Russ Verney, a former candidate for a Democratic seat in the House for New Hampshire. By early 1994, Perot again started making a few

---

*There is an earpiece in Gore's right ear, but Perot is referring instead to the left ear, closest to him during the debate. Perot allowed my wife, Trisha, and me to watch a videotape of the debate in his office conference room. The "twinkle" in Gore's left ear appeared to us to clearly be just a reflection of light on his skin. When Perot stopped by to see whether we had spotted the device, we told him it just looked like skin to us. "Maybe so," he said. "Maybe it is just the light."

public appearances. When asked by reporters if he would run again in 1996, Perot sidestepped the question. "I would say the only reason I would ever run again is if the members who've worked so hard and effectively just really, really, really felt that," Perot told C-SPAN host Brian Lamb in January 1994. "I am not driven to be an elected official."[18] In March he told Larry King, "I have no interest in being a political candidate. . . . My dream is that the Republicans and Democrats will both have great candidates in 1996."[19]

Perot had also begun talking regularly with Georgia congressman Newt Gingrich. The Republicans had rehired Perot's 1992 pollster, Frank Luntz, who was familiar with the issues that drove the Perot voters. Gingrich wanted those voters.

"Perot had a tremendous involvement in getting the Contract with America done," says Clay Mulford. "In United We Stand America we were talking about getting a contract of issues that candidates would have to sign in order to get an endorsement from the UWSA party if one was formed. That is what was going on in much of 1993 and early 1994. So that idea was transferred to the Republicans, and of course, Perot was delighted by it, that something might get done."[20] Perot thought Clinton was weak, criticized him frequently, and was prepared to give the Republicans a chance at cleaning up the mess in Washington.

Initially in 1994, Perot busied himself with a new issue: health care. As Hillary Clinton's task force considered possible overhauls of the existing health care system, Perot wanted to run television programs that offered a nonpartisan mix of experts. He tried to buy more television time to run infomercials, but having sold him time for three programs the previous year, all the networks now declined. He then offered to spend $1 million to have the Republicans produce a program about health care. The Republicans were also turned down. "All the networks have shut us off," says Russ Verney. "If you are a candidate, you can get the time. But not as a political party. That was an important message."[21] (Perot had had the same problem in 1992, in that no network would sell him time during the summer months when he was out of the race.)

That autumn, Perot went on another tour, again doing the talk show circuit, and visiting states to endorse some candidates in the

1994 midterm elections. (His success rate was mixed and, in one instance, controversial—his own United We Stand America followers were infuriated when he supported Texas governor Ann Richards in her failed race against George W. Bush, the ex-president's son.) It was his most concerted burst of activity since the NAFTA debate. He was careful to keep his options open about his own political future. "If the members in 1996 insist that I run again," he said on National Public Radio, "I will do it for them. If that's what we have to do to shock the system, and to get the changes, we'll do it."[22]

The unexpectedly strong Republican election results in the 1994 elections seemed to take some of the steam out of Perot's call for radical change in Washington. Not only had the voters brought about the most dramatic shift in decades (for which Perot claimed credit by dubbing his United We Stand America voters the swing vote), but the Republicans had addressed so many of Perot's issues that there was the possibility his movement could be coopted by Newt's revolution.

Publicly, Perot wished the Republicans well, and he concentrated instead on hosting a nationally syndicated radio call-in program. It started in October, and received solid ratings. Every week, Perot invited Washington's leading politicians to talk about national issues. As a host, he was not combative, was a careful listener, refrained from interjecting his own opinion, and allowed his guests ample opportunity to make their points. The radio program was a good vehicle for Perot to enhance his image. His rehabilitation was slow but steady—a California poll in October 1994 showed that 31 percent would consider voting for Perot in 1996.

Even so, by early 1995 most commentators had concluded that Perot was no longer a force in national politics. With the exception of campaign finance reform, the Republicans had brought everything in the contract up for a vote within the first one hundred days of their term (the balanced budget amendment failed to pass by a single vote). But Perot had quietly started canvassing United We Stand America members to discover whether there was sentiment for starting a third party. In February 1995, Gordon Black gave Perot and Mulford a strong pitch on forming a new centrist party, urging Perot to break the "stranglehold" of the

Republicans and Democrats. Perot said no, but he did suggest that Black visit major United We Stand America chapters to give lectures on the mechanics of establishing a third party.* Perot was familiar with the obstacles. California had a very early deadline. Every state had a different process (some had no defined procedure, which meant entrenched Republicans and Democrats had discretion over a third party's standing). Quite a few had stricter requirements for third-party qualification than running an independent candidacy. In Ohio, for instance, an independent candidate must collect 5,000 signatures by August 22 of the year of the presidential race, but a third party must collect over 33,000 by December of the preceding year. In some, like New York, the major parties can maneuver to keep a new party off the ballot no matter how many signatures are gathered. By the spring, Perot was leaning against undertaking the massive expense and effort required to put a third party on the ballot in all fifty states.

That summer, as the two parties returned to more traditional bickering and less productivity, talk of an independent candidacy increased, but it did not involve Perot. It centered instead on the popular former chairman of the Joint Chiefs of Staff, General Colin Powell, whose long-anticipated autobiography was due out in the autumn. As the Powell bandwagon boomed, Perot tried to avoid a complete eclipse by inviting all the Republican presidential candidates and Democratic party leaders to Dallas for a three-day United We Stand America conference ("Kiss the Ring, the Sequel," Mary Matalin dubbed it). Every major Republican candidate (and some minor ones), plus Democratic leaders in the House and Senate and in the party, gathered in Dallas from August 11–13, 1995 (but President Clinton declined to attend). Covered extensively by the national press, the conference put Perot and his organization back on the political map. The repre-

---

* If Perot had decided to create a third party in 1992, he would be able to make another run in 1996 with very little effort. One of the ways to qualify as a "party" in a state is to get a certain amount of the vote in the last similar election (percentages vary, but often hover around 10 percent). Perot's 1992 vote totals were high enough that he would have automatically qualified to be on the ballot in forty-one states in 1996. As a result of running as an independent, he qualified in only five.

sentatives of both parties courted Perot and his members, address-ing their specific concerns of term limits, a balanced budget amendment, and campaign finance reform. During the confer-ence, a new national poll showed that 62 percent of the American public wanted a third political party.[23] And once again Perot had made a surprising comeback from his nadir in late 1994—in a three-way race, Clinton took 37 percent, Dole 33 percent, and Perot 26 percent.

On NBC's *Meet the Press,* broadcast from the United We Stand America conference on its final day, Perot refused to rule out another run for the White House. "I can't say that I'm going to go away."[24] He closed the conference by challenging the Republicans and Democrats to sign a bipartisan "Contract for America," and encouraged them to tackle the key issues in the next one hundred days. It was a challenge the parties ignored, giving Perot reason to stay involved.

In late August, Colin Powell's popularity was still rising. "Powell is a fine guy, I've known him forever," say Perot. "But when all that was going on, I told some people we have a third party, it is the press party, they already have their nominee."[25]* Perot, however, was not waiting for events to catch up to him, but was aggressively reviewing his options at the end of the summer. He briefly considered challenging Clinton or running for the Republican nomination. At one point, Perot even toyed with run-ning in both party primaries, in some states as a Democrat and in others as a Republican, in order to discuss the issues and "be in the game." All of those ideas were rejected.

The quandary left for Perot was straightforward. If he did not act quickly to form a third party, the opportunity would be lost, as California's deadline (the first in the nation, at October 31) was

---

* Actually, while Perot speaks highly of Powell, he is wary of him because Powell counts as his closest friend Richard Armitage, Perot's target in the Pentagon. Powell, in a 1992 deposition to the Senate Select Committee on POWs/MIAs, said: "My view of Rich Armitage is that he's one of the finest men I've ever known, one of the most dedicated public servants and Americans I've ever known, and I would always be in his camp whether he was clean as a whis-tle or in trouble." A Powell administration would almost certainly mean a high post for Armitage, a nightmarish thought for Perot.

fast approaching. Since it is the largest electoral state, failing to qualify on that ballot would significantly diminish the importance of his third party. And having eliminated a Democratic or Republican challenge, Perot's only option would be to run as an independent. If he did not run at all, he risked being totally excluded from the issues since, as he had discovered the previous year, the networks would not sell him time unless he was a candidate. The question mark was Colin Powell, who was still toying with the idea of an independent run. Perot's legitimate concern was that if he missed the third-party cutoff, he would be overshadowed as an independent in the event that Powell made that run.

It was Gordon Black who gave Perot the final impetus to form a third party. Black, a longtime advocate for a third party, had been a key part of the support for millionaire businessman Tom Golisano's run for New York governor in 1994 (Golisano had spent almost $7 million of his own money on that unsuccessful race). Although he received only 4 percent of the vote, it was enough to qualify the banner he ran under, the Independence party, for a place on the New York ballot in 1996. Black enlisted Golisano's support to put together a network of major states for creating a limited third party for the 1996 presidential race. "It would be too costly to do all fifty states, we figured, with the deadlines being so close," says Black. "However, it was fairly simple to pull together thirty, minus California and Florida. Fifteen or sixteen require fewer than fifteen thousand signatures. The cost difference between getting thirty and forty is huge, largely with California and Florida adding to the expense."[26]

Black and Golisano estimated it would cost between $500,000 and $1 million to qualify in the thirty states. Such a strategy meant they obviously could not field a winning candidate for the 1996 election, but they viewed it as an effective first step that would attract substantial media attention and lead to a full party for the 2000 election.

Black approached Clay Mulford and demonstrated how simple it could be to qualify in the thirty states. He showed Mulford the exact dates for qualifying for the ballots in each state, and also provided information about some existing third parties in different states that might be willing to work with a new national party.

"I showed him the list," recalls Black, "of New York, Minnesota, Utah, Oregon, Connecticut, and Pennsylvania. They all have centrist third parties, so working together is not a big deal."[27] Black's presentation convinced Mulford that putting together a third party for the 1996 elections was doable, although difficult. The imminent California deadline meant that Perot had to act quickly.

Within a week, Mulford called Black and told him Perot wanted to meet with him and Golisano, in Dallas. On Wednesday, September 20, Perot and Russ Verney talked with Black and Golisano for two hours. The California deadline was only a month away. There were two options for qualifying, each difficult—either obtain 900,000 signatures on petitions, or nearly 90,000 registered voters had to leave their current parties and join the new party. For Perot, there were also other complications. He and Gingrich spoke two or three times a week, and the Republicans had applied constant pressure on him not to form a third party. Also, Perot worried because a new party would be expected to field candidates for Congress and the Senate, and Black says that "he feared that kooks and nuts—he always mentioned David Duke—would run as candidates of the new party and be associated with him. Ross said they had already spent two solid years filtering out weirdos in United We Stand."[28] Black tried to persuade Perot that there were significant advantages for his establishment of a third party. It would put him back into the spotlight and guarantee he had a voice in the 1996 election. A third party would also provide Perot with a strategic advantage. An independent candidate has to reveal his or her hand by early spring, since Texas, with a May 11 deadline for its petitions, forces a candidate to begin collecting signatures by late March. Perot believed that was one of his major mistakes in 1992—his running so early allowed the press and other candidates to build negative stories, leaving him seriously damaged by the summer. With a third party in place, Perot could hold a convention similar to the major parties and select a candidate at the end of the summer. Then it would be a two-month sprint for the White House. If Perot were the candidate, with his tens of millions compressed into a much shorter campaign, he could fundamentally alter the 1996 race.

At the end of the meeting, Perot told Black and Golisano that he would think about it. A few days later he called Black and told him he would form a third party. "Are you happy now?" Perot asked. "Yes, I am happy now," Black said with a chuckle.[29]

On September 25, 1995, Perot used his favorite venue for major announcements, *Larry King Live*. He announced, "We're at a critical time in our country's history, and tonight we're going to start the process of starting a new party" [which would be known as the Reform party].[30]*

Once again, Perot had captured the headlines and the attention of independent voters. In the first five minutes after he flashed an 800 number on the screen, he claimed, 800,000 callers jammed the line. As political reporter Richard Berke noted two days later in *The New York Times,* Perot's announcement was described, "even by his detractors, as a masterly maneuver that allows Mr. Perot to insert himself as a power broker into the 1996 residential campaign and shake up the calculations over who will make it to the White House."[31]

And when Colin Powell announced on November 9 that he would not seek the presidency in 1996, Perot and his fledgling party were alone in the independent spotlight.

"Most reporters do not understand what is involved in forming a third party or running an independent candidacy," says Gordon Black. "It is all about money, and if you don't have it, you can't get on the ballot, and even if you get there, like John Anderson did in 1980, then you don't have any money left to run a campaign. Perot's money puts him in a league of his own."[32] Several former and current politicians, ranging from ex-senators Lowell Weicker and Paul Tsongas to Senator Bill Bradley, briefly flirted with the idea of a third-party or independent run, but by December 19, 1995, the financial realities sank in, and they settled merely for an

---

* The original name, the Independence Party, was suggested by Golisano and Black, who had already qualified for ballot status under that name in New York. However, because of conflicts in several states, most notably California, Perot changed the name in November to the Reform party. Black was mildly disappointed: "Our research shows the Reform party is a lousy choice. American party or America party is good, but three states have banned it. The Patriot party tested as too right-wing."

"announcement of principles" they hoped the candidates would address in the campaign.

The reaction to Perot's decision from the two major parties differed sharply. Republicans were infuriated, believing they had done all they could to satisfy Perot and he had betrayed them. "I can't figure this fellow out," said an angry Bob Dole when told the news.[33] But the Democrats saw a possible advantage: splitting the anti-Clinton vote. Dick Morris, one of the president's aides, even called Gordon Black within a week of Perot's announcement and asked if any help was needed on petition gathering. Black flatly rejected the offer, but Morris's interest showed that the Democrats did not think a third party was a bad development for its chances of retaining the White House.

California, with an October 31 deadline, was Perot's major hurdle. On Sunday, October 1, Perot paid to have petitions for his new party printed in 6 million newspapers around the state. He encouraged voters to mail them to the California secretary of state—900,000 signatures were needed. Four days later, the secretary of state changed the rules and announced that Perot did not have the option of collecting the 900,000 signatures but instead had to utilize the more difficult process of convincing 89,007 voters to abandon their current party affiliations and sign with the new party.

Perot believes the rules were changed when it became clear that "we were going to make it [in collecting 900,000 signatures]. We had to start all over again."[34] The secretary of state, however, did not have the voter registration forms necessary to switch party allegiance, and Perot had to print them at his own expense. No longer trusting the California authorities, he kept photocopies of every signature turned in to the state ("It is going to be pretty hard to play games with us," he says). "They kept dramatically underreporting the numbers we had," says Perot. "They underreported and underreported. There was also a Republican resolution in California that anyone who helped us would never get any more business from the Republican party. Every state is controlled by one of the two parties. The people in those parties don't want a third party. So this is to be expected. . . . The temptation to keep the status quo is pretty strong."[35]

But Perot had no intention of failing in California, and viewed it as a test of what his volunteers could accomplish. On November 1, 1995, California secretary of state Bill Jones announced that Perot had qualified his party for the 1996 ballot. It was a remarkable feat, especially since it was accomplished in three weeks.

"We have trained hundreds of people in California," says Perot. "We brought them in, it was sort of like basic training, so a lot of people have done it now and they are ready to go back to their own states and do it there. California is so big, it is like trying to register a nation. It was done in the field, in eighteen days. . . . Says a lot about the desire for a third party."[36]*

Some of the states that followed presented even more difficulty for Perot's fledgling effort. Maine disqualified so many Reform party petitions that the effort to get on the ballot there fell 515 votes short. In Ohio, the Reform party turned in more than 50,000 signatures (33,463 are required), yet state officials eliminated 20,000 on a host of minor technicalities. But Perot had the money to fight. In both states he conclusively showed that thousands of signatures were improperly scrubbed, but before the Reform party was certified for the ballot, he had to take both states to court. "It's Ballotgate," says Russ Verney, now the national chairman of the Citizens to Establish the Reform Party. "The Republican and Democratic voter registrars have been stealing signatures from us—anything they can think of to keep us off the ballot."[37]

Perot, however, did not appear concerned with the obstacles, and was instead convinced that the Reform party will not only have its candidate on all fifty state ballots for the 1996 election but will also be a majority party within a generation. "People say

---

* When Perot's party qualified in California, it received little news coverage outside of California, part of what Gordon Black calls the "bias in the mainstream media against anything that comes outside the two-party system." As further evidence, Black points to the much wider press coverage when Perot failed to make a December deadline to qualify for spring primaries in Ohio, even though, as Black pointed out, "it was a nothing story, since Perot had no intention of running anyone in the state primaries, and he will certainly be on the ballot for the November election. Most reporters just don't understand how to cover this since it is so new, and they haven't mastered the details."

three parties won't work," he boldly predicts, "and we say, 'We don't think there will be three.' "[38]

Perot's rules for selecting the Reform party's candidate are unique, as expected. Anyone who wants to run will have to obtain signatures from 10 percent of those who have signed up with the party. Then, after agreeing to support a platform of issues that were at the core of Perot's 1992 race and forswearing any personal attacks on other candidates, that person can run for the nomination at an electronic convention planned for August. Party members, each given a personal identification number to counter any fraud, will be able to vote by fax, telephone, and even e-mail.

As Perot continued working for the Reform party, speculation increased in the spring that he would be the candidate. In March he indicated he would be willing to run if his party selected him as its candidate. Some who have worked with him on the new party would be shocked if Perot was not the Reform standard-bearer. "When Ross Perot does his convention, it is going to be unlike anything this country has ever seen," says Gordon Black. "He will hold a two-day national primary, carried on cable television, with 3 to 4 million people voting on who the candidate will be. The media will ignore it until they can't ignore it any longer. And that candidate will be Perot, no doubt about it. He will come roaring out by Labor Day with $100 million in television time, and it will be a locomotive that will change that election completely."[39]

Early in September 1995, Gordon Black asked Perot if he could imagine being the vice-president on a 1996 ticket. "Gordon, can you really imagine me as a vice-president?" Perot said.[40] Ken Follett, who wrote the book about Perot's rescue of his workers from revolutionary Iran, got to know him well during their project and cannot imagine him at anything other than the top spot on the ticket. "I've heard him say it," recalls Follett. " 'If I could run for king, I would do it.' "[41] Unfortunately for Perot, reaching for the presidency will have to suffice.

Acknowledgments

Because Ross Perot wields sizable power, especially in Texas, and has a reputation for aggressively contesting those who cross him, researching this book posed a unique problem. Dozens of people—primarily former business associates or government officials who had dealt with Perot over the years—agreed to be interviewed only under the condition that they not be identified in the book. The information they provided was often important enough to use despite this restriction. As a result, quotations sometimes appear without attribution in this book. In no case, however, did I use material from one of these interviews unless I independently corroborated its accuracy through another person or documentary source.

As for those people who agreed to speak on the record, some deserve specific mention. Foremost is Ross Perot himself. He was initially reluctant to be interviewed, but once he decided to cooperate he made himself freely available, and I owe him a debt of gratitude for his substantial help. His two executive secretaries, Sally Bell and Barbara Conly, never hesitated to track down the smallest details about Perot's life or the history of EDS.

A number of people were unusually generous with their time. They granted repeated interviews and were always available to answer questions. Among these, I owe special thanks to Ken Riedlinger, a former EDS executive who remains a supporter of Perot's. He agreed to talk frankly about what he views as Perot's strengths and weaknesses. Others also close to Perot—Mort Meyerson, Bill Gayden, and Murphy Martin—all had insights that were central to understanding Perot. Tom Meurer, with his superb recall, aided in reconstructing stories about EDS and Perot's adventures in Southeast Asia.

With regard to the early years of Perot's life, Claude Pinkerton, Hayes McClerkin, and Dr. J. B. Rochelle provided me with an appreciation of the town and era in which Perot grew up. I am especially grateful to Tom Downtain, Tom Marquez, Ron Sperberg, and Rob Brooks for explaining the corporate culture of EDS. And Tom Beauchamps, Gene Aune, Wesley Hjornevik, and James Naughton guided me through the complexities of the relationship between EDS and Blue Cross/Blue Shield.

The POW/MIA story weaves a steady thread through Perot's life, and a number of people went out of their way to provide details of their encounters with Perot. Key to my research were Jim Cannon, Ann Mills Griffiths, Frank Carlucci, Stephen Solarz, Robinson Risner, Jim Badey, Richard Childress, and Richard Armitage and his assistant, Brenda Mitchell. William Codinha and Frances Zwenig shared their knowledge about the 1992 POW/MIA Senate Select Committee investigation. Bob Doubek, Jan Scruggs, and Terry O'Donnell unraveled the related matter of Perot and the Vietnam Memorial in Washington, D.C.

Another important event in Perot's life was the rescue of two of his kidnapped workers from Iran. I could not have gotten the full story without the unselfish assistance of Ken Follett, Professor Bahman "Buzz" Fozouni, Reza Neghabat, Dr. Shoja Sheikh, Henry Precht, Charles Naas, David Newson, and Ward Christensen.

For the inside story of Perot's 1992 campaign, I am indebted to Tom Luce, Joe Canzeri, Sal Russo, Jim Squires, Liz Noyer, Orson Swindle, Ed Rollins, Jack Gargan, John Jay Hooker, James Carville and Mary Matalin, and Larry King. Bob Barkin and Charlie Leonard provided personal files, correspondence, and papers from their work on the campaign. Problems swamped many of the Perot volunteers in 1992, and some of those affected shared their experiences with me, among them Larry Way, Kevin Laughlin, Paige Pell, John Opincar, Kathy Jaeger, Bob Penn, Joyce Shepard, Roger Yane, Lloyd Wells, and Cliff Arneback. Dawn

Larsen was especially valuable in giving me a fuller appreciation of that situation.

On the issue of third-party politics, thanks are due to Sharon Holman and Russ Verney for their unique perspective on the independent/third-party political process, and on Perot himself. In addition, Richard Winger, the nation's leading expert on ballot access, and Gordon Black, a political science professor and pollster, had seemingly endless patience with my numerous questions. And Clay Mulford took considerable time from his hectic schedule to provide significant information about the 1992 campaign and the movement toward a new party.

The claims of dirty tricks that arose during the 1992 campaign created a hornet's nest of conflicting stories from apparently credible sources. For their help in sorting out what happened, several people deserve particular thanks, including Oliver "Buck" Revell, the former chief of the Dallas FBI office; Farris Rookstool, an analyst also previously with the Dallas office; and former agent Jim Siano, who has since done investigative work for Perot. Former police chief Bill Rathburn and two of his top officers, Rudy Diaz and Eddie Walt, presented the Dallas police angle. Scott Barnes has been called a "mystery box" by Perot, and the former soldier of fortune must be approached warily by any credible journalist, but Barnes did provide documents whose authenticity I confirmed, and after many conversations, he made some startling admissions about his own role. David Taylor, a BBC producer, must also be thanked for finally talking about a subject he was reluctant to discuss on the record. Finally, Jim Oberwetter, a Hunt Oil executive who was the 1992 Texas chief for the Bush-Quayle campaign, relived a very painful experience in his interviews with me.

Others who helped on a variety of issues are Felix Rohatyn, Caspar Weinberger, Peter du Pont, Walt Newport, Garey Gilley, J. D. James, and Steve Wolens.

Many journalists have written about Perot, and the key ones are listed in the bibliography, but a few merit individual mention. Tracy Everbaugh of *The Dallas Morning News* loaned me her file of Freedom of Information requests covering a variety of subjects relating to Perot. Allen Pusey, the assistant projects editor of the *Morning News,* referred me to several people who were valuable in developing a complete picture of Perot's life. Also, two authors, Carolyn Barta (*Perot and His People,* 1993) and Todd Mason (*Perot,* 1990), were generous in pointing me toward knowledgeable sources as well as helping me to avoid pitfalls along the way. And further appreciation goes to Todd Mason for supplying his research materials from his unauthorized biography of Perot—even small details such as his telephone list saved innumerable hours.

James S. Rosen, a New York writer at work on a biography of former attorney general John Mitchell, was kind enough to let me use his materials from the Nixon administration that related to Perot.

Those in charge of special collections and archives were instrumental in finding relevant documents. I was aided by Cliff Vanderpool, director, and Jamie A. Simmons, curator, of the Texarkana Museums System, Texarkana, Texas; Dr. David Wigdor, assistant chief of the Library of Congress; Charles E. Schamel, archivist, Archival Projects Branch of the Center for Legislative Archives, National Archives, Washington, D.C.; Karl Weissenbach, acting director, and William M. Joyner, archivist, Nixon Presidential Papers, National Archives, College Park, Maryland; Mr. Robert Schacht, director and archivist, Sam Houston Regional Library and Research Center, Austin, Texas; Linda Hanson, archivist, Lyndon B. Johnson Presidential Library, Austin, Texas; Kathy Struss, audiovisual archivist, Dwight Eisenhower Presidential Library, Abilene, Kansas; and Katherine Carothers, information clerk, Federal Election Commission, Washington, D.C. Elvis Brathwaite, of Wide World Photos, was diligent in finding interesting pictures of Perot and the events that have marked his life.

Charles Schwartz, a good friend, helped me whenever I encountered a particularly vexing computer problem. Unfortunately for him, those only seemed to occur in the middle of the night.

John Dodson and David Davis, of the Adolphus Hotel, deserve mention for accommodating my many requests and virtually converting my hotel room into a second office during my extended stays in Dallas.

I am fortunate to count Fredric Dannen as one of my closest friends. He is a constant source of support. His critical review of the manuscript, with his keen eye as a journalist, made it a better book.

My agent, Owen Laster, of the William Morris Agency, placed this book with the right publisher. He was also able to negotiate a contract that allowed me to complete it without having to cut corners on research. As for my publishers, Random House, I am delighted to have yet another book with them. Random House encourages a truly collaborative effort in publishing, even allowing me to become involved in decisions about publicity, advertising, and marketing. Harry Evans, the president and publisher, had the foresight to sign this book at a time when Ross Perot and third-party politics seemed to be on no one's mind but my own. Also at Random House, there is a tremendous support team, ranging from Andy Carpenter, who somehow designs innovative yet appropriate book covers, to Ivan Held in publicity, whose knowledge and enthusiasm were a steady encouragement. Bernie Klein created the elegant interior design. Editorial associate Barbé Hammer always had an answer for my many queries. Managing editor Amy Edelman remained cheerfully unflappable, even when I was wreaking havoc on the schedule by constantly rewriting. Beth Pearson, who oversaw the editorial production, significantly improved the manuscript with her constant nit-picking. Her sense of humor made the long hours that were necessary to meet our tight deadline pass easily.

Most of all, though, I owe a great debt to my friend and editor, Robert Loomis. No writer should expect to receive the time and attention to detail that Bob spent in reviewing my manuscript. His suggestions, comments, and editing—and the debate in which he engaged me over the contents—were indispensable contributions. I cannot imagine working on a book without his guidance.

Finally, I must pay tribute to my wife, Trisha. She works on each of my books, travels with me to conduct the interviews and archival work, organizes the file cabinets of information at home, and scans hundreds of documents into the computer. She listens to my own interminable self-doubts, and then reads every draft of the manuscript, always improving it with her insightful criticisms. She was responsible for first turning my attention to Ross Perot and third-party politics. I am blessed to have her as my partner. This book is as much hers as mine.

Notes

Chapter 1:
The Boy from Texarkana

1. Carolyn Barta, *Perot and His People: Disrupting the Balance of Political Power* (Fort Worth, Texas: The Summit Group, 1993), p. 8.
2. Margot Perot, interviewed on *Larry King Live,* CNN, October 22, 1992.
3. Interview with Mort Meyerson, April 30, 1995.
4. Interview with Tom Luce, August 12, 1995.
5. Interview with Clay Mulford, March 9, 1995.
6. Interview with Jack Gargan, April 20, 1995.
7. Ibid.
8. Steve Nicely, "Campaign Launched in KC Pushes Perot for President," *Kansas City Star,* June 2, 1991, p. B7.
9. Interview with Jack Gargan, April 20, 1995.
10. Interview with John Jay Hooker, April 25, 1995.
11. Interview with John Jay Hooker, April 26, 1995.
12. Interview with John Jay Hooker, April 25, 1995.
13. Interview with John Jay Hooker, April 26, 1995.
14. Interview with John Seigenthaler, August 17, 1995.

15. Interview with Larry King, August 12, 1995.
16. Jim Squires, interviewed by Michael Isikoff, "Unlikely Suitors Pushed Perot Bid," *The Washington Post,* May 31, 1992, p. A1.
17. Interview with Ross Perot, August 22, 1995.
18. Interview with John Jay Hooker, April 26, 1995.
19. Interview with Ross Perot, November 29, 1995.
20. Ross Perot, interviewed by Jennifer Andrews of KTAL television, Shreveport, Louisiana, January 18, 1995.
21. Interview with Ross Perot, November 29, 1995.
22. Ibid.
23. Interview with B. W. "Sonny" Atchley, September 1, 1995.
24. Interview with Bette Perot, April 26, 1996.
25. KTAL interview with Ross Perot, op. cit.
26. Interview with Ross Perot, November 29, 1995.
27. Ibid.
28. Interview with Bette Perot, April 26, 1996.
29. KTAL interview with Ross Perot, op. cit.
30. Interviews with Ross Perot, November 29 and 30, 1995.

31. Interview with Bette Perot, April 26, 1996.

32. Ellen Crow, interviewed by David Von Drehle, "The Texas-Arkansas Line: Birthplace of Presidents?," *The Washington Post National Weekly Edition,* June 22–28, 1992, p. 13.

33. Interview with Dr. Herbert Wren, March 11, 1995.

34. Interview with Ross Perot, November 29, 1995.

35. Ibid.

36. Interviews with Ross Perot, August 9, November 29 and 30, 1995.

37. Nancy Perot, interviewed by David Remnick, "Our Nation Turns Its Lonely Eyes to H. Ross Perot," *The Washington Post Magazine,* April 12, 1987.

38. Paper drafted by Ross Perot titled "Ross Perot: Outline of His Life," undated, provided to author, p. 2.

39. Ed Overholser, interviewed by Marilyn Schwartz, "High School Classmates Get Back to Basics Recalling Ross Perot," *The Dallas Morning News,* April 9, 1984, p. 1C.

40. Interview with Herbert Wren, March 11, 1995.

41. Todd Mason, *Perot: An Unauthorized Biography* (Homewood, Illinois: Business One Irwin, 1990), pp. 20, 21, 24.

42. Interview with Hayes McClerkin, March 11, 1995.

43. Interview with Jamie Simmons, curator, Texarkana Historical Museum, August 29, 1995.

44. Interview with B. W. "Sonny" Atchley, September 1, 1995.

45. Interview with Ross Perot, November 29, 1995.

46. KTAL interview with Perot, op. cit.; also, interview with Ross Perot, November 30, 1995.

47. Interview with Claude Pinkerton, February 27, 1995.

48. Interview with Jimmy Crowson, March 1, 1995.

49. Ross Perot, "Perot on Perot," *U.S. News & World Report,* June 29, 1992, pp. 24–25.

50. Interview with Claude Pinkerton, February 27, 1995.

51. Interview with Jane Maxwell, September 1, 1995.

Chapter 2:
The Godless Navy

1. Ross Perot, "Perot on Perot," *U.S. News & World Report,* June 29, 1992, p. 26.

2. Interview with Bob Lowell, February 13, 1995.

3. Arlis Simmons, quoted by Todd Mason, *Perot: An Unauthorized Biography* (Homewood, Illinois: Business One Irwin, 1990), p. 30.

4. Interview with Mark Royston, February 13, 1995.

5. Interview with Bob Lowell, February 13, 1995.

6. Margot Perot, quoted by Ken Gross, *Ross Perot: The Man Behind the Myth* (New York: Random House, 1992), pp. 41, 43–44.

7. Ibid., pp. 44–45.

8. Bette Perot, quoted by Gross, op. cit., p. 45.

9. Interview with Ross Perot, November 30, 1995.

10. Ross Perot, quoted by Gross, op. cit., p. 46; also, interview with Ross Perot, November 30, 1995.

11. Interview with Ross Perot, November 30, 1995.

12. Eric Schmitt, "Perot in Navy: Dynamic and Popular," *The New York Times,* June 8, 1992, p. A12.

13. Interview with Ross Perot, November 30, 1995.

14. Ross Perot, quoted by Gross, op. cit., p. 47; also, interview with Ross Perot, November 30, 1995.

15. Interview with Ross Perot, November 30, 1995.

16. Gerald Scott, quoted by Schmitt, op. cit., p. A12.

17. Ed Ditzel quoted by Art Pine, "Collision with the Navy Gives Insight into Perot," *Los Angeles Times,* June 4, 1992, p. A1.

18. Pine, "Collision with the Navy," op. cit. p. A1.

19. Letter, Ross Perot, Sr., to Wright Patman, March 7, 1955, Papers of Wright Patman, Ross Perot/Texas, Texarkana 1955 File, LBJ Library.

20. Letter, Wright Patman to Ross Perot, Sr., March 8, 1955, Papers of Wright Patman, Ross Perot/Texas, Texarkana 1955 File, LBJ Library.

21. Letter, Ross Perot, Sr., to Wright Patman, May 3, 1955, Papers of Wright Patman, Ross Perot/Texas, Texarkana 1955 File, LBJ Library.

22. Undated memorandum/letter, Papers of Wright Patman, Ross Perot/Texas, Texarkana 1955 File, LBJ Library.

23. Memo, Lt. Henry Ross Perot to secretary of the navy, April 27, 1955, Papers of Wright Patman, Ross Perot/Texas, Texarkana 1955 File, LBJ Library.

24. Letter, Ross Perot, Sr., to Wright Patman, July 27, 1955, Papers of Wright Patman, Ross Perot/Texas, Texarkana 1955 File, LBJ Library.

25. Written conclusion of Captain G. H. Miller, quoted by Art Pine, "Officers Judged Perot Too Immature for Naval Career," Los Angeles Times, July 2, 1992, p. A1.

26. Written decision of Rear Admiral J. C. Daniel, quoted by Art Pine, "Officers Judged Perot Too Immature," op. cit. p. A1.

27. Letter of Captain Gerald Scott, quoted by Art Pine, "Officers Judged Perot Too Immature," op. cit. p. A1.

28. Letter, Ross Perot, Sr., to Wright Patman, July 27, 1955, Papers of Wright Patman, Ross Perot/Texas, Texarkana 1955 File, LBJ Library.

29. Interview with Ross Perot, November 30, 1995.

30. Ibid.

31. Bette Perot, quoted by Gross, op. cit., p. 58.

32. Margot Perot, quoted by Gross, op. cit. pp. 58–59.

33. Certified copy of marriage certificate of Henry Ross Perot and G. Margot Birmingham, September 13, 1956, from the Office of Register of Wills and Clerk of the Orphans Court, Westmoreland County, Pennsylvania.

34. Conversation recounted by Ross Perot, interviewed on November 30, 1995.

Chapter 3: "Bring Me the Guys Who Love to Win"

1. Interview with Jane Onofrey, February 27, 1995.

2. Todd Mason, Perot: An Unauthorized Biography (Homewood, Illinois: Business One Irwin, 1990), p. 36.

3. Marty Primeau, "Ross Perot," The Dallas Morning News, June 29, 1986, p. 2E.

4. Dean Campbell, quoted by Mason, op. cit., p. 40.

5. Interview with Tom Marquez, June 16, 1995.

6. Ross Perot, quoted by Bryan Wooley, The Edge of the West and Other Texas Stories (El Paso, Texas: Texas Western Press, 1990), p. 183.

7. Henry Wendler, quoted by Primeau, op. cit., p. 2E.

8. George J. Church, "The Other Side of Perot," Time, June 29, 1992.

9. Ross Perot, quoted by Ken Gross, Ross Perot: The Man Behind The Myth (New York: Random House, 1992), pp. 74–75.

10. Interview with Ross Perot, November 30, 1995.

11. Ross Perot, quoted by David Remnick, "Our Nation Turns Its Lonely Eyes to H. Ross Perot," The Washington Post Magazine, April 12, 1987.

12. Interview with Ross Perot, November 30, 1995.

13. Interview with Murphy Martin, March 8, 1995.

14. Interview with Ross Perot, November 30, 1995.

15. Ross Perot, quoted in Dallas Times Herald, March 14, 1974, per Tony Chiu, Ross Perot: In His Own Words (New York: Warner Books, 1992), p. 11.

16. Interview with Ross Perot, November 30, 1995.

17. Ross Perot, quoted by Bo Burlingham and Curtis Hartman, "Cowboy Capitalist," Inc., January 1989.

18. Interview with Tom Beauchamps, March 9, 1995.

19. Garry Wills, "The Rescuer," *The New York Review of Books,* June 25, 1992.

20. Ross Perot, quoted in "Ross Perot: Dallasite of the Year," *D Magazine,* January 1984, p. 113.

21. Interview with Tom Marquez, June 16, 1995.

22. Ross Perot, quoted in *Dallas Times Herald,* February 9, 1986, per Chiu, op. cit., p. 13.

23. Tom Marquez, quoted by Primeau, op. cit., p. 2E.

24. Interview with Tom Downtain, March 14, 1995.

25. Tom Marquez, quoted by Primeau, op. cit., p. 2E.

26. Interview with Tom Marquez, June 16, 1995.

27. Interview with Anne Ellis, February 21, 1995.

28. Interview with Ross Perot, November 30, 1995.

29. Interview with Tom Marquez, June 16, 1995.

30. Interview with Tom Downtain, March 14, 1995.

31. Interview with Tom Marquez, June 16, 1995.

32. Interview with Tom Downtain, March 15, 1995.

33. Interview with Ross Perot, November 30, 1995.

34. Interview with Tom Downtain, March 15, 1995.

35. Ross Perot, quoted in *The Dallas Morning News,* May 3, 1970, per Chiu, op. cit., p. 15.

36. Doron P. Levin, *Irreconcilable Differences: Ross Perot Versus General Motors* (Boston: Little, Brown, 1989), p. 30; Jack Hight, quoted by Mason, op. cit., p. 45.

Chapter 4: Welfare Billionaire

1. Letter, to George Lusk from Milledge A. Hart, February 25, 1963, VP Papers, Case File: Hart–Has, LBJ Library.

2. Memo to the files from George Lusk, March 15, 1963, VP Master File, Pen–Per, 1963, LBJ Library.

3. Memo, to Paul M. Popple from Elmer B. Staats, April 23, 1965, White House Central Files, Ex WH 5-1, 4/9/65– 9/7/65, LBJ Library.

4. Letter, to Paul M. Popple from Jack Hight, April 23, 1965, White House Central Files, Ex WH 5-1, 4/9/65–9/7/65, LBJ Library.

5. Memo, to Paul M. Popple from Elmer B. Staats, May 4, 1965, White House Central Files, Ex WH 5-1, 4/9/65–9/7/65, LBJ Library.

6. Interview with Tom Downtain, March 14, 1995.

7. Interview with Ken Riedlinger, October 16, 1995.

8. Testimony of Thomas Tierney, Administration of Federal Health Benefit Programs, Hearings Before a Subcommittee of the Committee on Government Operations, Part 3—Data Processing, House of Representatives, Ninety-second Congress, First Session, September 28, 1971, p. 26.

9. Testimony of Thomas Tierney, Administration of Federal Health Benefit Programs, Part 3, First Session, September 28, 1971, pp. 5, 9, 19, 22.

10. Testimony of Thomas Tierney, Administration of Federal Health Benefit Programs, Part 3, First Session; September 28, 1971, p. 26; Steven Holmes, "Federal Contracts Gave Perot His Big Break," *The New York Times,* May 5, 1992, p. 1.

11. Excerpts Relating to Costs of Computer Services, from HEW Audit Reports for Administrative Costs of Part A and Part B of the Medicare Program at Texas Blue Cross–Blue Shield During Calendar Years 1966 and 1967, p. 280, reprinted as Appendix 2, Administration of Federal Health Benefit Programs, Part 3, First Session, September 28, 1971.

12. Testimony of Thomas Tierney, Administration of Federal Health Benefit Programs, Part 3, First Session, September 28, 1971, pp. 28–31, and Appendix 2, pp. 281–83.

13. Report of William J. McQuay regarding Visit to Dallas Regional Office and Group Medical Services, Inc. (Texas Blue Shield), November 15–16, 1967, reprinted in Hearings Before a Subcommittee of the Committee on Government Operations, Part

3—Data Processing, House of Representatives, Ninety-second Congress, First Session, September 28, 1971, pp. 53–54.

14. Testimony of Thomas Tierney, Administration of Federal Health Benefit Programs, Part 3, First Session, September 28, 1971, pp. 33–34.

15. Testimony of Walker Evans, Administration of Federal Health Benefit Programs, Part 3, First Session, November 9, 1971, pp. 97–98.

16. Report of Meeting with Electronic Data Systems, Inc., Baltimore, Md., April 24, 1967, reprinted in full in Administration of Federal Health Benefit Programs, Part 3, First Session, November 9, 1971, pp. 118–19.

17. Interview with Tom Beauchamps, March 9, 1995; testimony of Thomas Tierney, Administration of Federal Health Benefit Programs, Part 3, First Session; September 28, 1971, pp. 5, 22; testimony of Walker Evans, Administration of Federal Health Benefit Programs, Part 3, First Session. November 9, 1971, pp. 84–85, 90.

18. Interview with Tom Beauchamps, March 9, 1995.

19. Testimony of Walker Evans, Administration of Federal Health Benefit Programs, Part 3, First Session, November 9, 1971, pp. 97–98.

20. Interview with Tom Beauchamps, March 9, 1995.

21. Testimony of Walker Evans, Administration of Federal Health Benefit Programs, Part 3, First Session, November 9, 1971, p. 85.

22. Testimony of Thomas Tierney, Administration of Federal Health Benefit Programs, Part 3, First Session, September 28, 1971, pp. 35–36; testimony of Walker Evans, Administration of Federal Health Benefit Programs, Part 3, First Session, November 9, 1971, pp. 85–87, 96–97; memo, to Robert M. Mayne from George E. Rawson, June 13, 1968, reproduced at pp. 123–24.

23. Testimony of Thomas Tierney, Administration of Federal Health Benefit Programs, Part 3, First Session, September 28, 1971, pp. 50–52.

24. Letter, to Tom L. Beauchamps from Thomas M. Tierney, July 29, 1968, reprinted in Hearings Before a Subcommittee of the Committee on Government Operations, Part 3—Data Processing, House of Representatives, Ninety-second Congress, First Session, September 28, 1971, pp. 59–60; also, testimony of Walker Evans, Administration of Federal Health Benefit Programs, Part 3, First Session, November 9, 1971, p. 89.

25. Robert Fitch, "H. Ross Perot: America's First Welfare Billionaire," *Ramparts,* November 1971, p. 49.

26. Testimony of Walker Evans, Administration of Federal Health Benefit Programs, Part 3, First Session, November 9, 1971, p. 98.

27. Ibid., pp. 88–89.

28. Interview with Ross Perot, November 30, 1995.

29. Testimony of Walker Evans, Administration of Federal Health Benefit Programs, Part 3, First Session, November 9, 1971, pp. 94–95.

30. Interview with Ross Perot, November 30, 1995.

31. Testimony of Thomas Tierney, Administration of Federal Health Benefit Programs, Part 3, First Session, September 28, 1971, pp. 27, 65; testimony of Walker Evans, Administration of Federal Health Benefit Programs, Part 3, First Session, November 9, 1971, pp. 95, 99, 101.

32. Interview with Tom Downtain, March 14, 1995.

33. Testimony of Thomas Tierney, Administration of Federal Health Benefit Programs, Part 3, First Session, September 28, 1971, p. 10.

34. Interview with Eugune Aune, June 14, 1995.

35. Interview with James Naughton, September 14, 1995; Fitch, op. cit., p. 44.

36. Interview with James Naughton, September 14, 1995.

37. Bo Burlingham and Curtis Hartman, "Cowboy Capitalist," *Inc.,* January 1989.

38. Fitch, op. cit., pp. 45–47.

39. HEW Audit Agency Reviews of EDSF Medicare Costs at California Blue Shield and Pennsylvania Blue Shield, October 30, 1970, reprinted in Administration of Federal Health Benefit Programs, Part 4, Second Session, Appendix 19, pp. 543–44;

newsletter, *The Gallagher President's Report,* August 21, 1973, Volume IX, Number 34, Papers of Wright Patman, Ross Perot Folder, Container 773B, LBJ Library.

40. Newsletter, *The Gallagher President's Report,* August 21, 1973, Volume IX, Number 34, Papers of Wright Patman, Ross Perot Folder, Container 773B, LBJ Library.

41. Ross Perot, quoted by Roy Rowan, "The World According to Ross Perot," *Life,* February 1988, p. 66.

42. Interview with Ross Perot, August 8, 1995.

43. Interview with Bill Gayden, March 10, 1995.

44. Ross Perot, quoted by David Remnick, "Our Nation Turns Its Lonely Eyes to H. Ross Perot," *The Washington Post Magazine,* April 12, 1987.

45. David Firestone, "So Who Is This Guy?" *Newsday,* May 17, 1992.

46. Fitch, op. cit., pp. 47–48.

47. Hardy Green, quoted by Firestone, op. cit.

48. Interview with Ross Perot, August 8, 1995.

49. Ibid.

50. Interview with Ken Riedlinger, October 16, 1995.

51. Interview with Ross Perot, August 8, 1995.

52. Interview with Ken Riedlinger, October 16, 1995.

53. Review of registration document (prospectus) Electronic Data Systems Corp., on file with the Securities and Exchange Commission, Washington, D.C.

54. John Brooks, *The Go-Go Years* (New York: Weybright and Talley, 1973), p. 18.

55. Interview with James Naughton, September 14, 1995.

56. Arthur M. Louis, "The Fastest Richest Texan Ever," *Fortune,* November 1968, p. 170.

Chapter 5:
The Ultimate Insider

1. Interview with Tom Meurer, March 8, 1995.

2. Interview with Rob Brooks, March 9, 1995.

3. Interview with Ross Perot, November 30, 1995.

4. Interview with Rob Brooks, March 9, 1995.

5. *The New York Times,* September 10, 1971, quoted by Tony Chiu, *Ross Perot: In His Own Words* (New York: Warner Books, 1992), p. 23.

6. Interview with Tom Meurer, March 8, 1995.

7. Portia Isaacson, quoted by Laura Berman and Paul Lienert, "Ross Perot Rides Again," *The Detroit Free Press,* April 27, 1986, p. 14.

8. Tom Peters, quoted by Berman and Lienert, op. cit., p. 24.

9. Interview with Tom Meurer, March 8, 1995.

10. Ibid.

11. Ross Perot conversation recounted by Tom Meurer, interviewed March 8, 1995.

12. Interview with Tom Meurer, March 8, 1995.

13. See generally, Subject Files: Confidential Files, 1969–74, Political Affairs 1-20-69 to 4-30-70, White House Central Files, Box 46, Nixon Presidential Materials Staff, National Archives.

14. See generally, "File Search on Ross Perot," four pages, undated, folder: Peter Flanigan, Staff Members and Office Files, Box 9, White House Special Files, Nixon Presidential Materials Staff, National Archives.

15. For general attitude of White House aides to Perot, see memo, to Haldeman, Erlichman, Kissinger, et al., from Alexander Butterfield, January 17, 1970, Subject Files: Confidential Files, 1969–74, Political Affairs 1-20-69 to 4-30-70, White House Central Files, Box 46, Nixon Presidential Materials Staff, National Archives.

16. Memo, handwritten, titled "HRH," November 4, 1969.

17. Undated handwritten notes, titled "ABC," Subject Files: Confidential Files, 1969–74, Political Affairs 1-20-69 to 4-30-70, White House Central Files, Box 46, Nixon Presidential Materials Staff, National Archives.

18. Letter, to Ross Perot from Tod R. Hullin, October 7, 1969, Subject Files: Confidential Files, 1969–74, Political Affairs 1-20-69 to 4-30-70, White House Central Files, Box 46, Nixon Presidential Materials Staff, National Archives.

19. Interview with Ross Perot, February 12, 1996.

20. Memo, to John Erlichman from Jim Atwater, Subject: Meeting with Ross Perot, May 26, 1969, Subject Files: Confidential Files, 1969–74, Political Affairs 1-20-69 to 4-30-70, White House Central Files, Box 46, Nixon Presidential Materials Staff, National Archives.

21. Twenty-seven pages of handwritten notes relating to the preparation of Gordon Strachan's January 1972 memo to H. R. Haldeman regarding an assessment of the Perot/administration relationship, Ross Perot Folder, White House Special Files, Staff Member and Office Files, H. R. Haldeman, Alpha Subject Files, Box 133, Nixon Presidential Materials Staff, National Archives.

22. Letter, to John Erlichman from Ross Perot, June 4, 1969, Subject Files: Confidential Files, 1969–74, Political Affairs 1-20-69 to 4-30-70, White House Central Files, Box 46, Nixon Presidential Materials Staff, National Archives.

23. Memo, to H. R. Haldeman from Alexander P. Butterfield, January 30, 1970, Ross Perot Folder, White House Special Files, Staff Member and Office Files, Alpha Subject Files, H. R. Haldeman, Box 133, Nixon Presidential Materials Staff, National Archives.

24. Letter, to Richard Nixon from Ross Perot, April 19, 1971; see also memo, to H. R. Haldeman from Gordon Strachan, January 12, 1972, Ross Perot Folder, White House Special Files, Staff Member and Office Files, Alpha Subject Files, H. R. Haldeman Box 133, Nixon Presidential Materials Staff, National Archives.

25. Twenty-seven pages of handwritten notes relating to the preparation of Gordon Strachan's January 1972 memo to H. R. Haldeman regarding an assessment of the Perot/administration relationship, Ross Perot Folder, White House Special Files, Staff Member and Office Files, H. R. Haldeman, Alpha Subject Files, Box 133, Nixon Presidential Materials Staff, National Archives.

26. Stephen A. Holmes, "White House Aides' Memos Paint Perot as Nixon Insider," The New York Times, May 8, 1992, p. 1.

27. Memo, to H. R. Haldeman from Gordon Strachan, September 1, 1972, Ross Perot Folder, White House Special Files, Staff Member and Office Files, H. R. Haldeman, Alpha Subject Files, Box 133, Nixon Presidential Materials Staff, National Archives.

28. Twenty-seven pages of handwritten notes relating to the preparation of Gordon Strachan's January 1972 memo to H. R. Haldeman regarding an assessment of the Perot/administration relationship, Ross Perot Folder, White House Special Files, Staff Member and Office Files, H. R. Haldeman, Alpha Subject Files, Box 133, Nixon Presidential Materials Staff, National Archives.

29. Memorandum to the Special Assistant to the Secretary and the Deputy Secretary of Defense from Robert E. Jordan, III, Special Assistant, Civil Functions, Department of the Army, April 23, 1969, Subject Files: Confidential Files, 1969–74, Political Affairs 1-20-69 to 4-30-70, White House Central Files, Box 46, Nixon Presidential Materials Staff, National Archives.

30. Letter, to Lt. General William F. Cassidy from John Erlichman, April 18, 1969, Subject Files: Confidential Files, 1969–74, Political Affairs 1-20-69 to 4-30-70, White House Central Files, Box 46, Nixon Presidential Materials Staff, National Archives.

31. Memo, to Ed Morgan from Tom Cole, April 9, 1969; see also letter, to Col. James D. Hughes from Ross Perot, May 6, 1969, Ross Perot Folder, White House Special Files, Staff Member and Office Files, H. R. Haldeman, Alpha Subject Files, Box 133, Nixon Presidential Materials Staff, National Archives.

32. Memo, to John Erlichman from Col. James D. Hughes, September 27, 1969, Subject Files: Confidential Files, 1969–74, Political Affairs 1-20-69 to 4-30-70, White House Central Files, Box 46, Nixon Presidential Materials Staff, National Archives.

33. See generally, memo, to Staff Secretary from John Erlichman, May 15, 1969, Administratively Confidential Memo from Gordon Strachan to H. R. Haldeman, January 12, 1972, p. 4, Ross Perot Folder, White House Special Files, Staff Member and Office Files, H. R. Haldeman, Alpha Subject Files, Box 133, Nixon Presidential Materials Staff, National Archives; see also phone message to the President from SAW, Subject Files: Confidential Files, 1969–74, Political Affairs 1-20-69 to 4-30-70, White House Central Files, Box 46, Nixon Presidential Materials Staff, National Archives; also, *Issues and Answers*, ABC News interview with Ross Perot, January 11, 1970.

34. Memo, to Staff Secretary from John Erlichman, re: Ross Perot Meeting with the President; May 15, 1969, Ross Perot Folder, White House Special Files, Staff Member and Office Files, H. R. Haldeman, Alpha Subject Files, Box 133, Nixon Presidential Materials Staff, National Archives; see also H. R. Haldeman, *The Haldeman Diaries: Inside the Nixon White House* (New York: Berkley Books, 1995), p. 71.

35. Typed sheet, titled "Richard Nixon Foundation," May 12, 1969, page 2 of two, gathered from the Weekly Compilation of Presidential Documents, May 19, 1969, Ross Perot Folder, White House Special Files, Staff Member and Office Files, H. R. Haldeman, Alpha Subject Files, Box 133, Nixon Presidential Materials Staff, National Archives.

36. Memo, to Rogers Morton from Peter Flanigan, July 10, 1969, Ross Perot Folder, White House Special Files, Staff Member and Office Files, H. R. Haldeman, Alpha Subject Files, Box 133, Nixon Presidential Materials Staff, National Archives.

37. Memo, to President Nixon from Harry Flemming, December 8, 1969; see also memo, to Rogers Morton from Peter Flanigan, December 4, 1969; White House Special Files, Staff Member and Office Files, H. R. Haldeman, Alpha Subject Files, Box 133, Nixon Presidential Materials Staff, National Archives.

38. Letter, to Ross Perot from John Erlichman, June 17, 1969, Ross Perot Folder, White House Special Files, Staff Member and Office Files, H. R. Halde-

man, Alpha Subject Files, Box 133, Nixon Presidential Materials Staff, National Archives.

39. Memo, to President Nixon from Alexander P. Butterfield, November 24, 1969, White House Special Files, Alexander Butterfield, November 1969, Nixon Presidential Materials Staff, National Archives.

40. Memo, to Staff Secretary from Peter Flanigan, June 30, 1969, Ross Perot Folder, White House Special Files, Staff Member and Office Files, H. R. Haldeman, Alpha Subject Files, Box 133, Nixon Presidential Materials Staff, National Archives.

41. Interview with Murphy Martin, March 8, 1995.

42. Ibid.

43. Interview with Tom Meurer, March 8, 1995.

44. Memo, to Haldeman, Erlichman, Kissinger, Harlow from Alexander P. Butterfield, October 24, 1969, Ross Perot Folder, White House Special Files, Staff Member and Office Files, Alpha Subject Files, Box 133, Nixon Presidential Materials Staff, National Archives.

45. Ibid.

46. Ibid.

47. Memo, to H. R. Haldeman from Alexander Butterfield, December 1, 1969, Correspondence File, Staff Member and Office Files, Box 1, December 1969, Nixon Presidential Materials Staff, National Archives.

48. See generally, memos, to H. R. Haldeman from Alexander P. Butterfield, December 15 and 16, 1969, Ross Perot Folder, White House Special Files, Staff Member and Office Files, Alpha Subject Files, Box 133, Nixon Presidential Materials Staff, National Archives.

49. Twenty-seven pages of handwritten notes relating to the preparation of Gordon Strachan's January 1972 memo to H. R. Haldeman regarding an assessment of the Perot/administration relationship, Ross Perot Folder, White House Special Files, Staff Member and Office Files, H. R. Haldeman, Alpha Subject Files, Box 133, Nixon Presidential Materials Staff, National Archives.

50. Interview with Tom Meurer, March 8, 1995.

51. Ibid.; see also television script, "United We Stand," broadcast date November 16, 1969, eleven pages, Ross Perot Folder, White House Special Files, Staff Member and Office Files, Alpha Subject Files, Box 133, Nixon Presidential Materials Staff, National Archives.

52. Interview with Tom Meurer, March 8, 1995; interview with William Safire, October 5, 1995; see also memo, to H. R. Haldeman from Alexander P. Butterfield, November 14, 1969, Ross Perot Folder, White House Special Files, Staff Member and Office Files, Alpha Subject Files, Box 133, Nixon Presidential Materials Staff, National Archives.

53. Memo, to H. R. Haldeman from Alexander P. Butterfield, November 14, 1969, Ross Perot Folder, White House Special Files, Staff Member and Office Files, Alpha Subject Files, Box 133, Nixon Presidential Materials Staff, National Archives.

54. Television script, "United We Stand," broadcast date November 16, 1969, eleven pages, Ross Perot Folder, White House Special Files, Staff Member and Office Files, Alpha Subject Files, Box 133, Nixon Presidential Materials Staff, National Archives.

55. Memo, to H. R. Haldeman from Alexander P. Butterfield, December 3, 1969, Alexander Butterfield Correspondence File, Staff Member and Office Files, Box 1, White House Special Files, December 1969, Nixon Presidential Materials Staff, National Archives.

56. Haldeman, op. cit., p. 127.

57. Memo, to Stephen B. Bull and John Brown from Dwight Chapin, November 25, 1969, Ross Perot Folder, White House Special Files, Staff Member and Office Files, H. R. Haldeman, Alpha Subject Files, Box 133, Nixon Presidential Materials Staff, National Archives; see also H. R. Haldeman, op. cit., p. 134.

58. Deposition of H. Ross Perot, July 1, 1992, pp. 16–19, 21, 50, Senate Select Committee on POW/MIA Affairs, Center for Legislative Archives, National Archives.

59. Interview with Murphy Martin, March 8, 1995; see also deposition of Murphy Martin, June 24, 1992, pp. 42–43, Senate Select Committee on POW/MIA Affairs, Center for Legislative Archives, National Archives.

60. Memo, to the President from Alexander P. Butterfield, December 22, 1969, Alexander Butterfield Correspondence File, Staff Member and Office Files, Box 1, White House Special Files, December 1969, Nixon Presidential Materials Staff, National Archives.

61. Deposition of H. Ross Perot, July 1, 1992, p. 18, Senate Select Committee on POW/MIA Affairs, Center for Legislative Archives, National Archives.

62. Memo, to the President from Alexander P. Butterfield, December 27, 1969, 3:30 P.M., Alexander Butterfield Correspondence File, Staff Member and Office Files, Box 1, White House Special Files, December 1969, Nixon Presidential Materials Staff, National Archives.

63. Memo, to the President from Alexander P. Butterfield, December 29, 1969, 9:00 A.M., Alexander Butterfield Correspondence File, Staff Member and Office Files, Box 1, White House Special Files, December 1969, Nixon Presidential Materials Staff, National Archives.

64. Interview with Tom Meurer, March 8, 1995.

65. Interview with Murphy Martin, March 8, 1995.

66. Interview with Tom Meurer, March 8, 1995.

67. Interview with Murphy Martin, March 8, 1995.

68. Memo, to the President from Alexander P. Butterfield, January 10, 1970, Ross Perot Folder, White House Special Files, Staff Member and Office Files, H. R. Haldeman, Alpha Subject Files, Box 133, Nixon Presidential Materials Staff, National Archives.

69. Memo, to H. R. Haldeman from Alexander P. Butterfield, January 23, 1970, Ross Perot Folder, White House Special Files, Staff Member and Office Files, H. R. Haldeman, Alpha Subject Files, Box 133, Nixon Presidential Materials Staff, National Archives.

70. Memo, to H. R. Haldeman from Alexander P. Butterfield, January 30, 1970, Ross Perot Folder, White House Special Files, Staff Member and Office Files, Alpha

Subject Files, Box 133, Nixon Presidential Materials Staff, National Archives.

71. Memo, to the president from Alexander P. Butterfield, January 31, 1970, "re: Your Scheduled Meeting with Ross Perot, 12:15 P.M. Sunday, February 1, 1970," January 31, 1970 (shorter version), Ross Perot Folder, White House Special Files, Staff Member and Office Files, H. R. Haldeman, Alpha Subject Files, Box 133, Nixon Presidential Materials Staff, National Archives.

72. Ibid. (extended version).

73. Memo, to the president from Alexander P. Butterfield, January 10, 1970, Ross Perot Folder, White House Special Files, Staff Member and Office Files, H. R. Haldeman, Alpha Subject Files, Box 133, Nixon Presidential Materials Staff, National Archives.

74. Memo, to the president from Alexander P. Butterfield, February 1, 1970, Ross Perot Folder, White House Special Files, Staff Member and Office Files, Alpha Subject Files, Box 133, Nixon Presidential Materials Staff, National Archives.

75. Letter, to H. R. Haldeman from H. Ross Perot, February 24, 1970, Ross Perot Folder, White House Special Files, Staff Member and Office Files, Alpha Subject Files, Box 133, Nixon Presidential Materials Staff, National Archives.

76. Deposition of H. Ross Perot, July 1, 1992, pp. 18–19, Senate Select Committee on POW/MIA Affairs, Center for Legislative Archives, National Archives.

77. Oral History Interview with Charles W. Colson on September 21, 1988, Nixon Presidential Materials Staff, National Archives.

78. Ibid.

79. Ibid.

80. Ibid.

81. Deposition of H. Ross Perot, July 1, 1992, pp. 53–54, Senate Select Committee on POW/MIA Affairs, Center for Legislative Archives, National Archives.

82. Herb Klein, interviewed by Murphy Martin, May 19, 1976, transcript made available by Ross Perot.

83. See generally, Dinner at the White House list, Thursday, July 16, 1970, one page; letter, to Ross Perot from John Erlichman, June 18, 1970; also, memo, to Hugh

Sloan from General Alexander M. Haig, September 24, 1970; letter, to Ross Perot from George T. Bell, January 12, 1971; letter, to Ross Perot from Harry S. Dent, November 18, 1971, Ross Perot Folder, White House Special Files, Staff Member and Office Files, H. R. Haldeman, Alpha Subject Files, Box 133, Nixon Presidential Materials Staff, National Archives.

84. Copy of telegram from Richard Nixon, stamp-dated February 13, 1970, one page; also, February 15, 1970, draft of telegram, Executive SO3, Ross Perot Folder, White House Special Files, Staff Member and Office Files, H. R. Haldeman, Alpha Subject Files, Box 133, Nixon Presidential Materials Staff, National Archives.

85. List of May 26, 1970, setting forth forty names of appointments to the Advisory Committee on the Arts; also twenty-seven pages of handwritten notes relating to the preparation of Gordon Strachan's January, 1972, memo to H. R. Haldeman regarding an assessment of the Perot/administration relationship, Ross Perot Folder, White House Special Files, Staff Member and Office Files, H. R. Haldeman, Alpha Subject Files, Box 133, Nixon Presidential Materials Staff, National Archives.

86. Letter, to Ross Perot from Rose Mary Woods, January 20, 1971, Ross Perot Folder, White House Special Files, Staff Member and Office Files, H. R. Haldeman, Alpha Subject Files, Box 133, Nixon Presidential Materials Staff, National Archives.

87. Contributor checklist, undated, Watergate Special Prosecution Force, Record Group 460, Townhouse File #807 Documentary Evidence, Gleason Records, 1970 memorandum; see also two-page document titled "Gleason Records"; letter to H. R. Haldeman from Herbert W. Kalmbach, November 6, 1970, Watergate Special Prosecution Force, Record Group 460, Townhouse File #807, Campaign Contribution Task Force, Planning and Coordination, Investigative Correspondence, Box 1, Nixon Presidential Materials Staff, National Archives.

88. Memorandum, to Harry S. Dent from Jack A. Gleason, June 16, 1970, Watergate Special Prosecution Force, Record Group 460, Townhouse File #807,

Documentary Evidence, Gleason Records, 1970 Memorandum, Nixon Presidential Materials Staff, National Archives.

89. Memorandum, to Leon Jaworski from Thomas McBride, August 19, 1974; also, untitled two pages of handwritten notes about a meeting with Ross Perot in Dallas, May 11, 1970, Watergate Special Prosecution Force, Record Group 460, Townhouse File #807, Campaign Contribution Task Force, Planning and Coordination, Investigative Correspondence, Box 1, Nixon Presidential Materials Staff, National Archives.

90. Memorandum, to Harry S. Dent from Jack A. Gleason, July 27, 1970, Watergate Special Prosecution Force, Record Group 460, Townhouse File #807, Documentary Evidence, Gleason Records, 1970 Memorandum, Nixon Presidential Materials Staff, National Archives.

91. Dan Thomasson, "Nixon Fan Got No-bid U.S. Plum," *Washington Daily News,* January 17, 1972, Ross Perot Folder, White House Special Files, Staff Member and Office Files, H. R. Haldeman, Alpha Subject Files, Box 133, Nixon Presidential Materials Staff, National Archives.

92. Ibid.

93. Scott Lehigh, "Medicare Pacts Prompted Battle over Firm's Books," *The Boston Globe,* June 16, 1992, p. 25.

94. Memo, to Gordon Strachan from Kenneth Cole, undated, with fifteen handwritten pages, Ross Perot Folder, White House Special Files, Staff Member and Office Files, H. R. Haldeman, Alpha Subject Files, Box 133, Nixon Presidential Materials Staff, National Archives.

95. Twenty-seven pages of handwritten notes relating to the preparation of Gordon Strachan's January 1972 memo to H. R. Haldeman regarding an assessment of the Perot/administration relationship, Ross Perot Folder, White House Special Files, Staff Member and Office Files, H. R. Haldeman, Alpha Subject Files, Box 133, Nixon Presidential Materials Staff, National Archives.

96. Ibid.

97. Testimony of Thomas Tierney, Administration of Federal Health Benefit Programs, Hearing Before a Subcommittee of the Committee on Government Operations, Part 3—Data Processing, House of Representatives Ninety-second Congress, First Session, September 28, 1971, pp. 14, 61, 73–74, 90.

98. Memo, to H. R. Haldeman from Gordon Strachan, September 1, 1972, Ross Perot Folder, White House Special Files, Staff Member and Office Files, H. R. Haldeman, Alpha Subject Files, Box 133, Nixon Presidential Materials Staff, National Archives.

99. Interview with Ross Perot, February 12, 1996.

100. Memo, to Dwight Chapin from Tom Lias, April 9, 1971, Ross Perot Folder, White House Special Files, Staff Member and Office Files, H. R. Haldeman, Alpha Subject Files, Box 133, Nixon Presidential Materials Staff, National Archives.

101. Memo, to John Mitchell and H. R. Haldeman from Murray M. Chotiner, January 10, 1971, Ross Perot Folder, White House Special Files, Staff Member and Office Files, H. R. Haldeman, Alpha Subject Files, Box 133, Nixon Presidential Materials Staff, National Archives.

102. Twenty-seven pages of handwritten notes relating to the preparation of Gordon Strachan's January 1972 memo to H. R. Haldeman regarding an assessment of the Perot/administration relationship, Ross Perot Folder, White House Special Files, Staff Member and Office Files, H. R. Haldeman, Alpha Subject Files, Box 133, Nixon Presidential Materials Staff, National Archives.

103. Memo, to Ronald Walker from Dwight Chapin, February 2, 1971, Ross Perot Folder, White House Special Files, Staff Member and Office Files, H. R. Haldeman, Alpha Subject Files, Box 133, Nixon Presidential Materials Staff, National Archives.

104. Memo, to H. R. Haldeman from Gordon Strachan, "Subject: H. Ross Perot," January 12, 1972, Ross Perot Folder, White House Special Files, Staff Member and Office Files, H. R. Haldeman, Alpha Subject Files, Box 133, Nixon Presidential Materials Staff, National Archives.

105. Ibid.

106. Twenty-seven pages of handwritten notes relating to the preparation of Gordon Strachan's January 1972 memo to H. R. Haldeman regarding an assessment of the Perot/administration relationship, Ross Perot Folder, White House Special Files, Staff Member and Office Files, H. R. Haldeman, Alpha Subject Files, Box 133, Nixon Presidential Materials Staff, National Archives.

107. H. R. Haldeman, op. cit., p. 478.

Chapter 6: Wall Street Fiasco

1. New York Stock Exchange Fact Book, available from the media information office of the New York Stock Exchange.

2. William G. Smith, "Ross Perot: Where He's Steering EDS—the Tightest Ship in Texas," *Texas Business,* December 1978, p. 34.

3. Interview with Peter du Pont, February 22, 1995.

4. Ibid.

5. John Brooks, *The Go-Go Years* (New York: Weybright and Talley, 1973), p. 318.

6. Interview with Felix Rohatyn, May 24, 1995.

7. Ibid.

8. "H. Ross Perot Turns His Back on Wall Street," *Business Week,* January 26, 1974, p. 63.

9. Interview with Felix Rohatyn, May 24, 1995.

10. Memorandum, to the President from Peter M. Flanigan, December 4, 1970, Ross Perot Folder, White House Special Files, Staff Member and Office Files, H. R. Haldeman, Alpha Subject Files, Box 133, Nixon Presidential Materials Staff, National Archives.

11. John Solomon, "Nixon Administration Documents Show Perot as 'Ultimate Insider,' " Associated Press, appeared in *The Washington Post,* May 8, 1992, p. A4.

12. Ross Perot, quoted by Seth Faison, Jr., "How Perot Took Wrong Turn in Effort to Bail Out Wall Street," *The New York Times,* May 18, 1992; interview with Ross Perot, February 12, 1996.

13. Twenty-seven pages of handwritten notes relating to the preparation of Gordon Strachan's January 1972 memo to H. R. Haldeman regarding an assessment of the Perot/administration relationship, Ross Perot Folder, White House Special Files, Staff Member and Office Files, H. R. Haldeman, Alpha Subject Files, Box 133, Nixon Presidential Materials Staff, National Archives.

14. Ross Perot, quoted in "Financial Planning (A Special Report): Risk Taking," *The Wall Street Journal,* November 13, 1987, p. 20D.

15. Interview with Felix Rohatyn, May 24, 1995.

16. Interview with Bill Gayden, March 10, 1995.

17. Brooks, op. cit., p. 342.

18. Interview with Felix Rohatyn, May 24, 1995.

19. Interview with Peter du Pont, February 22, 1995.

20. Memorandum, to the President from Peter Flanigan, December 15, 1970, Ross Perot Folder, White House Special Files, Staff Member and Office Files, H. R. Haldeman, Alpha Subject Files, Box 133, Nixon Presidential Materials Staff, National Archives.

21. Interview with Felix Rohatyn, May 24, 1995.

22. Twenty-seven pages of handwritten notes relating to the preparation of Gordon Strachan's January 1972 memo to H. R. Haldeman regarding an assessment of the Perot/administration relationship, Ross Perot Folder, White House Special Files, Staff Member and Office Files, H. R. Haldeman, Alpha Subject Files, Box 133, Nixon Presidential Materials Staff, National Archives.

23. Interview with Felix Rohatyn, May 24, 1995.

24. Lawrence Wright, "The Man from Texarkana," *The New York Times Magazine,* July 2, 1992; Hugh Aynesworth and Stephen G. Michaud, "Perot's Power Play," *Texas Monthly,* March 1981, p. 60.

25. Interview with Felix Rohatyn, May 24, 1995.

26. Interview with Peter du Pont, February 22, 1995.

27. Twenty-seven pages of handwritten notes relating to the preparation of Gordon Strachan's January 1972 memo to H. R. Haldeman regarding an assessment of the Perot/administration relationship, Ross Perot Folder, White House Special Files, Staff Member and Office Files, H. R. Haldeman, Alpha Subject Files, Box 133, Nixon Presidential Materials Staff, National Archives.

28. Doron P. Levin, *Irreconcilable Differences: Ross Perot Versus General Motors* (Boston: Little, Brown, 1989), p. 43.

29. Robert Fitch, "H. Ross Perot: America's First Welfare Billionaire," *Ramparts,* November 1971.

30. Todd Mason, *Perot: An Unauthorized Biography* (Homewood, Illinois: Business One Irwin, 1990), p. 110.

31. *Dun's Review,* March 1, 1973, per Mason, op. cit.

32. Mason, op. cit., p. 111.

33. Walter Auch, quoted by Faison, op. cit., p. A1.

34. *The Dallas Morning News,* October 15, 1972, and *Dun's Review,* March 1, 1973, both per Mason, op. cit.

35. Advertisement for du Pont–Glore, Forgan that appeared in *Time,* June 4, 1973.

36. Donald Morrison, "Ambush on Wall Street," *Texas Monthly,* April 1974, p. 73.

37. *The Dallas Morning News,* October 15, 1972, as cited in Tony Chiu, *Ross Perot: In His Own Words* (New York: Warner Books, 1992), p. 22.

38. Faison, op. cit., p. A1; see also Mason, op. cit., p. 113.

39. Interview with Peter du Pont, February 22, 1995.

40. Interview with Felix Rohatyn, May 24, 1995.

41. "H. Ross Perot Turns His Back on Wall Street," op. cit., p. 62.

42. Ibid., p. 63.

43. Allan J. Mayer, "Savior or Swindler?," *Newsweek,* July 14, 1975, p. 64.

44. Mason, op. cit., p. 115; interview with Jack Walston, August 9, 1989.

45. "H. Ross Perot Turns His Back on Wall Street," op. cit., p. 62.

46. Interview with Peter du Pont, February 22, 1995.

47. "H. Ross Perot Turns His Back on Wall Street," op. cit., p. 64.

48. Ibid., p. 61.

49. Interview with Felix Rohatyn, May 24, 1995.

50. *Barron's,* "Word from the Wise: Ross Perot on Insider Trading, Takeovers, and Other Choice Topics," February 23, 1987.

51. Scott Lehigh, "Medicare Pacts Prompted Battle over Firm's Books," *The Boston Globe,* June 16, 1992, p. 25.

52. FEC records of contributions, 1972–1975; see also Margaret Carlson, "Perot and His Presidents," *Time,* May 25, 1992, p. 34.

53. "The Outsider with Insider Pull," *Orlando Sentinel Tribune,* May 24, 1992, p. A8.

54. Review of Congressional Record, Ways and Means Committee, November 4, 1975, Government Printing Office; see also Carlson, op. cit., p. 34.

55. See generally, "Ross Perot's Problem Child," *Newsweek,* February 18, 1974; "H. Ross Perot Turns His Back on Wall Street," op. cit.

56. "Ross Perot's Problem Child," *Newsweek,* February 18, 1974, p. 71.

57. Interview with Ken Riedlinger, October 16, 1995.

58. Conversation as recounted by Caspar Weinberger, interviewed on February 21, 1995.

59. Ross Perot, quoted in "Ross Perot: Dallasite of the Year," *D Magazine,* January 1984, p. 113.

Chapter 7: "I'm Not an Investigative Personality"

1. Deposition of H. Ross Perot, July 1, 1992, p. 102, Senate Select Committee on POW/MIA Affairs, Center for Legislative Archives, National Archives; also, interview with Ross Perot, February 12, 1996.

2. Ross Perot, quoted by David Remnick, "Our Nation Turns Its Lonely Eyes to H. Ross Perot," *The Washington Post Magazine,* April 12, 1987.

3. Interview with Tom Meurer, March 8, 1995.

4. Ibid.

5. Deposition of H. Ross Perot, July 1, 1992, p. 102, Senate Select Committee on POW/MIA Affairs, Center for Legislative Archives, National Archives.

6. William G. Smith, "Ross Perot," *Texas Monthly,* December 1978, p. 38.

7. Todd Mason, *Perot: An Unauthorized Biography* (Homewood, Illinois: Business One Irwin, 1990), pp. 117–118.

8. Interview with Tom Meurer, March 8, 1995.

9. Interview with Rob Brooks, March 9, 1995.

10. Ken Follett, *On Wings of Eagles* (New York: Signet, 1984), pp. 89–90.

11. Interview with Tom Downtain, March 14, 1995.

12. Interview with Rob Brooks, March 9, 1995.

13. Interview with Tom Marquez, June 16, 1995.

14. Ibid.

15. Ibid.

16. "How H. Ross Perot Builds Fierce Loyalty at EDS in Dallas," *International Management,* March 1983; Mason, op. cit., p. 101.

17. Interview with Ken Riedlinger, August 14, 1995.

18. Mason, op. cit., p. 170.

19. Mort Meyerson, quoted by David Remnick, op. cit., p. 25.

20. Interview with Mort Meyerson, April 20, 1995.

21. Ibid.

22. Ibid.

23. Testimony of Ross Perot, *EDS v. Henry Ross Perot and Perot Systems Corp.,* In Chancery No. 108556, Fairfax, Virginia, October 19, 1988, p. 141.

24. Interview with Ken Riedlinger, October 16, 1995.

25. Doron P. Levin, *Irreconcilable Differences: Ross Perot Versus General Motors* (Boston: Little, Brown, 1989), pp. 54–55.

26. *Facts On File World News Digest,* Section: "Presidential Campaign," June 11, 1992.

27. Elizabeth Bailey, "Getting EDS into Washington," *Forbes,* May 14, 1979, p. 178.

28. Robert Pear, "Audits of Federal Contracts Indicate Major Failures by Perot Companies," *The New York Times,* June 24, 1992, p. A14.

29. Saul Friedman, "Perot's Power Plays," *Newsday,* May 18, 1992, p. 6; Pear, op. cit., p. 14.

30. Interview with Ken Riedlinger, October 16, 1995.

31. Bailey, op. cit., p. 178.

32. EDS Annual Report, 1978.

Chapter 8: Escape from Iran

1. Ken Follett, *On Wings of Eagles* (New York: Signet, 1994), p. 49.

2. Ibid., p. 14.

3. Ibid., p. 22.

4. Ken Gross, *Ross Perot: The Man Behind the Myth* (New York: Random House, 1992), p. 154.

5. Follett, op. cit., p. 172.

6. Follett, op. cit., p. 73.

7. Interview with John Stempel, October 3, 1995.

8. Interview with Clyde Taylor, October 4, 1995.

9. Interview with Henry Precht, October 4, 1995.

10. Interview with David Newsom, October 5, 1995.

11. Interview with John Stempel, October 3, 1995.

12. Interview with Henry Precht, October 4, 1995.

13. Interview with Roger Brewin, October 13, 1995; Joseph Albright, "Perot Failed to Investigate Partner's Scandals in 1970s," *The Houston Chronicle,* June 29, 1992, p. B8.

14. Ross Perot statement, second of two-part CNN Special Assignment Investigation, May 15, 1992; Albright, op. cit., p. B8.

15. Follett, op. cit., p. 72.

16. Dan Morgan and Walter Pincus, "Friend of Shah Was Enriched by 'High Tech' Deals," *The Washington Post,* p. A1; Follett, op. cit., p. 72.

17. Paul Bucha, quoted in second of two-part CNN Special Assignment Investigation, May 15, 1992.

18. Second of two-part CNN Special Assignment Investigation, May 15, 1992.

19. Interview with Reza Neghabat, October 13, 1995.

20. Interview with Ken Follett, April 6, 1995.

21. Ross Perot, quoted by Tim Boxer, " 'Wings of Eagles' Celebrates Perot's Real-Life Derring-Do," *New York Post,* April 8, 1986.

22. Follett, op. cit., p. 85.

23. Ibid., pp. 96–97.

24. Ibid., p. 137.

25. Ibid., p. 141.

26. Interview with David Newsom, October 5, 1995.

27. Interview with Charles Naas, October 4, 1995.

28. Follett, op. cit., p. 166.

29. Interview with Charles Naas, October 4, 1995.

30. Ibid.

31. Follett, op. cit., p. 182.

32. Gross, op. cit., p. 158.

33. Follett, op. cit., p. 197.

34. Interview with John Stempel, October 3, 1995.

35. Follett, op. cit., p. 205.

36. Ibid., p. 213.

37. Interview with John Stempel, October 3, 1995.

38. Follett, op. cit., p. 247.

39. Interview with John Stempel, October 3, 1995.

40. Follett, op. cit., pp. 260–62.

41. Ross Perot, quoted in "How H. Ross Perot Builds Fierce Loyalty at EDS in Dallas," *International Management,* March 1983.

42. Interview with Reza Neghabat, October 13, 1995.

43. Ross Perot, quoted by William Gaines and Mike Dorning, "The Myth of Iran's Rescue," *Chicago Tribune,* July 9, 1992, p. M1.

44. Interview with John Stempel, October 3, 1995.

45. Interview with David Newsom, October 5, 1995.

46. Interview with Ken Johnson, October 16, 1995.

47. Sidney Blumenthal, "On Wings of Bull: Perot's Phony Iranian Rescue," *The New Republic,* July 13, 1992, p. 12.

48. Speech by Ross Perot, Washington D.C., May 24, 1981.

49. David Remnick, "Our Nation Turns Its Lonely Eyes to H. Ross Perot," *The Washington Post Magazine,* April 12, 1987.

50. Interview with David Newsom, October 5, 1995.

51. Interview with Ken Follett, April 6, 1995.

52. Ibid.

53. Ibid.

54. Ibid.

55. Interview with Ron Sperberg, October 17, 1995.

56. Interview with John Stempel, October 3, 1995.

57. Interview with Ken Follett, April 6, 1995.

58. Interview with Henry Precht, October 4, 1995.

59. Interview with John Stempel, October 3, 1995.

60. Gaines and Dorning, op. cit., p. M1.

61. Interview with Bahman Fozouni, October 13, 1995.

62. Ross Perot as quoted in second of two-part CNN Special Assignment Investigation, May 15, 1992.

63. Edgar Sherick, quoted by Ed Bark, " 'On Wings of Eagles' Is a Bumpy Flight," *The Dallas Morning News,* May 18, 1986, p. C1.

Chapter 9:
Waging a Holy War

1. Ross Perot, quoted in *The Dallas Morning News,* February 5, 1981, per Tony Chiu, *Ross Perot: In His Own Words* (New York: Warner Books, 1992), pp. 66–67.

2. Doron P. Levin, *Irreconcilable Differences: Ross Perot Versus General Motors* (Boston: Little, Brown, 1989), p. 62.

3. Interview with Ken Riedlinger, October 16, 1995.

4. Interview with Rick Salwen, October 15, 1995.

5. Rick Salwen, quoted by Michael Isikoff, "Perot Championed Unorthodox

War on Drugs," *The Washington Post*, June 10, 1992, p. A1.

6. Ross Perot, quoted by Ken Gross, *Ross Perot: The Man Behind the Myth* (New York: Random House, 1992), op. cit., p. 182.

7. Ross Perot, quoted in *The Dallas Morning News*, April 16, 1980, per Chiu, op. cit., p. 66.

8. Sidney Blumenthal, "The Mission: H. Ross Perot's Vietnam Obsession," *The New Republic*, July 6, 1992, p. 16.

9. "Reports Say Perot Offered Island in U.S. Drug Fight," *The New York Times*, May 31, 1992, p. A21.

10. Interview with Rick Salwen, October 15, 1995.

11. Ross Perot, quoted in *The Dallas Morning News*, April 16, 1980, per Chiu, op. cit., p. 67.

12. Ross Perot, quoted by Marty Primeau, "Ross Perot," *The Dallas Morning News*, July 6, 1986, p. E1.

13. Interview with Ken Riedlinger, October 16, 1995.

14. Ross Perot, quoted by Hugh Aynesworth and Stephen G. Michaud, "Perot's Power Play," *Texas Monthly*, March 1981, p. 51.

15. Ross Perot, Jr., quoted by Todd Mason, Russell Mitchell, William Hampton, and Marc Frons, "Ross Perot's Crusade," *Business Week*, October 6, 1986, p. 60.

16. Les Alberthal, quoted by Todd Mason, *Perot: An Unauthorized Biography* (Homewood, Illinois: Business One Irwin, 1990), p. 167.

17. Levin, op. cit., p. 63; interviews with other executives present at the meeting.

18. Interview with Ken Riedlinger, October 16, 1995.

19. Interview with Wesley Hjornevik, March 16, 1995.

20. Ibid.

21. Ibid.

22. Ibid.

23. Ibid.

24. Ibid.

25. Interview with Ken Riedlinger, October 16, 1995.

26. Ibid.

27. Aynesworth and Michaud, op. cit., pp. 51–52.

28. Interview with Ken Riedlinger, October 16, 1995.

29. Ross Perot, quoted by Aynesworth and Michaud, op. cit., pp. 52, 57.

30. Ibid., p. 52.

31. Ibid.

32. Aynesworth and Michaud, op. cit., p. 49.

33. David Young, quoted by Aynesworth and Michaud, op. cit., p. 52.

34. Interview with Ken Riedlinger, October 16, 1995.

35. Ibid.

36. Ibid.

37. Ross Perot, quoted by Aynesworth and Michaud, op. cit., p. 52.

38. Frank Ikard, quoted by Mike Droning and William Gains, "Perot's Style a Mix of Carrot and Stick," *Chicago Tribune*, June 28, 1992, p. 1.

39. Interview with Hilmar Moore, May 30, 1995.

40. Conversation recounted in interview with Ron Sperberg, December 1, 1995.

41. Interview with Ross Perot, August 8, 1995.

42. Interview with Bill Smith, October 18, 1995.

43. Ibid.; interview with Brux Austin, October 18, 1995.

44. Interview with Brux Austin, October 18, 1995.

45. Levin, op. cit., p. 64.

46. Ross Perot, quoted by Aynesworth and Michaud, op. cit., p. 52.

Chapter 10: Memorial for the Dead

1. Interview with Ross Perot, February 12, 1996.

2. Interview with Bob Doubek, May 18, 1995.

3. Jan Scruggs quoted by Elisabeth Bumiller, "The Memorial, Mirror of Vietnam," *The Washington Post*, November 9, 1984, p. F1.

4. Interview with Bob Doubek, May 18, 1995.

5. Interview with Jan Scruggs, August 3, 1995.

6. Interview with Bob Doubek, May 18, 1995.

7. Conversation between Ross Perot and Bob Doubek, recounted in an interview with Bob Doubek, May 18, 1995.

8. Ibid.

9. Interview with Jan Scruggs, August 3, 1995.

10. Typed three-page "chronology of events/history of the involvement of Mr. H. Ross Perot with the Vietnam Veterans Memorial Fund," Vietnam Veterans Memorial Fund Office Files, Memorial Design, Controversy and Criticism, Perot, H. Ross, 1981–83, Box 30, Manuscript Division, Library of Congress, p. 1.

11. Ibid.

12. Ibid.

13. Letter, to James G. Watt from Jan C. Scruggs, December 2, 1981, five pages, Vietnam Veterans Memorial Fund, Controversy and Other Problems, Attachment to VVMF letter to Watt, December 18, 1981, Files of Project Director, Box 62, Manuscript Division, Library of Congress.

14. Typed three-page "chronology of events/history of the involvement of Mr. H. Ross Perot with the Vietnam Veterans Memorial Fund," Vietnam Veterans Memorial Fund Office Files, Memorial Design, Controversy and Criticism, Perot, H. Ross, 1981–83, Box 30, Manuscript Division, Library of Congress, p. 2.

15. Ibid.

16. Ibid.

17. VVFM Call Report, Jan Scruggs and Ross Perot conversation recounted, May 13, 1981, Vietnam Veterans Memorial Fund Office Files, Memorial Design, Controversy and Criticism, Perot, H. Ross, 1981–83, Box 30, Manuscript Division, Library of Congress.

18. Interview with Ross Perot, February 12, 1996.

19. Letter, to H. Ross Perot from Jan C. Scruggs, May 21, 1981, Vietnam Veterans Memorial Fund Office Files, Memorial Design, Controversy and Criticism, Perot, H. Ross, 1981–83, Box 30, Manuscript Division, Library of Congress.

20. Letter, to H. Ross Perot from Jan C. Scruggs, July 21, 1981, Vietnam Veterans Memorial Fund Office Files, Memorial Design, Controversy and Criticism, Perot, H. Ross, 1981–83, Box 30, Manuscript Division, Library of Congress.

21. VVMF Call Report, conversation between Ross Perot and Jan Scruggs, July 17, 1981, Vietnam Veterans Memorial Fund Office Files, Memorial Design, Controversy and Criticism, Perot, H. Ross, 1981–83, Box 30, Manuscript Division, Library of Congress.

22. Typed three-page "chronology of events/history of the involvement of Mr. H. Ross Perot with the Vietnam Veterans Memorial Fund"; VVMF Call Report of conversation between Ross Perot and Jan Scruggs, November 11, 1981, Vietnam Veterans Memorial Fund Office Files, Memorial Design, Controversy and Criticism, Perot, H. Ross, 1981–83, Box 30, Manuscript Division, Library of Congress, p. 3.

23. See, for example, letter to H. Ross Perot from Jan C. Scruggs, with enclosures, November 9, 1981, Vietnam Veterans Memorial Fund Office Files, Memorial Design, Controversy and Criticism, Perot, H. Ross, 1981–83, Box 30, Manuscript Division, Library of Congress.

24. Typed three-page "chronology of events/history of the involvement of Mr. H. Ross Perot with the Vietnam Veterans Memorial Fund," Vietnam Veterans Memorial Fund Office Files, Memorial Design, Controversy and Criticism, Perot, H. Ross, 1981–83, Box 30, Manuscript Division, Library of Congress, p. 3.

25. Typed three-page "chronology of events/history of the involvement of Mr. H. Ross Perot with the Vietnam Veterans Memorial Fund"; see also VVMF Call Report of conversation between Ross Perot and Jan Scruggs, December 11, 1981, Vietnam Veterans Memorial Fund Office Files, Memorial Design, Controversy and Criticism, Perot, H. Ross, 1981–83, Box 30, Manuscript Division, Library of Congress, p. 3.

26. "Vietnam Memorial Inappropriate, Millionaire Sympathizer Protests," Associated Press, December 17, 1981, Vietnam Veterans Memorial Fund Office Files, Memorial Design, Controversy and Criticism, Perot, H. Ross, 1981–83, Box 30, Manuscript Division, Library of Congress.

27. Interview with Bob Doubek, May 18, 1995.

28. Ibid.

29. Ibid.

30. Ibid.

31. Interview with Jan Scruggs, August 3, 1995.

32. Interview with Bob Doubek, May 18, 1995.

33. Meeting described in interview with Jan Scruggs, August 3, 1995.

34. "Watt Raises Obstacle on Vietnam Memorial," Associated Press, January 13, 1982, Vietnam Veterans Memorial Fund Office Files, Memorial Design, Controversy and Criticism, Perot, H. Ross, 1981–83, Box 30, Manuscript Division, Library of Congress.

35. Telephone conversation with General Davison, recounted in interview with Jan Scruggs, August 3, 1995.

36. Interview with Ross Perot, February 12, 1996.

37. VVMF Call Report, prepared by Jan Scruggs, recounting a conversation with Ed Debolt, February 1, 1982; see also VVMF Call Report, conversation between Jack Wheeler and Roy Adams, May 6, 1982, Veterans Memorial Fund Office Files, Memorial Design, Controversy and Criticism, Perot, H. Ross, 1981–83, Box 30, Manuscript Division, Library of Congress.

38. VVMF Call Report, prepared by Jan Scruggs, recounting a conversation with General Michael Davison, February 2, 1982, Vietnam Veterans Memorial Fund Office Files, Memorial Design, Controversy and Criticism, Perot, H. Ross, 1981–83, Box 30, Manuscript Division, Library of Congress.

39. Ibid.

40. VVMF Call Report, recounting a conversation between Jack Wheeler and Ross Perot, May 5, 1982, Vietnam Veterans Memorial Fund Office Files, Memorial Design, Controversy and Criticism, Perot, H. Ross, 1981–83, Box 30, Manuscript Division, Library of Congress.

41. Letter, to Jack Wheeler from Ross Perot, May 7, 1982, Vietnam Veterans Memorial Fund Office Files, Memorial Design, Controversy and Criticism, Perot, H. Ross, 1981–83, Box 30, Manuscript Division, Library of Congress.

42. VVMF Call Report, conversation between Elliot Richardson and J. C. Scruggs, subject: "H. Ross Perot and our dealings with him," May 10, 1982, Vietnam Veterans Memorial Fund Office Files, Memorial Design, Controversy and Criticism, Perot, H. Ross, 1981–83, Box 30, Manuscript Division, Library of Congress.

43. VVMF Call Report, conversation between Cyrus Vance and Jan Scruggs, June 9, 1982, Vietnam Veterans Memorial Fund Office Files, Memorial Design, Controversy and Criticism, Perot, H. Ross, 1981–83, Box 30, Manuscript Division, Library of Congress.

44. Letter, to H. Ross Perot from Jan C. Scruggs, June 24, 1982, Vietnam Veterans Memorial Fund Office Files, Memorial Design, Controversy and Criticism, Perot, H. Ross, 1981–83, Box 30, Manuscript Division, Library of Congress.

45. VVMF Call Report, conversation between General Davison and Jan Scruggs, regarding Davison talk with Perot, June 7, 1982, Vietnam Veterans Memorial Fund Office Files, Memorial Design, Controversy and Criticism, Perot, H. Ross, 1981–83, Box 30, Manuscript Division, Library of Congress.

46. VVMF Call Report, prepared by Jan Scruggs, recounting a conversation with Ray Grace, June 1, 1983, Vietnam Veterans Memorial Fund Office Files, Memorial Design, Controversy and Criticism, Perot, H. Ross, 1981–83, Box 30, Manuscript Division, Library of Congress.

47. Letter, to Elliot Richardson from Jan C. Scruggs, June 14, 1982, Vietnam Veterans Memorial Fund Office Files, Memorial Design, Controversy and Criticism, Perot, H. Ross, 1981–83, Box 30, Manuscript Division, Library of Congress.

48. VVMF Call Report, notes of conversation between Elliot Richardson and Jan Scruggs, subject: "Perot's latest demand," June 8, 1982, Vietnam Veterans Memorial Fund Office Files, Memorial Design, Controversy and Criticism, Perot, H. Ross, 1981–83, Box 30, Manuscript Division, Library of Congress.

49. Letter, to H. R. Perot from John P. Wheeler, June 8, 1982, Vietnam Veterans Memorial Fund Office Files, Memorial

Design, Controversy and Criticism, Perot, H. Ross, 1981–83, Box 30, Manuscript Division, Library of Congress.

50. Letter, to H. Ross Perot from Jan Scruggs, June 11, 1982, Vietnam Veterans Memorial Fund Office Files, Memorial Design, Controversy and Criticism, Perot, H. Ross, 1981–83, Box 30, Manuscript Division, Library of Congress.

51. Letter, to H. R. Perot from Richard E. Radez, July 12, 1982, Vietnam Veterans Memorial Fund Office Files, Memorial Design, Controversy and Criticism, Perot, H. Ross, 1981–83, Box 30, Manuscript Division, Library of Congress.

52. Memorandum for the record, from Richard Radez, subject: RER Telephone Conversation with Mr. H. Ross Perot, July 12, 1982, Vietnam Veterans Memorial Fund Office Files, Memorial Design, Controversy and Criticism, Perot, H. Ross, 1981–83, Box 30, Manuscript Division, Library of Congress.

53. Letter, to Board of Directors, Vietnam Veterans Memorial Fund, from Ross Perot, July 23, 1982, Vietnam Veterans Memorial Fund Office Files, Memorial Design, Controversy and Criticism, Perot, H. Ross, 1981–83, Box 30, Manuscript Division, Library of Congress.

54. See, for example, VVMF Call Report of conversation with Lloyd Unsell, August 25, 1982, Vietnam Veterans Memorial Fund Office Files, Memorial Design, Controversy and Criticism, Perot, H. Ross, 1981–83, Box 30, Manuscript Division, Library of Congress.

55. Memo, to Independent Audit Committee from Jan C. Scruggs, subject: "Recent Actions by Mr. H. Ross Perot," September 21, 1982, Vietnam Veterans Memorial Fund Office Files, Memorial Design, Controversy and Criticism, Perot, H. Ross, 1981–83, Box 30, Manuscript Division, Library of Congress.

56. Letter, to Richard P. Shlakman from Steven M. Umin, September 17, 1982; see also Shlakman's clarification of what he meant regarding Ross Perot's relationship to charities, letter to Steven M. Umin, from Richard P. Shlakman, September 28, 1982, Vietnam Veterans Memorial Fund Office Files, Memorial Design, Controversy and

Criticism, Perot, H. Ross, 1981–83, Box 30, Manuscript Division, Library of Congress.

57. Memo, to Independent Audit Committee from Jan C. Scruggs, subject: "Recent Actions by Mr. H. Ross Perot," September 21, 1982, Vietnam Veterans Memorial Fund Office Files, Memorial Design, Controversy and Criticism, Perot, H. Ross, 1981–83, Box 30, Manuscript Division, Library of Congress.

58. Letter, to Richard P. Shlakman from Steven M. Umin, September 17, 1982, Vietnam Veterans Memorial Fund Office Files, Memorial Design, Controversy and Criticism, Perot, H. Ross, 1981–83, Box 30, Manuscript Division, Library of Congress.

59. Memo, to Independent Audit Committee from Jan C. Scruggs, subject: "Recent Actions by Mr. H. Ross Perot," September 21, 1982, Vietnam Veterans Memorial Fund Office Files, Memorial Design, Controversy and Criticism, Perot, H. Ross, 1981–83, Box 30, Manuscript Division, Library of Congress.

60. Ross Perot, quoted in "Lest We Forget," *60 Minutes*, CBS, Sunday, October 10, 1982.

61. "Poll Shows Former POWs Dislike Vietnam Memorial," *The Florida Times-Union*, October 12, 1982, Vietnam Veterans Memorial Fund Office Files, Memorial Design, Controversy and Criticism, Perot, H. Ross, 1981–83, Box 30, Manuscript Division, Library of Congress.

62. Interview with Jan Scruggs, August 3, 1995.

63. Jan Scruggs, on "Vietnam Veterans Memorial Controversy," *Nightline*, ABC, October 14, 1982.

64. Ross Perot, on "Vietnam Veterans Memorial Controversy," *Nightline*, ABC, October 14, 1982.

65. Memorandum, for the Record from Jan C. Scruggs, subject: "Perot," November 1, 1982; see also VVMF Call Report, regarding conversation between Paul Thayer and Jan Scruggs, subject: "Thayer's talk with Perot," October 4, 1982; also, Elliot Richardson and Jan Scruggs conversation, subject: "Richardson's talk with Joe Allbritton," October 29, 1982, Vietnam Veterans Memorial Fund Office

Files, Memorial Design, Controversy and Criticism, Perot, H. Ross, 1981–83, Box 30, Manuscript Division, Library of Congress.

66. Letter, to Terrence O'Donnell from Roy M. Cohn, March 29, 1983, Vietnam Veterans Memorial Fund Office Files, Memorial Design, Controversy and Criticism, Perot, H. Ross, 1981–83, Box 30, Manuscript Division, Library of Congress.

67. Letter, to Jan Scruggs from Elliot Richardson, March 14, 1983, Vietnam Veterans Memorial Fund Office Files, Memorial Design, Controversy and Criticism, Perot, H. Ross, 1981–83, Box 30, Manuscript Division, Library of Congress.

68. VVMF Call Report, conversation with Chuck Bailey, February 25, 1983, Vietnam Veterans Memorial Fund Office Files, Memorial Design, Controversy and Criticism, Perot, H. Ross, 1981–83, Box 30, Manuscript Division, Library of Congress.

69. See, for example, VVMF Call Report, conversation with Terry Yates, March 7, 1982, Vietnam Veterans Memorial Fund Office Files, Memorial Design, Controversy and Criticism, Perot, H. Ross, 1981–83, Box 30, Manuscript Division, Library of Congress.

70. VVMF Call Report, conversation between Cyrus Vance and Jan Scruggs, subject: "Discussion with Roy Cohn re: Audit," Vietnam Veterans Memorial Fund Office Files, Memorial Design, Controversy and Criticism, Perot, H. Ross, 1981–83, Box 30, Manuscript Division, Library of Congress.

71. VVMF Call Report, Jack Wheeler recounting information about Baines correspondence relating to Roy Cohn, March 7, 1983, Vietnam Veterans Memorial Fund Office Files, Memorial Design, Controversy and Criticism, Perot, H. Ross, 1981–83, Box 30, Manuscript Division, Library of Congress.

72. Todd Mason, *Perot: An Unauthorized Biography* (Homewood, Illinois: Business One Irwin, 1990), p. 177.

73. Letter to Roy M. Cohn from Terrence O'Donnell, July 1, 1983, Vietnam Veterans Memorial Fund Office Files, Memorial Design, Controversy and Criti-

cism, Perot, H. Ross, 1981–83, Box 30, Manuscript Division, Library of Congress.

74. Memorandum, to Independent Audit Committee from Jan C. Scruggs, July 1, 1983, Vietnam Veterans Memorial Fund Office Files, Memorial Design, Controversy and Criticism, Perot, H. Ross, 1981–83, Box 30, Manuscript Division, Library of Congress.

75. Affidavit of David A. Christian, September 23, 1983, six pages, Vietnam Veterans Memorial Fund Office Files, Memorial Design, Controversy and Criticism, Christian, David A., 1983–84, Box 29, Manuscript Division, Library of Congress.

76. Carlton Sherwood, quoted by Elisabeth Bumiller, "The Memorial, Mirror of Vietnam," *The Washington Post,* November 9, 1984, p. F1.

77. See, for example, memo to file, from Jan C. Scruggs, subject: "Mr. Perot," undated, Vietnam Veterans Memorial Fund Office Files, Memorial Design, Controversy and Criticism, Perot, H. Ross, 1981–83, Box 30, Manuscript Division, Library of Congress.

78. Letters, to Ross Perot from Jan Scruggs, June 7, 1984, and to Jan Scruggs from Sally Walther, June 14, 1984, Vietnam Veterans Memorial Fund Office Files, Memorial Design, Controversy and Criticism, Perot, H. Ross, 1981–83, Box 30, Manuscript Division, Library of Congress.

79. Letter, from Jan Scruggs to H. Ross Perot, November 2, 1992, from the files of Jan Scruggs.

80. Ross Perot, quoted by Bumiller, op. cit., p. F1.

81. Interview with Ross Perot, November 30, 1995.

Chapter 11:
The Detroit Invasion

1. Ross Perot, quoted in *The Dallas Morning News,* March 26, 1984, per Tony Chiu, *Ross Perot: In His Own Words* (New York: Warner Books, 1992), p. 72.

2. Ross Perot, quoted in *The Dallas Morning News,* January 11, 1983, per Chiu, op. cit., p. 75.

3. Ross Perot, quoted in *The Dallas Morning News,* October 1, 1983, and May 13, 1984, and *The New York Times,* October 9, 1983, per Chiu, op. cit., pp. 76–77.

4. Ross Perot, quoted in *The Dallas Morning News,* August 25, 1983, per Chiu, op. cit., p. 78.

5. Ross Perot, quoted in *The Dallas Morning News,* June 6, 1984, per Todd Mason, *Perot: An Unauthorized Biography* (Homewood, Illinois: Business One Irwin, 1990), p. 127.

6. Ross Perot, quoted in *The Dallas Morning News,* September 11, 1983, per Chiu, op. cit., p. 79.

7. Annette Cootes, quoted by Jamie Dettmer, "Man-made Champion of the American Dream," *The New York Times,* June 20, 1992.

8. Interview with John Leedom, October 26, 1995.

9. Ross Perot, in a speech in Washington, D.C., November 20, 1984, quoted by Mason, op. cit., pp. 127–28.

10. Eddie Joseph, quoted in an ABC News special hosted by Peter Jennings, June 29, 1992.

11. Raymon Bynum, quoted by Mason, op. cit., p. 126.

12. Ross Perot, quoted in ABC News special hosted by Peter Jennings, June 29, 1992.

13. Interview with John Leedom, October 26, 1995.

14. Ibid.

15. Mark White, quoted by Scot Lehigh, "Beyond Aura, Accounts of a Combative, Rigid Perot," *The Boston Globe,* June 16, 1992, p. 24.

16. O. H. "Ike" Harris, quoted by David Firestone, "Taking Apart the Billionaire Who Would Be President," *Newsday,* May 17, 1992, p. 3.

17. Ross Perot, quoted by David Remnick, "H. Ross Perot to GM: 'I'll Drive'; GM to H. Ross: 'Oh, Yeah?,' " *The Washington Post Magazine,* April 19, 1987.

18. Interview with John Leedom, October 26, 1995.

19. Mark White, quoted by Scot Lehigh, op. cit., p. 24.

20. Interview with Ross Perot, November 30, 1995.

21. Interview with John Leedom, October 26, 1995.

22. Interview with Mort Meyerson, April 20, 1995.

23. Roger Smith, quoted by Albert Lee, *Call Me Roger* (Chicago: Contemporary Books, 1988), p. 28.

24. Doron P. Levin, *Irreconcilable Differences: Ross Perot Versus General Motors* (Boston: Little, Brown, 1989), p. 98.

25. Review of stock market record for EDS closing share price and volume, maintained by New York Stock Exchange.

26. Levin, op. cit., p. 122.

27. Bill Gayden, quoted by Levin, op. cit., p. 107.

28. Interview with Felix Rohatyn, May 24, 1995.

29. Interview with Mort Meyerson, April 20, 1995.

30. Testimony of Ross Perot, *EDS* v. *Henry Ross Perot and Perot Systems Corp.,* In Chancery No. 108556, Fairfax, Virginia, October 19, 1988, p. 161.

31. Ross Perot, quoted by Levin, op. cit., p. 108.

32. Interview with Mort Meyerson, April 20, 1995.

33. Les Alberthal, quoted by Mason, op. cit., p. 132.

34. Interview with Ken Riedlinger, October 31, 1995.

35. Roger Smith, quoted by Lee, op. cit., p. 157.

36. Interview with Ken Riedlinger, October 31, 1995.

Chapter 12: "The Tar Baby"

1. Ross Perot, quoted by Albert Lee, *Call Me Roger* (Chicago: Contemporary Books, 1988), p. 169.

2. Alex Mair, quoted by Doron P. Levin, *Irreconcilable Differences: Ross Perot Versus General Motors* (Boston: Little, Brown, 1989), p. 170.

3. Levin, op. cit., p. 174.

4. Interview with Ken Riedlinger, October 31, 1995.

5. Alex Cunningham, quoted by Levin, op. cit., p. 178.

6. Gary Fernandes, quoted by Todd Mason, *Perot: An Unauthorized Biography* (Homewood, Illinois: Business One Irwin, 1990), p. 136.

7. Interview with Ken Riedlinger, October 31, 1995.

8. Ibid.

9. Mason, op. cit., p. 145.

10. Lee, op. cit., p. 164.

11. Ibid.

12. Interview with Ken Riedlinger, October 31, 1995.

13. Ibid.

14. Interview with Ross Perot, August 8, 1995.

15. Ibid.

16. Ross Perot, quoted by Levin, op. cit., p. 178.

17. Ibid., p. 192.

18. Interview with Ross Perot, August 8, 1995.

19. Interview with Mort Meyerson, April 20, 1995.

20. Mort Meyerson, quoted by Levin, op. cit., p. 213.

21. Interview with Ken Riedlinger, October 31, 1995.

22. Ross Perot, quoted by Levin, op. cit., p. 218.

23. Ken Riedlinger, quoted by Levin, op. cit., p. 221.

24. Interview with Ken Riedlinger, October 31, 1995.

25. Ibid.

26. Ibid.

27. Interview with Ross Perot, August 8, 1995.

28. David E. Davis, quoted by David Remnick, "H. Ross Perot to GM: 'I'll Drive,'; GM to H. Ross: 'Oh, Yeah?,' " *The Washington Post Magazine,* April 19, 1987.

29. Ross Perot, quoted by Levin, op. cit., p. 236.

30. Interview with Bill Gayden, March 10, 1995.

31. Ross Perot, quoted by Remnick, op. cit.

32. Interview with Ken Riedlinger, October 31, 1995.

33. Ross Perot, quoted by Remnick, op. cit.

34. Ross Perot, quoted by Lee, op. cit., p. 167.

35. Letter, to Roger Smith from Ross Perot, October 23, 1985, quoted by Levin, op. cit., p. 248.

36. Ibid.

37. Deposition Exhibit 16 for Roger Smith, *EDS* v. *Henry Ross Perot and Perot Systems Corp.,* In Chancery No. 108556, Fairfax, Virginia, submitted March 3, 1989.

38. Lee, op. cit., p. 28.

39. See generally, four-page typed letter to J. T. Walter, chief financial officer of EDS, from J. R. Edman, General Motors vice-president, dated February 28, 1986, produced pursuant to discovery in *EDS* v. *Henry Ross Perot and Perot Systems Corp.,* In Chancery No. 108556, Fairfax, Virginia.

40. Lee, op. cit., p. 168.

41. Ross Perot, quoted by Remnick, op. cit.

42. Mort Meyerson, quoted by Levin, op. cit., p. 270.

43. EDS News Release, April 28, 1986.

44. Deposition of Roger Smith, *EDS* v. *Henry Ross Perot and Perot Systems Corp.,* In Chancery No. 108556, Fairfax, Virginia, March 3, 1989.

45. Letter, to Roger Smith from Ross Perot, May 7, 1986, quoted by Levin, op. cit., pp. 272–74.

46. Letter, to Roger Smith from Ross Perot, May 19, 1986, quoted by Levin, op. cit., pp. 276–77.

47. Ross Perot, quoted by J. Michael Kennedy, "Ross Perot: A Fighter All His Life," *Los Angeles Times,* May 11, 1986; N. R. Kleinfield, "The 'Irritant' They Call Perot," *The New York Times,* Section 3, April 27, 1986, p. 1.

48. Doron P. Levin and Paul Ingrassia, "Now on the Inside, Ross Perot Tells GM and Its Rivals How They Must Change," *The Wall Street Journal,* July 22, 1986, p. 1.

49. Ross Perot, quoted by Levin and Ingrassia, op. cit.

50. Levin, op. cit., p. 288.

51. Ross Perot, quoted by Levin, op. cit., p. 288.

52. Les Alberthal, quoted by Mason, op. cit., p. 206.

53. David Cole, quoted by Debra Whitefield, "The Great Mismatch," *Los Angeles Times,* December 2, 1986, part 4, p. 1.

54. See, for example, David C. Smith, "How Perot's Fling with GM Wound Up as a 5-Alarm Fire," *Ward's Auto World,* Volume 28, No. 7, July 1992, p. 7.

55. Roger Smith, quoted by David C. Smith, op. cit., p. 7.

56. Roger Smith, quoted by Lee, op. cit., p. 204.

57. Todd Mason, Russell Mitchell, William Hampton, and Marc Frons, "Ross Perot's Crusade," *Business Week,* October 6, 1986, p. 60.

58. Ross Perot, quoted by Lee, op. cit., p. 209.

59. Deposition of Les Alberthal, *EDS v. Henry Ross Perot and Perot Systems Corp.,* In Chancery No. 108556, Fairfax, Virginia, February 6, 1989.

60. Ibid.

61. Testimony of Ross Perot, *EDS v. Henry Ross Perot and Perot Systems Corp.,* In Chancery No. 108556, Fairfax, Virginia, October 19, 1995, p. 147.

62. Deposition of Elmer Johnson, *EDS v. Henry Ross Perot and Perot Systems Corp.,* In Chancery No. 108556, Fairfax, Virginia, February 3, 1989; Lee, op. cit., p. 213.

63. Elmer Johnson, quoted by R. C. Longworth, "Perot's Zeal Raises Doubts for Former GM Colleague," *Chicago Tribune,* July 2, 1992, Zone C, p. 1.

64. Ross Perot, quoted by Jon Lowell, "Rx for GM: Ross Perot," *Ward's Auto World,* November 1986.

65. Ross Perot, quoted by Remnick, op. cit.

66. Roger Smith, quoted by Lee, op. cit., p. 208.

67. Ibid., p. 206.

68. Ross Perot, quoted by Levin, op. cit., p. 311.

69. Ross Perot, quoted by Lee, op. cit., p. 198.

70. Ibid., p. 199.

71. Ibid., p. 214.

72. Ibid., p. 213.

73. Interview with Felix Rohatyn, May 24, 1995.

74. Testimony of Les Alberthal, *EDS v. Henry Ross Perot and Perot Systems Corp.,* In Chancery No. 108556, Fairfax, Virginia, October 13, 1988, p. 152.

75. Testimony of Malcolm Gudis, *EDS v. Henry Ross Perot and Perot Systems Corp.,* In Chancery No. 108556, Fairfax, Virginia, April 11, 1989, p. 106; see also testimony of Dean Linderman, April 11, 1989, p. 12; Stuart Reeves, April 11, 1989, p. 138; deposition statement of Claude Chappelear read into the record by Tom Barr, April 11, 1989, p. 156; testimony of Claude Chappelear, *Perot Systems v. General Motors Corporation, Electronic Data Systems, et al.,* District Court of Dallas County, Texas, 95th Judicial District, October 11, 1988, p. 158.

76. Testimony of Ross Perot, *EDS v. Henry Ross Perot and Perot Systems Corp.,* In Chancery No. 108556, Fairfax, Virginia, October 19, 1988, p. 147.

77. Testimony of Les Alberthal, *EDS v. Henry Ross Perot and Perot Systems Corp.,* In Chancery No. 108556, Fairfax, Virginia, October 13, 1988, p. 223.

78. Deposition of Gary Fernandes, *EDS v. Henry Ross Perot and Perot Systems Corp.,* In Chancery No. 108556, Fairfax, Virginia, February 15, 1989.

79. Testimony of Les Alberthal, *EDS v. Henry Ross Perot and Perot Systems Corp.,* In Chancery No. 108556, Fairfax, Virginia, October 13, 1988, p. 155; see also Alberthal testimony, April 11, 1989, pp. 88–90; statement of Tom Barr, Esq., April 11, 1989, p. 219.

80. Tom Luce and Elmer Johnson, quoted by Levin, op. cit., pp. 322–23.

81. Ross Perot, quoted by Levin, op. cit., p. 323.

82. Testimony of Les Alberthal, *EDS v. Henry Ross Perot and Perot Systems Corp.,* In Chancery No. 108556, Fairfax, Virginia, October 13, 1988, p. 149.

83. Press release by Ross Perot, December 1, 1986, quoted in full by Levin, op. cit., pp. 324–25.

84. Roger Smith, quoted by Lee, op. cit., p. 253.

85. Ibid., p. 215.

86. Deposition of Tom Luce, *EDS v. Henry Ross Perot and Perot Systems Corp.,* In Chancery No. 108556, Fairfax, Virginia, February 16, 1989.

87. Les Alberthal, quoted by Mason, op. cit., p. 221.

88. Elmer Johnson, quoted by Lee, op. cit., p. 254.

89. Transcript of Perot press conference, December 1, 1986, included as Plaintiff's Exhibit 19A, *EDS* v. *Henry Ross Perot and Perot Systems Corp.*, In Chancery No. 108556, Fairfax, Virginia, submitted October 19, 1988.

90. Ross Perot, quoted by William H. Inman, "Perot Says GM's Buyout Was Lousy Investment," UPI, P.M. cycle, Domestic News, December 2, 1986.

91. Ibid.

92. David C. Smith, op. cit., p. 7.

93. Ross Perot quoted by Jim Irwin, "Perot Knocks Automaker Again: GM Mum on Possible penalty," Associated Press Wire Service, Sunday A.M. cycle, Domestic News, December 7, 1986.

94. Roger Smith, quoted by Lee, op. cit., p. 219.

95. Ross Perot quoted by Levin, op. cit., p. 331.

Chapter 13:
Missing in Action

1. Deposition of Tom Meurer, June 24, 1992, p. 79, Senate Select Committee on POW/MIA Affairs, Center for Legislative Archives, National Archives.

2. Press conference by Roger Shields, chief of the Prisoner of War Task Force for the Pentagon, April 14, 1973.

3. Interview with Ross Perot, August 8, 1995; see also deposition of Ross Perot, July 1, 1992, p. 23, Senate Select Committee on POW/MIA Affairs, Center for Legislative Archives, National Archives.

4. Interview with Ross Perot, August 8, 1995.

5. Interview with Ann Mills Griffiths, February 4, 1995.

6. Ross Perot, quoted by Monika Jensen-Stevenson and William Stevenson, *Kiss the Boys Goodbye: How the United States Betrayed Its Own POWs in Vietnam* (New York: Penguin, 1991), p. 192.

7. Interview with Richard Childress, February 9, 1995.

8. Interview with Tom Meurer, March 14, 1995.

9. Interview with Ann Mills Griffiths, February 4, 1995; see also deposition of Tom Meurer, June 24, 1992, p. 14, and deposition of Richard Armitage, August 7, 1992, p. 53, Senate Select Committee on POW/MIA Affairs, Center for Legislative Archives, National Archives.

10. Interview with Ann Mills Griffiths, February 4, 1995.

11. Deposition of James Gordon "Bo" Gritz, November 23, 1992, p. 6, Senate Select Committee on POW/MIA Affairs, Center for Legislative Archives, National Archives.

12. Ibid., pp. 6–7.

13. Interview with Ann Mills Griffiths, February 4, 1995; see also deposition of Ann Mills Griffiths, October 6, 1992, pp. 42–43, Senate Select Committee on POW/MIA Affairs, Center for Legislative Archives, National Archives.

14. Deposition of James Gordon "Bo" Gritz, November 23, 1992, p. 7, Senate Select Committee on POW/MIA Affairs, Center for Legislative Archives, National Archives.

15. Ibid., p. 8.

16. Ibid., p. 162; see also deposition of Bobby Ray Inman, September 9, 1992, p. 79, Senate Select Committee on POW/MIA Affairs, Center for Legislative Archives, National Archives.

17. Deposition of James Gordon "Bo" Gritz, November 23, 1992, pp. 18, 93, Senate Select Committee on POW/MIA Affairs, Center for Legislative Archives, National Archives.

18. Deposition of Gen. Eugene Tighe, February 27, 1992, p. 171, Senate Select Committee on POW/MIA Affairs, Center for Legislative Archives, National Archives.

19. Interview with Richard Childress, February 9, 1995.

20. Ibid.; see also deposition of Richard Childress, July 30, 1992, p. 63, Senate Select Committee on POW/MIA Affairs, Center for Legislative Archives, National Archives.

21. Ross Perot, quoted by UPI, from San Antonio bureau, January 27, 1986.

22. Deposition of Ross Perot, July 1, 1992, p. 161, Senate Select Committee on POW/MIA Affairs, Center for Legislative Archives, National Archives.

23. Deposition of Leonard Peroots, June 15, 1992, pp. 81, 102, Senate Select Committee on POW/MIA Affairs, Center for Legislative Archives, National Archives.

24. Interview with Ross Perot, November 29, 1995.

25. Testimony of Ross Perot, the Tighe Report Hearings on American POW's and MIA's Before the Subcommittee on Asian and Pacific Affairs of the Committee on Foreign Affairs, House of Representatives, Ninety-ninth Congress, Second Session, October 15, 1986, p. 40.

26. Jensen-Stevenson and Stevenson, op. cit., p. 192.

27. Interview with Ross Perot, November 29, 1995.

28. Conversation between Ronald Reagan and Ross Perot, recounted by Ross Perot, interviewed on November 29, 1995.

29. Deposition of Frank Carlucci, June 26, 1992, pp. 88–90; see also deposition of Colin Powell, July 16, 1992, p. 62, Senate Select Committee on POW/MIA Affairs, Center for Legislative Archives, National Archives.

30. Interview with James Cannon, May 9, 1995; see also deposition of Frank Carlucci, June 26, 1992, p. 51, Senate Select Committee on POW/MIA Affairs, Center for Legislative Archives, National Archives.

31. Interview with Boyden Gray, July 25, 1995.

32. Interview with Ross Perot, November 29, 1995.

33. Ross Perot, quoted by Donald M. Rothberg, "Billionaire Offered $4.2 Million for Tape of American Captives," The Detroit Free Press, September 4, 1986, p. A14.

34. Interview with Ross Perot, November 29, 1995.

35. Ross Perot, quoted in Dallas Times Herald, September 4, 1986.

36. See generally, deposition of Ross Perot, July 1, 1992, pp. 150–54, Senate Select Committee on POW/MIA Affairs, Center for Legislative Archives, National Archives.

37. Conversation between Gen. Leonard Peroots and Ross Perot, recounted by Ross Perot in interview on November 29, 1995.

38. See generally, deposition of Ross Perot, July 1, 1992, pp. 129–30, Senate Select Committee on POW/MIA Affairs, Center for Legislative Archives, National Archives.

39. Ross Perot, quoted by Carl P. Leubsdorf, "Perot's MIA Quest," The Dallas Morning News, September 4, 1986, p. A8.

40. Interview with Richard Childress, February 9, 1995.

41. Deposition of Gen. Leonard H. Peroots, June 15, 1992, p. 96, Senate Select Committee on POW/MIA Affairs, Center for Legislative Archives, National Archives.

42. Deposition of Ross Perot, July 1, 1992, pp. 28–29, Senate Select Committee on POW/MIA Affairs, Center for Legislative Archives, National Archives.

43. Ross Perot, quoted by Jensen-Stevenson, op. cit., p. 237.

44. Ibid., p. 233.

45. Conversation between Ross Perot and William Webster, quoted by Monika Jensen-Stevenson, op. cit., p. 233.

46. Testimony of Ross Perot, August 11, 1992, Senate Select Committee on POW/MIA Affairs, Center for Legislative Archives, National Archives.

47. Ross Perot, quoted in George J. Church, "Perot's Private Probes: A Billionaire Pursues His Own Iran and MIA Trail," Time, May 4, 1987, p. 18.

48. Ross Perot, quoted by Jensen-Stevenson and Stevenson, op. cit., p. 233.

49. Interview with David Taylor, March 13, 1996.

50. Deposition of Ross Perot, July 1, 1992, p. 190, Senate Select Committee on POW/MIA Affairs, Center for Legislative Archives, National Archives; see also Ross Perot interview on C-SPAN with Brian Lamb, May 17, 1992.

51. Ross Perot, quoted by Jack Anderson and Michael Binstein, "Perot's Savaging of Richard Armitage," The Washington Post, July 5, 1992.

52. Ross Perot on C-SPAN, with Brian Lamb, May 17, 1992.

53. Interview with David Remnick, November 6, 1995.

54. Ross Perot on Today, NBC, June 24, 1992; see also deposition of Ross Perot, July 1, 1992, p. 190, Senate Select Committee on POW/MIA Affairs, Center for Legislative Archives, National Archives.

55. Ross Perot on C-SPAN, with Brian Lamb, May 17, 1992.

56. Daniel Sheehan recounting his conversation with Ross Perot, by Karen De Witt and Michael Kelly, "Perot Pursued Charges Against Official for Years," *The New York Times,* June 28, 1992.

57. Daniel Sheehan, quoted by Jensen-Stevenson and Stevenson, op. cit., p. 233; see also Daniel Sheehan, quoted by De Witt and Kelly, op. cit.

58. Interview with David Taylor, March 13, 1996.

59. Ross Perot, quoted by Brian Duffy, "The World According to Ross," *U.S. News & World Report,* June 1, 1992, p. 27.

60. Testimony of Ross Perot, the Tighe Report Hearings on American POW's and MIA's Before the Subcommittee on Asian and Pacific Affairs of the Committee on Foreign Affairs, House of Representatives, Ninety-ninth Congress, Second Session, October 15, 1986, p. 46.

61. Ibid., p. 45.

62. Letter to author, from George Bush, October 3, 1995.

63. Interview with Ross Perot, February 12, 1996.

64. Ibid.

65. Interview with Caspar Weinberger, February 21, 1995.

66. Deposition of Gen. Leonard H. Peroots, June 15, 1992, pp. 123, 125, Senate Select Committee on POW/MIA Affairs, Center for Legislative Archives, National Archives.

67. Interview with Richard Armitage, February 10, 1995.

68. Recollection of conversation between Perot and Armitage by Richard Armitage, interviewed on February 10, 1995.

69. Deposition of Richard Armitage, August 7, 1992, p. 83, Senate Select Committee on POW/MIA Affairs, Center for Legislative Archives, National Archives.

70. Deposition of Ross Perot, July 1, 1992, pp. 285–86, Senate Select Committee on POW/MIA Affairs, Center for Legislative Archives, National Archives.

71. Interview with Buck Revell, March 13, 1995.

72. Interview with Frank Carlucci, February 9, 1995; see also deposition of James

Cannon, August 6, 1992, p. 51; deposition of Frank Carlucci, June 26, 1992, pp. 55–57, 62, Senate Select Committee on POW/MIA Affairs, Center for Legislative Archives, National Archives.

73. Deposition of Frank Carlucci, June 26, 1992, pp. 53–54, Senate Select Committee on POW/MIA Affairs, Center for Legislative Archives, National Archives.

74. Deposition of James Cannon, August 6, 1992, pp. 115–16, Senate Select Committee on POW/MIA Affairs, Center for Legislative Archives, National Archives.

75. Letter, to Edwin Meese from Craig Fuller, March 2, 1987, listed as an exhibit to the deposition of James Cannon, August 2, 1992, Senate Select Committee on POW/MIA Affairs, Center for Legislative Archives, National Archives.

76. Morton Kondracke, "Perot vs. Armitage: Epic Confrontation May Affect Election, *Roll Call,* June 29, 1992, p. 6; see also deposition of Richard Armitage, August 7, 1992, pp. 112–13, Senate Select Committee on POW/MIA Affairs, Center for Legislative Archives, National Archives.

77. Deposition of Richard Armitage, August 7, 1992, pp. 72–73, Senate Select Committee on POW/MIA Affairs, Center for Legislative Archives, National Archives.

78. Ross Perot, quoted by Rita Beamish, "Bush Aide Confirms Report on Armitage," *The Boston Globe,* January 12, 1987, p. 4.

79. George J. Church, "Perot's Private Probes: A Billionaire Pursues His Own Iran and MIA Trail," *Time,* May 4, 1987, p. 18.

80. Interview with James Cannon, May 9, 1995.

81. Ibid.

82. Deposition of James Cannon, August 6, 1992, p. 62, Senate Select Committee on POW/MIA Affairs, Center for Legislative Archives, National Archives.

83. Interview with James Cannon, May 9, 1995.

84. Office of the Vice President, Memorandum for the Files, from the Vice President, regarding phone call from Ross Perot, March 21, 1987, 2:00 P.M.; see also letter, to Ross Perot from George Bush, March 23, 1987 (both documents listed as exhibits to the deposition of James Can-

non, August 2, 1992, Senate Select Committee on POW/MIA Affairs, Center for Legislative Archives, National Archives).

85. Office of the Vice President, Memorandum for the Files, from the Vice President, regarding phone call from Ross Perot, March 21, 1987, 2:00 P.M., listed as an exhibit to the deposition of James Cannon, August 2, 1992, p. 3, Senate Select Committee on POW/MIA Affairs, Center for Legislative Archives, National Archives.

86. Telephone summary list of conversations with Colin Powell, prepared by James Cannon, March 21, 1987, listed as an exhibit to deposition of James Cannon, August 6, 1992, Senate Select Committee on POW/MIA Affairs, Center for Legislative Archives, National Archives.

87. Letter to the author, from Howard Baker, August 14, 1995.

88. Interview with James Cannon, May 9, 1995.

89. Ibid.

90. Interview with Ross Perot, August 8, 1995.

91. Interview with Richard Childress, February 9, 1995.

92. Interview with Frank Carlucci, February 9, 1995; see also deposition of Frank Carlucci, June 26, 1992, pp. 43, 45, Senate Select Committee on POW/MIA Affairs, Center for Legislative Archives, National Archives.

93. Deposition of Colin Powell, July 16, 1992, pp. 53–55, Senate Select Committee on POW/MIA Affairs, Center for Legislative Archives, National Archives.

94. Deposition of Richard Childress, July 30, 1992, p. 137, Senate Select Committee on POW/MIA Affairs, Center for Legislative Archives, National Archives.

95. Deposition of Colin Powell, July 16, 1992, p. 87, Senate Select Committee on POW/MIA Affairs, Center for Legislative Archives, National Archives.

96. Exhibit Seven, draft of proposed statement for the president, April 19, 1987, deposition of Ross Perot, July 1, 1992, Senate Select Committee on POW/MIA Affairs, Center for Legislative Archives, National Archives.

97. Interview with Ross Perot, February 12, 1996.

98. Ibid.

99. Interview with Frank Carlucci, February 9, 1995, see also deposition of Frank Carlucci, June 26, 1995, p. 65, Senate Select Committee on POW/MIA Affairs, Center for Legislative Archives, National Archives.

100. Interview with Ross Perot, February 12, 1996; see also deposition of Colin Powell, July 16, 1992, pp. 121–22, Senate Select Committee on POW/MIA Affairs, Center for Legislative Archives, National Archives.

101. Ross Perot, quoted by Jensen-Stevenson and Stevenson, op. cit., p. 337.

102. Interview with James Cannon, May 9, 1995.

103. Interview with Boyden Gray, July 25, 1995.

104. Interview with Frank Carlucci, February 9, 1995.

105. Deposition of Ross Perot, July 1, 1992, p. 258, Senate Select Committee on POW/MIA Affairs, Center for Legislative Archives, National Archives.

106. Patrick E. Tyler, "Perot, in Vietnam, Sought Business," *The New York Times,* June 4, 1992, p. A1.

107. Deposition of Ross Perot, July 1, 1992, p. 262, Senate Select Committee on POW/MIA Affairs, Center for Legislative Archives, National Archives.

108. Exhibit 30, attached to deposition of Harry McKillop, June 30, 1992, Senate Select Committee on POW/MIA Affairs, Center for Legislative Archives, National Archives.

109. Deposition of Ross Perot, July 1, 1992, pp. 260, 263, 265, 270, Senate Select Committee on POW/MIA Affairs, Center for Legislative Archives, National Archives.

110. Deposition of Ross Perot, July 1, 1992, p. 302, Senate Select Committee on POW/MIA Affairs, Center for Legislative Archives, National Archives; see also p. 300.

111. Author's review of deposition of Harry McKillop, June 30, 1992, Senate Select Committee on POW/MIA Affairs, Center for Legislative Archives, National Archives.

112. Deposition of Harry McKillop, June 30, 1992, p. 243, Senate Select Com-

mittee on POW/MIA Affairs, Center for Legislative Archives, National Archives.

113. Deposition of Harry McKillop, June 30, 1992, p. 152, Senate Select Committee on POW/MIA Affairs, Center for Legislative Archives, National Archives.

114. Le Van Bang, quoted by Pete Engardio, "Was Perot Looking for More Than Missing G.I.'s in Vietnam?," *Business Week,* June 15, 1992, pp. 37–38.

115. Ross Perot, quoted by Engardio, op. cit., p. 38.

Chapter 14: "Vacuum It Up"

1. Ross Perot, quoted in the Associated Press, per "Don't Bring Back 'Pet Rock Crowd,' Perot Urges," Fort Worth *Star-Telegram,* October 15, 1987.

2. Charles Siler, "You Don't Lose 'Em All," *Forbes,* August 10, 1987, p. 34.

3. "Perot Property Targeted," *The Houston Chronicle,* September 14, 1987; see also "Perot Annexation Costly," *Odessa American,* September 14, 1987.

4. Interview with Robert Bolen, January 26, 1995.

5. Ibid.

6. Interview with Garey Gilley, January 25, 1995.

7. Interview with Robert Bolen, January 26, 1995.

8. William Garrison, quoted by Dan Malone, "FW Official Benefited from Land Sale to Perots," *The Dallas Morning News,* February 12, 1989, p. A1.

9. Dan Malone, "FW Officials' Firms Did Work for Perot Project," *The Dallas Morning News,* January 28, 1989, p. 1A.

10. Interview with Steve Wollens, January 27, 1995.

11. "In Brief: Some Pork Went Perot's Way," editorial, *Oakland Press,* February 13, 1988.

12. Review of FEC records, maintained on file in Washington, D.C.

13. Robert V. Camuto, J. Lynn Lunsford, and Dave Montgomery, "Perot's, White House: Uneasy Alliance," Fort Worth *Star-Telegram,* April 19, 1992, p. A1.

14. Interview with Reed Pigman, January 26, 1995.

15. Richard Connor, "Ross Perot Might Be More Menace Than Hero," *The Houston Chronicle,* May 8, 1992, p. 13.

16. Interview with Reed Pigman, January 26, 1995.

17. Interview with Robert Bolen, January 26, 1995.

18. J. Lynn Lunsford, "Manager Sought for Alliance," *The Dallas Morning News,* December 15, 1992, p. 32A.

19. Bob Hullet, quoted by J. Lynn Lunsford, "Board Advises Against Perot Offer to Manage Alliance," *The Dallas Morning News,* March 19, 1993, p. 32A.

20. Dean Baquet, "Perot Investments in Land Thrive with Public Funds," *The New York Times,* May 29, 1992, p. A1.

21. J. Lynn Lunsford, "Deal May Reopen Old Airport Wounds; Federal Express Plan Irks Some in Dallas," *The Dallas Morning News,* December 17, 1993, p. 27A.

22. Richard A. Oppel, Jr., "Agency OKs Trade Zone at Alliance," *The Dallas Morning News,* September 8, 1993, p. 1D.

23. Thomas C. Hayes, "New Perot Project: Airport for Industry," *The New York Times,* July 11, 1989, p. D1.

24. Ross Perot, quoted by Laura Miller, "More Ideas from Amazing Ross Perot," *Dallas Times Herald,* March 13, 1988.

25. James Ragland, quoted by Michael Isikoff, "Perot Championed Unorthodox War on Drugs," *The Washington Post,* June 10, 1992, p. A1.

26. Monica Smith, quoted by Miller, "More Ideas from Amazing Ross Perot," op. cit.

27. Ibid.

28. Domingo Garcia, quoted by Isikoff, op. cit., p. A1.

29. See generally, Robert V. Camuto, "Perot Meets Hispanic City Leaders," *Dallas Times Herald,* March 17, 1988, p. B1.

30. Ross Perot, quoted by Lori Montgomery, "Perot on Police: All I Want Is a Better City," *Dallas Times Herald,* March 16, 1988, p. A1.

31. Ibid., p. A18.

32. Ross Perot, quoted by Laura Miller, "How They See Perot's Views at City Hall," *Dallas Times Herald,* March 18, 1988.

33. Billy Powell, quoted by Laura Miller, "All About the Police Perot Review Board," *Dallas Times Herald,* June 29, 1988, p. B3.

34. Miller, "All About the Police Perot Review Board," op. cit., p. B3.

35. Interview with Ross Perot, November 30, 1995.

36. Ross Perot, quoted by Miller, "All About the Police Perot Review Board," op. cit., p. B3.

37. John Wiley Price, quoted by Lawrence E. Young, "Price Complaint Says Police Failed to Enforce Law on Perot Relative," *The Dallas Morning News,* June 29, 1988, p. A19.

38. Interview with Ross Perot, November 30, 1995.

39. Tom Luce, quoted by Isikoff, op. cit., p. A1.

40. Peter Johnson, quoted by Helen Fogel, "Perot-GM Fight Seen as Even Match," *The Detroit News,* July 31, 1988, p. 1.

Chapter 15: Free the Slaves

1. Testimony of Ross Perot, *EDS* vs. *Henry Ross Perot and Perot Systems Corp.,* In Chancery No. 108556, Fairfax, Virginia, October 19, 1988, p. 189.

2. Bill of Complaint for Injunctive Relief, *EDS* v. *Henry Ross Perot and Perot Systems Corp.,* In Chancery No. 108556, Fairfax, Virginia, filed September 27, 1988, p. 7.

3. Interview with Ross Perot, February 12, 1996.

4. Gary Anthes, "GAO Scrutinizes USPS Contract with Perot Firm," *Federal Computer Week,* June 13, 1988, pp. 1, 69.

5. "Super Patriot: Ross Perot—How He'll Make His Next Billion," *U.S. News & World Report,* June 20, 1988.

6. Testimony of DeSoto S. Jordan, Jr., *Perot Systems* v. *General Motors Corpora-tion, Electronic Data Systems, et. al.,* District Court of Dallas County, Texas, 95th Judicial District, October 11, 1988, pp. 71, 81.

7. Deposition of Ross Perot, February 9, 1989, *EDS* v. *Henry Ross Perot and Perot Systems Corp.,* In Chancery No. 108556, Fairfax, Virginia.

8. Interview with Ross Perot, February 12, 1996.

9. Testimony of Les Alberthal, *EDS* v. *Henry Ross Perot and Perot Systems Corp.,* In Chancery No. 108556, Fairfax, Virginia, October 13, 1988, p. 196.

10. Ibid., p. 197.

11. Joseph White, "Perot's No-Bid Contract with the Postal Service Is Suspended Under Pressure from Capitol Hill," *The Wall Street Journal,* July 11, 1988, p. 36.

12. Cyrus E. Phillips IV, quoted in "No Stamp of Approval," *Federal Computer Week,* June 20, 1988.

13. Carl Levin, quoted by Patricia Edmonds, "Senate Stalls Perot's 'Sweet Deal,' " *The Detroit Free Press,* June 23, 1988, p. A3.

14. Ross Perot, quoted by Bob Drummond, "Perot Says EDS Now Fair Game," *Dallas Times Herald,* July 8, 1989, p. A1.

15. Perot Systems document, quoted, in part, by John Spelich, "Perot: New Firm Will Depose EDS," *The Detroit Free Press,* June 21, 1988, p. 11.

16. Ross Perot, quoted by Robert Dodge, "Perot Threatens 'War' After Pact Suspended," *The Dallas Morning News,* July 8, 1988, p. A1.

17. Ross Perot, quoted by Kevin Maney and John Killrirk, "Perot: Full Speed Ahead," *USA Today,* June 22, 1988.

18. Bill Wright, quoted by Todd Mason, *Perot: An Unauthorized Biography* (Homewood, Illinois: Business One Irwin, 1990), p. 264.

19. Les Alberthal, quoted by Peter Elkind, "Ross Perot: Can He Save America?," *Texas Monthly,* December 1988, p. 196.

20. Ross Perot, quoted by Lise Olson, "Perot Accuses Giant of Plot to Crush New Firm," *The Detroit Free Press,* June 25, 1989, p. A1.

21. Ibid.

22. Ross Perot, quoted by Jim Mitchell and Robert Dodge, "Perot Says 'Fight Is On' with EDS," *The Dallas Morning News,* June 25, 1988, p. 1A.

23. Ross Perot, quoted by Robert Dodge, "Perot Threatens 'War' After Pact Suspended," *The Dallas Morning News,* July 8, 1988, p. A1.

24. Ross Perot, Jr., quoted by Kevin Kelly and Frances Seghers, "Look Out, Roger Smith—Perot Is Still Mad," *Business Week,* September 26, 1988, p. 108.

25. "Executives of the Month," *Gallagher Report,* July 25, 1988.

26. Paul Farhi, "Postal Service Bows to Pressure, Formally Suspends Contract with Perot," *The Washington Post,* July 9, 1988, Business Section, p. 1; Ross Perot, quoted by Marcia Stepanek, "EDS Sues Perot, Claiming He's in Competition," *The Detroit Free Press,* September 28, 1988, p. 1.

27. Ross Perot, quoted by Joseph White, "G.M.'s EDS Unit Sues Founder Perot, Saying He Broke Terms of Parting Pact," *The Wall Street Journal,* September 28, 1988, p. 3; see also Perot, quoted in "EDS Sues Perot," *USA Today,* September 28, 1988; Perot, quoted by Harihar Krishnan, UPI business writer, "EDS Files Lawsuit Against Perot," September 28, 1988.

28. Testimony of Les Alberthal, *EDS* v. *Henry Ross Perot and Perot Systems Corp.,* In Chancery No. 108556, Fairfax, Virginia, October 13, 1988, p. 192; see also testimony of Malcolm Gudis, October 19, p. 26.

29. Testimony of Ross Perot, *EDS* v. *Henry Ross Perot and Perot Systems Corp.,* In Chancery No. 108556, Fairfax, Virginia, April 10, 1989, p. 136.

30. Ross Perot, quoted by James Risen, "GM Unit Sues to Close Perot's Firm," *Los Angeles Times,* September 28, 1988, p. 1.

31. Testimony of Elmer Johnson, *EDS* v. *Henry Ross Perot and Perot Systems Corp.,* In Chancery No. 108556, Fairfax, Virginia, April 11, 1989, p. 83.

32. Testimony of Elmer Johnson, Hearing for a Preliminary Injunction, *EDS* v. *Henry Ross Perot and Perot Systems Corp.,* In Chancery No. 108556, Fairfax, Virginia, October 13, 1988, p. 79.

33. Testimony of Les Alberthal, *EDS* v. *Henry Ross Perot and Perot Systems Corp.,* In Chancery No. 108556, Fairfax, Virginia, October 13, 1988, p. 166; see also testimony of Malcolm Gudis, October 19, pp. 14–17.

34. Testimony of Les Alberthal, *EDS* v. *Henry Ross Perot and Perot Systems Corp.,* In Chancery No. 108556, Fairfax, Virginia, October 13, 1988, p. 168.

35. Preliminary Injunction Order, *EDS* v. *Henry Ross Perot and Perot Systems Corp.,* In Chancery No. 108556, Fairfax, Virginia, October 21, 1988, p. 2.

36. Ross Perot, quoted by Brian O'Reilly, "EDS After Perot: How Tough Is It?," *Fortune,* October 24, 1988, p. 72.

37. All comments quoted from Ross Perot are taken from a transcript of his appearance before the National Press Club, Washington, D.C., Thursday, November 17, 1988, reprinted in *New Technology Week,* November 21, 1988, pp. 3–11.

38. Excerpts from Perot's speech in Cambridge, at Harvard, reprinted in *The Boston Globe,* "Perot: Let's Make Our Country Strong," December 7, 1988.

39. Argument by Tom Barr, Esq., *EDS* v. *Henry Ross Perot and Perot Systems Corp.,* In Chancery No. 108556, Fairfax, Virginia, April 11, 1989, p. 223.

40. Ibid., p. 209.

41. Argument of David Fiske, Esq., *EDS* v. *Henry Ross Perot and Perot Systems Corp.,* In Chancery No. 108556, Fairfax, Virginia, April 11, 1989, p. 229.

42. Bench Order of Judge William Plummer, *EDS* v. *Henry Ross Perot and Perot Systems Corp.,* In Chancery No. 108556, Fairfax, Virginia, April 11, 1989, pp. 231–32.

43. Les Alberthal, quoted by Joseph White, "Perot Is Dealt Setback as Judge Limits Raids on Staff of EDS to Dec. 1, 1991," *The Wall Street Journal,* April 12, 1989, p. 1.

44. White, "Perot Is Dealt Setback as Judge Limits Raids on Staff of EDS to Dec. 1, 1991," op. cit., p. 1.

45. Interview with Ross Perot, August 8, 1995.

46. Oliver "Buck" Revell, quoted by Richard Whittle, "Perot Opposed Pentagon

Aide," *The Dallas Morning News,* June 28, 1992, p. 25A.

47. Ibid.; see also Oliver "Buck" Revell, quoted by Karen De Witt and Michael Kelly, "Perot Pursued Charges Against Official for Years," *The New York Times,* June 28, 1992.

48. Letter, from James D. Harmon, Jr., to I. Lewis Libby, April 28, 1989.

49. Dave McCurdy, quoted by Whittle, op. cit., p. 1A.

50. Ibid., p. 25A.

51. General Jack Merritt, quoted by Whittle, op. cit., p. 25A.

52. Richard Armitage, quoted by De Witt and Kelly, op. cit.

53. Interview with Richard Armitage, November 18, 1995.

Chapter 16: "Think Outside the Box"

1. Ross Perot on C-SPAN, March 23, 1992.

2. Interview with Sharon Holman, March 13, 1995.

3. Ross Perot on *Inside Politics,* CNN, March 4, 1992.

4. Interview with Clay Mulford, March 9, 1995.

5. Ibid.

6. Interview with Tom Luce, November 29, 1995.

7. Interview with Clay Mulford, March 9, 1995.

8. Ibid.

9. Ibid.

10. Interview with Tom Luce, November 29, 1995.

11. Interview with Clay Mulford, March 9, 1995.

12. Interview with Sharon Holman, March 13, 1995.

13. Carolyn Barta, *Perot and His People: Disrupting the Balance of Political Power* (Fort Worth: The Summit Group, 1993), p. 35.

14. Interview with Gordon Black, February 27, 1995.

15. Interview with Sharon Holman, March 13, 1995.

16. Ibid.

17. Interview with Jack Gargan, May 31, 1995.

18. Letter, to Ross Perot from Jack Gargan, March 22, 1992, provided to author by Mr. Gargan.

19. Letter to Ross Perot from Jack Gargan, June 26, 1992.

20. Interview with Marianne Garboff, February 14, 1995.

21. Interview with Jim Squires, April 25, 1995.

22. Barta, op. cit., p. 40.

23. Robin Toner, "Clinton Dogged by Voter Doubt, Poll of U.S. Says," *The New York Times,* April 1, 1992, p. A1.

24. Interview with Tom Luce, November 29, 1995.

25. Interview with James Squires, April 25, 1995.

26. Interview with Sal Russo, June 9, 1995.

27. Interview with James Squires, April 25, 1995.

28. The Texas poll, conducted from April 9 to April 18 among 674 Texans, sponsored by Hartke-Hanks Communications, released April 21, 1992.

29. *The New York Times* poll, published April 26, 1992, conducted from April 20 to April 23 among 1,151 registered voters.

30. *The Washington Post* poll, published April 27, 1992, conducted April 23 to April 26 among 1,003 people.

31. The *Los Angeles Times* poll, published April 28, 1992, conducted from April 23 to April 26 among 1,395 California registered voters.

32. Interview with Tom Luce, November 29, 1995.

33. Interview with James Squires, April 25, 1995.

34. Sharon Holman, quoted in Charles T. Royer, ed., *Campaign for President: The Managers Look at '92,* (Hollis, New Hampshire: Hollis Publishing, 1994), p. 137.

35. Interview with Sharon Holman, March 13, 1995.

36. Jack Nelson, "Perot's Swift Rise Draws GOP, Democratic Broadsides," *Los Angeles Times,* May 22, 1992, quoting Marlin Fitzwater.

37. Marilyn Quayle on *Fox Morning News,* May 28, 1992.

38. CNN/*Time* magazine poll, May 17, 1992, of 917 registered voters, by Yankelovich Clancy Shulman.

39. David Brinkley, *This Week with David Brinkley,* ABC, May 24, 1992.

40. Interview with Ross Perot, November 29, 1995.

41. Ross Perot on *20/20,* ABC, May 29, 1992.

42. David Gergen on *MacNeil/Lehrer NewsHour,* PBS, June 5, 1992.

Chapter 17:
Enter the Professionals

1. Interview with Mort Meyerson, April 20, 1995.

2. Interview with Tom Luce, November 29, 1995.

3. Interview with Mort Meyerson, April 20, 1995.

4. Interview with Ross Perot, November 29, 1995.

5. Interview with Ed Rollins, May 26, 1995.

6. David Shribman, "Perot Weighs Hiring Carter, Reagan Aides," *The Wall Street Journal,* May 28, 1992, p. A22.

7. Interview with Ed Rollins, May 26, 1995.

8. Interview with Tom Luce, February 18, 1996.

9. Interview with Ed Rollins, May 26, 1995.

10. Interview with Tom Luce, November 29, 1995.

11. Interview with Ed Rollins, May 26, 1995.

12. Ibid.

13. Ibid.

14. Interview with Jim Squires, April 25, 1995.

15. Interview with Tom Luce, November 29, 1995.

16. Interview with Ross Perot, February 12, 1996.

17. Interview with Charlie Leonard, June 1, 1995.

18. Interview with Jim Squires, April 25, 1995.

19. Interview with Charlie Leonard, June 1, 1995.

20. Meyerson and Leonard conversation recounted by Charlie Leonard, interviewed June 1, 1995.

21. Ross Perot, on CNN, June 3, 1992.

22. Interview with Charlie Leonard, June 1, 1995.

23. Interview with Joe Canzeri, May 15, 1995.

24. Interview with Charlie Leonard, June 1, 1995.

25. Interview with Sal Russo, June 9, 1995.

26. Ross Perot–Ed Rollins conversation recounted by Ed Rollins, interviewed on May 26, 1995.

27. Interview with Ed Rollins, May 26, 1995.

28. Interview with Sharon Holman, March 13, 1995.

29. Interview with Joe Canzeri, May 15, 1995.

30. Interview with Charlie Leonard, June 1, 1995.

31. Interview with Tony Marsh, June 5, 1995.

32. Interview with Tom Luce, November 29, 1995.

33. Interview with Jim Squires, April 25, 1995.

34. Interview with Murphy Martin, March 8, 1995.

35. Interview with Ross Perot, November 30, 1995.

36. Interview with Clay Mulford, March 9, 1995.

37. Interview with Jim Squires, April 25, 1995.

38. Tom Luce, quoted in Charles T. Royer, ed., *Campaign for President: The Manager's Look at '92,* (Hollis, New Hampshire: Hollis Publishing, 1994), p. 170.

39. Interview with Ed Rollins, May 26, 1995.

40. Ibid.

41. Hamilton Jordan, quoted by Jack Germond and Jules Witcover, *Mad as Hell: Revolt at the Ballot Box, 1992* (New York: Warner Books, 1993), p. 364.

42. Interview with Charlie Leonard, June 1, 1995.

43. Interview with Tony Marsh, June 5, 1995.

44. Interview with Ed Rollins, May 26, 1995.

45. Interview with Tom Luce, November 29, 1995.

46. Interview with Jim Squires, April 25, 1995.

47. Interview with Murphy Martin, March 8, 1995.

48. Interview with Sal Russo, September 7, 1995.

49. Interview with Tony Marsh, June 5, 1995.

50. Interview with Ed Rollins, May 26, 1995.

51. Interview with Jim Squires, April 25, 1995.

52. Interview with Liz Noyer, June 8, 1995.

53. Interview with Ed Rollins, May 26, 1995.

54. Interview with Bob Barkin, June 1, 1995.

55. Interview with Charlie Leonard, June 1, 1995.

56. Ibid.

57. Ibid.

58. Ibid.

59. Interview with Ed Rollins, May 26, 1995.

60. Interview with Charlie Leonard, June 1, 1995.

61. Interview with Sal Russo, June 9, 1995.

62. Ibid.

63. Interview with Jim Squires, April 25, 1995.

64. Ibid.

65. Interview with Liz Noyer, June 8, 1995.

66. Interview with Bob Barkin, June 1, 1995.

67. Interview with Tony Marsh, June 5, 1995.

68. Interview with Bob Barkin, June 1, 1995.

69. Conversation between Bob Barkin and Ed Rollins recounted by Bob Barkin, interviewed June 1, 1995.

70. One-page typed memo, at top marked "Important Memo," from personal files of Charlie Leonard.

71. Interview with Bob Barkin, June 1, 1995.

72. Interview with Charlie Leonard, June 1, 1995.

73. Ibid.

74. Ibid.; see also, generally, interview with Ed Rollins, May 26, 1995.

75. Interview with Sal Russo, June 9, 1995.

76. Interview with Bob Barkin, June 1, 1995.

77. Interview with Liz Noyer, June 8, 1995.

78. One-page typed document, from the personal files of Sal Russo.

79. Interview with Ed Rollins, May 26, 1995.

80. Conversation recounted by Ed Rollins, interviewed May 26, 1995.

81. Meeting among Ross Perot, Ed Rollins, Hal Riney, and Murphy Martin recreated from interview with Murphy Martin, March 8, 1995.

82. Ed Rollins, quoted by Carolyn Barta, *Perot and His People: Disrupting the Balance of Political Power* (Fort Worth: The Summit Group, 1993), p. 238.

83. Interview with Jim Squires, April 25, 1995.

84. Ibid.

85. Ibid.

86. Interview with Charlie Leonard, June 1, 1995.

87. Tom Luce, quoted in Royer, ed., op. cit., p. 174.

88. Interview with Mort Meyerson, April 20, 1995.

89. Interview with Bob Barkin, June 1, 1995.

90. Interview with Liz Noyer, June 8, 1995.

91. Ibid.

92. Interview with Murphy Martin, March 8, 1995.

93. Tom Luce, quoted in Royer, ed., op. cit., p. 165.

94. Interview with Mort Meyerson, April 20, 1995.

95. Ibid.

96. Transcript of remarks of Ross Perot at a press conference in Dallas, Texas, July 16, 1992.

Chapter 18:
The Second Coming

1. Ross Perot on *20/20*, ABC, July 17, 1992.

2. Ross Perot on *Larry King Live,* CNN, July 17, 1992.

3. Interview with Larry King, August 12, 1995.

4. Interview with Murphy Martin, March 8, 1995.

5. Interview with Mort Meyerson, April 20, 1995.

6. Interview with John Jay Hooker, April 26, 1995.

7. Murphy Martin, quoted by Carolyn Barta, *Perot and His People: Disrupting the Balance of Political Power* (Fort Worth: The Summit Group, 1993), p. 308.

8. Interview with Orson Swindle, August 1, 1995.

9. Ibid.

10. Review of Detailed Summary of Receipts and Disbursements (FEC Form 3P), Periods July 1 through September 30, 1992, maintained at the Federal Election Commission, Washington, D.C.

11. Interview with Ross Perot, November 29, 1995.

12. Interview with Jim Squires, April 25, 1995.

13. Interview with Felix Rohatyn, May 24, 1995.

14. Larry King, on *Larry King Live,* CNN, September 28, 1992.

15. Interview with Clay Mulford, March 13, 1995.

16. Interview with Sharon Holman, March 1, 1995.

17. Carolyn Barta, op. cit., p. 318.

18. Ross Perot, press conference in Dallas, October 1, 1992.

19. Interview with Mort Meyerson, April 20, 1995.

20. Clay Mulford, quoted by Peter Goldman, et al., *Quest for the Presidency* (College Station, Texas: Texas A&M University Press, 1994), p. 551.

21. Interview with Clay Mulford, March 13, 1995.

22. Interview with Ross Perot, November 30, 1995.

23. Interview with Murphy Martin, March 8, 1995.

24. Interview with Ross Perot, November 30, 1995.

25. James Carville quoted by Peter Goldman, et al., op. cit., p. 564.

26. Interview with Ross Perot, November 30, 1995.

27. Ibid.

28. Ibid.

29. Ross Perot on *60 Minutes,* CBS, October 25, 1992; see also Ross Perot, quoted in *Newsweek,* interviewed by Maynard Parker, July 27, 1992.

30. Ross Perot on *60 Minutes,* CBS, October 25, 1992.

Chapter 19:
The "Mystery Box"

1. Douglas E. Waller and Bob Cohn, "The Strange Tales of Mr. Barnes," *Newsweek,* November 9, 1992, pp. 24–25.

2. Ross Perot, quoted by Tom Morgenthau in "Citizen Perot," *Newsweek,* November 9, 1992, p. 25.

3. Scott Barnes, with Melva Libb, *Bohica: A True Account of One Man's Battle to Expose the Most Heinous Cover-up of the Vietnam Saga!* (Bohica Corporation: Canton, Ohio, 1987), pp. 6–7.

4. Deposition of Scott Barnes, March 6, 1992, pp. 44–47, 68–70, Senate Select Committee on POW/MIA Affairs, Center for Legislative Archives, National Archives; see also Exhibit 13 to the same deposition; Kern County District Attorney, Bureau of Investigation, case report regarding Scott Tracy Barnes, File No. I-95-064, dated June 28, 1995, prepared by Walt Newport.

5. Kern County District Attorney, Bureau of Investigation, case report regarding Scott Tracy Barnes, File No. I-95-064, dated June 28, 1995, prepared by Walt Newport, p. 2.

6. Interview with Scott Barnes, February 22, 1996.

7. Kern County District Attorney, Bureau of Investigation, case report regarding Scott Tracy Barnes, File No. I-95-064, dated June 28, 1995, prepared by Walt Newport, p. 3.

8. Barnes, *Bohica,* p. 135; see also Scott Barnes, quoted in *Covert Action Intelligence Bulletin,* Number 17, Summer 1982, p. 38.

9. "Bohica: The Facts Behind the Fantasies of the Author, Scott Barnes," a re-

search paper published by the National League of Families of American Prisoners and Missing in Southeast Asia, November 1988, p. 1, 16-A-5, 48-A-3 (hereinafter referred to as "Bohica," a research paper).

10. Ibid.

11. Robert Dornan, quoted by Susan Katz Keating, "The Source Who Bends Perot's Ear," *The Washington Times*, October 29, 1992, p. E1.

12. Scott Barnes, quoted in *Covert Action Intelligence Bulletin*, op. cit., p. 33.

13. Barnes, *Bohica*, p. 179.

14. Interview with David Taylor, March 13, 1996.

15. David Taylor, quoted by Monika Jensen-Stevenson and William Stevenson, *Kiss the Boys Goodbye* (New York: Plume, 1991), p. 84.

16. Interview with Ross Perot, October 24, 1995.

17. Ibid.

18. Interview with Scott Barnes, March 20, 1995.

19. Ibid.

20. Interview with Ross Perot, November 30, 1995.

21. Interview with Ross Perot, August 22, 1995.

22. Interview with Ross Perot, November 30, 1995.

23. Jensen-Stevenson and Stevenson, op. cit., p. 124.

24. Interview with David Taylor, March 13, 1996.

25. David Taylor, quoted by Jensen-Stevenson and Stevenson, op. cit., p. 199.

26. "Bohica," a research paper, p. 3; see also July 24, 1986, memorandum, from the Uniformed Services University of the Health Science Department of Defense, F. Edward Herbert School of Medicine, Psychiatry.

27. Robert Dornan, quoted by Keating, op. cit., p. E1.

28. Interview with Scott Barnes, March 17, 1995.

29. Interview with Scott Barnes, March 20, 1995.

30. Interview with David Taylor, March 13, 1996.

31. Ibid.

32. Letter, to Louise Van Hoozer from Colonel Joseph A. Schlatter, July 26, 1988, reprinted in "Bohica," a research paper, pp. 9, 12.

33. "Bohica," a research paper, p. 4.

34. Letter from David Taylor, dated February 27, 1987, addressed "To Whom It May Concern," reprinted in *Bohica*, Exhibit 13.

35. Kern County District Attorney, Bureau of Investigation, case report regarding Scott Tracy Barnes, File No. I-95-064, dated June 28, 1995, prepared by Walt Newport, p. 6.

36. Scott Barnes, comments recounted by Jensen-Stevenson and Stevenson, op. cit., p. 300.

37. Ibid.

38. Jensen-Stevenson and Stevenson, op. cit., p. 301.

39. David Taylor, quoted by Jensen-Stevenson and Stevenson, op. cit., pp. 300, 301, 325; also, interview with David Taylor, March 13, 1996.

40. Interview with Scott Barnes, March 20, 1995.

41. Interview with Scott Barnes, March 17, 1995; interview with David Taylor, March 13, 1996.

42. Kern County District Attorney, Bureau of Investigation, case report regarding Scott Tracy Barnes, File No. I-95-064, dated June 28, 1995, prepared by Walt Newport, p. 7.

43. Jensen-Stevenson and Stevenson, op. cit., p. 85.

44. Deposition of Scott Barnes, March 6, 1992, pp. 13, 19, Senate Select Committee on POW/MIA Affairs, Center for Legislative Archives, National Archives. Kern County District Attorney, Bureau of Investigation, case report regarding Scott Tracy Barnes, File No. I-95-064, dated June 28, 1995, prepared by Walt Newport, p. 7.

45. Deposition of Scott Barnes, March 6, 1992, p. 13, Senate Select Committee on POW/MIA Affairs, Center for Legislative Archives, National Archives.

Chapter 20: Dirty Tricks

1. Jim Oberwetter, quoted by Peter Applebome, "Perot, the 'Simple' Billion-

aire, Says Voters Can Force His Presidential Bid," *The New York Times,* March 29, 1992.

2. Transcript of Ross Perot speech before the American Society of Newspaper Editors, Washington, D.C., April 10, 1992.

3. Interview with James Oberwetter, March 10, 1995.

4. Ibid.

5. Interview with Terry O'Donnell, December 12, 1995; also, interview with O'Donnell, December 20, 1995.

6. Interview with Terry O'Donnell, December 12, 1995.

7. Interview with David Tell, March 13, 1996.

8. Interview with David Taylor, March 13, 1996.

9. Interview with Scott Barnes, March 17, 1995.

10. Interview with David Taylor, March 13, 1996.

11. Ibid.

12. Ibid.

13. Ibid.

14. Author's review of telephone bills for May 1992 for Scott Barnes and Jessica Lynn's High Fashion Store.

15. Interview with David Taylor, March 13, 1996.

16. Ibid.

17. Ross Perot, on *60 Minutes,* CBS, October 25, 1992.

18. Interview with David Taylor, March 13, 1996.

19. Ibid.

20. Interview with Scott Barnes, December 15, 1995.

21. Letter, undated, from David Taylor to the author.

22. Ross Perot, on *60 Minutes,* CBS, October 25, 1992.

23. Interview with Scott Barnes, March 17, 1995.

24. Interview with David Taylor, March 13, 1996.

25. Ibid.; letter, undated, from David Taylor, to the author.

26. Interview with Ross Perot, November 29, 1995.

27. Interview with Buck Revell, March 14, 1995.

28. Interview with David Taylor, March 13, 1996.

29. Ibid.

30. Interview with Ross Perot, August 22, 1995.

31. Interview with James Siano, June 15, 1995.

32. Ibid.

33. Interview with David Taylor, April 27, 1995; also, recounting of James Siano conversation with the Dallas police, interviews with Captain Eddie Walt and Chief Bill Rathburn, June 22, 1995, and Captain Rudy Diaz, July 5, 1995.

34. Letter, undated, from David Taylor to the author.

35. Interview with Scott Barnes, December 15, 1995.

36. Ibid.

37. Ibid.; interview with David Taylor, March 13, 1996.

38. Interview with David Taylor, March 13, 1996.

39. Interview with Captain Eddie Walt, June 22, 1995; interview with Captain Rudy Diaz, July 5, 1995.

40. Interviews with Captain Eddie Walt and Chief Bill Rathburn, June 22, 1995, and Captain Rudy Diaz, July 5, 1995.

41. Interview with Captain Eddie Walt, June 22, 1995.

42. Interview with Buck Revell, March 14, 1995.

43. Interview with David Taylor, March 13, 1996; interview with James Siano, June 15, 1995.

44. Interview with James Siano, June 15, 1995.

45. Testimony of W. Dennis Aiken Chief, Public Corruption Unit, before the Civil and Constitutional Rights Subcommittee of the House Committee on the Judiciary on FBI Undercover Operations, March 24, 1993, p. 9.

46. Interview with Jim Oberwetter, March 10, 1995.

47. Ibid.

48. Ibid.

49. Conversation between Jim Oberwetter and Scott Barnes recounted in an interview with Jim Oberwetter, March 10, 1995.

50. Testimony of W. Dennis Aiken Chief, Public Corruption Unit, before the Civil and Constitutional Rights Subcommittee of the House Committee on the Judiciary on FBI Undercover Operations, March 24, 1993, p. 9.

51. Ibid., p. 10.

52. Ibid., p. 11.

53. Interview with Jim Oberwetter, March 10, 1995.

54. Transcript of conversation between Jim Oberwetter, Wilbur Rainey, and undercover FBI agent, recorded on August 10, 1992, transcribed on August 18, 1992, by John Kubinsky, 27 pages.

55. Ibid., p. 6.

56. Ibid., p. 7.

57. Interview with Buck Revell, March 14, 1995.

58. Ross Perot, on *60 Minutes,* CBS, October 25, 1992.

59. Interview with Orson Swindle, August 1, 1995.

60. Background 1992 tracking poll conducted by Ed Goeas, reported in Peter Goldman, et al., *Quest for the Presidency, 1992* (College Station, Texas: Texas A & M University Press, 1994), p. 596.

61. Interview with Ross Perot, October 24, 1995.

62. Interview with Ross Perot, November 30, 1995.

Chapter 21:
Back in the Game

1. Interview with Orson Swindle, August 1, 1995.

2. Ross Perot, speech in Bangor, Maine on February 6, 1993, quoted by Carolyn Barta, *Perot and His People* (Fort Worth: The Summit Group, 1993), p. 427.

3. Interview with Joyce Shepard, February 23, 1995; interview with Lloyd Wells, February 16, 1995.

4. Ross Perot, quoted by Barta, op. cit., p. 442.

5. Interview with Gordon Black, February 27, 1995.

6. Interview with Jim Squires, April 25, 1995.

7. Ross Perot, quoted by Michael Isikoff, "Perot Tells Large Rally of Death Threat," *The Washington Post,* November 8, 1993, p. A4.

8. Buck Revell, quoted by Isikoff, op. cit., p. A4.

9. Interview with Sharon Holman, March 13, 1995.

10. Interview with Mort Meyerson, April 20, 1995.

11. Thomas V. DiBacco, "More Debacle Than Debate," Orlando *Sentinel,* November 11, 1993, p. A23; Kevin Willey, "Perot Revealed as Crew-Cut Mecham," *Arizona Republic,* November 11, 1993, p. B2.

12. Richard Benedetto, "Momentum Builds as 'Yes' Chorus Gets Louder," *USA Today,* November 17, 1993, p. 2A.

13. Interview with Jim Squires, April 25, 1995.

14. Interview with Ross Perot, November 29, 1995.

15. Interview with Gordon Black, February 27, 1995.

16. Interview with Larry King, August 12, 1995.

17. Ross Perot, on C-SPAN, January 23, 1994.

18. Ross Perot, on C-SPAN, January 21, 1994.

19. Ross Perot, on *Larry King Live,* CNN, March 17, 1994.

20. Interview with Clay Mulford, March 9, 1995.

21. Interview with Russell Verney, March 13, 1995.

22. Ross Perot on National Public Radio, September 27, 1994.

23. *USA Today*/CNN/Gallup poll, based on a poll of 1,210 voters, published in *USA Today,* August 11, 1995, p. 4A.

24. Ross Perot, on *Meet the Press,* NBC, August 13, 1995.

25. Interview with Ross Perot, November 29, 1995.

26. Interview with Gordon Black, November 6, 1995.

27. Ibid.

28. Interviews with Gordon Black, November 6 and December 20, 1995.

29. Interview with Gordon Black, November 6, 1995.

30. Ross Perot, on *Larry King Live,* CNN, September 25, 1995.

31. Richard L. Berke, "Even Perot's Detractors Praise Him for a Masterful Political Move," *The New York Times,* September 27, 1995, p. A1.

32. Interview with Gordon Black, December 20, 1995.

33. Senator Bob Dole, quoted by Berke, op. cit.

34. Interview with Ross Perot, October 24, 1995.

35. Ibid.

36. Ibid.

37. Interview with Russ Verney, February 22, 1996.

38. Interview with Ross Perot, November 29, 1995.

39. Interview with Gordon Black, December 20, 1995.

40. Interview with Gordon Black, November 6, 1995.

41. Interview with Ken Follett, April 6, 1995.

Selected Bibliography

Books and Articles

Instances in which a second edition is listed refer to the paperback used by the author for research.

Adler, Bill, and Bill Adler, Jr. *Ross Perot: An American Maverick Speaks Out.* New York: Citadel Press, 1994.

Aynesworth, Hugh. "Driving Mr. Perot: The Texarkana Years." *The Washington Times,* May 6, 1992.

————, with Stephen G. Michaud. "Perot's Power Play." *Texas Business,* March 1981.

Barnes, Scott (with Melva Libb). *Bohica: A True Account of One Man's Battle to Expose the Most Heinous Cover-up of the Vietnam Saga!* Canton, Ohio: Bohica Corporation, 1987.

Barta, Carolyn. *Perot and His People: Disrupting the Balance of Political Power.* Fort Worth: The Summit Group, 1993.

Black, Gordon S., and Benjamin D. Black. *The Politics of American Discontent: How a New Party Can Make Democracy Work Again.* New York: John Wiley & Sons, 1994.

Brooks, John. *The Go-Go Years.* New York: Weybright and Talley, 1973.

Burlingham, Bo, and Curtis Hartman. "Cowboy Capitalist." *Inc.,* January 1989.

Chiu, Tony. *Ross Perot: In His Own Words.* New York: Warner Books, 1992.

Church, George J. "The Other Side of Perot." *Time,* June 29, 1992.

————. "Perot's Private Probes: A Billionaire Pursues His Own Iran and MIA Trail." *Time,* May 4, 1987.

Dionne, E. J. *They Only Look Dead: Why Progressives Will Dominate the Next Political Era.* New York: Simon & Schuster, 1996.

Fitch, Robert. "H. Ross Perot: America's First Welfare Billionaire." *Ramparts,* November 1971.

Follett, Ken. *On Wings of Eagles.* New York: William Morrow and Company, 1983; Signet, 1984.

Germond, Jack W., and Jules Witcover. *Mad as Hell: Revolt at the Ballot Box, 1992.* New York: Warner Books, 1993.

Goldman, Peter (with Thomas M. DeFrank, Mark Miller, Andrew Murr, and Tom Matthews). *Quest for the Presidency 1992.* College Station, Texas: Texas A&M University Press, 1994.

Gross, Ken. *Ross Perot: The Man Behind the Myth.* New York: Random House, 1992.

Haldeman, H. R. *The Haldeman Diaries: Inside the Nixon White House.* New York: G. P. Putnam's Sons, 1994; Berkley, 1995; also, the CD-ROM version, Sony Imagesoft, 1994.

Jensen-Stevenson, Monika, and William Stevenson. *Kiss the Boys Goodbye: How the United States Betrayed Its Own POWs in Vietnam.* New York: Plume, 1991.

Keating, Susan Katz. *Prisoners of Hope: Exploiting the POW/MIA Myth in America.* New York: Random House, 1994.

Kelly, Michael. "Undeclared Candidate: Where Perot Exhibits a Lifetime of Memories." *The New York Times,* June 17, 1992.

Lee, Albert. *Call Me Roger.* Chicago: Contemporary Books, 1988.

Levin, Doron P. *Irreconcilable Differences: Ross Perot Versus General Motors.* Boston: Little, Brown, 1989.

Mason, Todd. *Perot: An Unauthorized Biography.* Homewood, Illinois: Business One Irwin Books, 1990.

Mintz, John. "Crusades of Ross Perot." *The Washington Post,* April 24, 1992.

Perot, Ross. *Intensive Care: We Must Save Medicare and Medicaid Now.* New York: HarperPerennial, 1995.

———. *Not for Sale at Any Price: How We Can Save America for Our Children.* New York: Hyperion, 1993.

———. "Perot on Perot." *U.S. News & World Report,* June 29, 1992.

United We Stand: How We Can Take Back Our Country. New York: Hyperion, 1992.

———. (with Pat Choate). *Save Your Job, Save Our Country: Why NAFTA Must Be Stopped—Now!* New York: Hyperion, 1993.

Primeau, Marty. "Ross Perot." *The Dallas Morning News,* June 29 and July 6, 1986.

Remnick, David. "Our Nation Turns Its Lonely Eyes to H. Ross Perot: How the Last Real Texan Grabbed the American Dream by the Neck, and Wrestled It to the Ground, and Made It Cry 'Uncle!' " *The Washington Post Magazine,* April 12, 1987.

————. "H. Ross Perot to GM 'I'll Drive'; GM to H. Ross Perot 'Oh, Yeah?' " *The Washington Post,* April 19, 1987.

Robinson, James W. *Ross Perot Speaks Out.* Rocklin, California: Prima Publishing, 1992.

Royer, Charles T. *Campaign for President: The Managers Look at '92.* Hollis, New Hampshire: Hollis Publishing Company, 1994.

Smith, William G. "Ross Perot Runs the Tightest Ship in Texas." *Texas Business,* December 1978.

Wills, Garry. "The Rescuer." *The New York Review of Books,* June 25, 1992.

Wooley, Bryan. *The Edge of the West, and Other Texas Stories.* El Paso, Texas: Texas Western Press, 1990.

Wright, Lawrence. "The Man from Texarkana." *The New York Times Magazine,* June 28, 1992.

Government Reports

"Administration of Federal Health Benefit Programs," Hearings Before a Subcommittee of the Committee on Government Operations, House of Representatives, Ninety-second Congress, Sessions One and Two, September 28 and 30; November 9; and December 1, 1971. U.S. Government Printing Office, 1972.

"Hearings Before the Civil and Constitutional Rights Subcommittee of the House Committee on the Judiciary on FBI Undercover Operations," March 1993.

"Report of the Select Committee on POW/MIA Affairs," U.S. Senate, 103rd Congress, January 13, 1993. U.S. Government Printing Office, 1993.

Court Transcripts

Electronic Data Systems v. *Henry Ross Perot and Perot Systems Corp.,* In Chancery Case Number 108556, Circuit Court, Fairfax County, Virginia, 1988, 1989.

INDEX

About the Author

GERALD POSNER, a former Wall Street lawyer, is the author of *Case Closed* (1993), a critically acclaimed reexamination of the JFK assassination. His other books include a 1988 exposé of the heroin trade (*Warlords of Crime*) and a 1991 collection of interviews with the children of Nazi leaders (*Hitler's Children*). He is also co-author of *Mengele: The Complete Story*, the definitive biography of Auschwitz's "Angel of Death." His novel, *The Bio-Assassins*, was published in 1989.

Mr. Posner's articles have appeared in numerous magazines and newspapers, including *The New York Times, The New Yorker*, and *U.S. News & World Report*. He lives in New York City with his wife, Trisha. More information about Mr. Posner and his work is available on the Internet at http://www.posner.com.

About the Type

This book was set in Sabon, a typeface designed by the well-known German typographer Jan Tschichold (1902–74). Sabon's design is based upon the original letter forms of Claude Garamond and was created specifically to be used for three sources: foundry type for hand composition, Linotype, and Monotype. Tschichold named his typeface for the famous Frankfurt typefounder Jacques Sabon, who died in 1580.